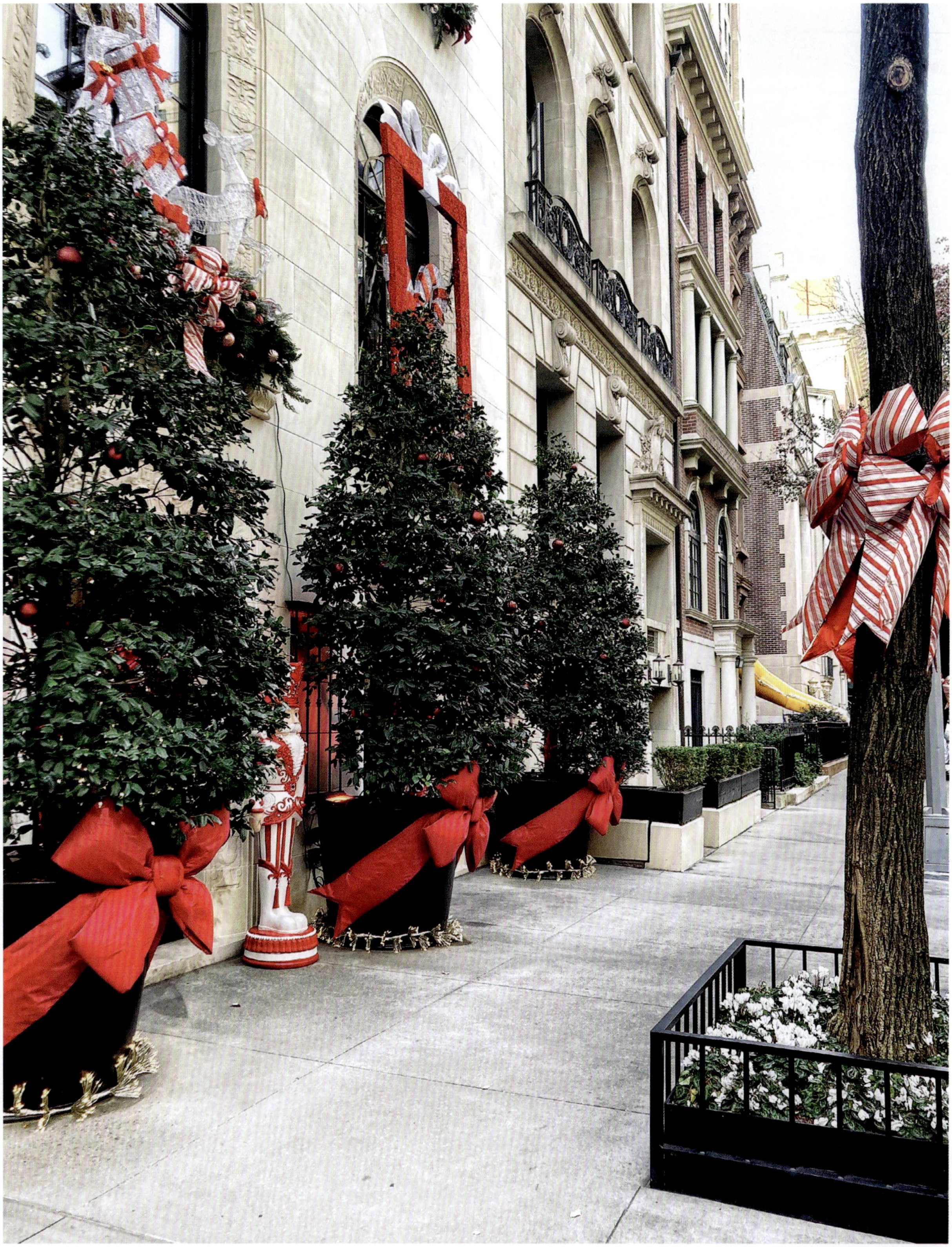

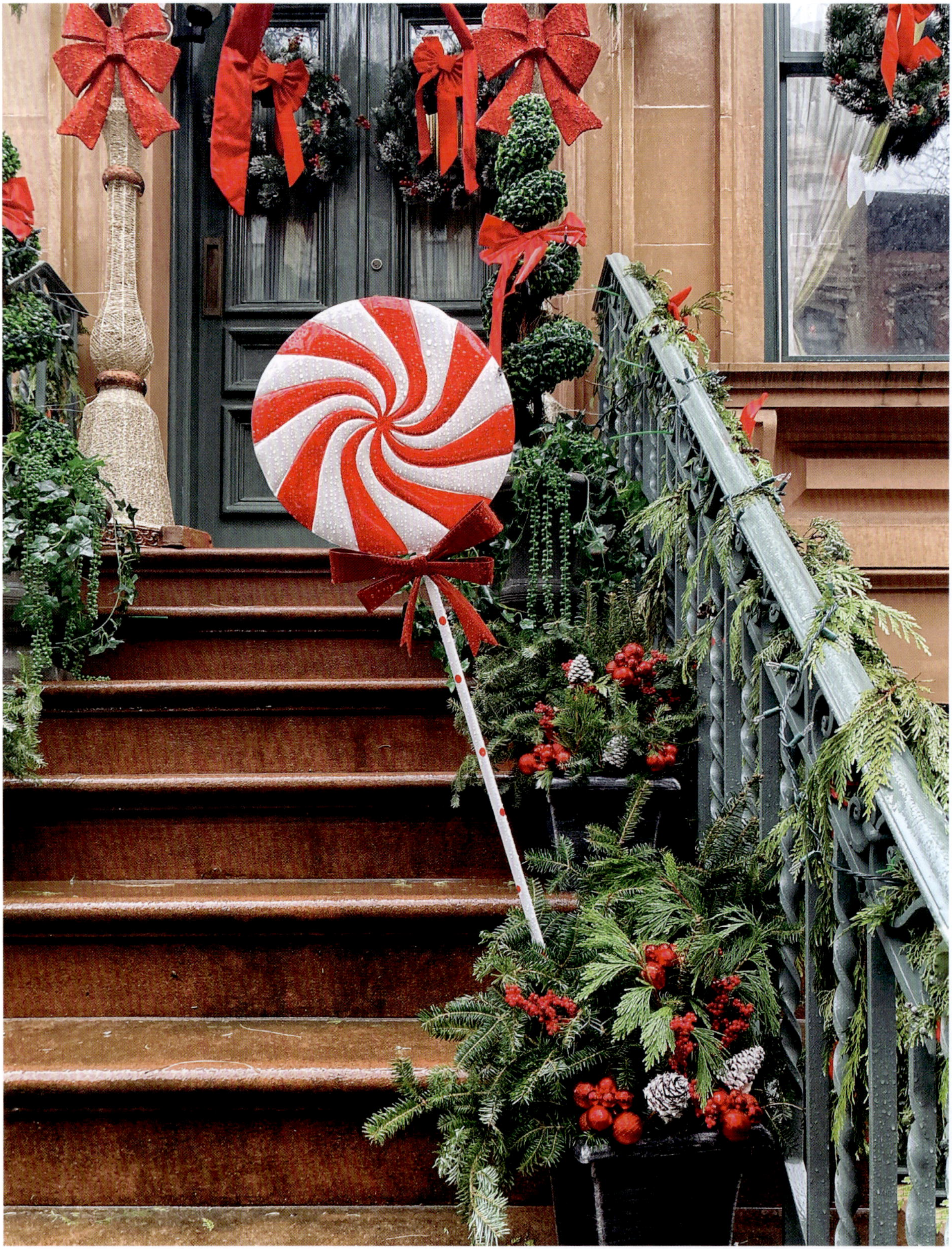

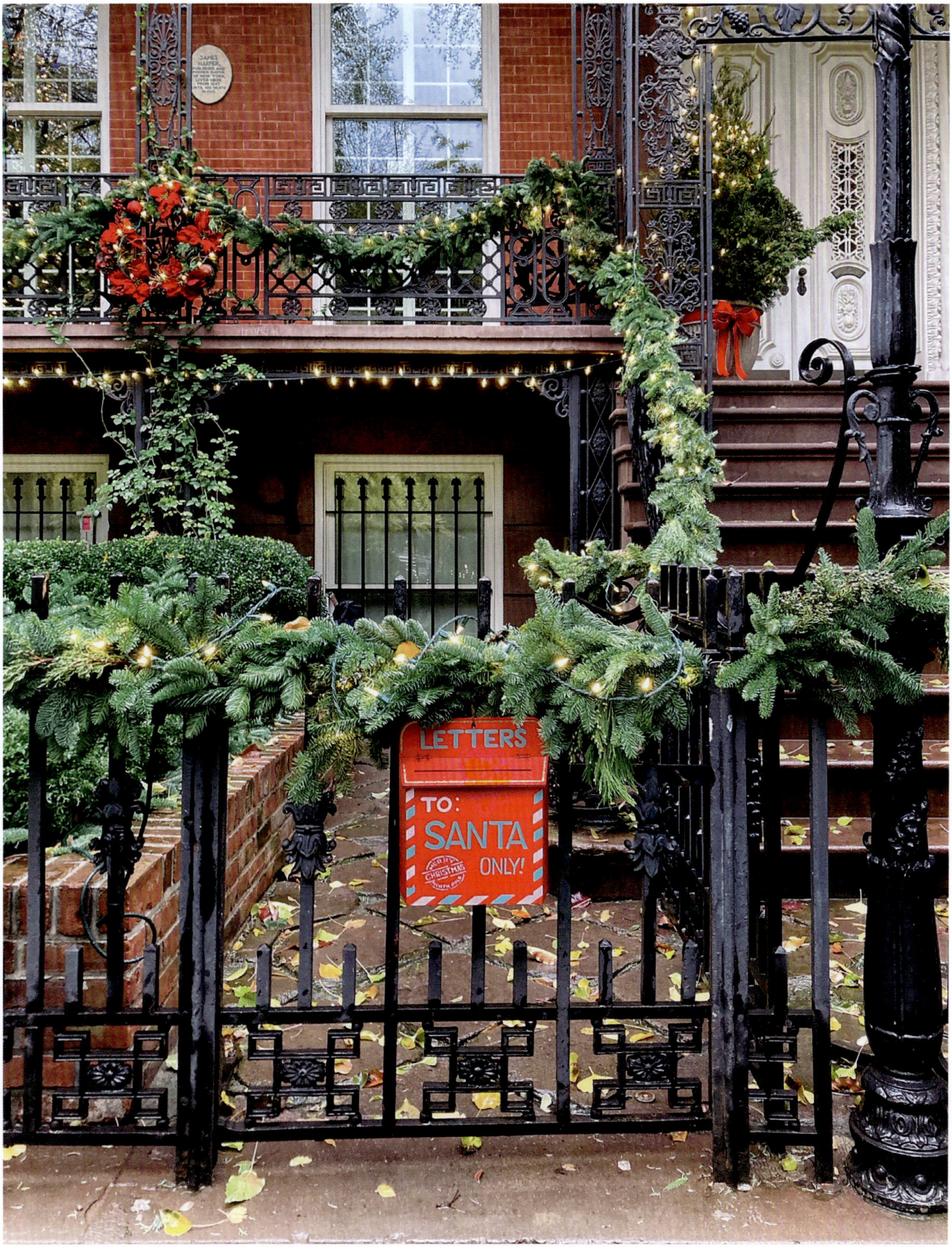
LETTERS
TO:
SANTA
ONLY!

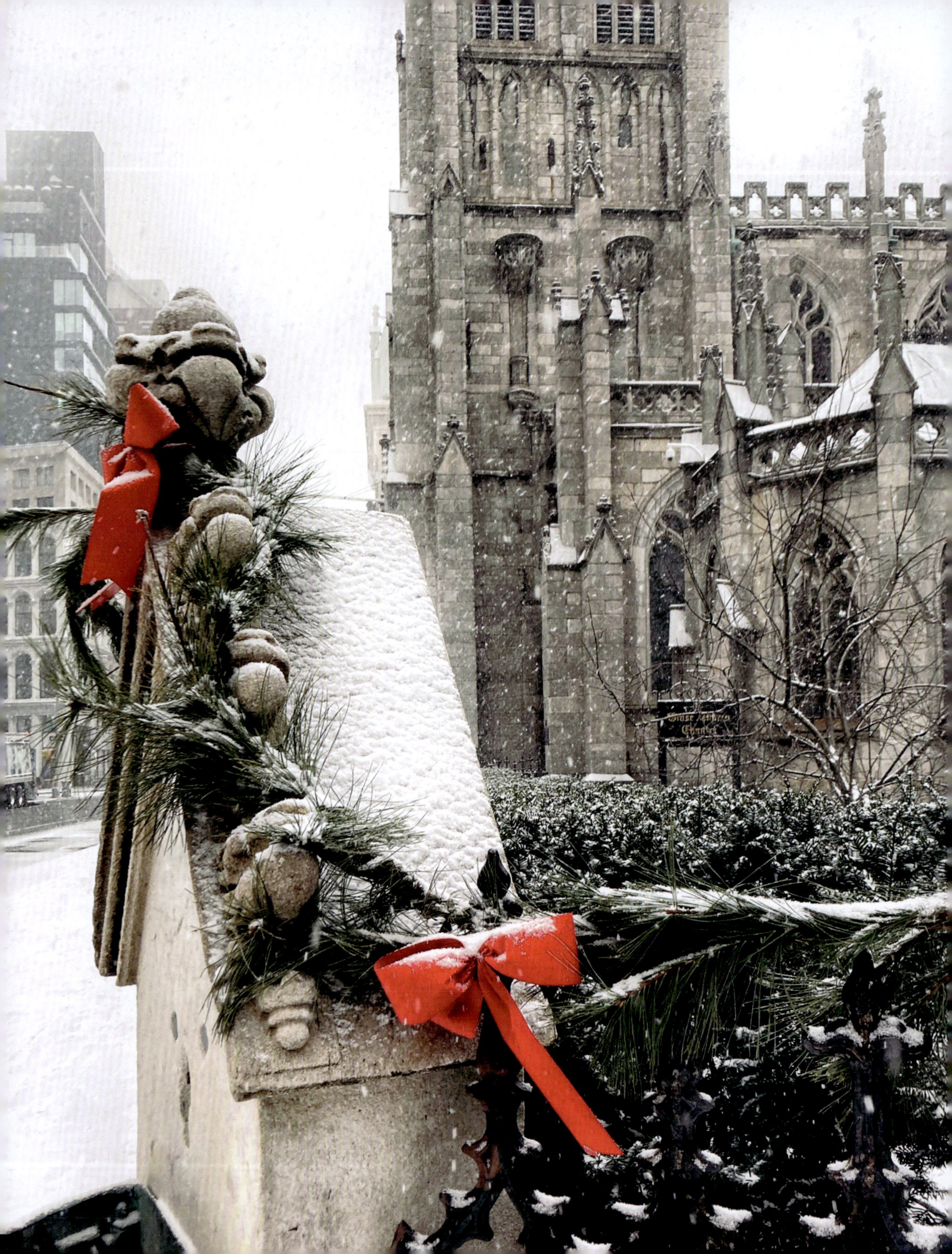

Walk With Me NEW YORK *Holiday*

THE BEAUTY OF THE SEASON THROUGH THE LENS OF

SUSAN KAUFMAN

ABRAMS, NEW YORK

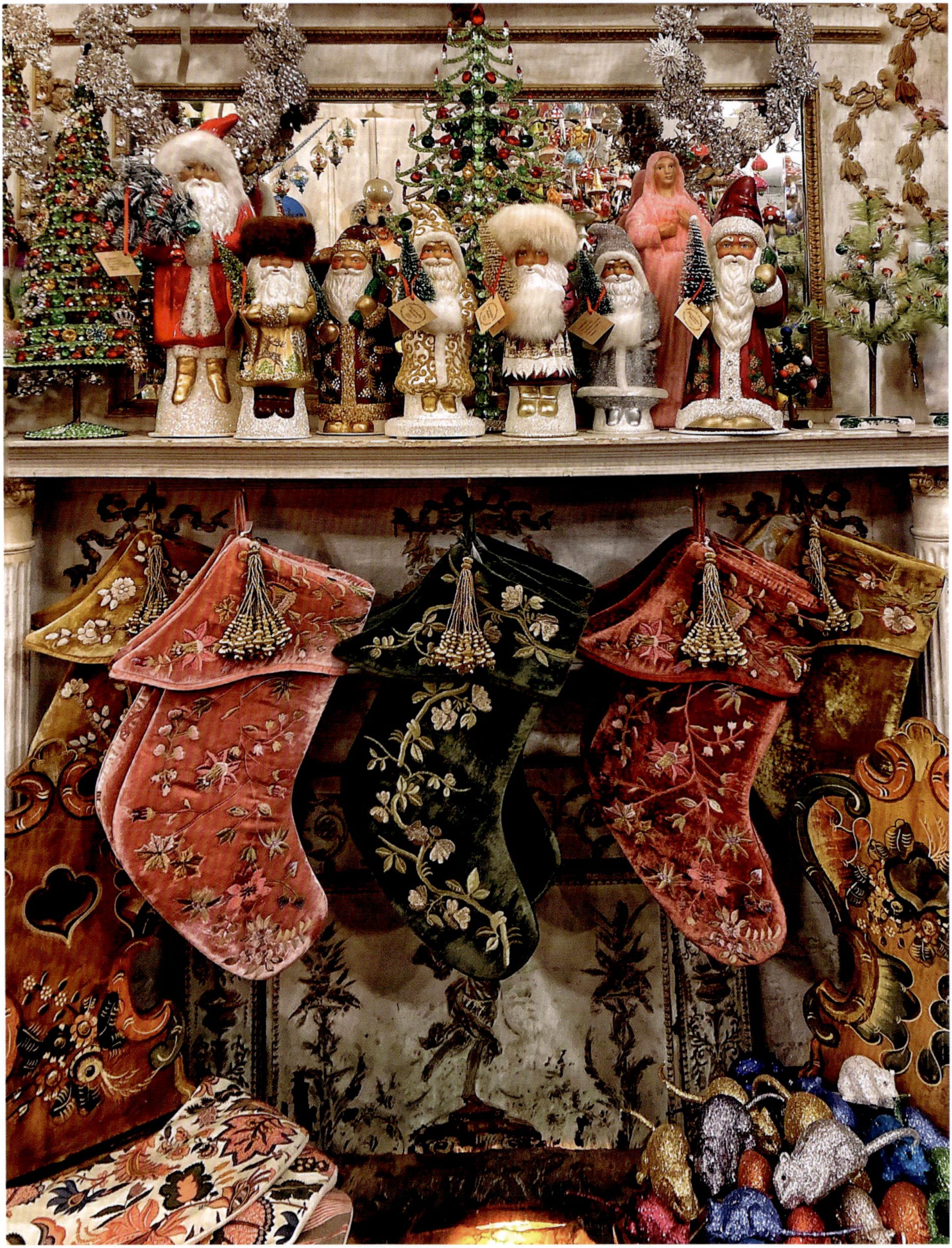

Contents

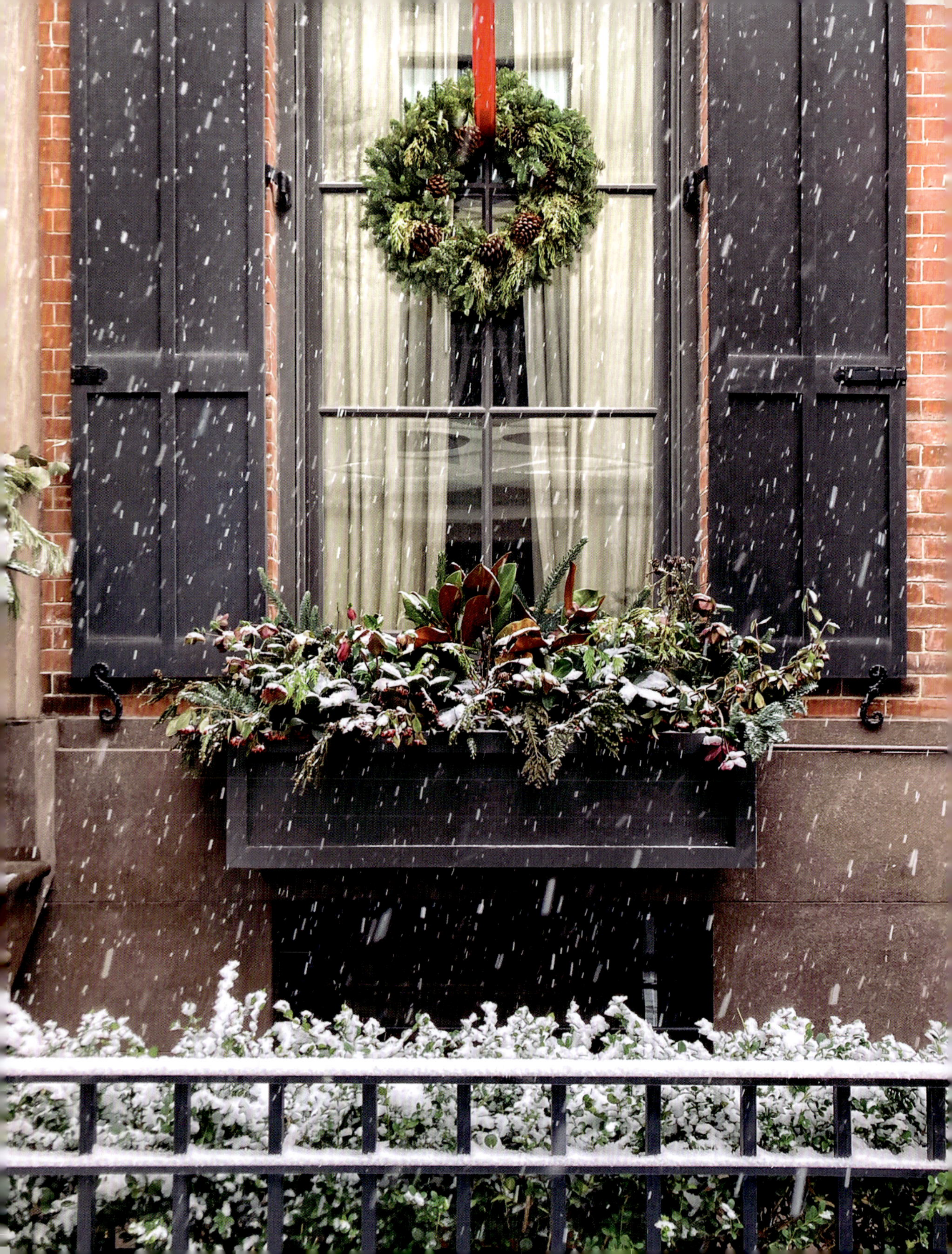

Introduction

I can still remember that childhood feeling of giddy anticipation as I awaited Santa's arrival on Christmas Eve, and the thrill of waking up Christmas morning to find stuffed stockings and presents under the tree. Now, as a grown-up, I get that same feeling every year around mid-November when I start to see festive decorations popping up all over New York City—signaling that the magical holiday season is just around the corner!

Whatever holiday you celebrate, I think it's the most wonderful time of year to be in the city—and so do the more than sixty-four million tourists who come from all over the world to experience its energy and spirit. Even jaded locals catch the buzz of excitement in the air. To be here during the holidays is to feel like a kid again—there's so much to delight the senses and bring joy.

In the weeks leading up to the Macy's Thanksgiving Day Parade, which kicks off the official start to the season, stores, restaurants, hotels, and public spaces get to work preparing their creative displays for the mad rush of visitors to come. Twinkling lights are hung, garlands are draped, Nutcrackers stand ready, red bows are tied, and wreaths are put up. Christmas tree vendors line the sidewalks with rows of fresh-cut pines that fill the air with their wonderful aroma. Skating rinks open and holiday markets in Union Square, Bryant Park, and Grand Central Terminal set up their stalls for gift buying.

By early December, Midtown--the epicenter of holiday attractions--is dressed up and ready to wow the crowds who come to snap photos of the iconic Rockefeller Center Christmas Tree (more than 125 million visits in just six weeks!), gawk at Saks Fifth Avenue's spectacular light show, and admire the fabulous store windows along Fifth Avenue. But beyond Midtown there are many other enchantingly decorated areas of the city to discover: from the lavishly decked out townhouses and brownstones on the Upper East and Upper West Sides, to the stylishly adorned indie boutiques and restaurants in the West Village and SoHo.

OPPOSITE: Snow falling on classic seasonal trimmings on Bank Street in the West Village

These holiday gems are what you'll find in this book, along with the classic must-sees made famous on film. (Who hasn't seen Macy's in *Miracle on 34th Street*, or the Plaza hotel in *Home Alone 2: Lost in New York*?)

Over the years I've traversed Manhattan with my trusty iPhone from Uptown (60th to 95th Streets) to Midtown (23rd to 59th Streets) to Downtown (below 23rd Street), to capture and share on Instagram the most charming, iconic, and delightful holiday decorations and winter scenes. And every year my Instagram followers have enthusiastically commented, "You need to do a New York City holiday book!" And so, I have!

The photos in this book include my favorite shots taken on those walks. In fact, many of those favorite images were taken on one picture-perfect December day during a snowfall. I was so energized and inspired by seeing the city transform into a winter wonderland that I walked more than twelve miles—from the Upper East Side, into Central Park, and down to the West Village without any fatigue. What could be better than experiencing a white Christmas in New York? Holiday decorations are ephemeral by nature; they are here and gone within six weeks. (Most decorations come down in early January.) Since many places switch things up every year, you may not be able to find the exact versions of the scenes captured in this book, but if you visit the lists of spots included on the "Holiday Favorites" page at the end of each section, you'll be sure to find something equally beautiful and inspiring.

I hope you'll have as much fun looking through this book as I had shooting the photos in it, and I hope it will convey the spirit and magic of my hometown at my favorite time of the year. Maybe it will inspire you to visit one day, or it will bring back happy memories of past visits, or maybe it will just provide a little eye candy to enjoy in your own home. I'd like to think of it as a heartfelt celebration of the city I love, and my little present to you.

—Susan Kaufman
New York City, 2026

OPPOSITE, CLOCKWISE FROM TOP LEFT: Magnolia-covered columns and wreaths on East 95th Street; shimmering berries and velvet bow at the LoveShackFancy boutique on Bleecker Street; old-fashioned Christmas lights on Bank Street; a decorated evergreen garland on Charles Street

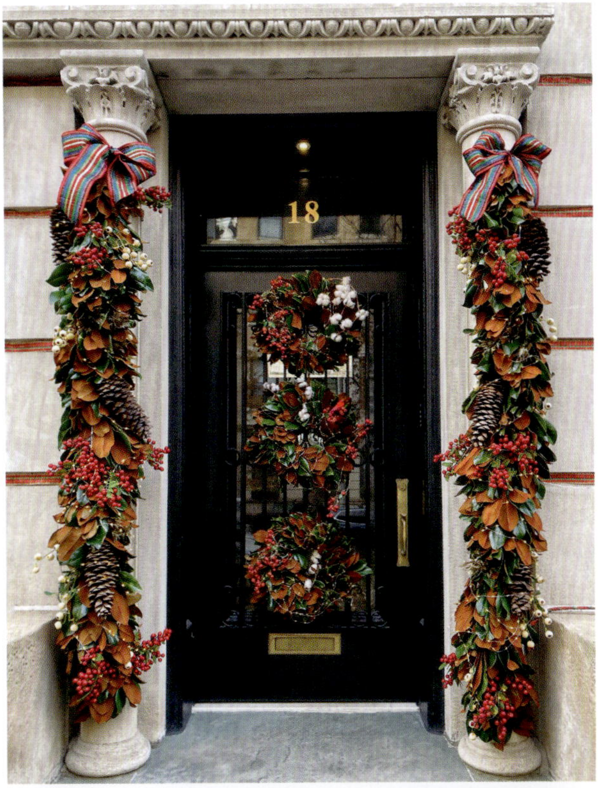
18
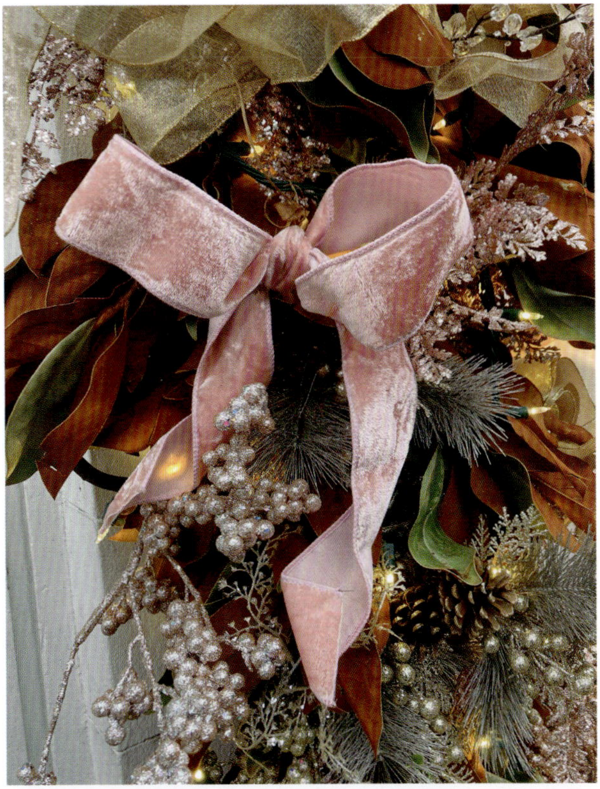
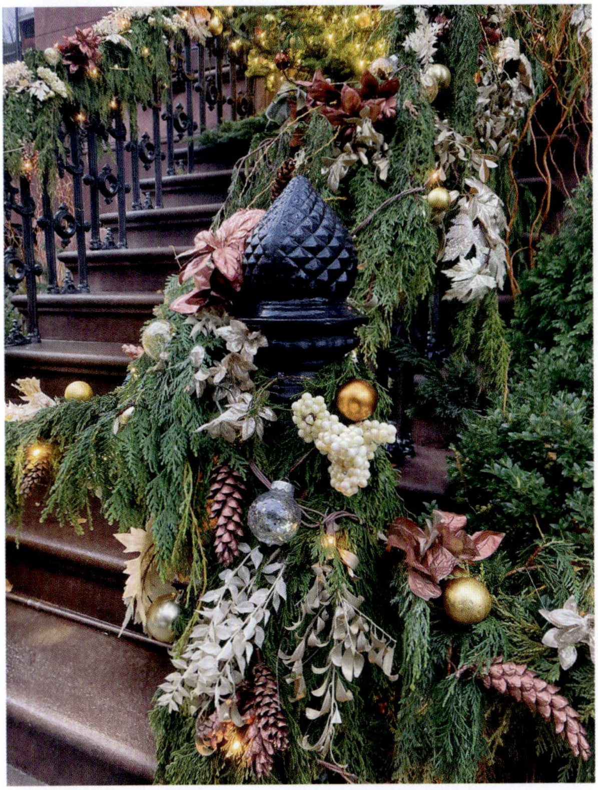
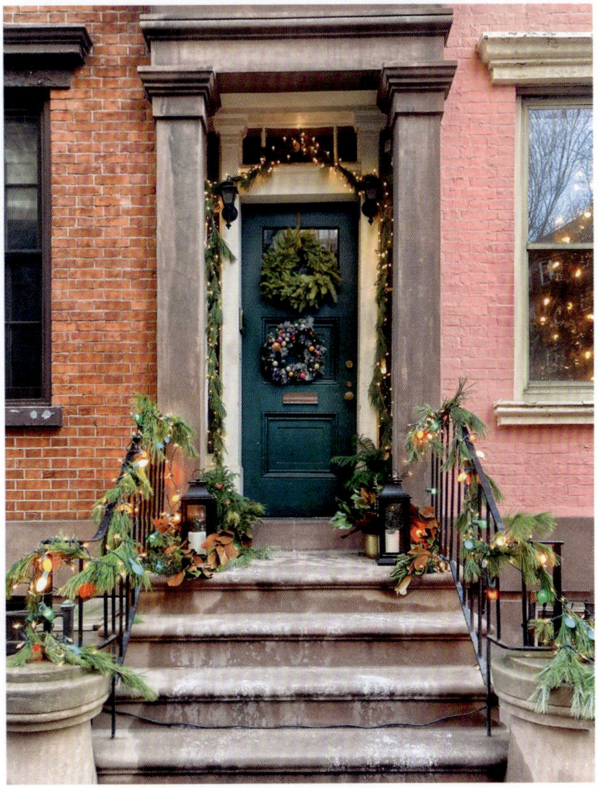

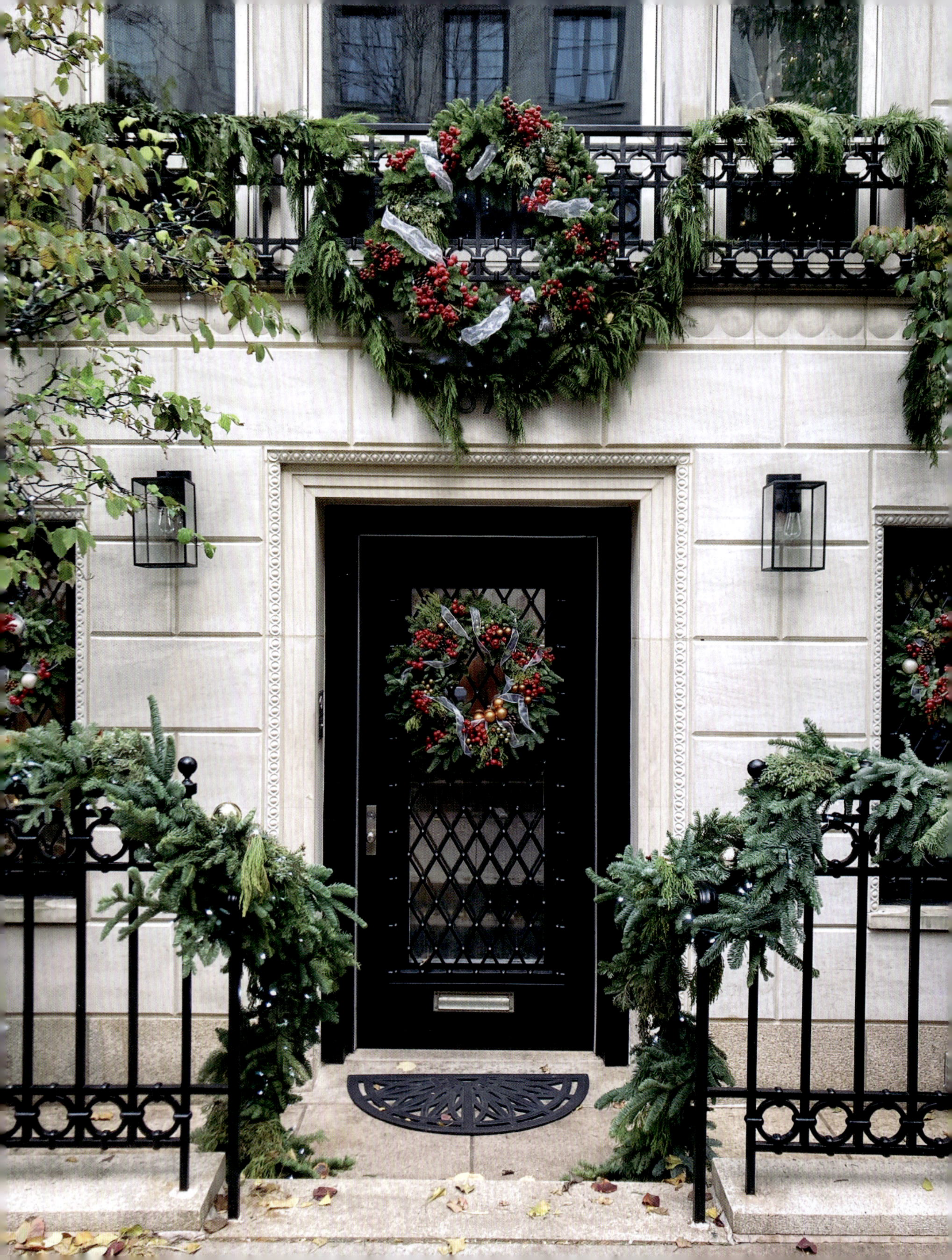

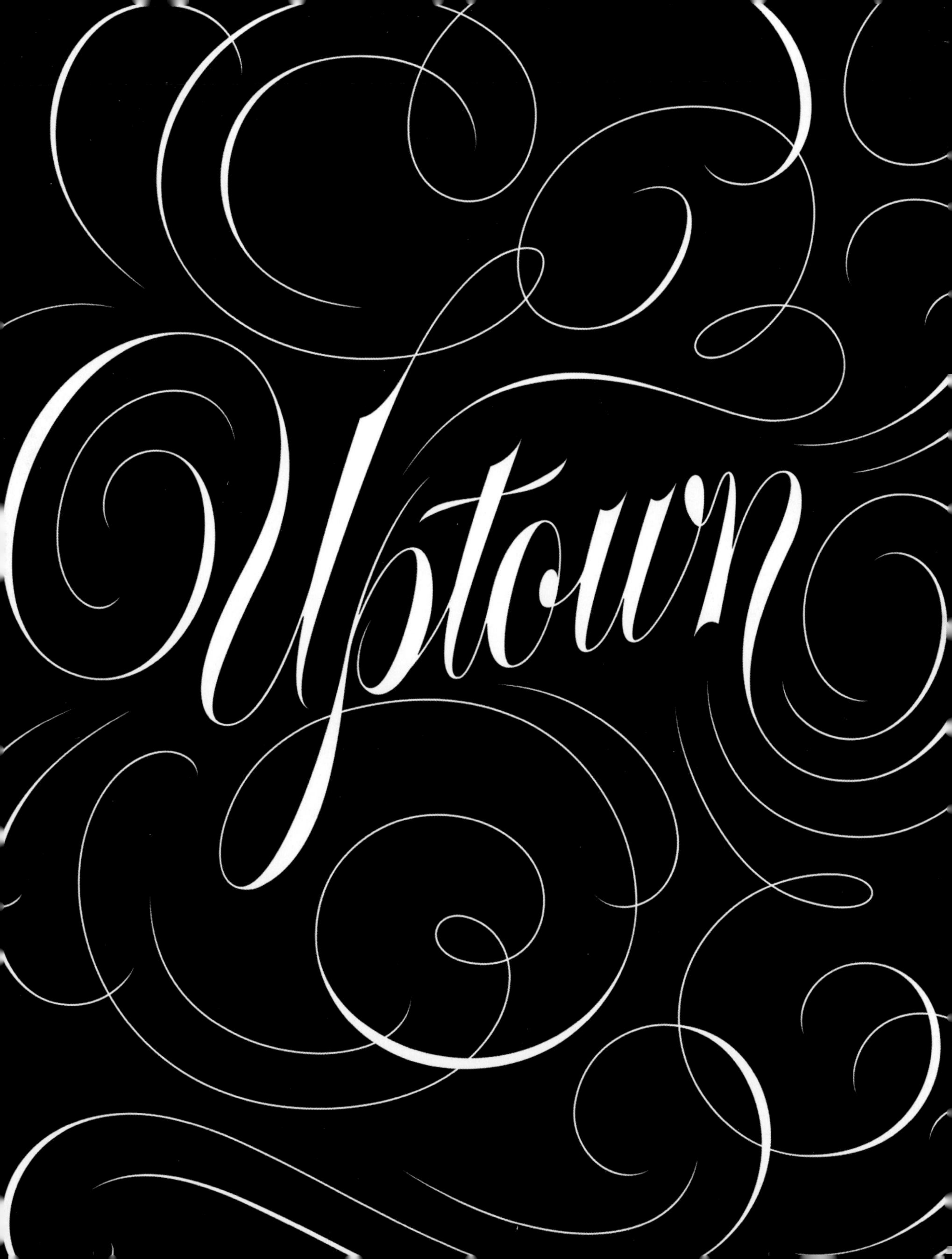
Uptown

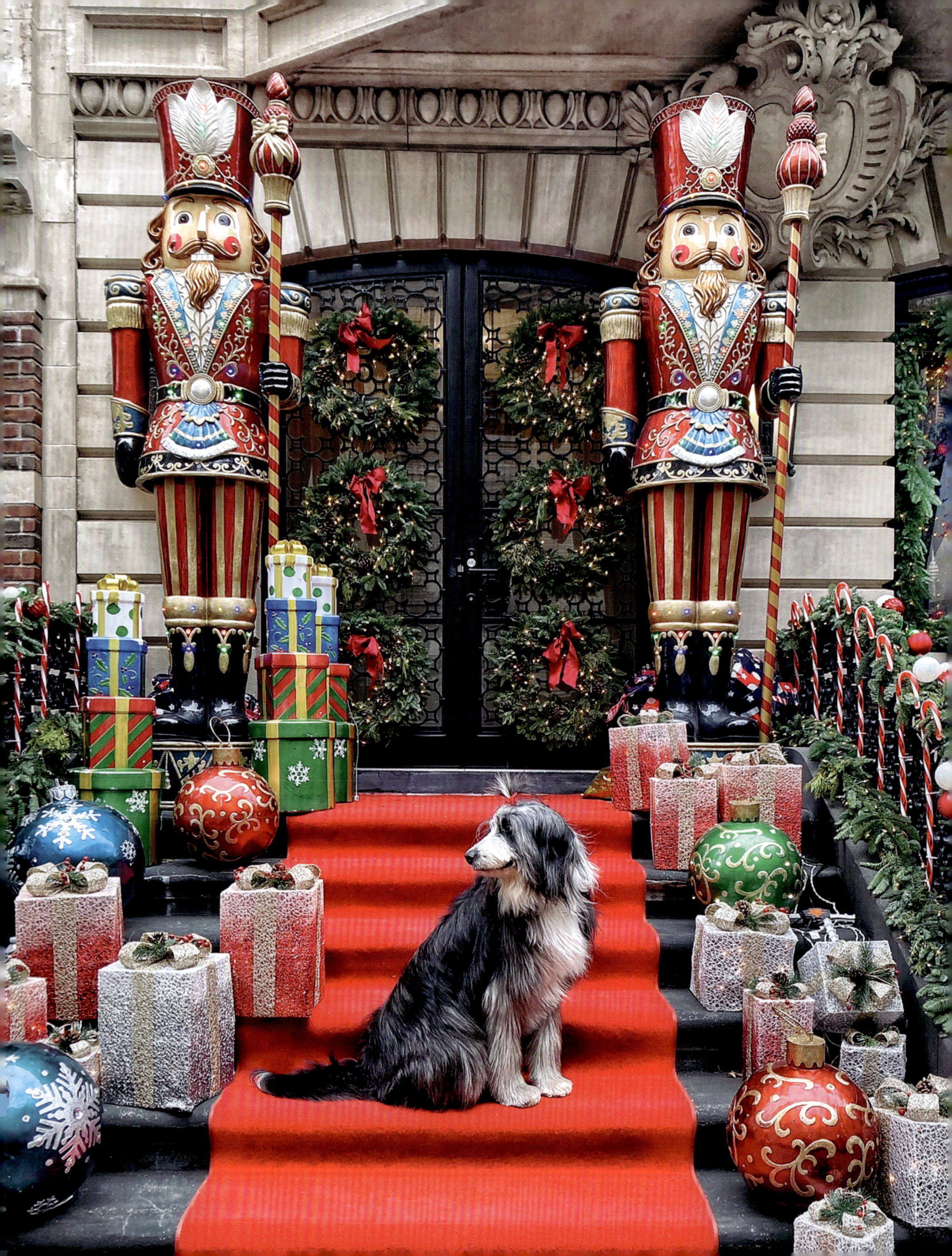

Uptown

One of my favorite things to do during the holiday season is to stroll around the quiet streets of the Upper East Side from 60th Street up to 95th in search of fabulous Christmas decorations to photograph. It's like being on a treasure hunt—and treasures abound!

This mostly residential part of the city is filled with stunning limestone townhouses whose owners spare no expense dressing up their stoops and facades with every style of ornamentation imaginable—from over-the-top and whimsical to simple and elegant. Some of New York City's most talented floral and event designers, and even a few D.I.Y. homeowners, create these wonderful and imaginative displays for all to enjoy. And every year more and more homes are joining in the fun.

I also love taking a leisurely walk up Madison Avenue (the less grand but equally festive alternative to Midtown's Fifth Avenue) to window-shop and admire the tastefully decked-out luxury boutiques and hotels, and to pop into Ralph's Coffee for a tasty cappuccino. (Unless the line is too long!) While uptown, I always visit the Metropolitan Museum of Art to see the stunning Neapolitan Christmas tree—it's one of my favorite holiday traditions.

If we're lucky enough to get a December snowfall, there's no place more magical to be than Central Park. It's like a Currier and Ives print come to life with dogs frolicking, children sledding, and people enjoying themselves in a true winter wonderland.

When I've had my festive fill of the Upper East Side, I can always take a walk through the park to check out more festively adorned brownstones on the Upper West Side—with a stop along the way to check out the iconic Tavern on the Green in all its holiday glory. Walking uptown and taking in the holiday sights is a perfect way to spend a day, or even two.

PREVIOUS: Elaborate garlands and wreaths dress up this simple townhouse façade on East 82nd Street between Park and Madison Avenues. **OPPOSITE:** This must-see townhouse on East 76th Street between Madison and Fifth Avenues pulls out all the decorating stops, including a photo-op-worthy red carpet, even for cute pooches.

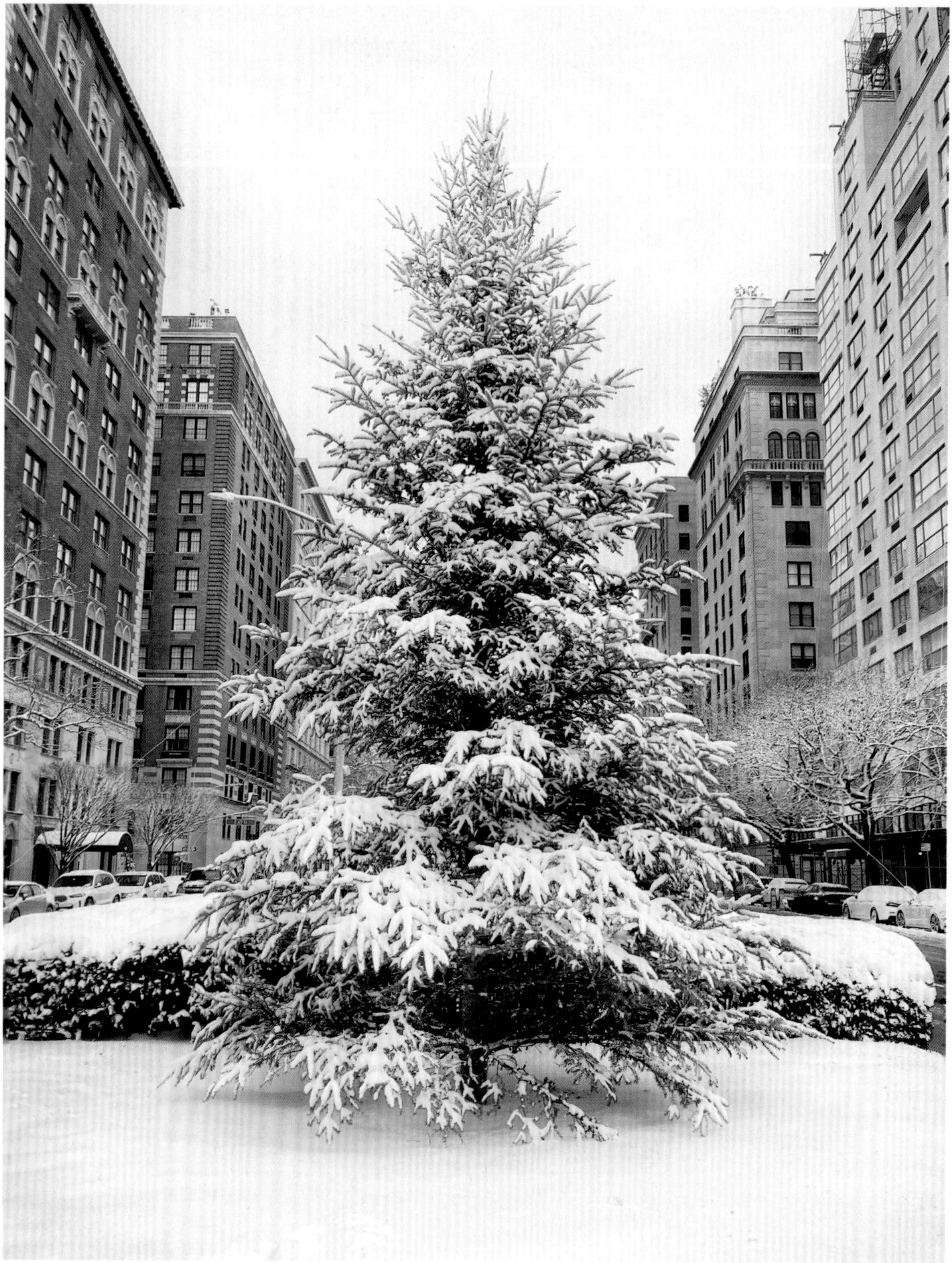

ABOVE: A snow-covered Christmas tree on the Park Avenue Mall and East 64th Street. Every year trees are put up along the Mall from 54th to 97th Streets. **OPPOSITE:** A simple white townhouse with traditional wreaths on East 61st Street between Park and Lexington Avenues

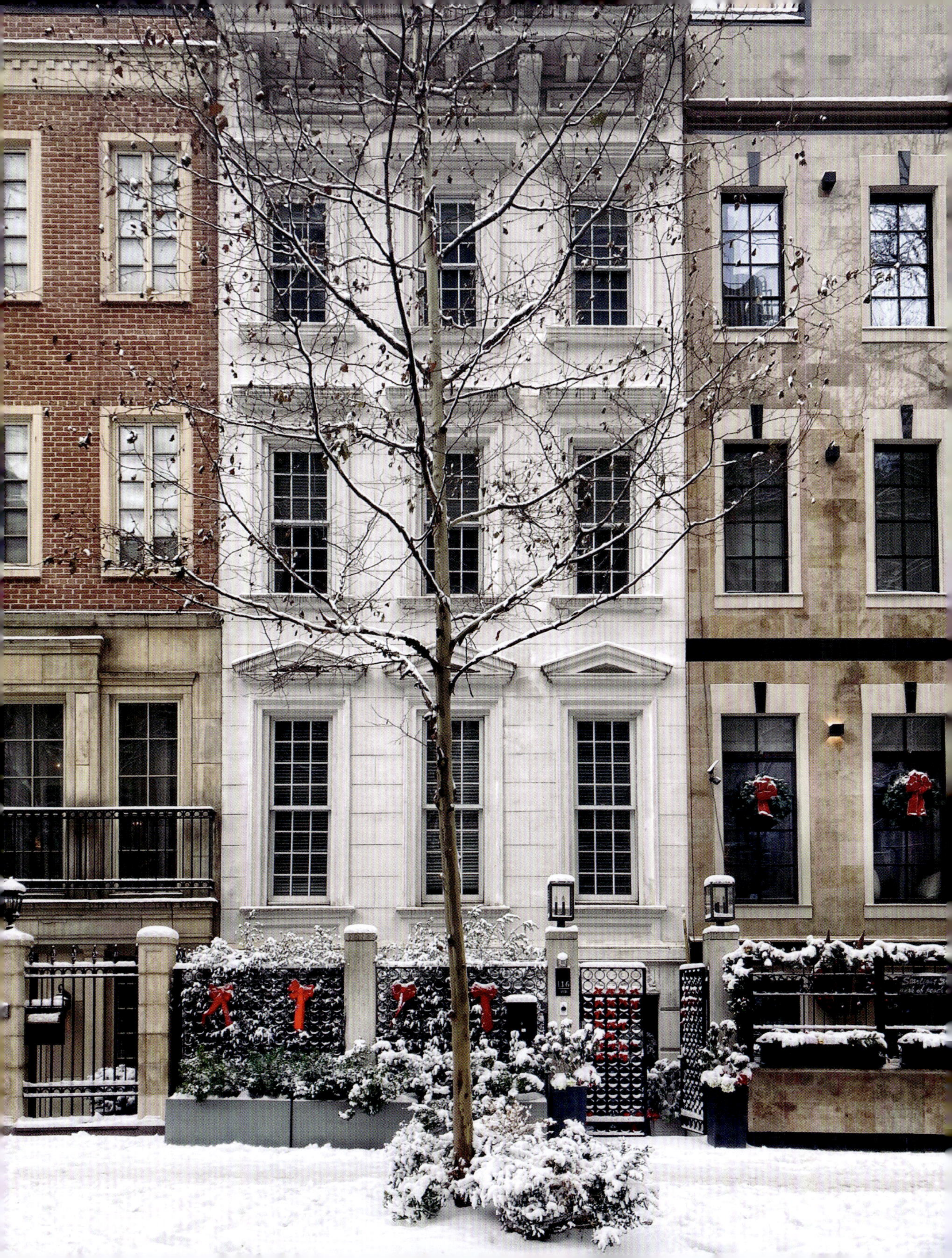
116

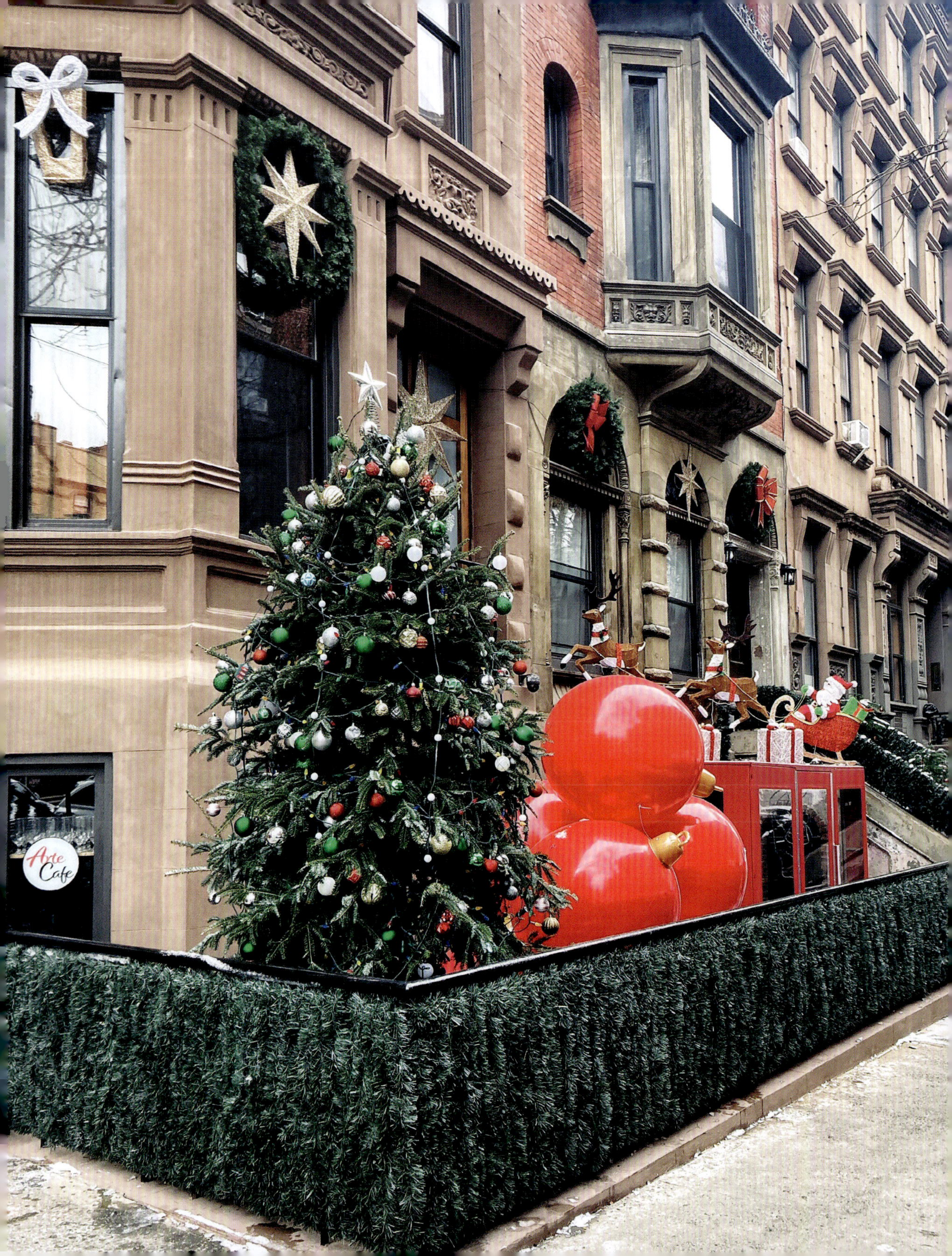
Arte
Cafe

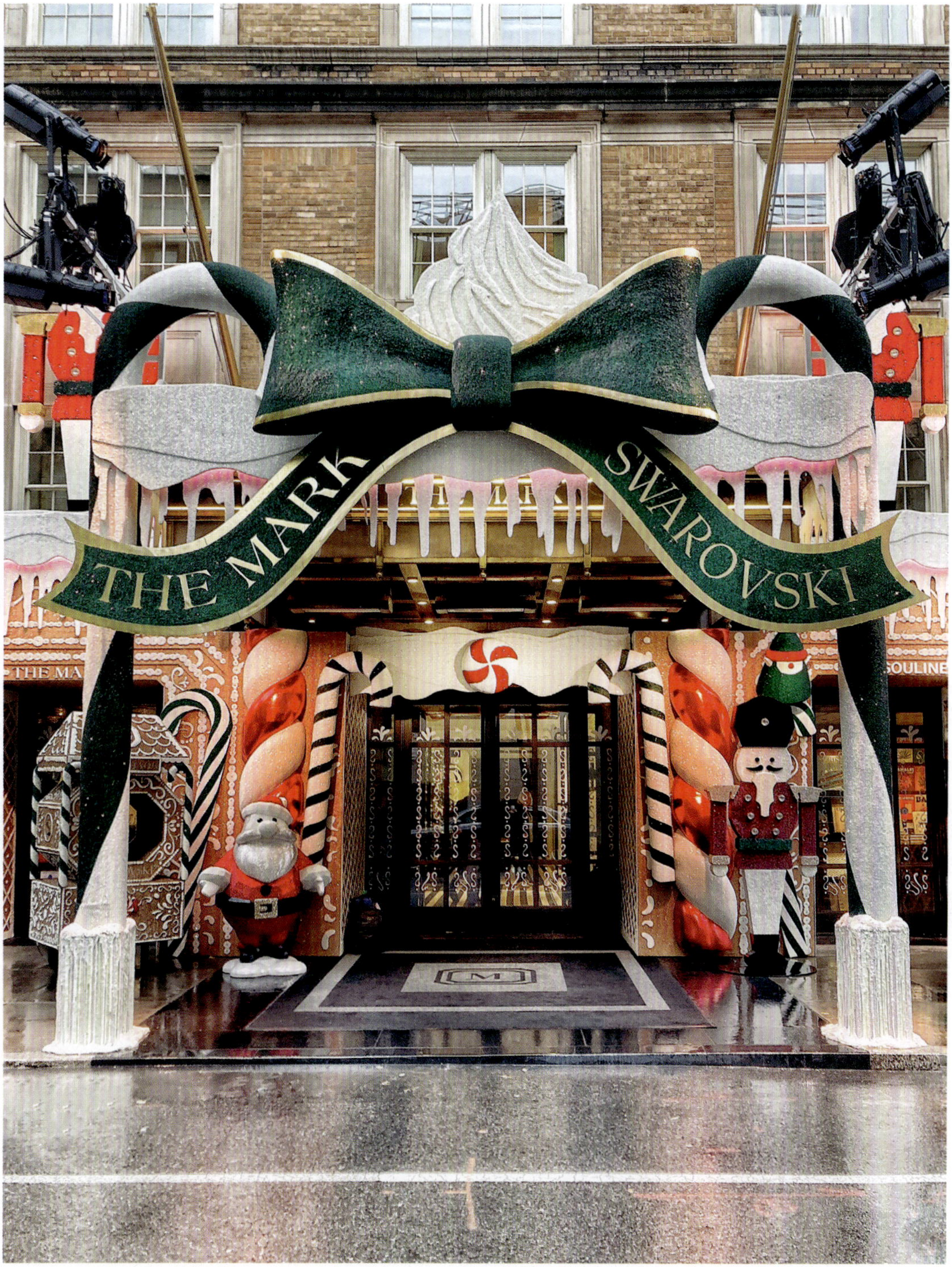

OPPOSITE: Arte Cafe on West 73rd Street and Columbus Avenue adds a holly-jolly good time to the Upper West Side. **ABOVE:** Jewelry brand Swarovski created a gingerbread-house facade covered in crystals for the exclusive Mark Hotel on East 77th Street between Madison and Fifth Avenues.

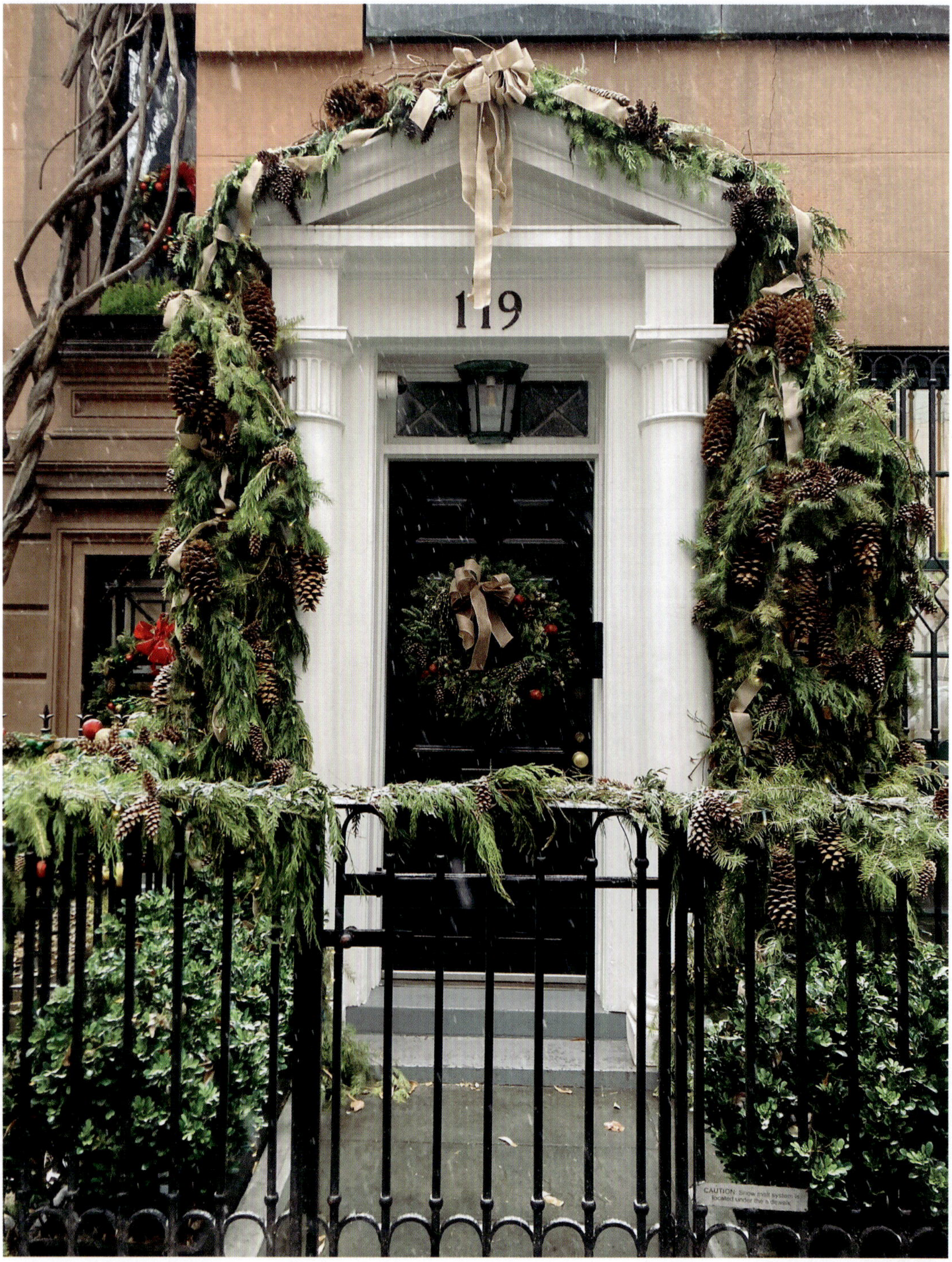

ABOVE: Pretty garlands, ribbons, and pine cones frame a doorway on East 78th Street between Lexington and Park Avenues. **OPPOSITE, CLOCKWISE FROM TOP LEFT:** Topiaries and ribbons on East 70th Street; gold ribbons on green wreaths on East 66th Street; a garland-swathed fence on East 73rd Street; Christmas trees and sparkly snowflakes on East 78th Street

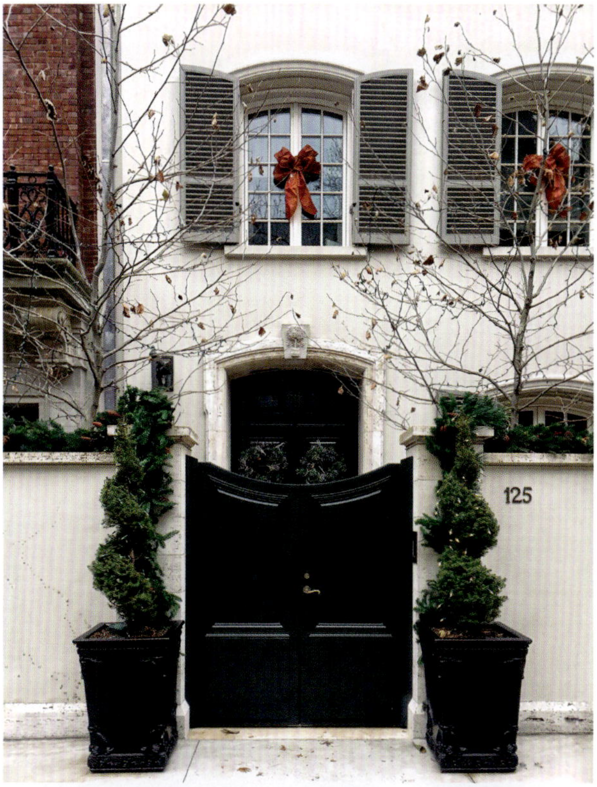
125
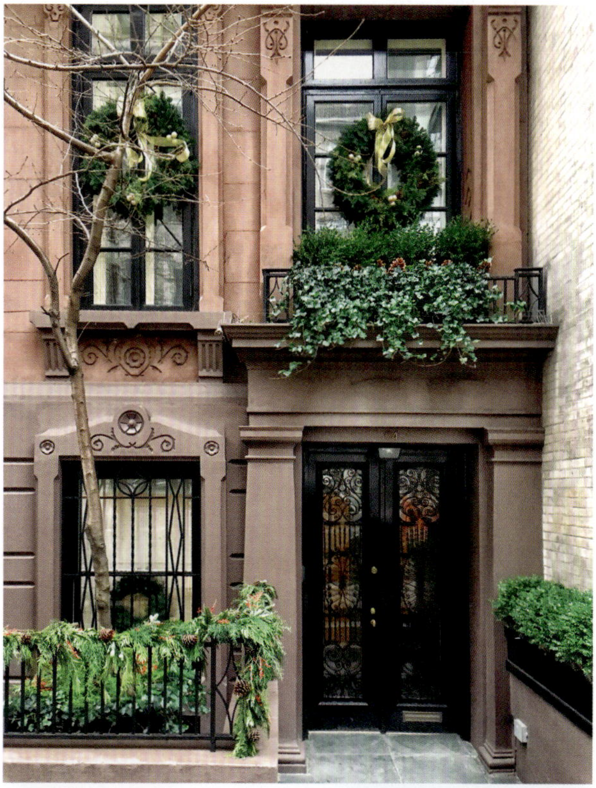
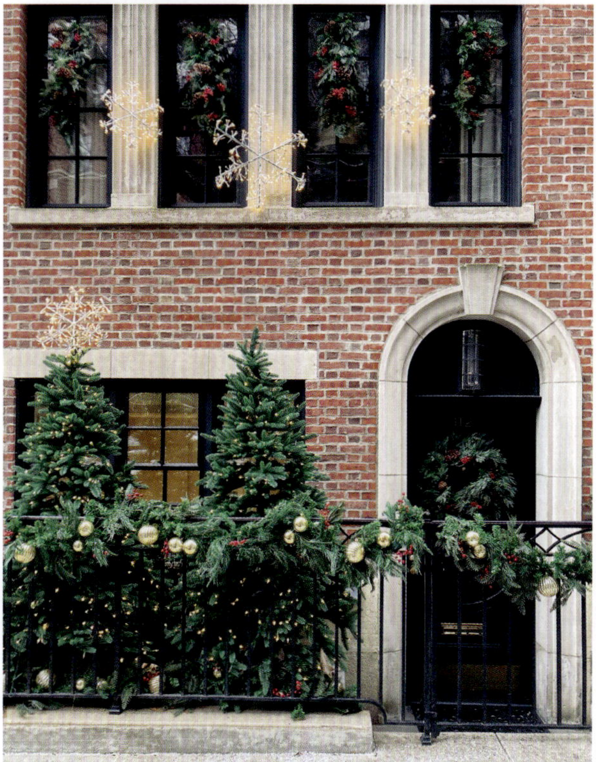
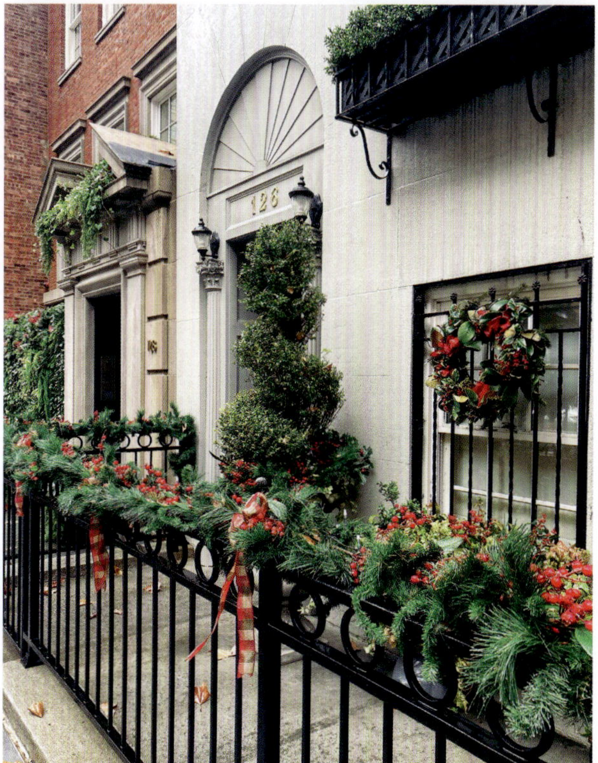
126

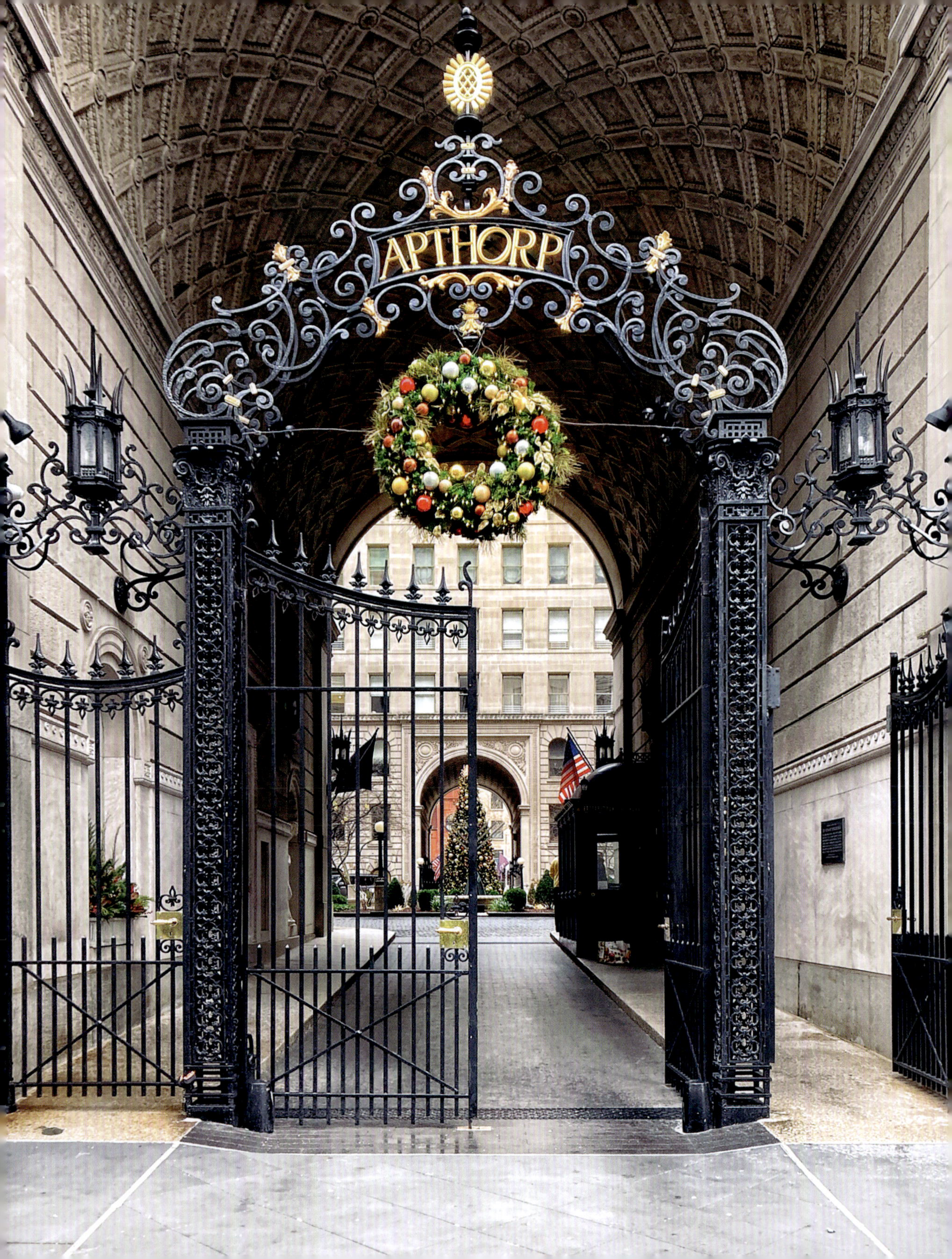
APTHORP

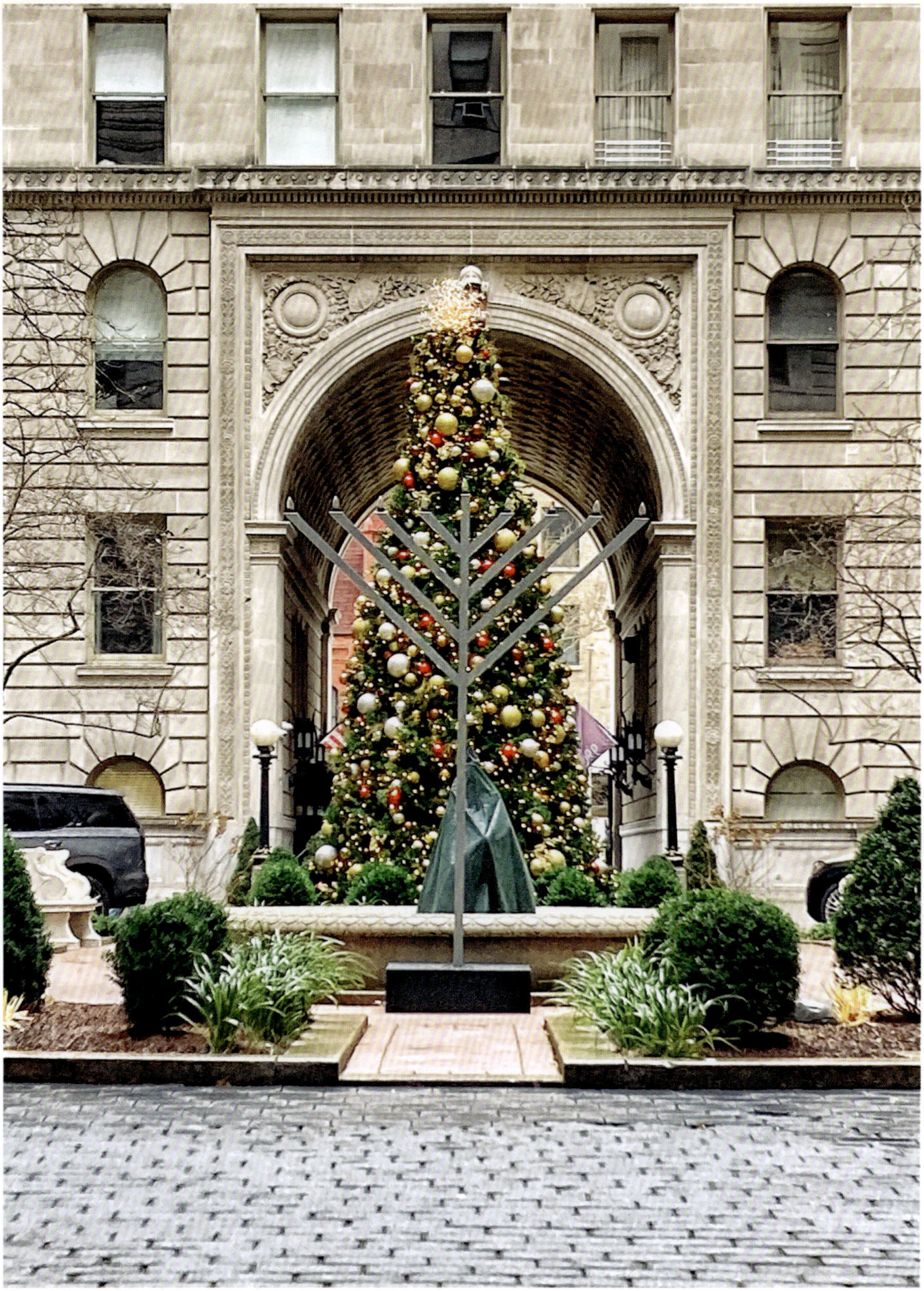

OPPOSITE AND ABOVE: A colorful wreath hangs from the elaborate wrought-iron gate of the Apthorp, an Italian Renaissance Revival building (ca. 1905–1908). A giant menorah and Christmas tree in the courtyard of the historic Apthorp building on Broadway between West 78th and 79th Streets.

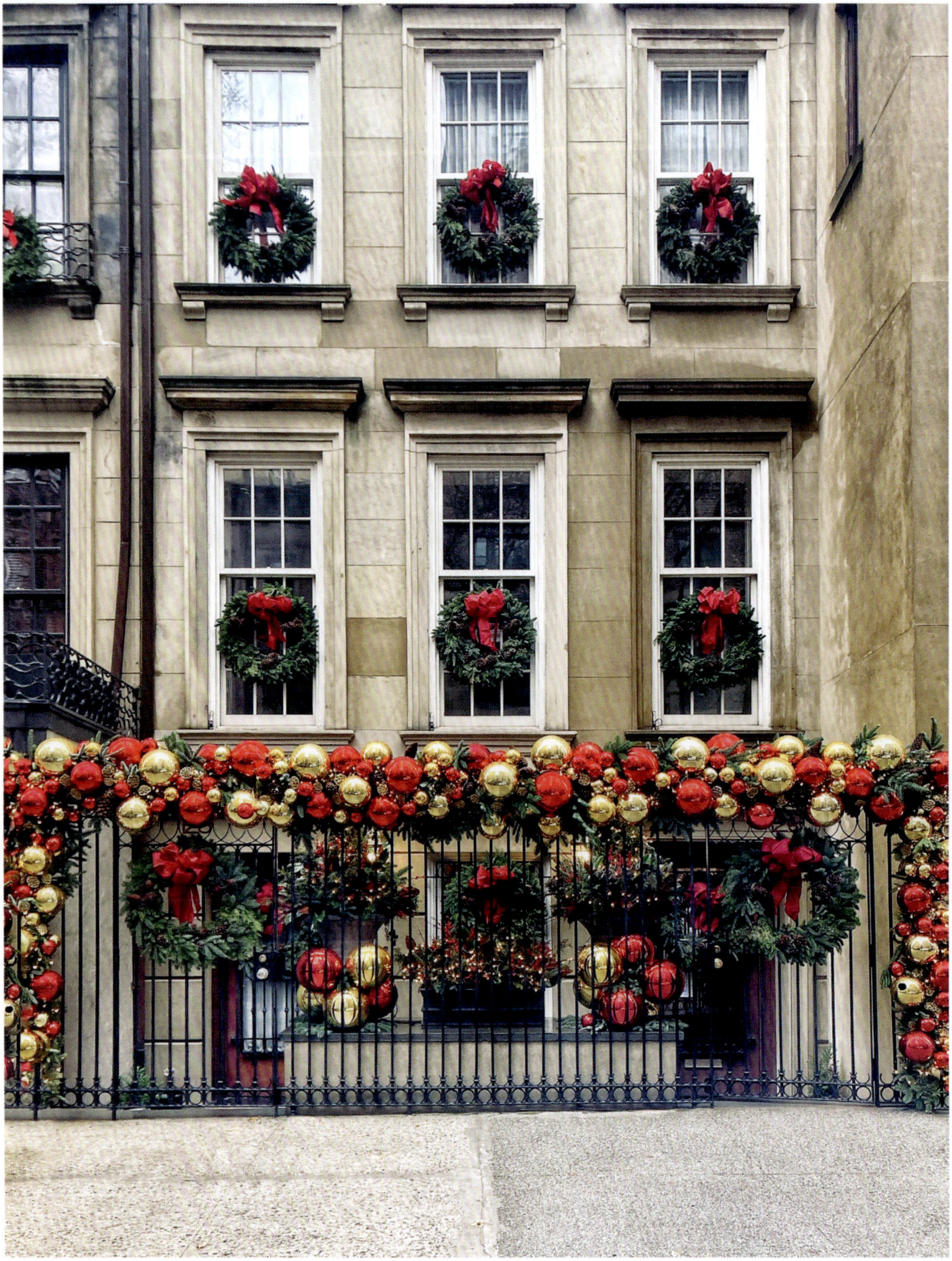

ABOVE: Red and gold baubles cover a gate, and wreaths are in every window on East 74th Street between Lexington and Park Avenues. **OPPOSITE:** Pulling out all the festive stops on East 72nd Street between Second and Third Avenues

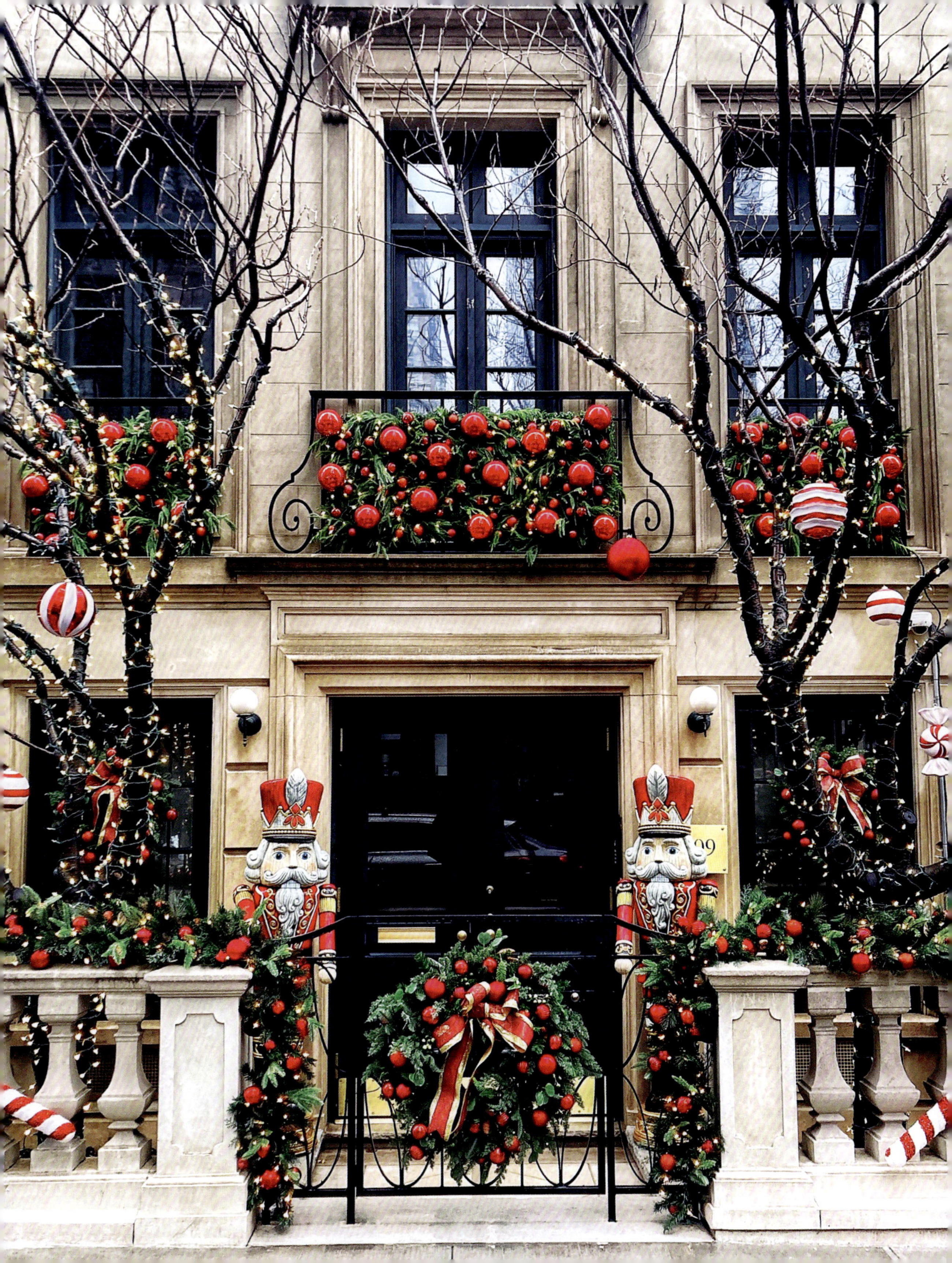

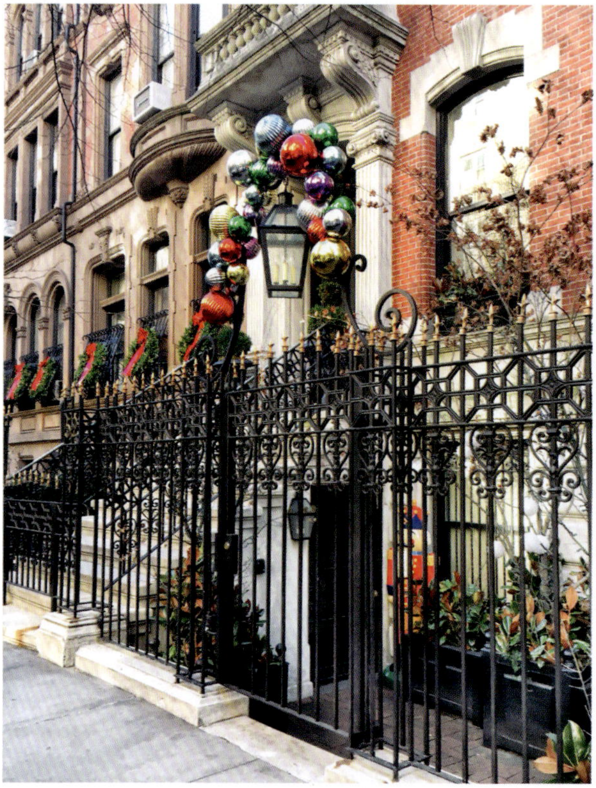
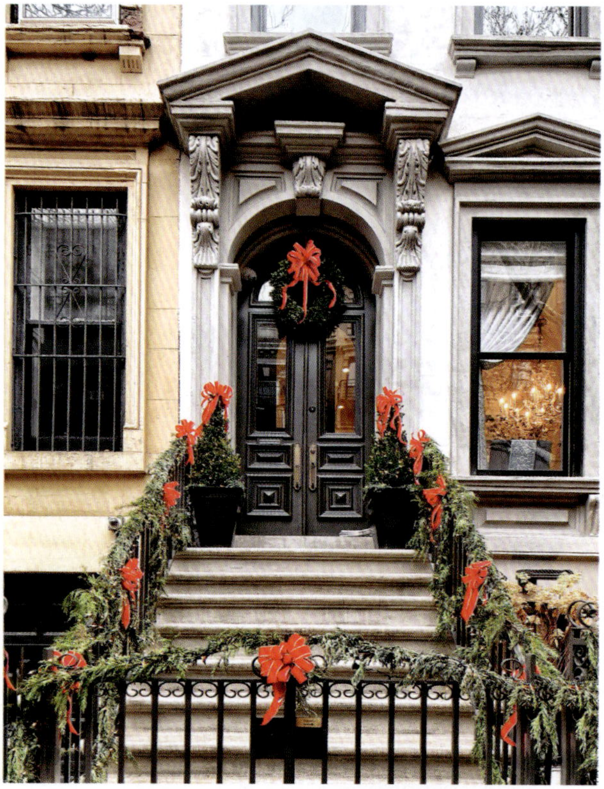
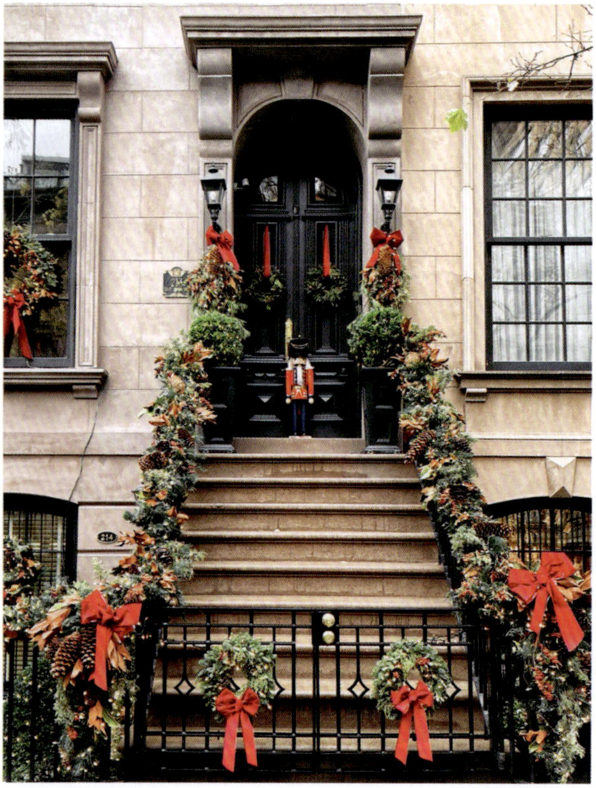
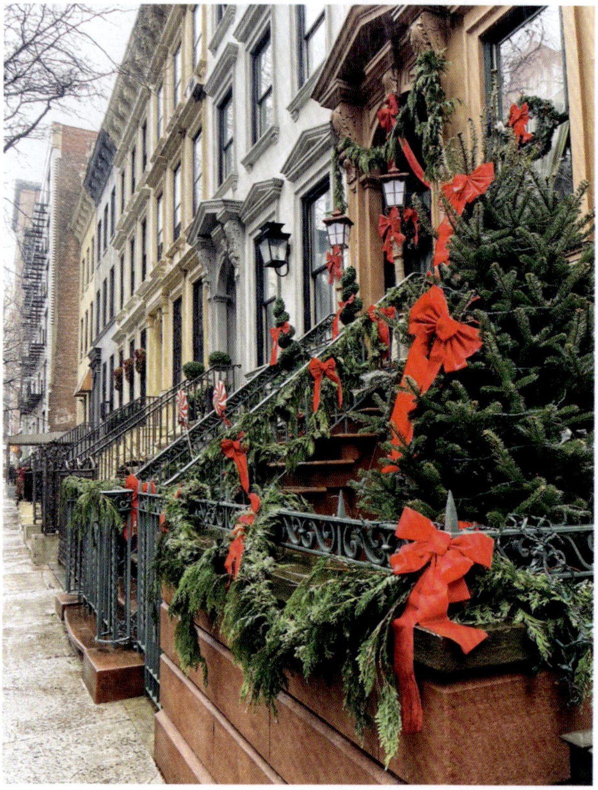

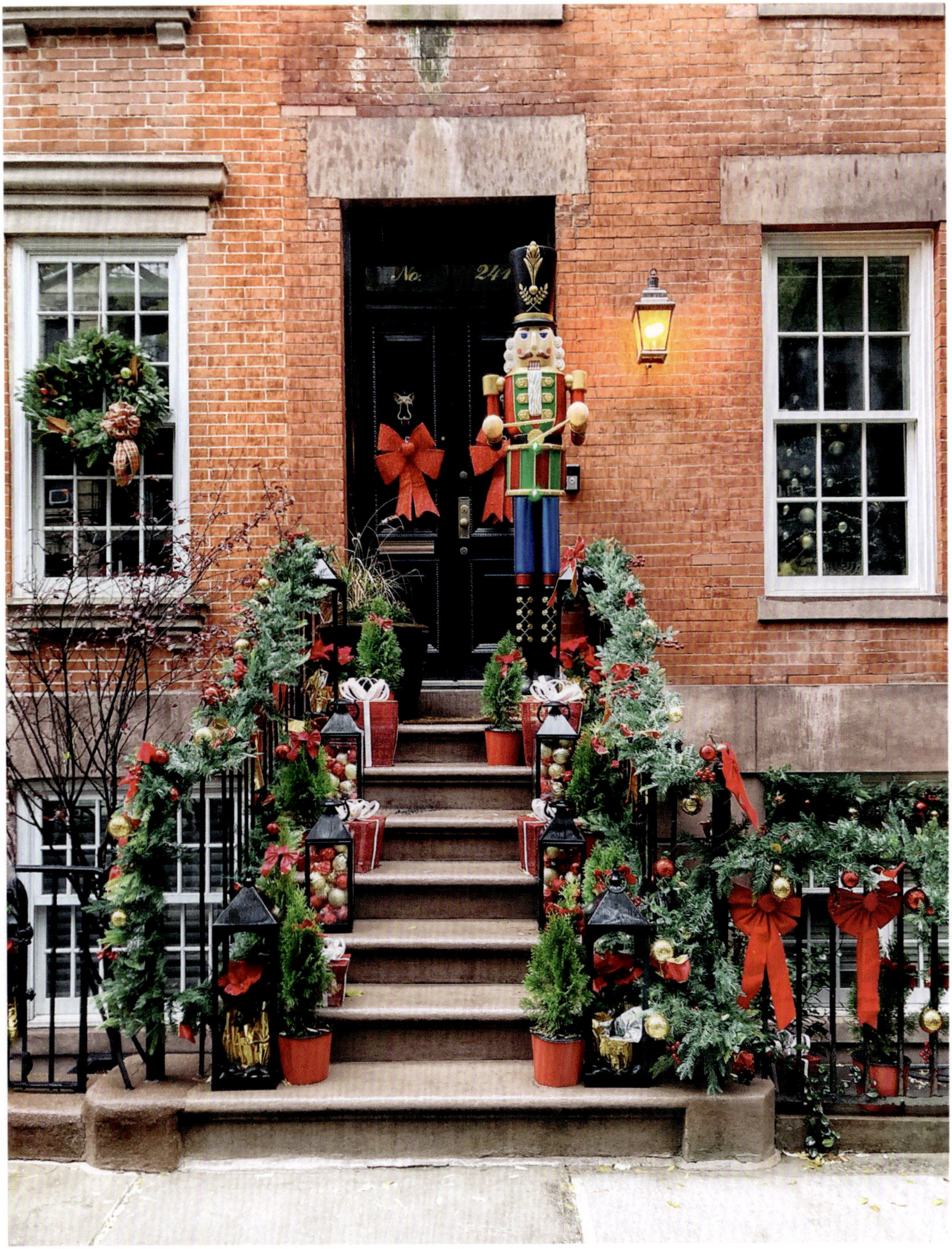

OPPOSITE, CLOCKWISE FROM TOP LEFT: An arch of colorful baubles on East 83rd Street; classic red bows on East 83rd Street; greenery covered in red bows on East 83rd Street; a mini nutcracker guards the door on East 61st Street. **ABOVE:** The owners of this townhouse on East 78th Street between Second and Third Avenues change up their stoop decor every year, and it's always a must-see destination.

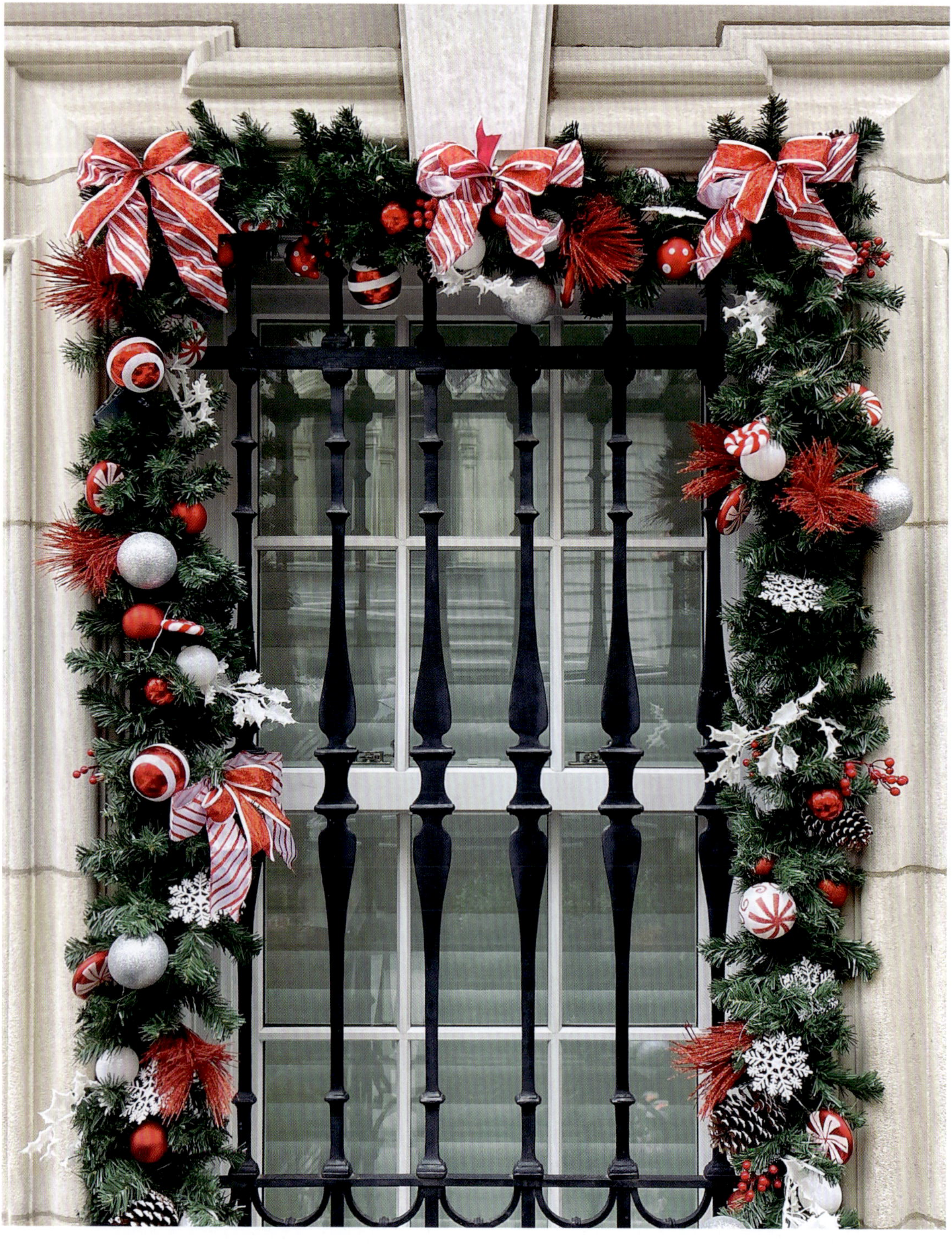

ABOVE: A charmingly trimmed window in classic Christmas colors on East 73rd Street between Madison and Fifth Avenues. **OPPOSITE:** Red wreaths in a rich garnet shade adorn a lovely cream-colored townhouse on East 64th Street between Lexington and Third Avenues.

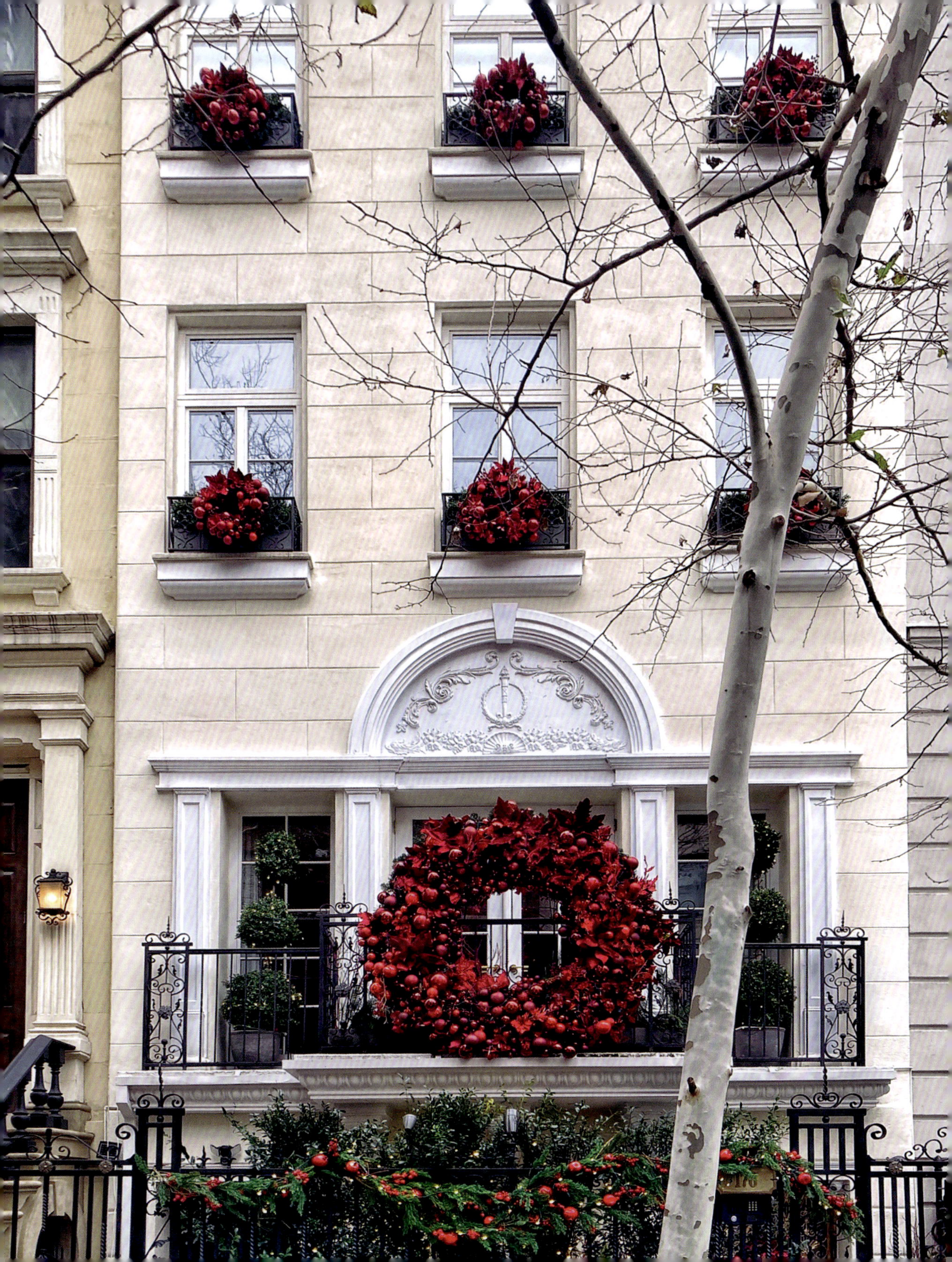

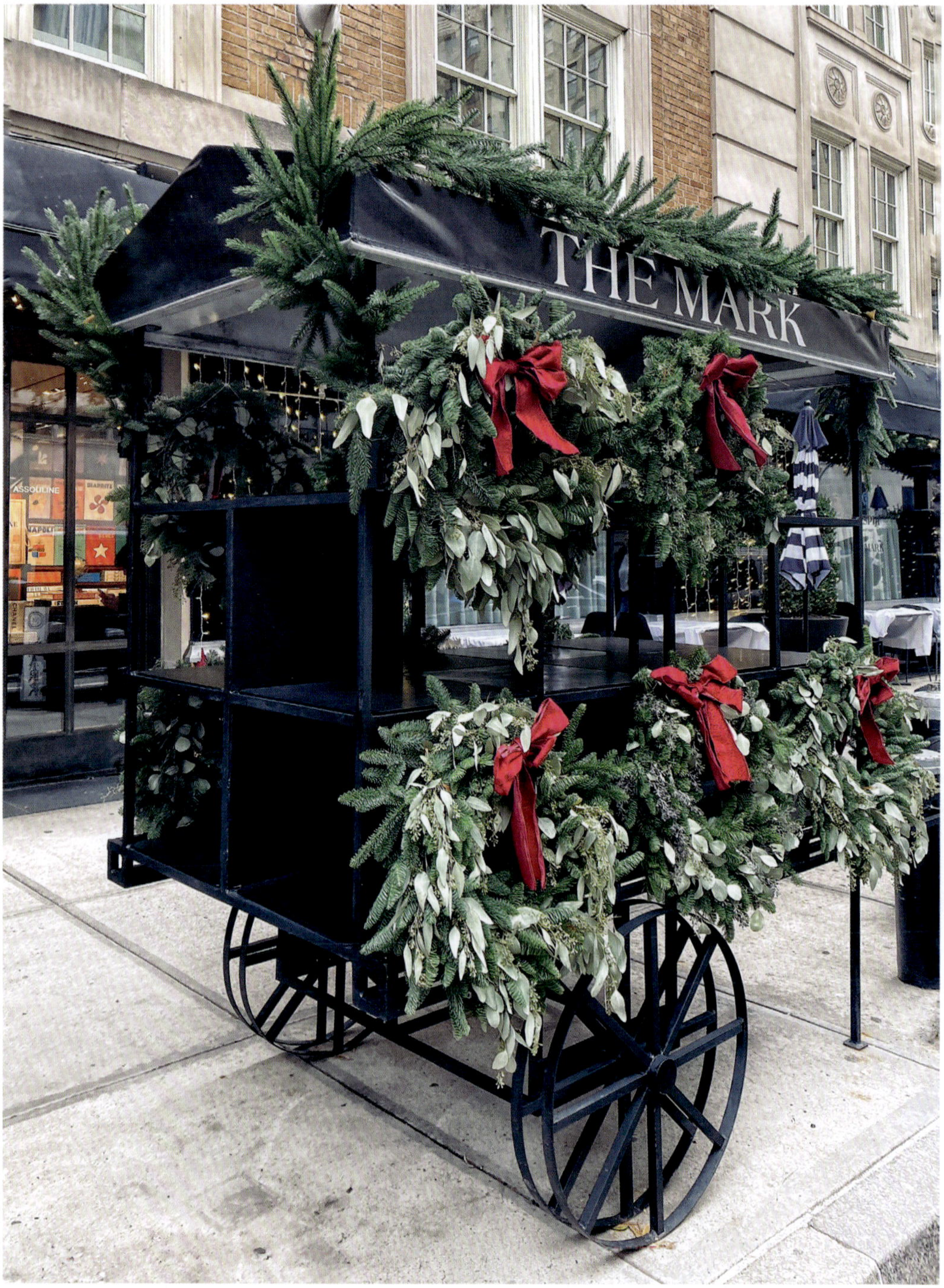

ABOVE: A selection of eucalyptus and pine wreaths on the Mark Hotel's charming flower cart.
OPPOSITE, CLOCKWISE FROM TOP LEFT: Big bows and greenery on shops and restaurants along Madison Avenue: Frank & Eileen's boutique at East 65th Street; the Frances Valentine women's shop at East 73rd Street; French restaurant Match Brasserie on East 65th Street off Madison Avenue; Altesi, a classic Italian restaurant on East 64th Street and Madison Avenue

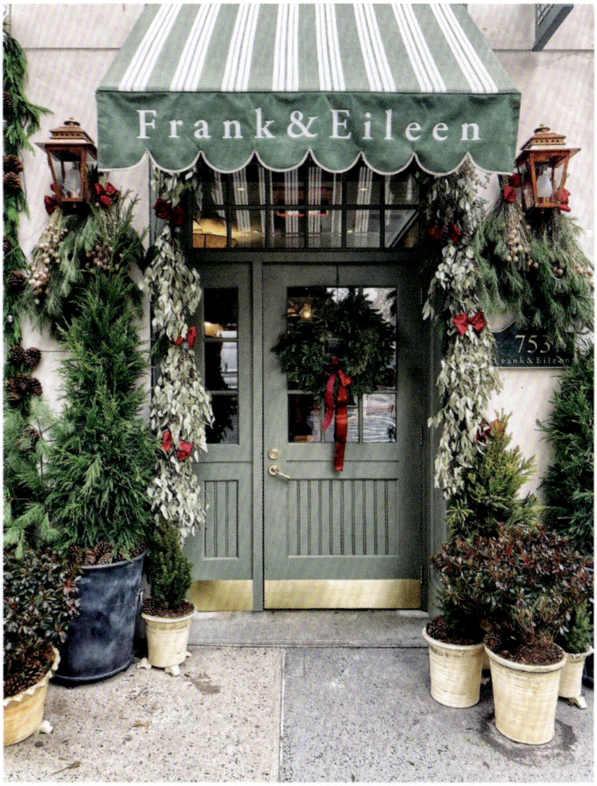
Frank&Eileen
753
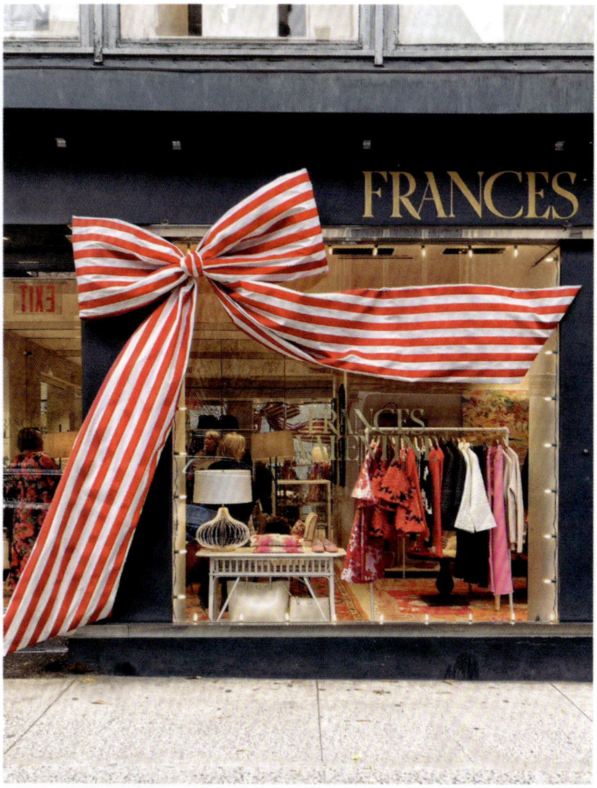
FRANCES
EXIT
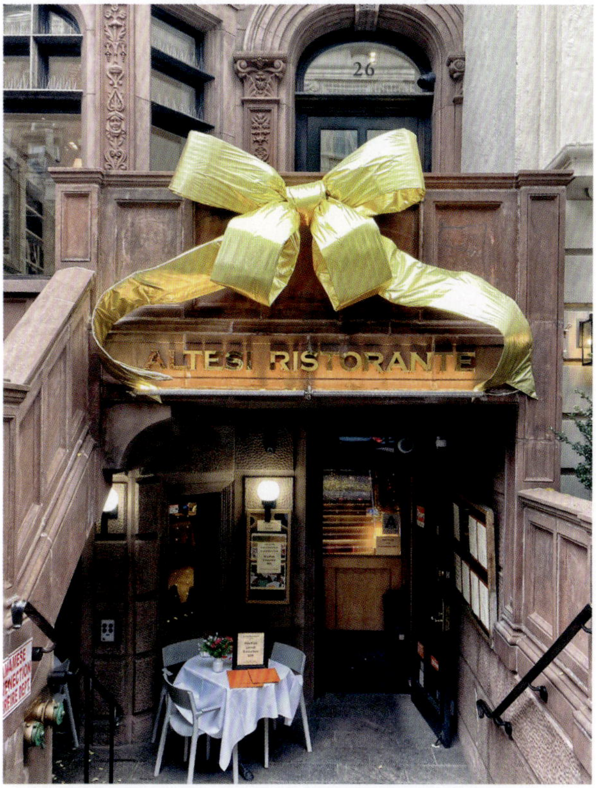
26
ALTESI RISTORANTE
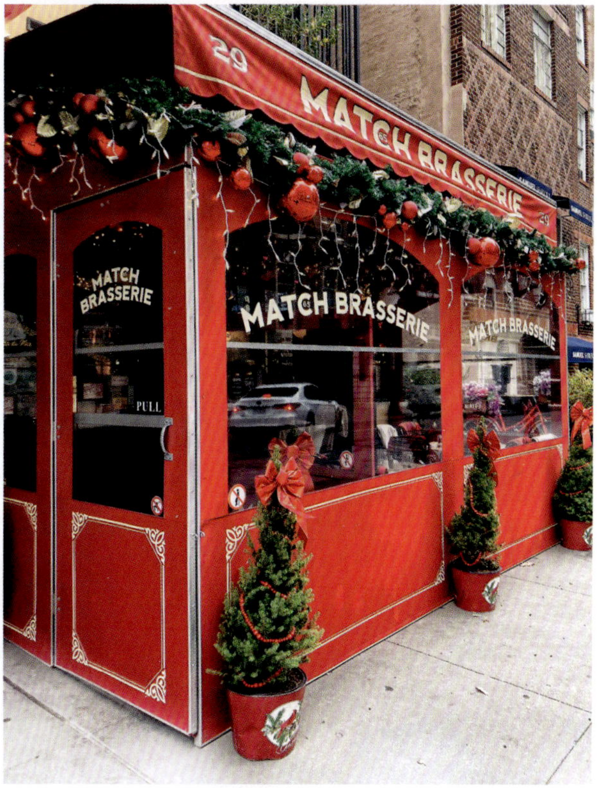
29
MATCH BRASSERIE
MATCH BRASSERIE
MATCH BRASSERIE
MATCH BRASSERIE
PULL

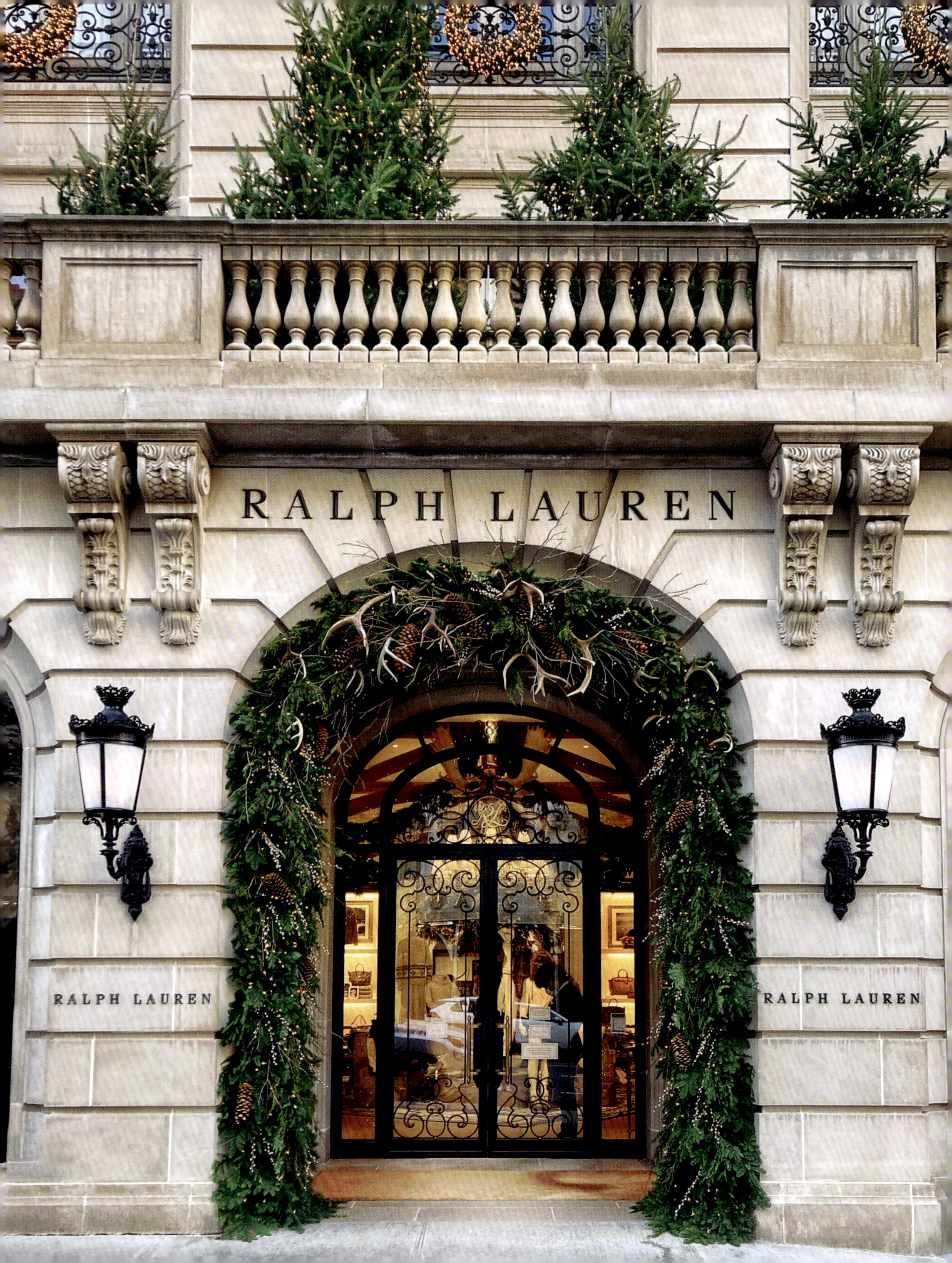
RALPH LAUREN
RALPH LAUREN
RALPH LAUREN

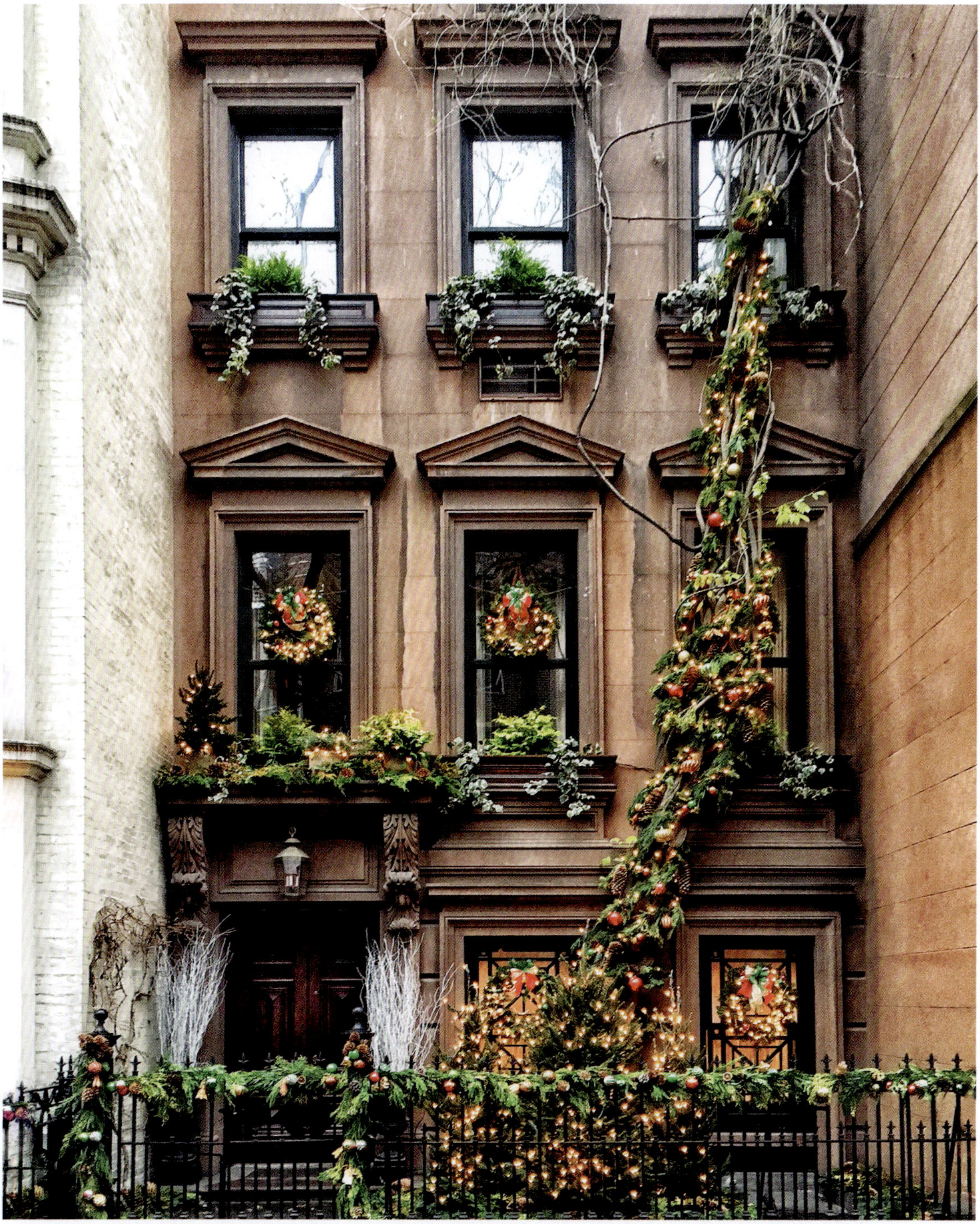

OPPOSITE: A "very Ralph" garland accessorized with pine cones, white berries, and antlers enhances the entrance to the Ralph Lauren women's store on Madison Avenue and East 72nd Street. **ABOVE:** Glittering wreaths and a wisteria vine festooned with lights, ornaments, and garlands give a warm holiday glow to this handsome townhouse on East 78th Street between Lexington and Park Avenues.

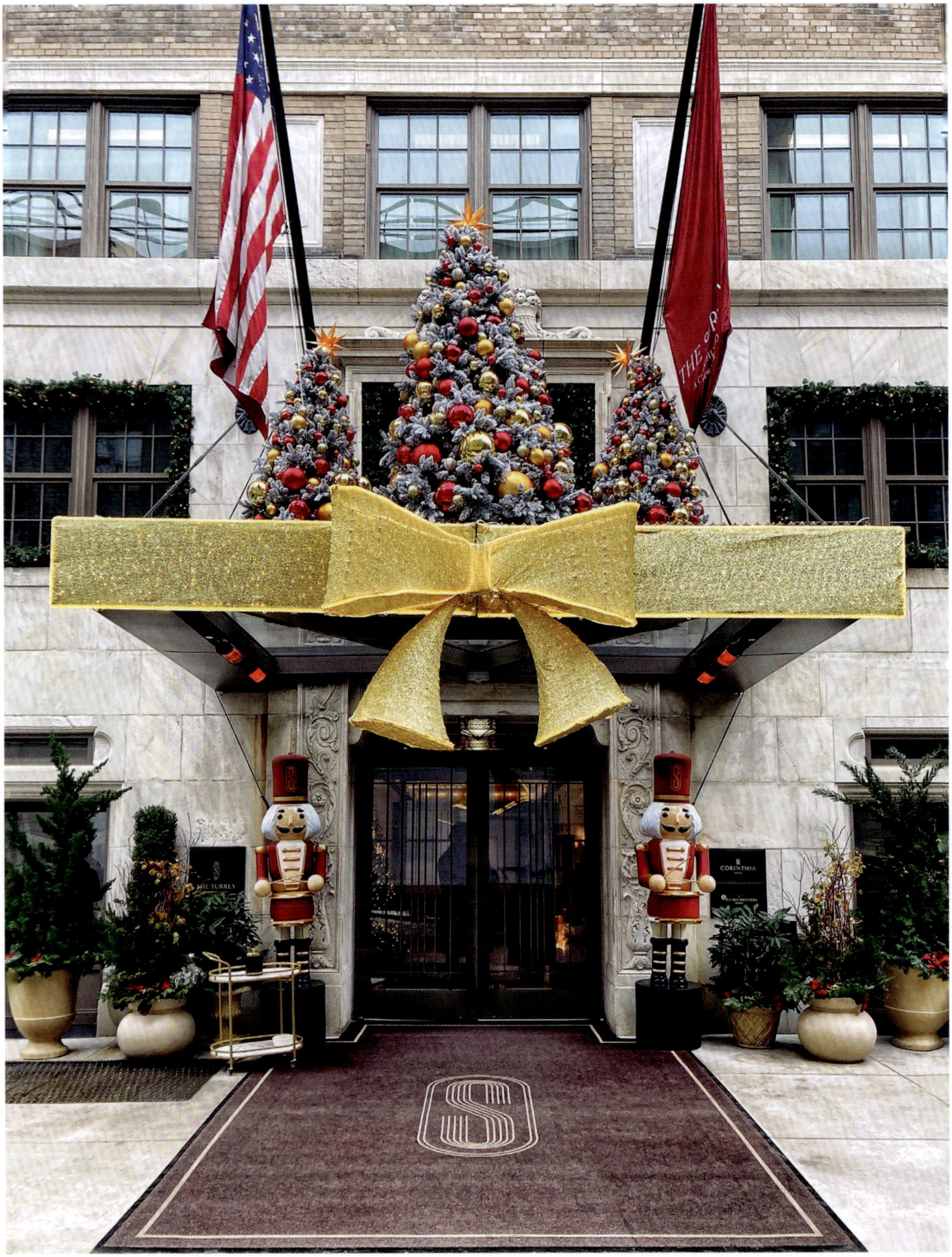

ABOVE: A giant gold bow and colorful Christmas trees welcome guests to the Surrey Hotel on East 76th Street between Madison and Fifth Avenues. **OPPOSITE, CLOCKWISE FROM TOP LEFT:** Birley Bakery, a French bakery and café on East 69th Street with a window displaying baked goods; a decorated Christmas tree and banister downstairs; a cozy café with fireplace upstairs; a fun selection of whimsical ornaments

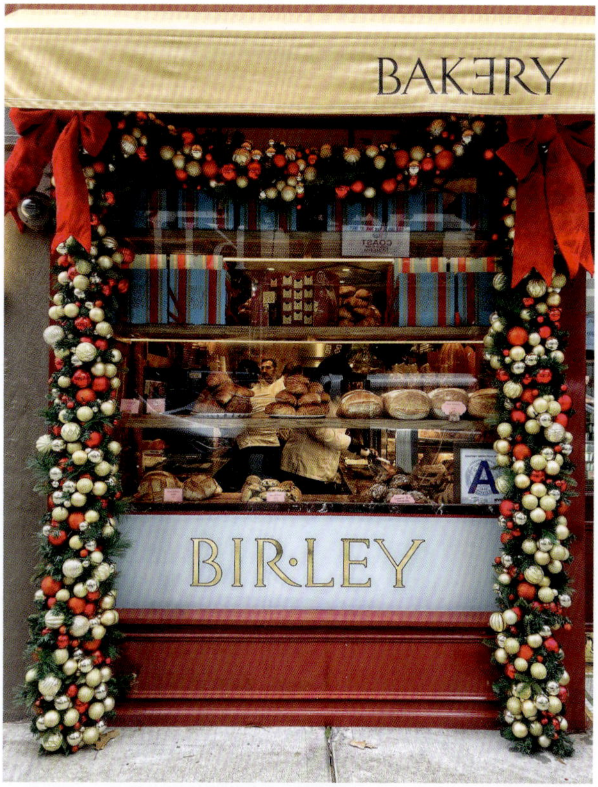
BAKERY
BIRLEY
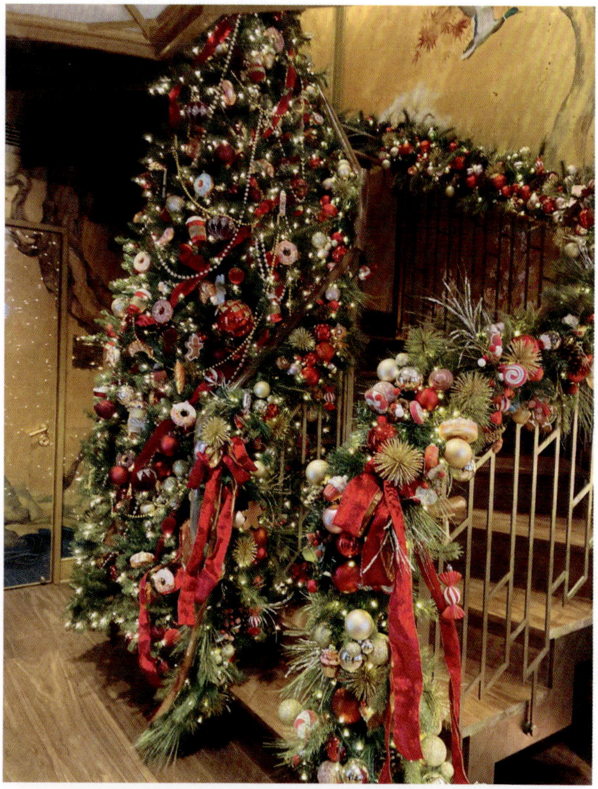
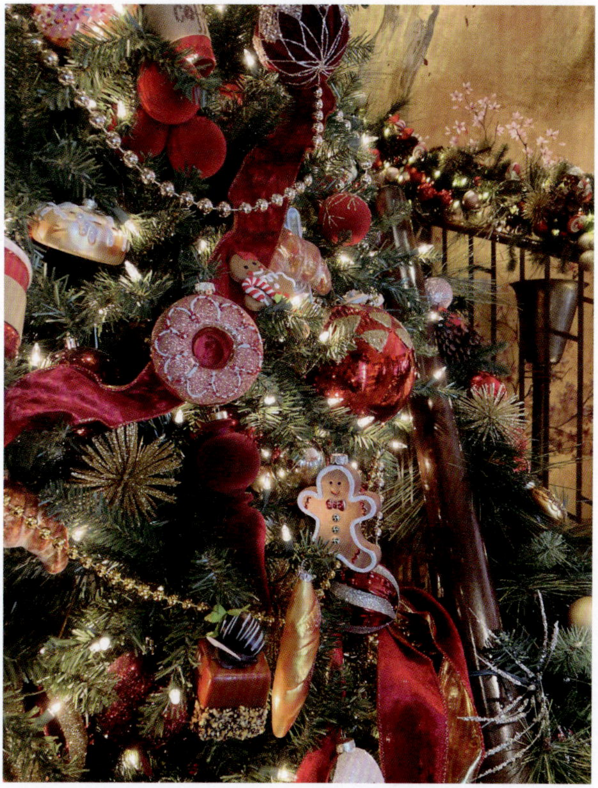
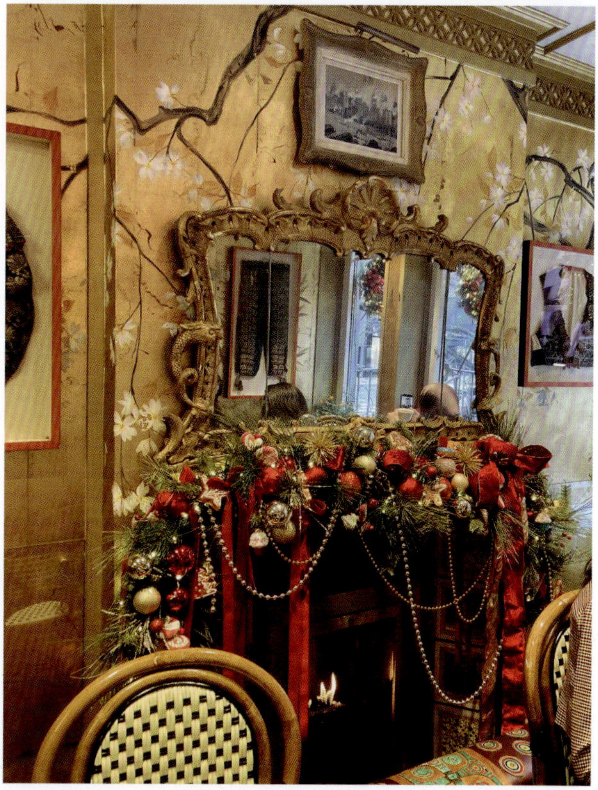

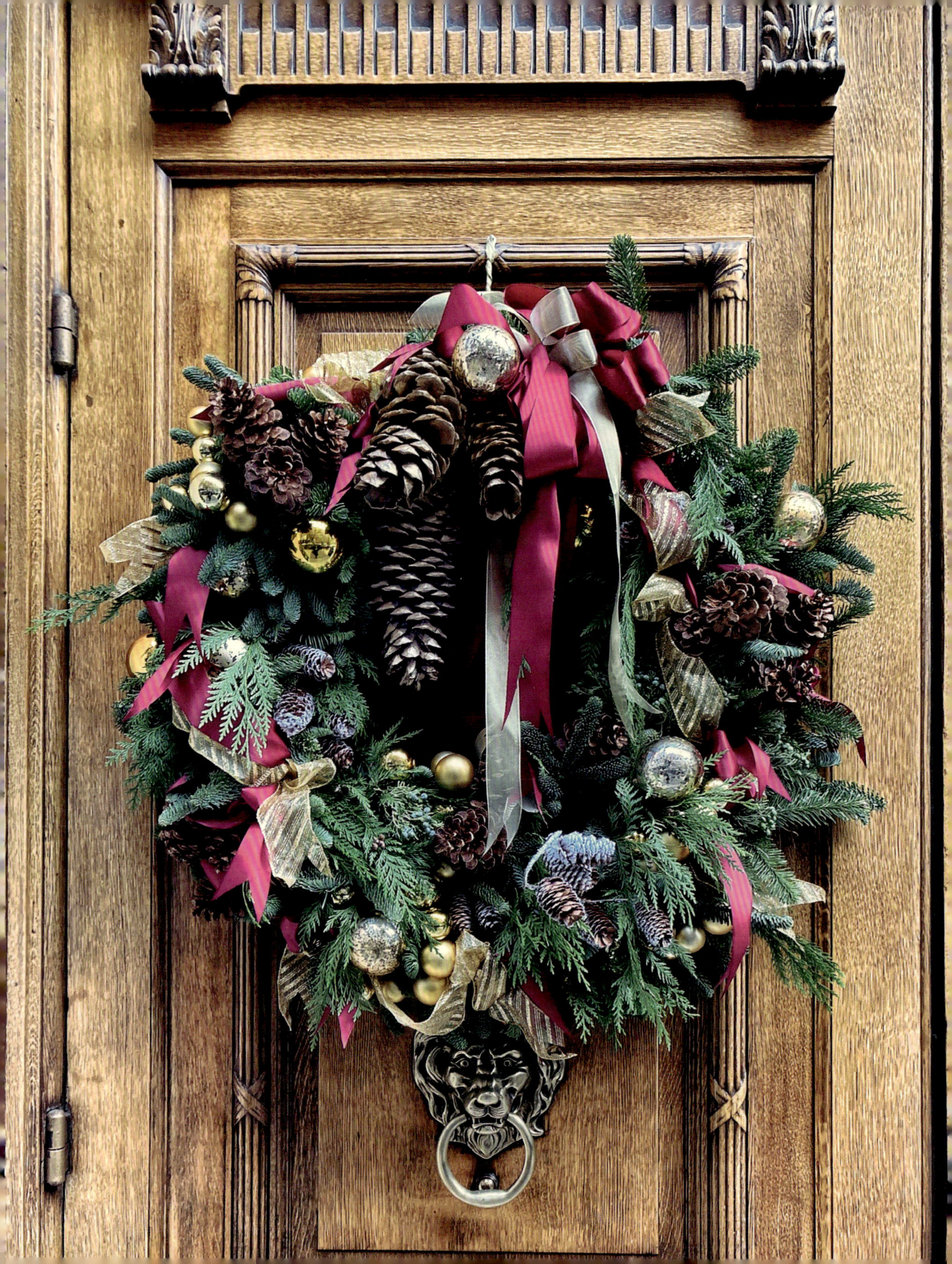

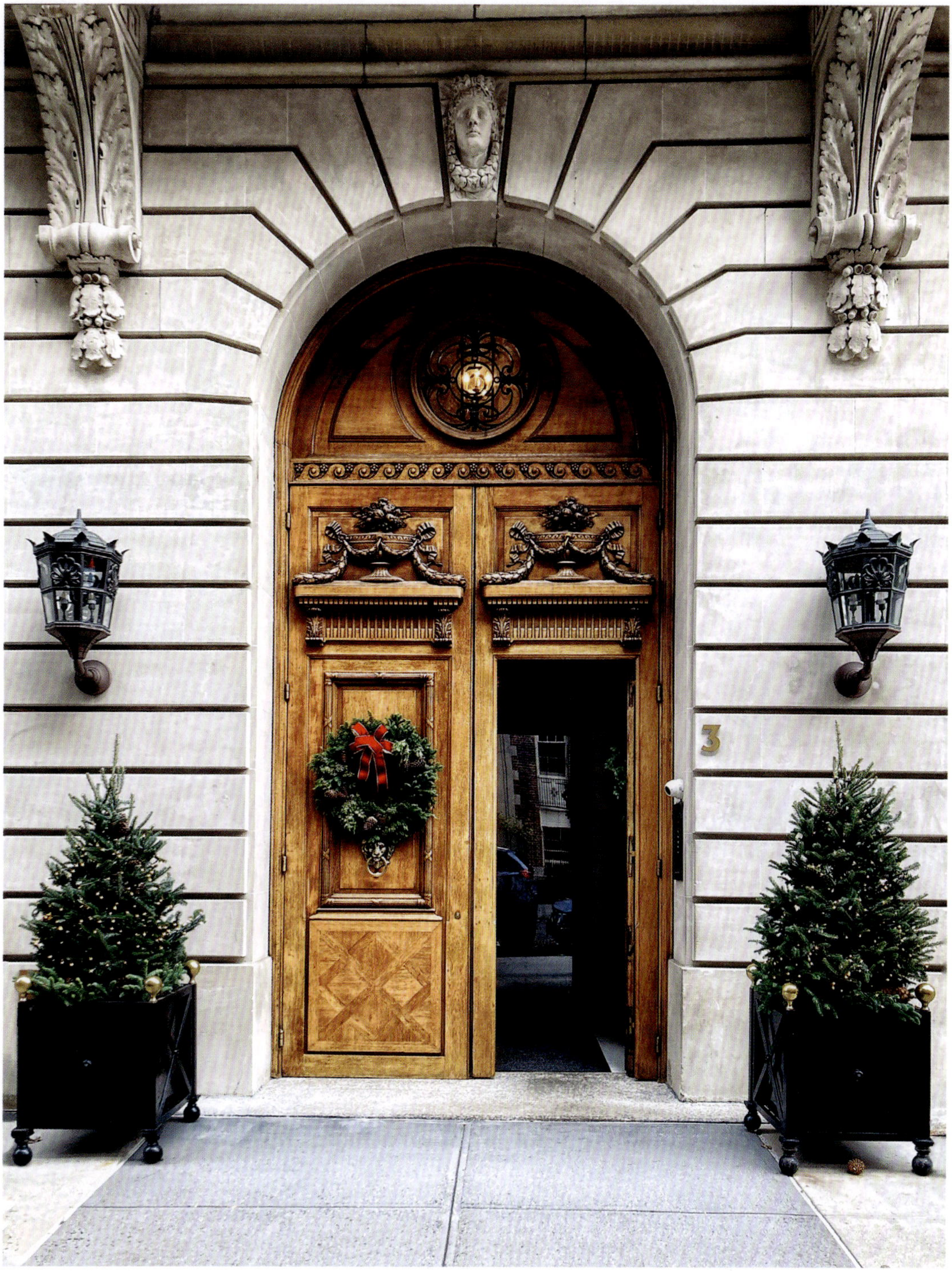

OPPOSITE: This exquisite wreath is just one of many that grace the above door during the holiday season—a new one is displayed every two weeks. **ABOVE:** Mini Christmas trees in planters flank an elegant limestone mansion's beautiful carved wood door on East 95th Street between Madison and Fifth Avenues.

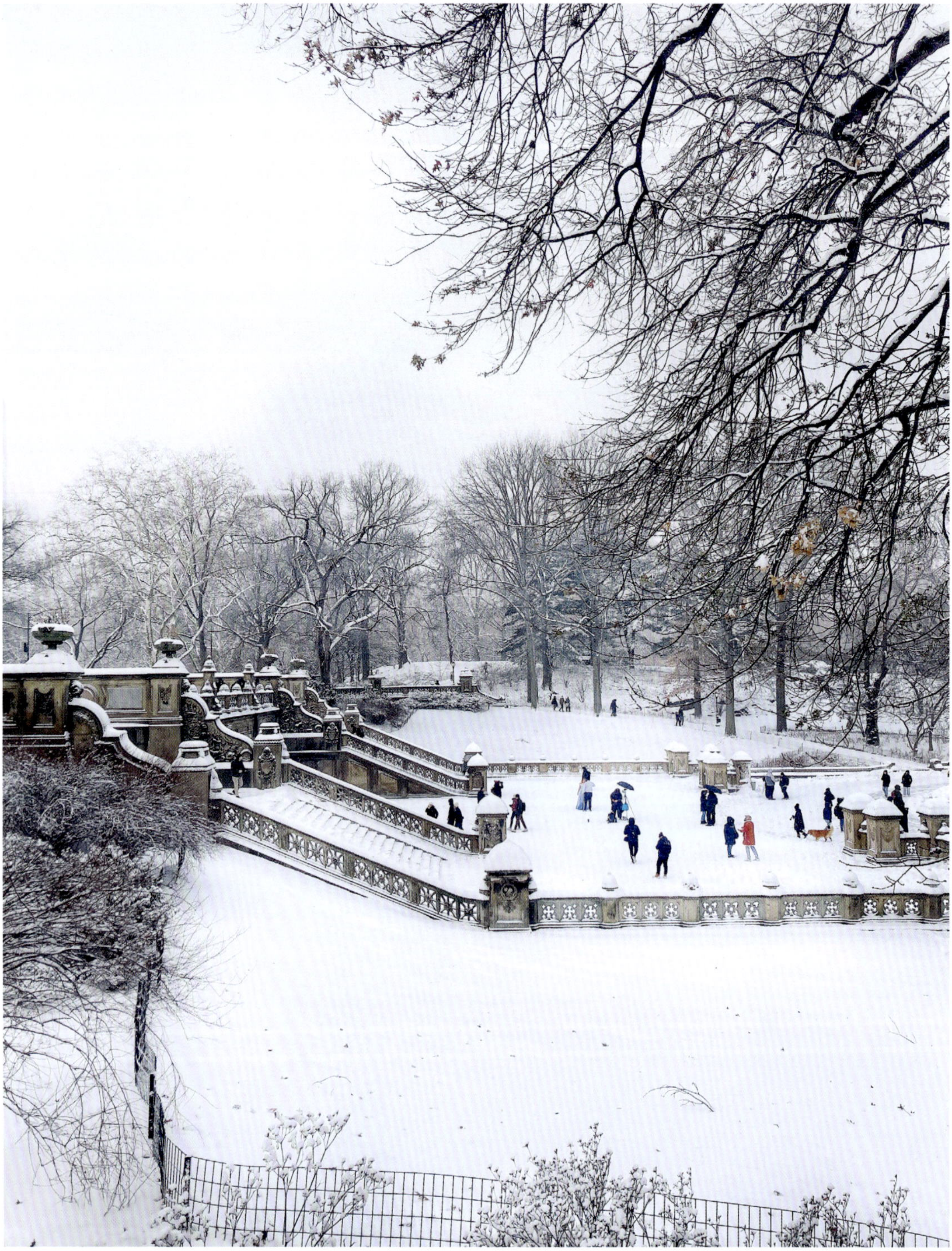

ABOVE: Bethesda Terrace in Central Park during a snowfall on a late December day. **OPPOSITE:** Walking along a quiet snow-covered Fifth Avenue sidewalk after sledding in Central Park

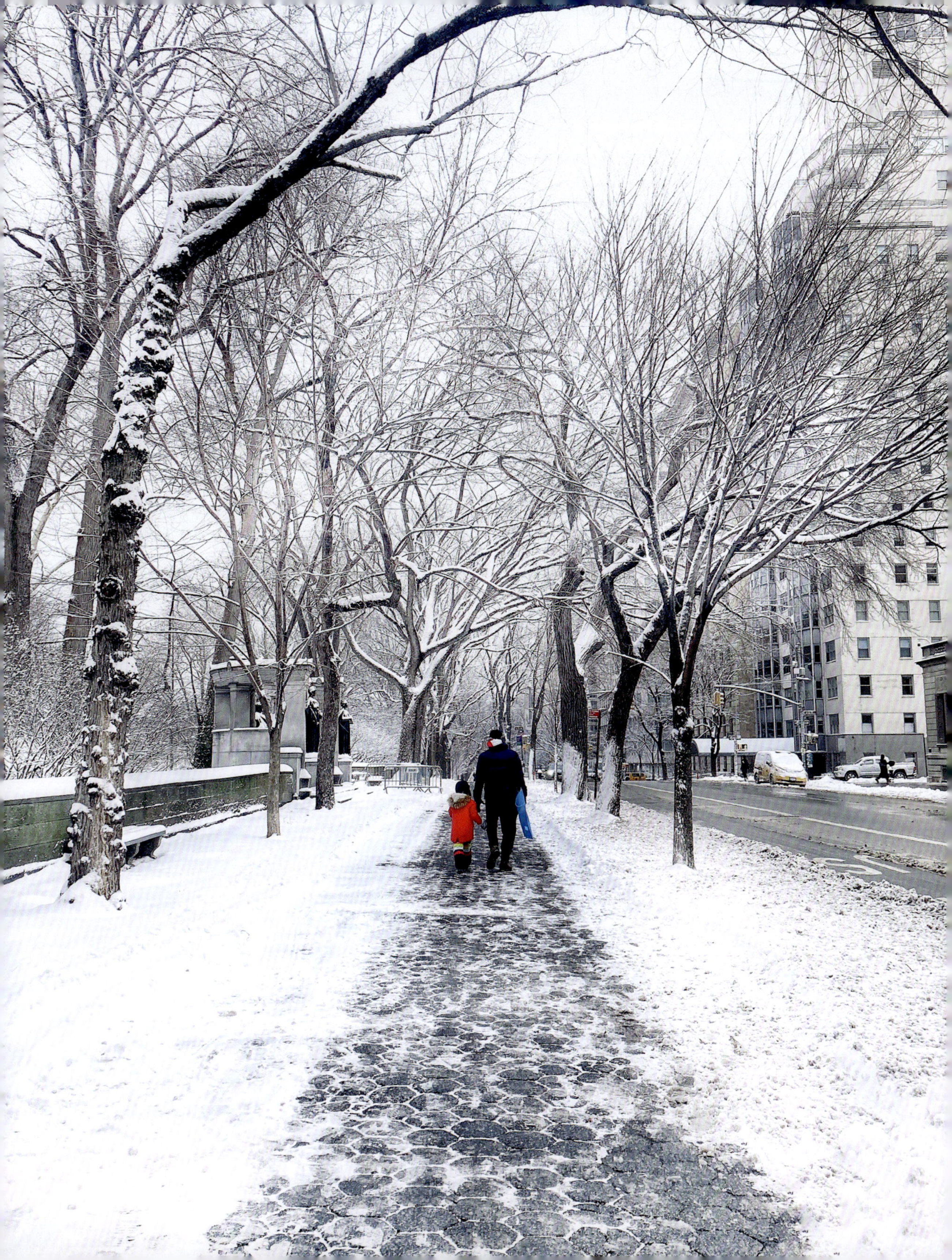

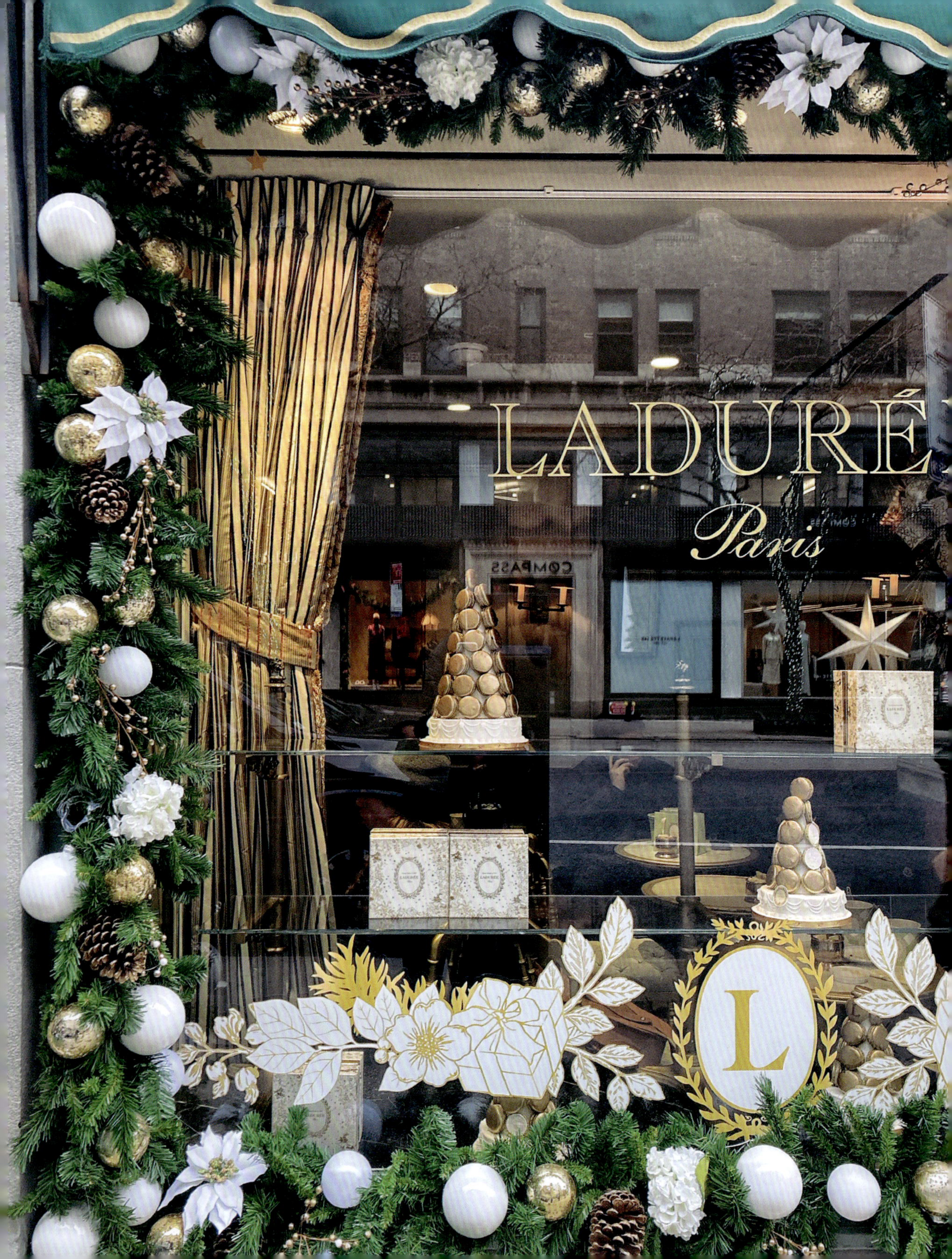
LADURÉE
Paris
L

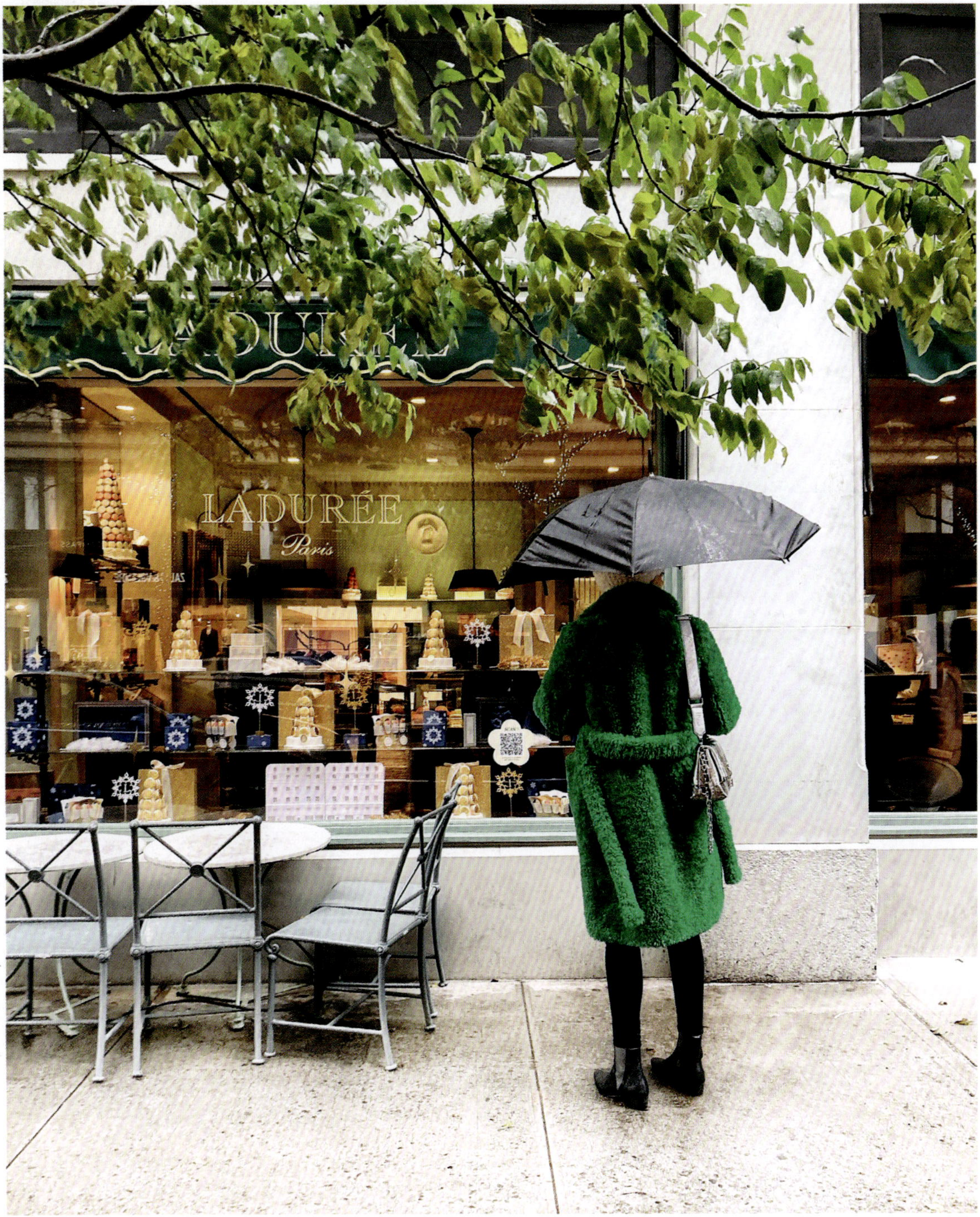

OPPOSITE AND ABOVE: A tasteful mix of gold and white ornaments frames the window of Ladurée, a French pastry shop and tea salon on Madison Avenue and 70th Street. The cute snowflakes and gold macaron Christmas trees in their window attract a passerby on a rainy day.

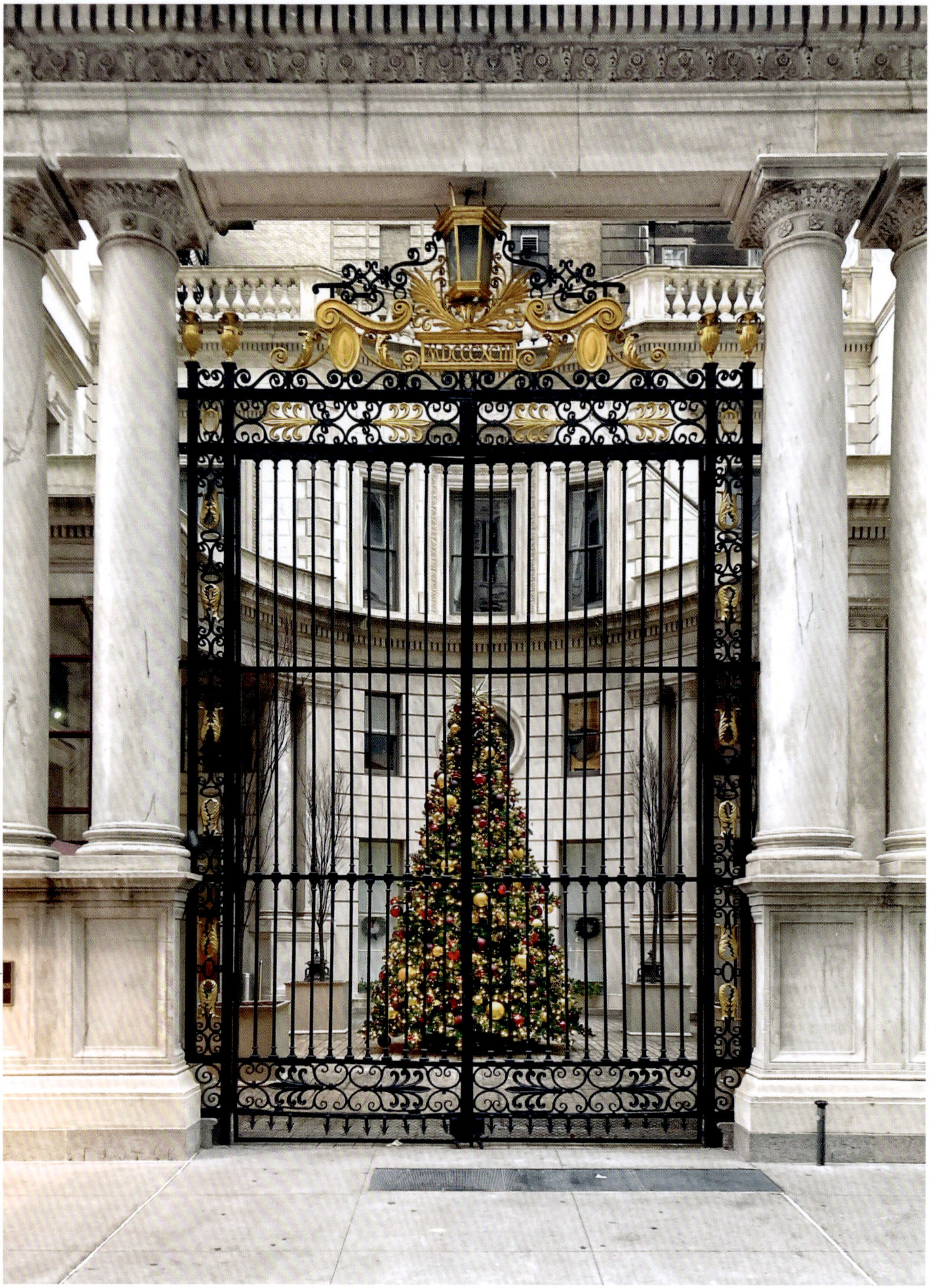

ABOVE: An opulent Christmas tree stands in the courtyard of the Metropolitan Club on East 60th Street, a private social club founded by J. P. Morgan in 1861. **OPPOSITE, CLOCKWISE FROM TOP LEFT:** The iconic Carlyle Hotel on East 76th Street; a townhouse dripping in gold lights on East 66th Street; wreaths and wrought iron on East 82nd Street; Ralph's Coffee on East 72nd Street

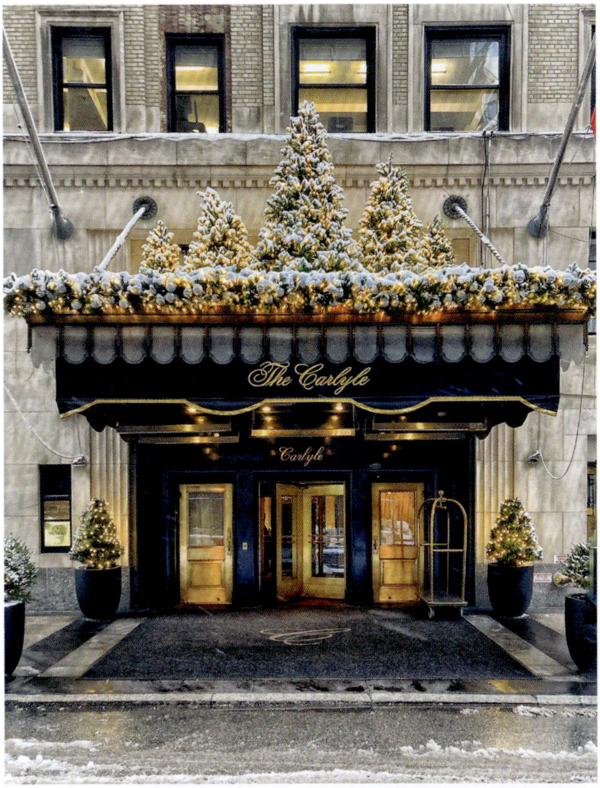
The Carlyle
Carlyle

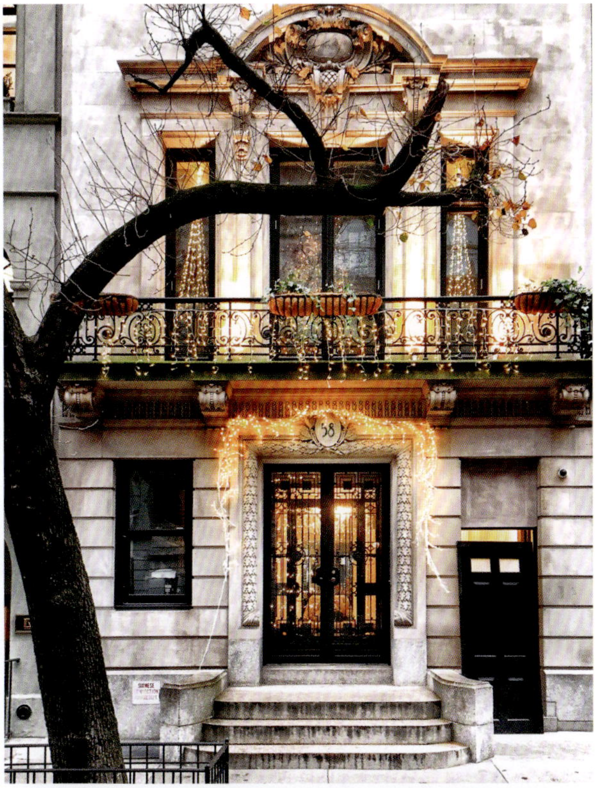
38

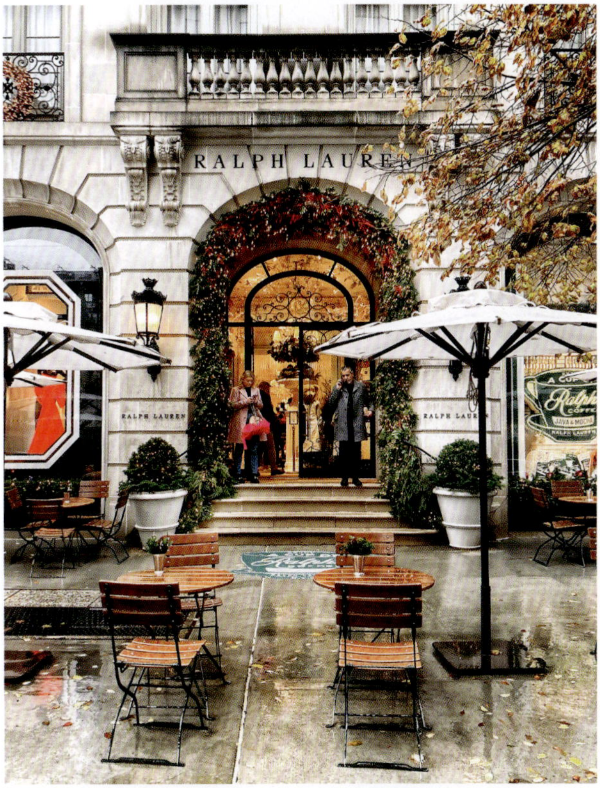
RALPH LAUREN

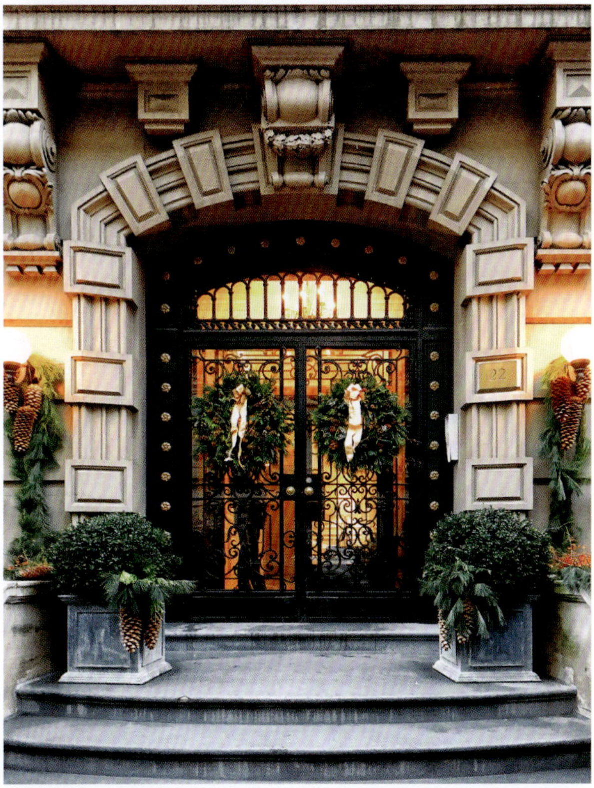
22

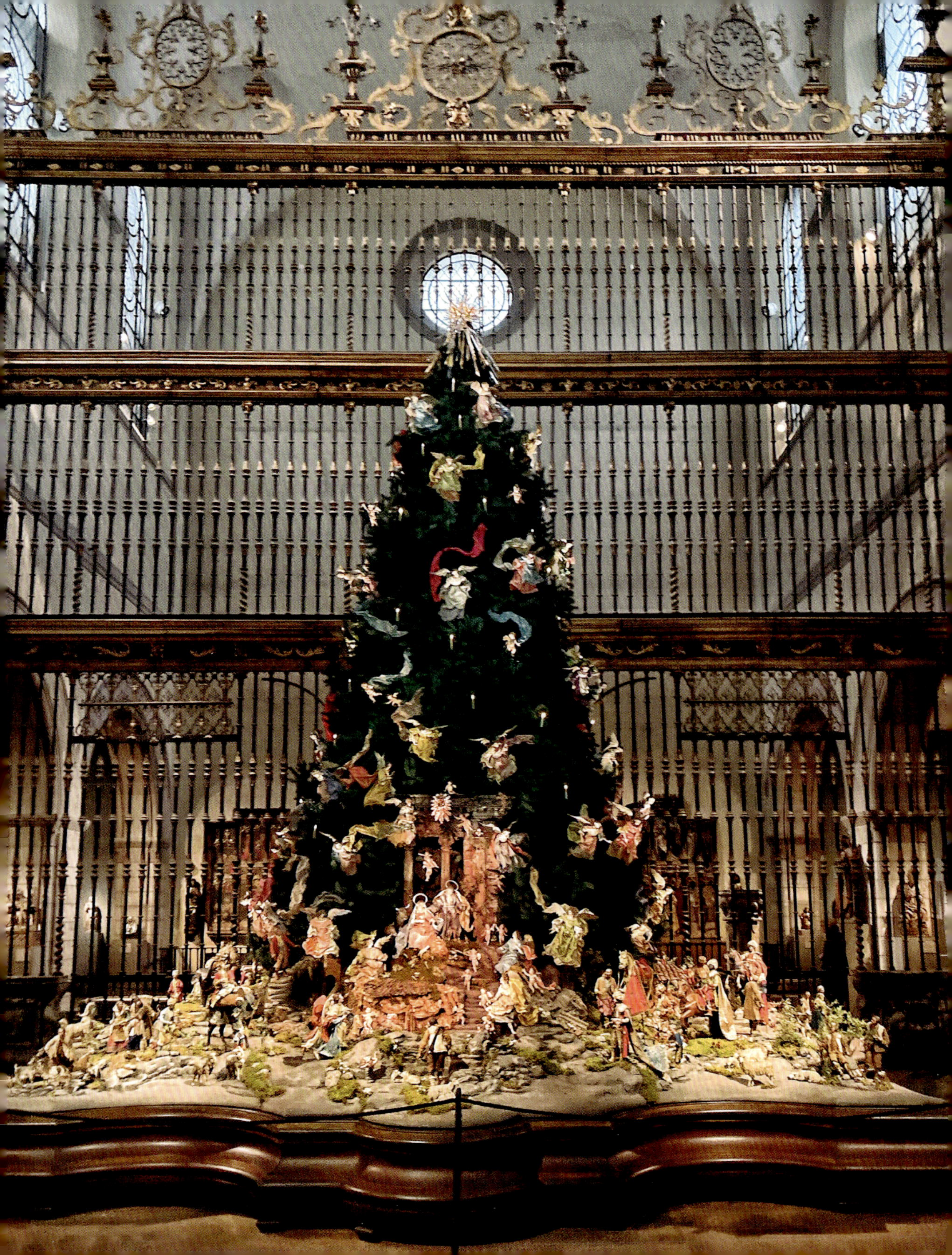

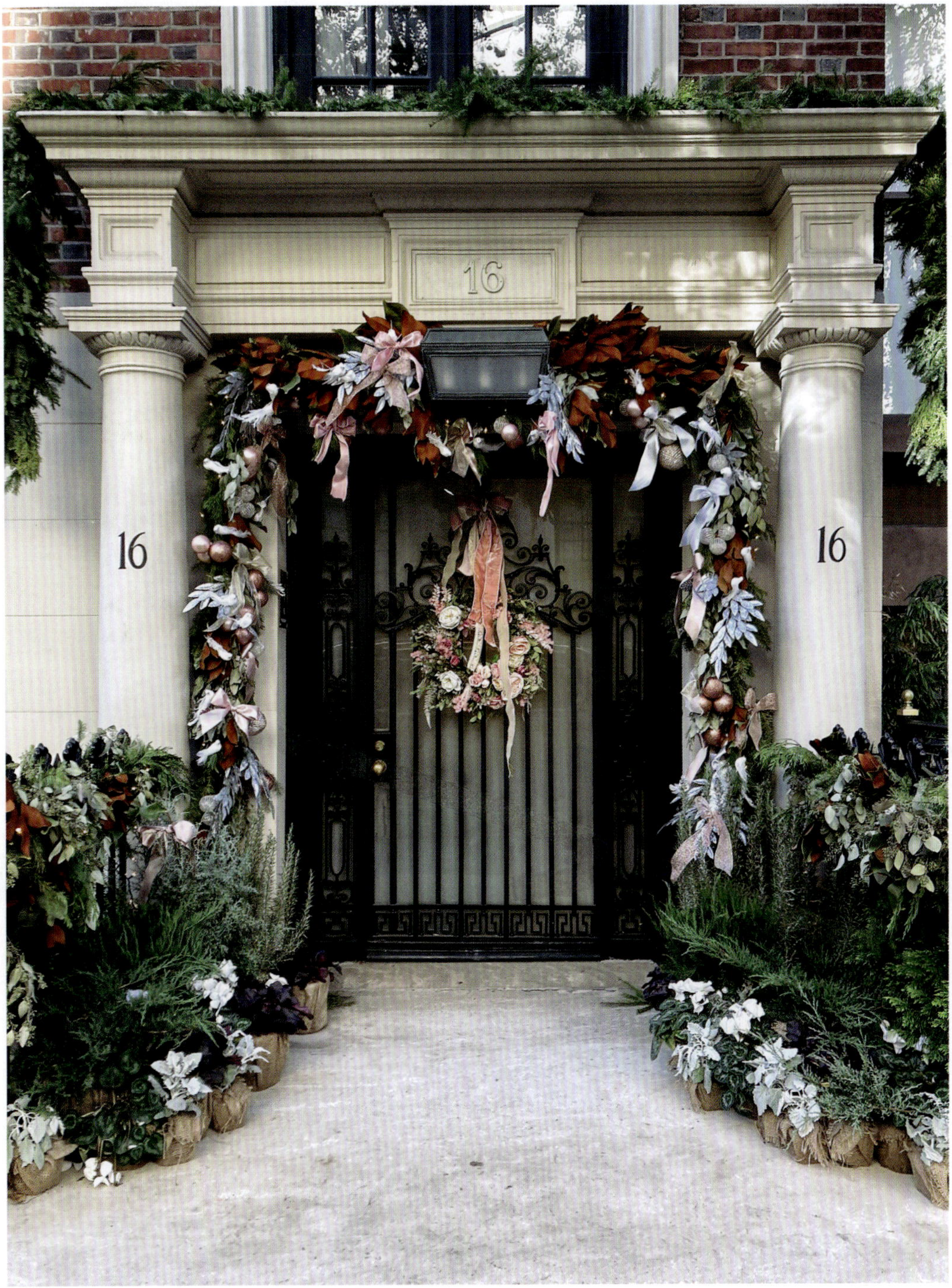

OPPOSITE: The Metropolitan Museum of Art's Christmas tree is adorned with sixty eighteenth-century angels and twenty cherubs and is set against an eighteenth-century Spanish choir screen from the Cathedral of Valladolid. **ABOVE:** A romantic entrance on East 64th Street between Madison and Fifth Avenues, decorated with pastel ribbons and magnolia leaves.

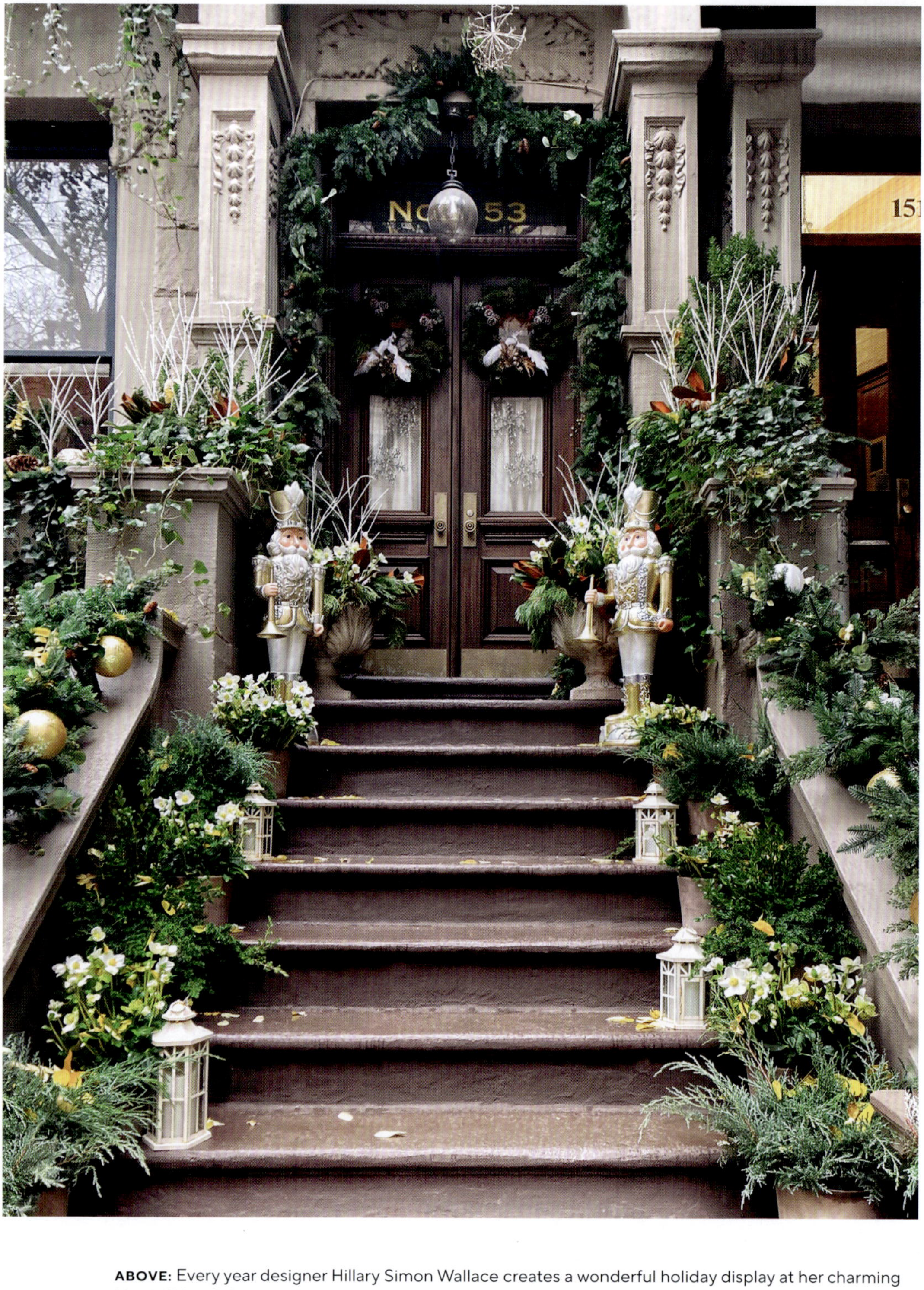

ABOVE: Every year designer Hillary Simon Wallace creates a wonderful holiday display at her charming Upper West Side townhouse on West 82nd Street between Columbus and Amsterdam Avenues.
OPPOSITE: A pretty, natural wreath adds a festive touch to an elegant limestone townhouse on East 73rd Street between Madison and 5th Avenues.

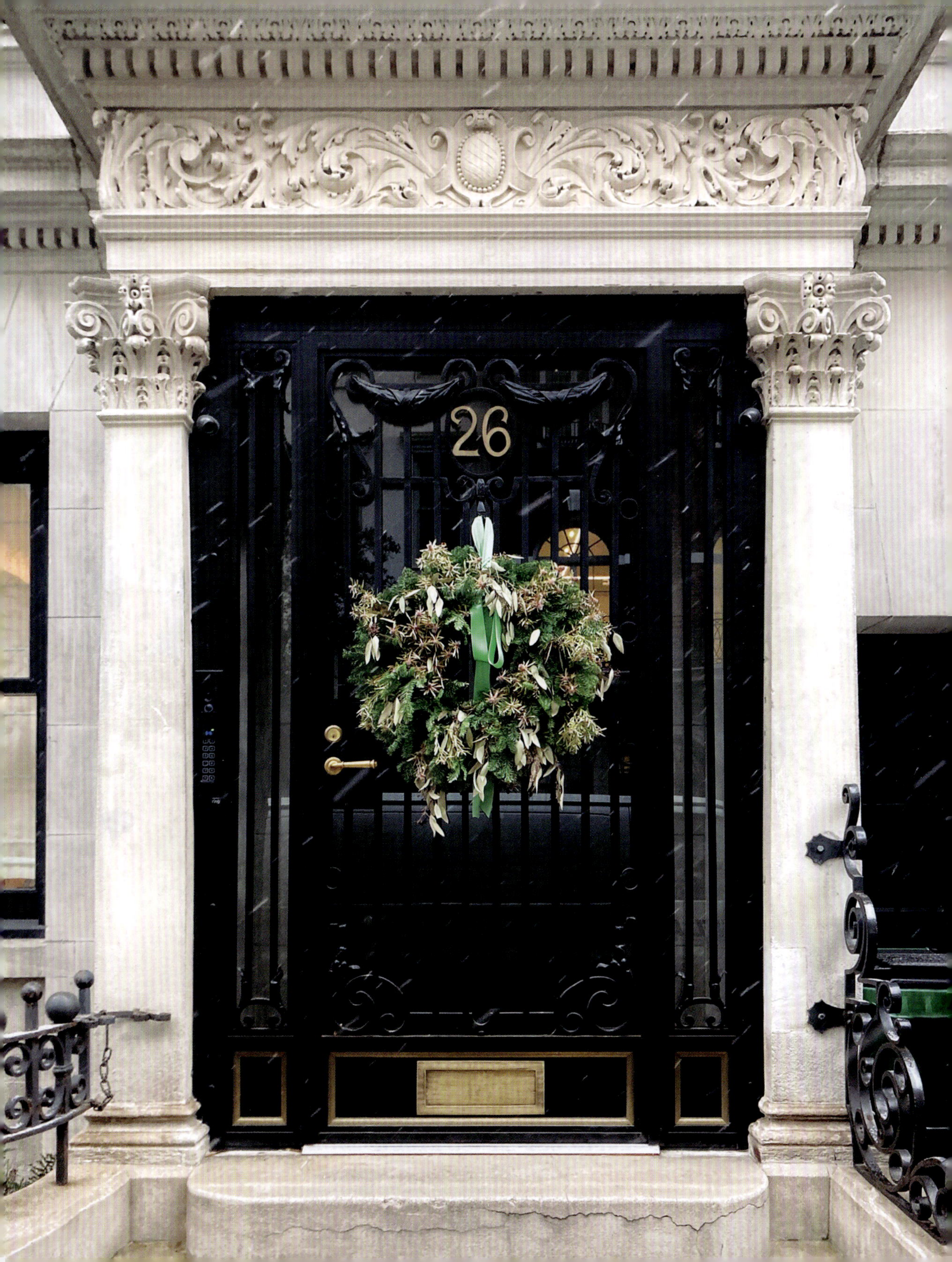
26

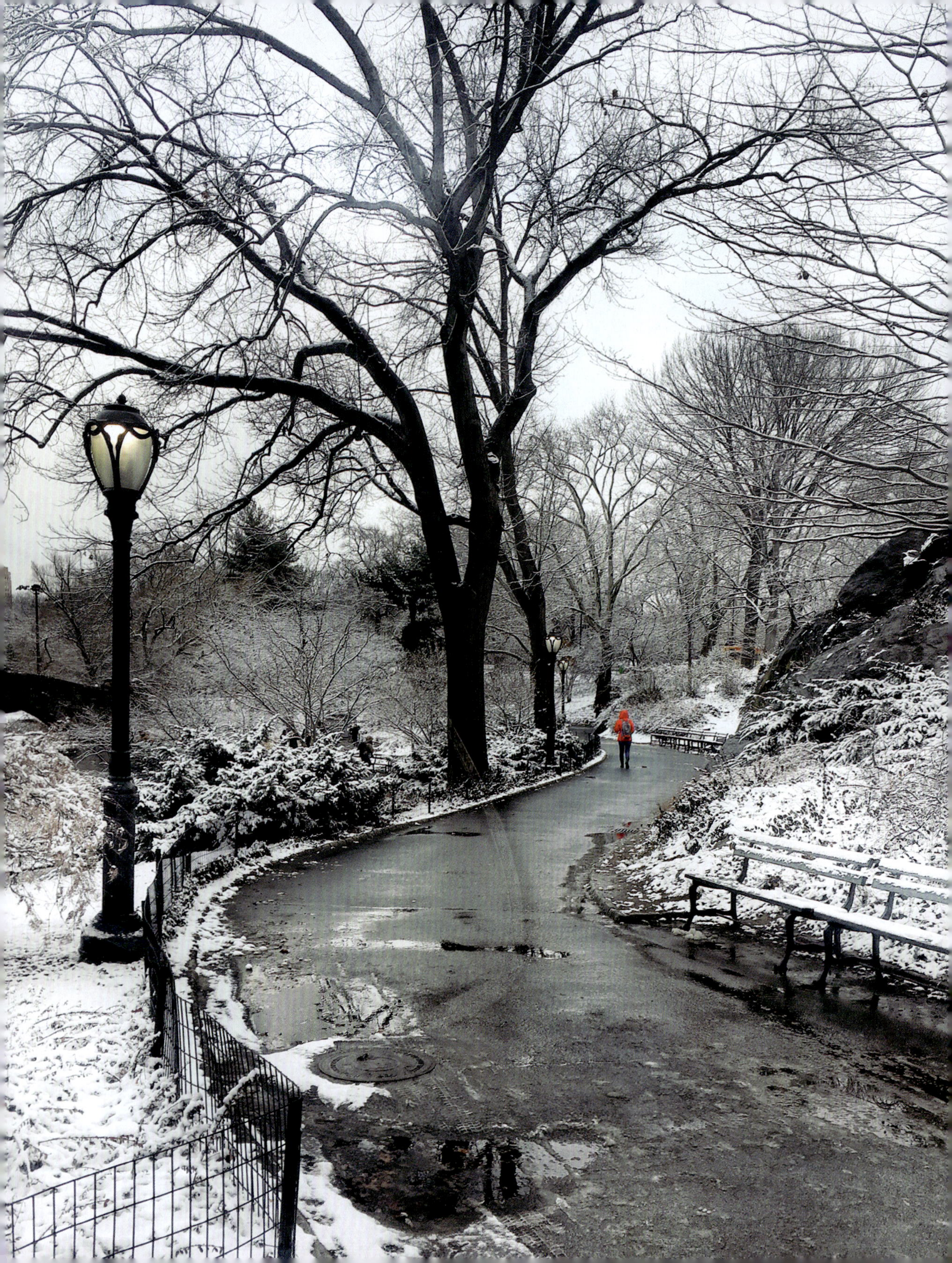

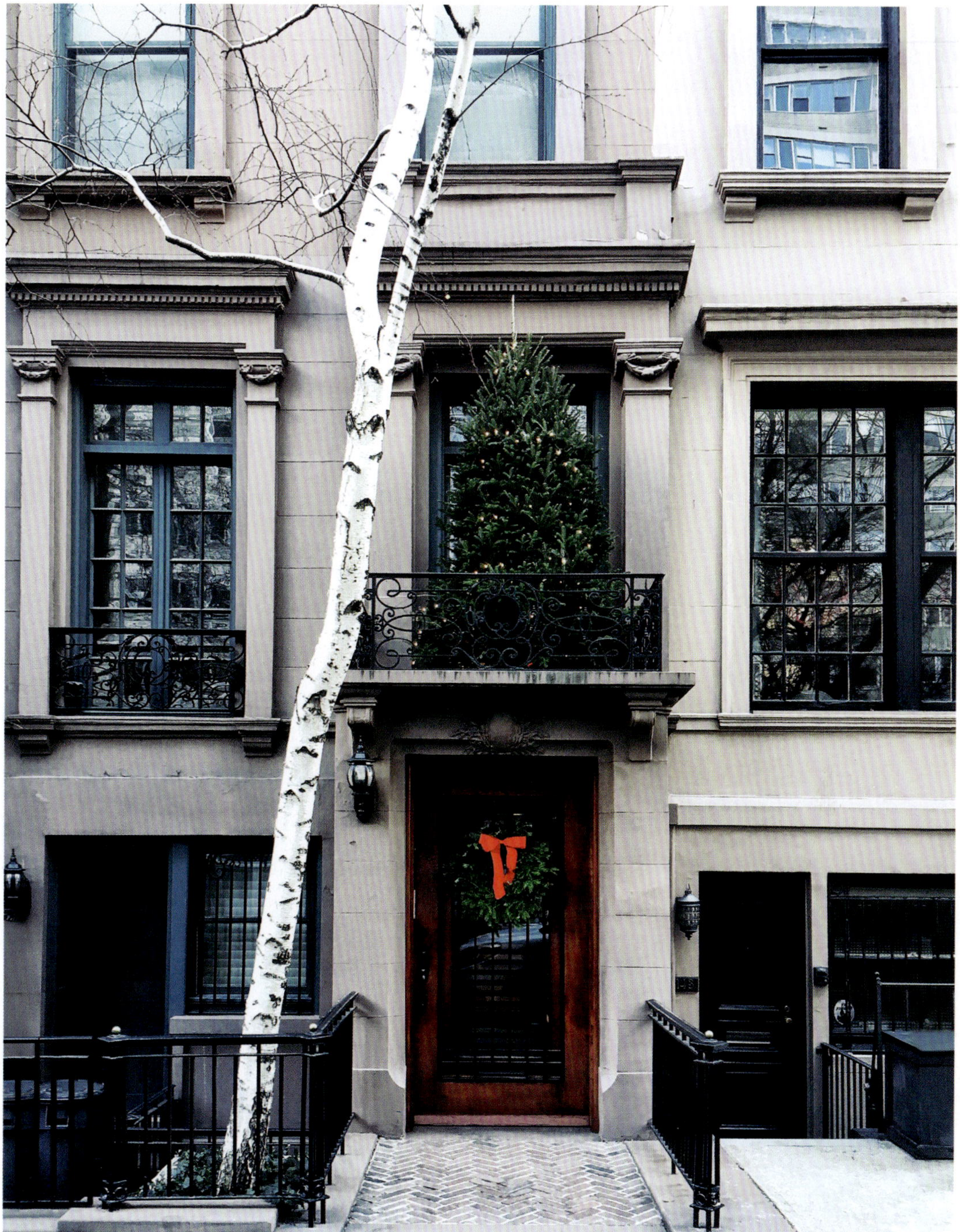

OPPOSITE: A quiet moment walking along the path by the Pond in Central Park near East 60th Street and Fifth Avenue. **ABOVE:** A classic wreath on the door with an unexpected Christmas tree on the Juliet balcony above it, on East 69th Street between Third and Lexington Avenues.

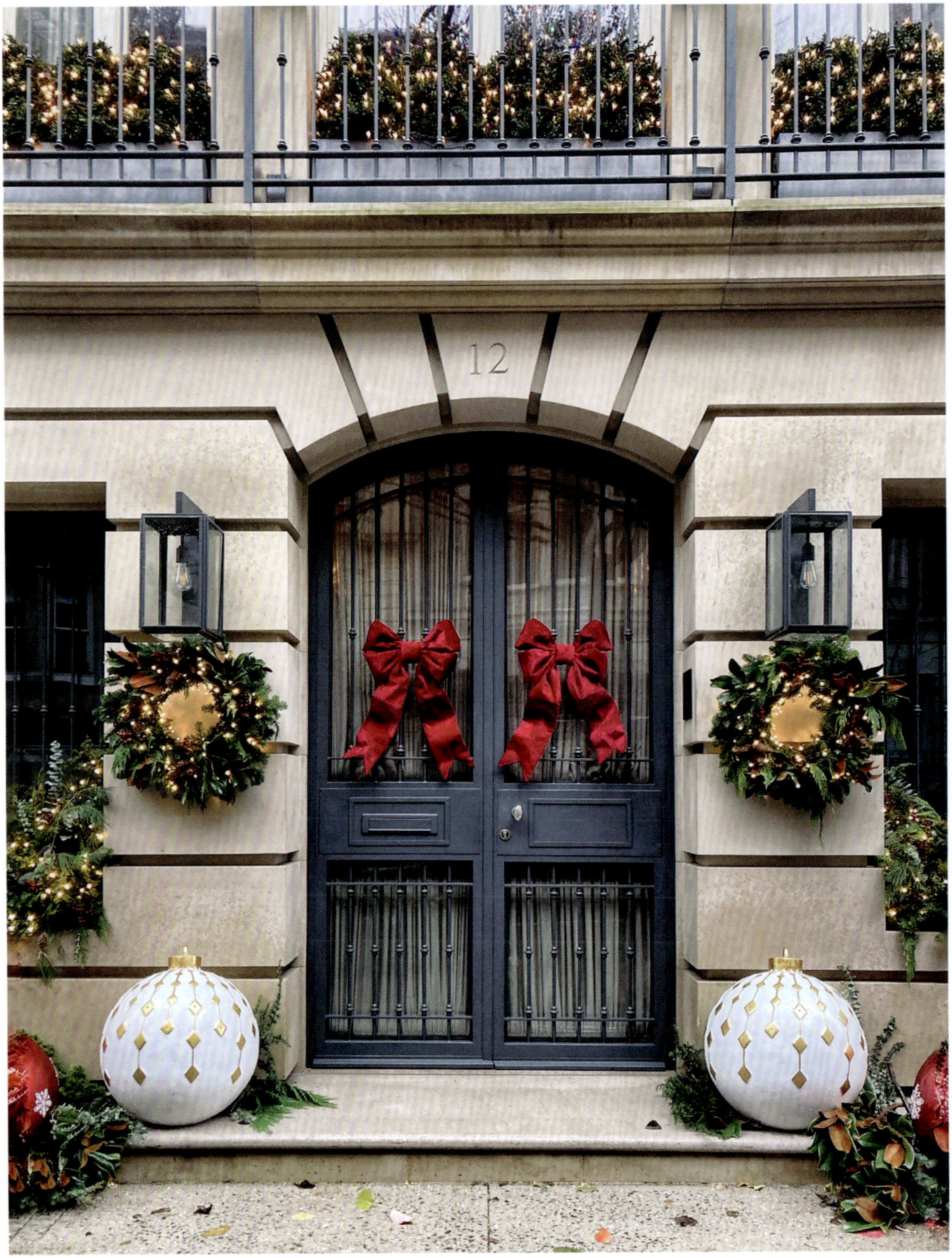

ABOVE: Double the fun: two wreaths, two red bows, and two oversized ornaments add a touch of whimsy to a modern metal door on East 76th Street between Madison and Fifth Avenues. **OPPOSITE:** Garlands, baubles, and wreaths galore in traditional red, green, and white Christmas colors make a cheerful scene on East 83rd Street between Park and Madison Avenues.

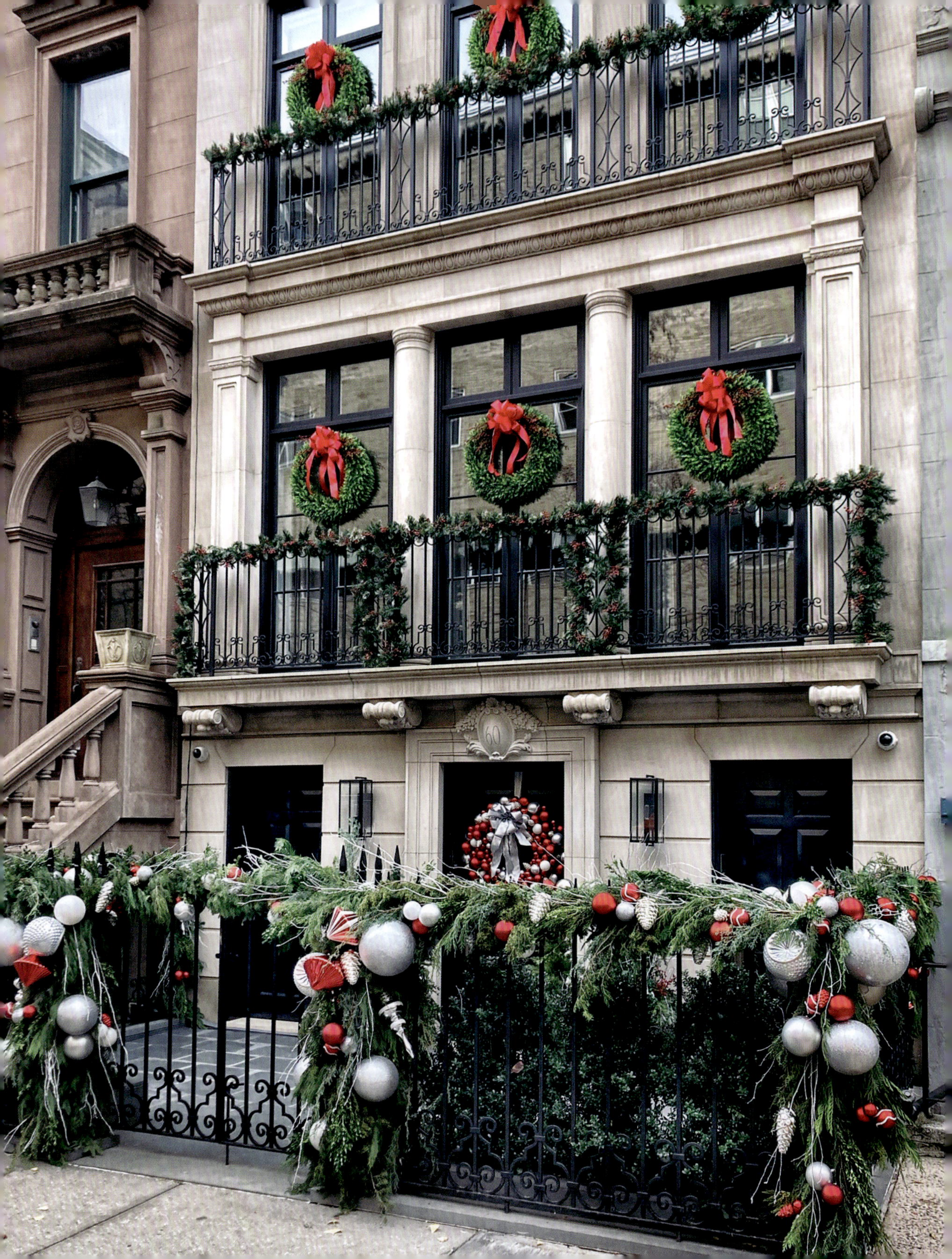
60

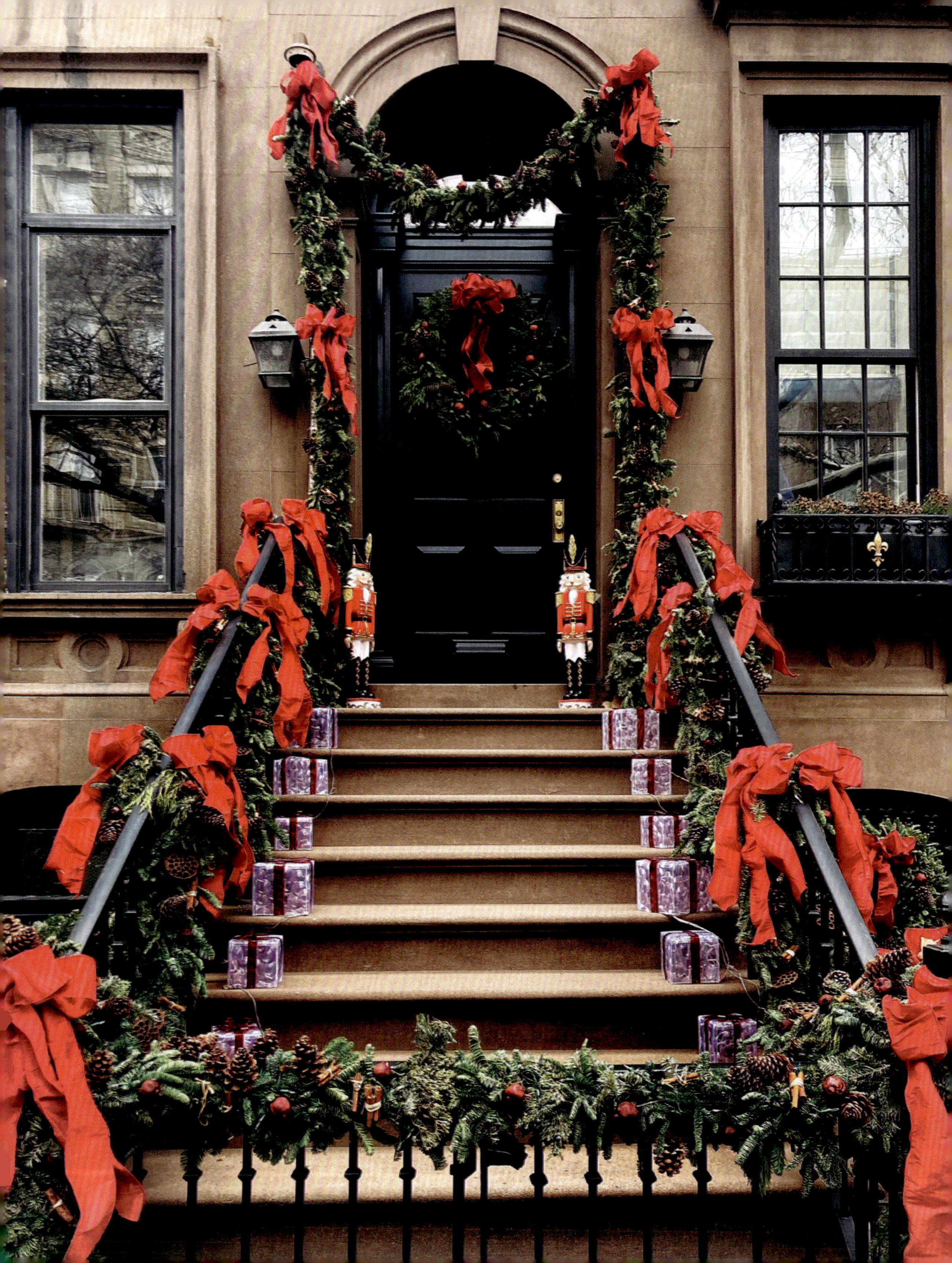

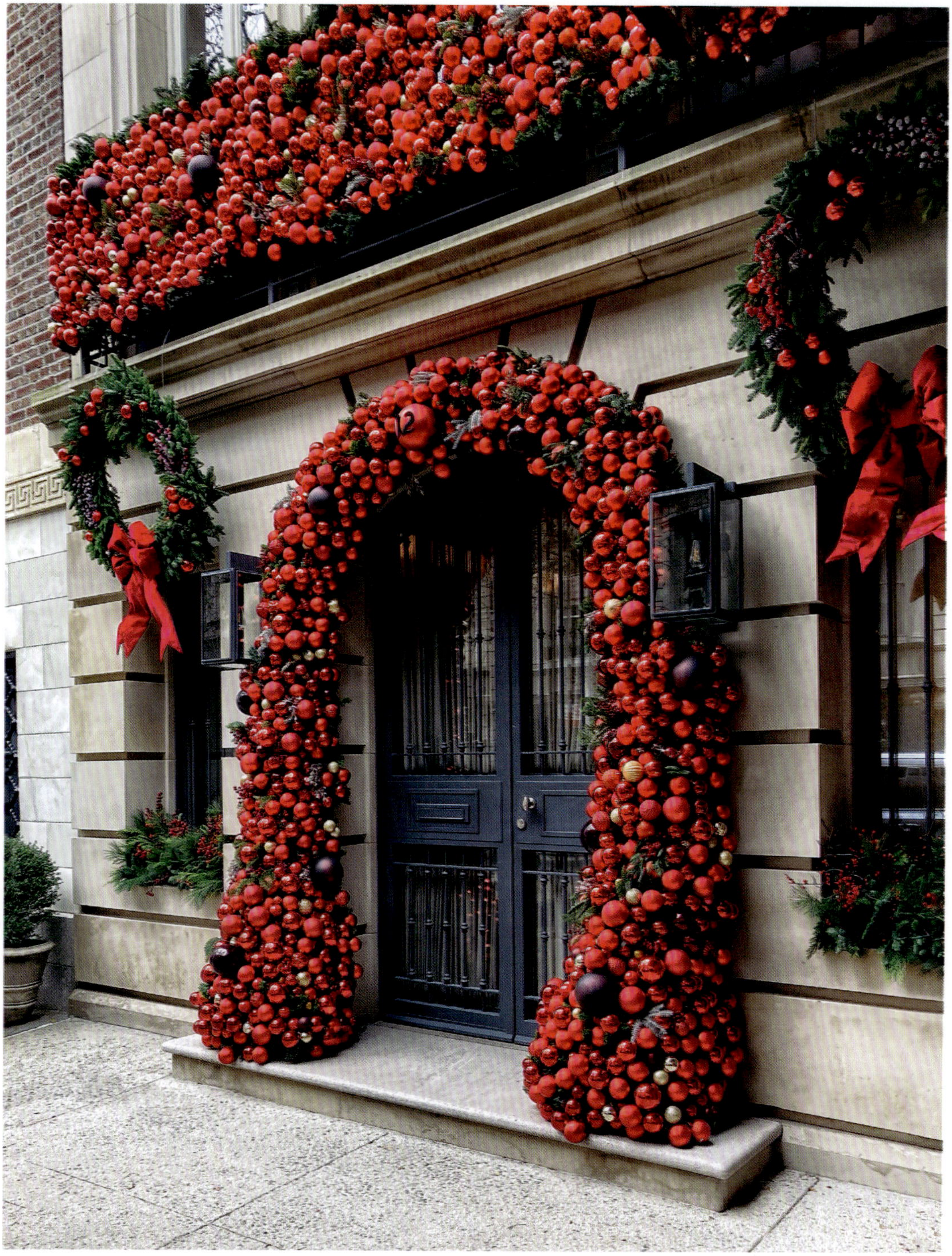

OPPOSITE: Red bows and garlands decorated with pine cones and cinnamon sticks create an old-fashioned Christmas feeling on East 62nd Street between Second and Third Avenues. **ABOVE:** Clusters of cheerful red baubles make a fun and festive statement on East 76th Street between Madison and Fifth Avenues.

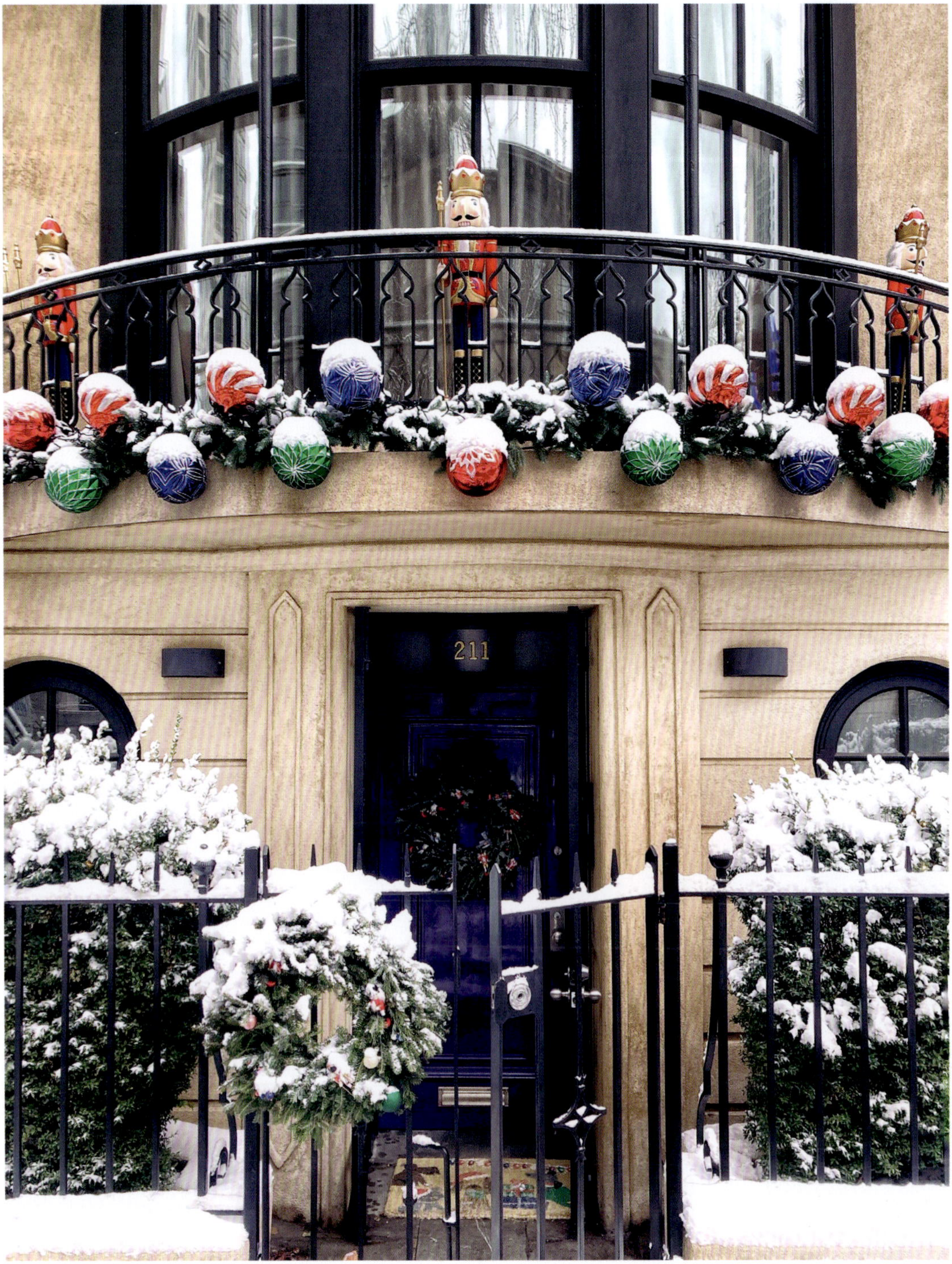

ABOVE: Intrepid Nutcrackers stand guard on the snowy balcony of this charming townhouse on East 61st Street between Second and Third Avenues. **OPPOSITE, CLOCKWISE FROM TOP LEFT:** Whimsical wreaths: colorful and cute on West 82nd Street; mini Nutcrackers (closeup of previous page); a red ribbon and snowflakes on East 64th Street; holiday candy theme on East 73rd Street

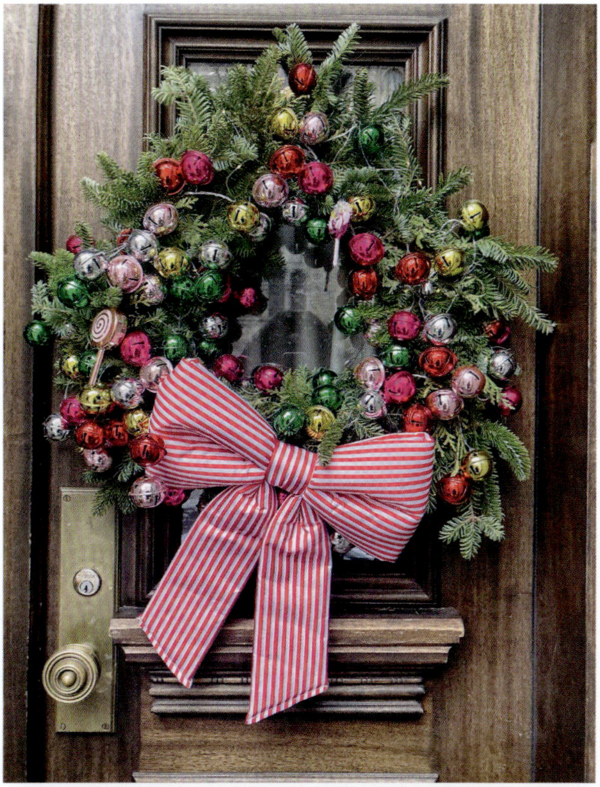
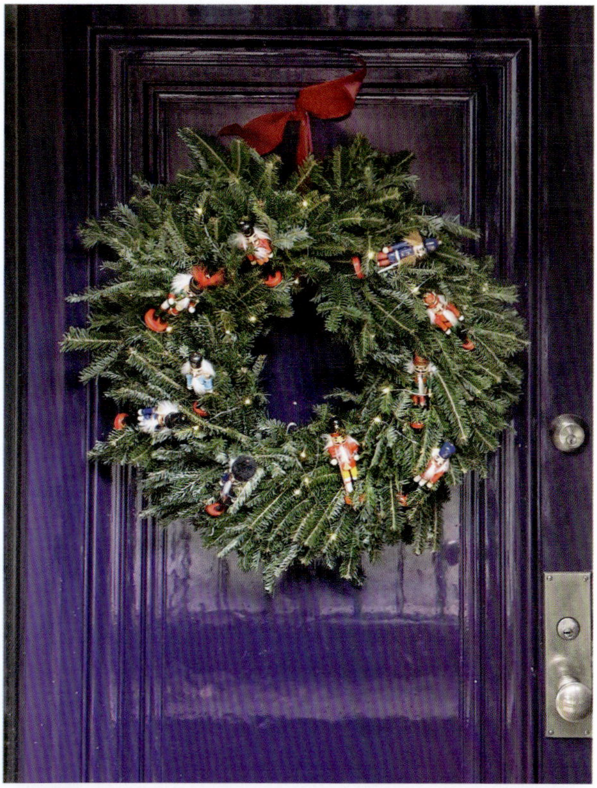
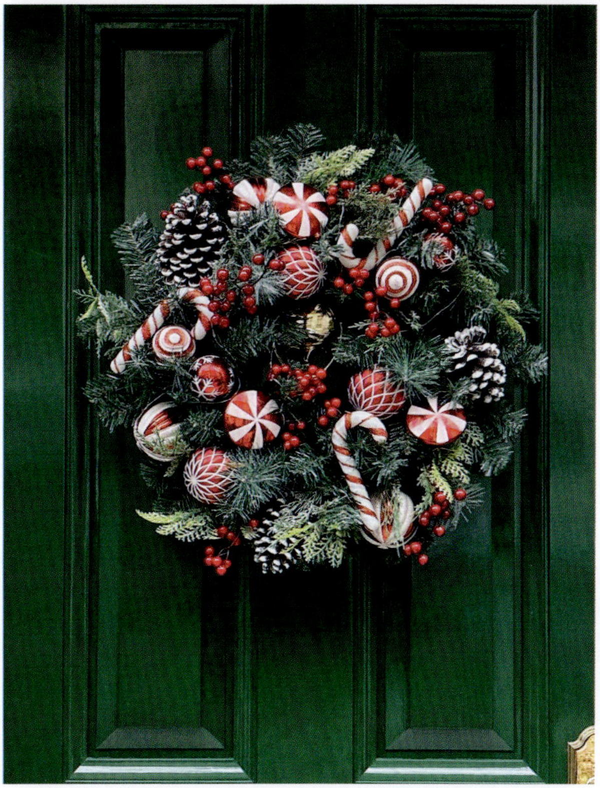
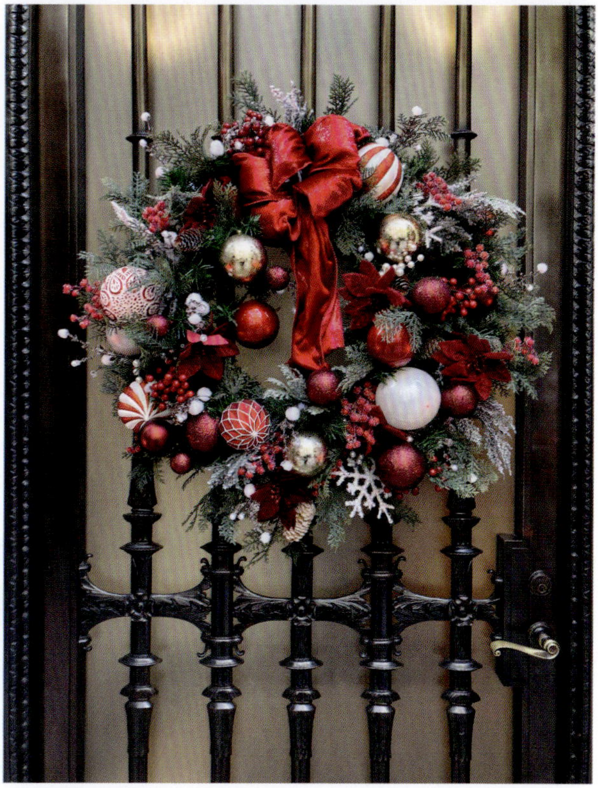

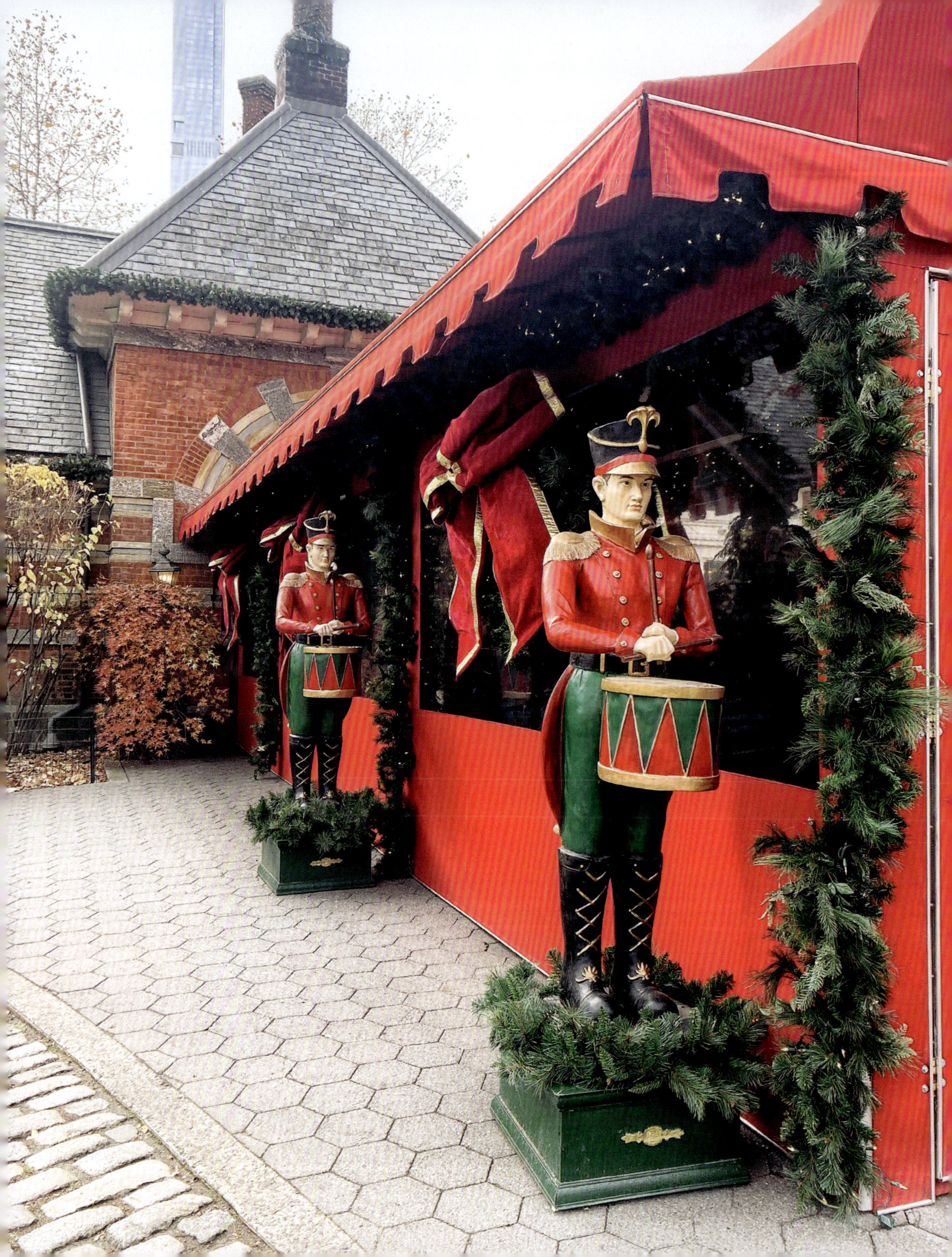

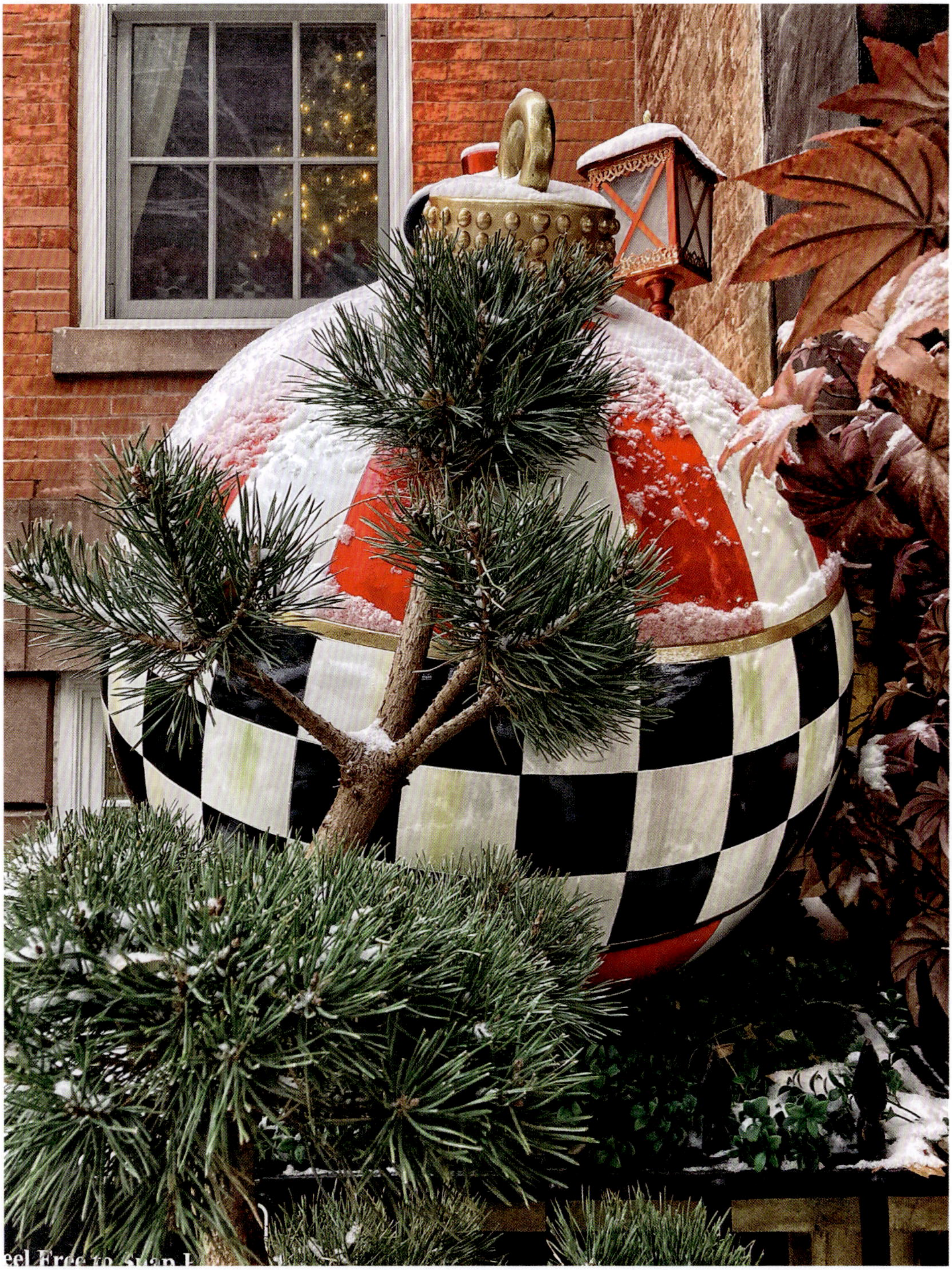

OPPOSITE: Traditional wooden soldiers bang their drums at the tented entrance to the iconic Tavern on the Green in Central Park at West 67th Street. **ABOVE:** A giant Mackenzie-Childs ornament covered with a dusting of snow on East 78th Street between Second and Third Avenues.

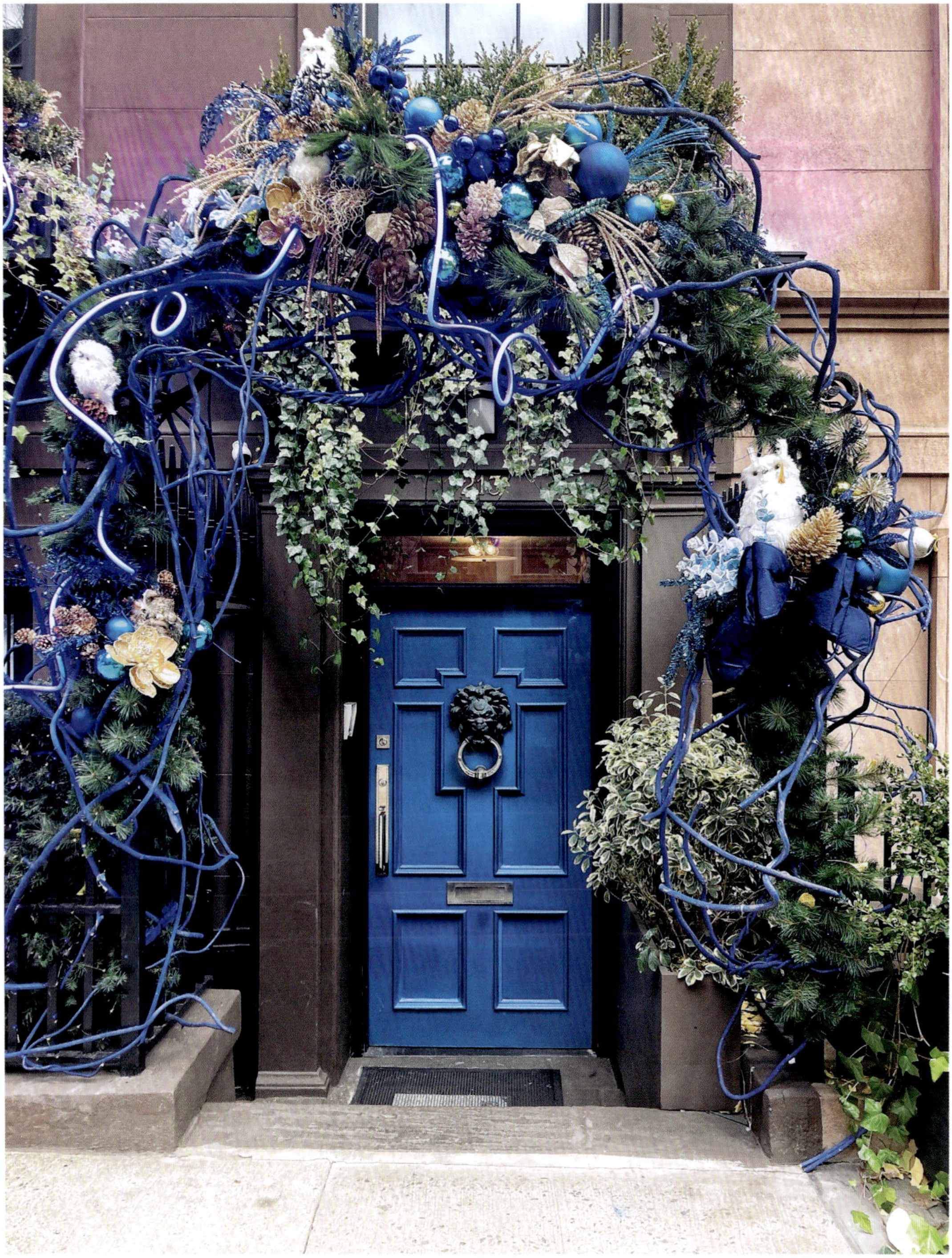

ABOVE: This townhouse with its eye-catching blue door on East 61st Street between Second and Third Avenues always delivers the most unique and creative blue-themed decorations year after year. **OPPOSITE:** An owl sits atop a mix of natural winter greenery on East 73rd Street between Madison and Park Avenues.

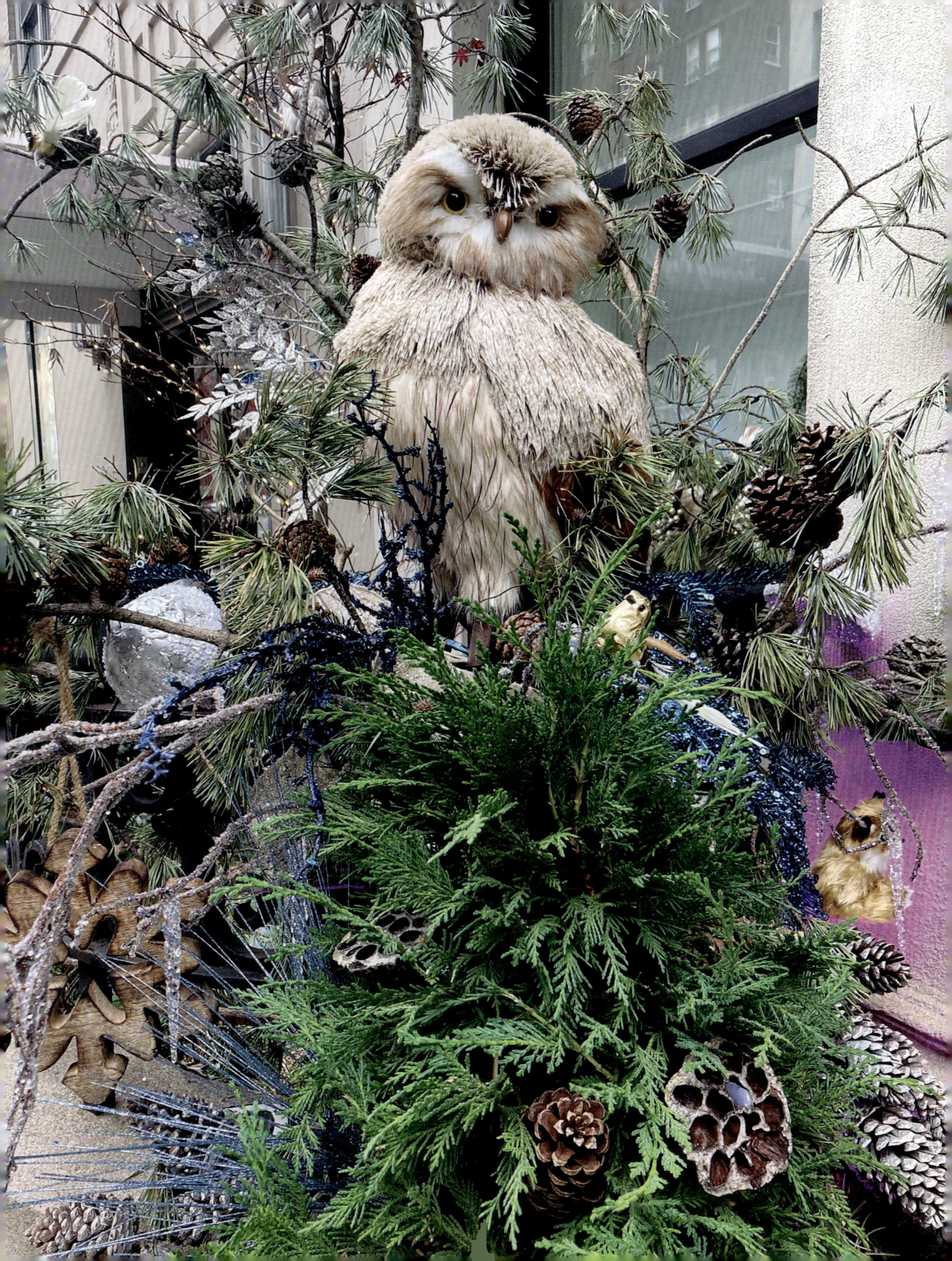

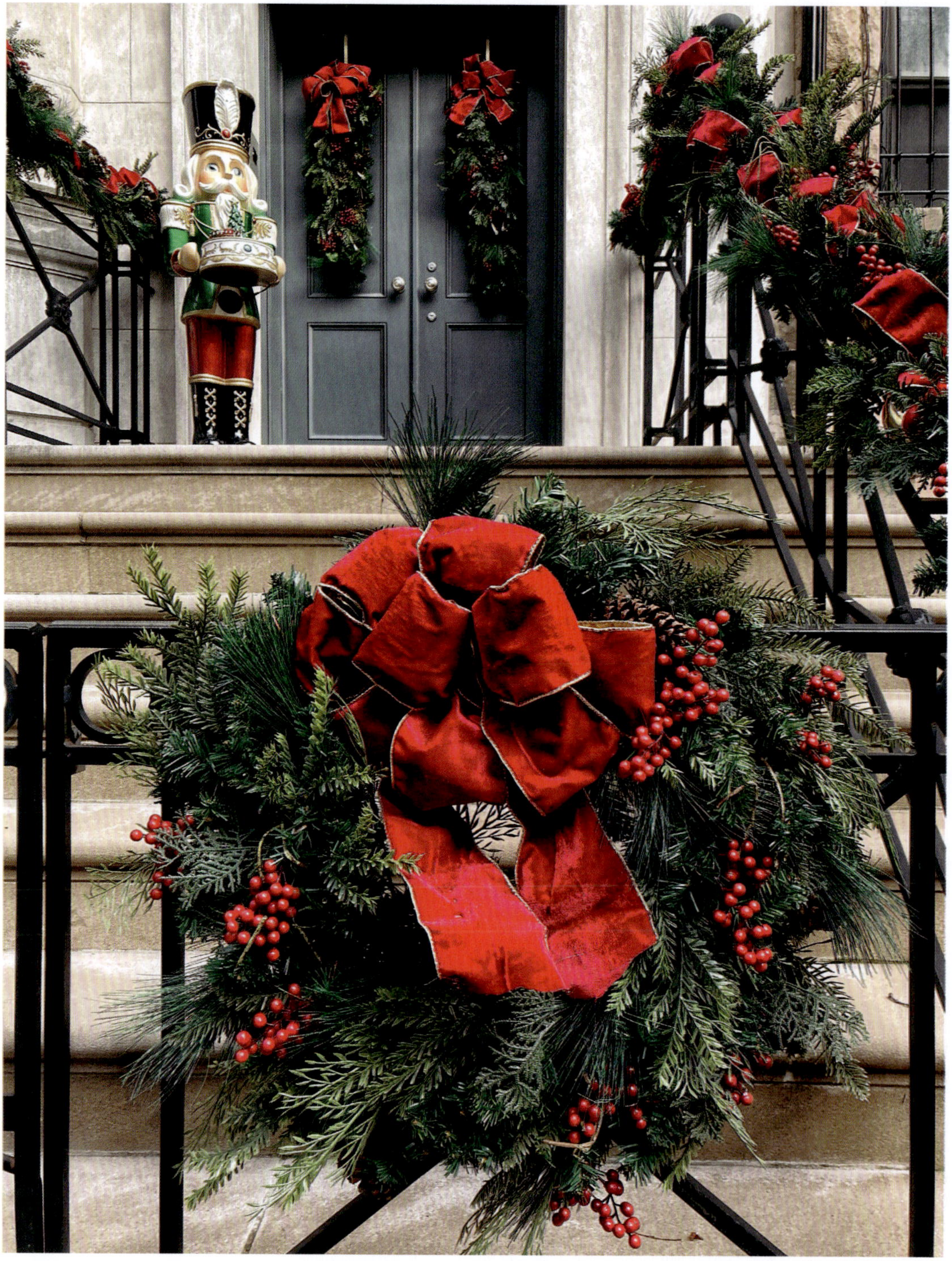

ABOVE: Above: Traditional Christmas décor on East 94th Street between Madison and Fifth Avenues. **OPPOSITE, CLOCKWISE FROM TOP LEFT:** Classic evergreen wreaths with red bows: on the windows, West 80th Street; hung on the door and balcony, East 76th Street; with twinkling lights, East 69th Street; on a red door with red bells, East 61st Street

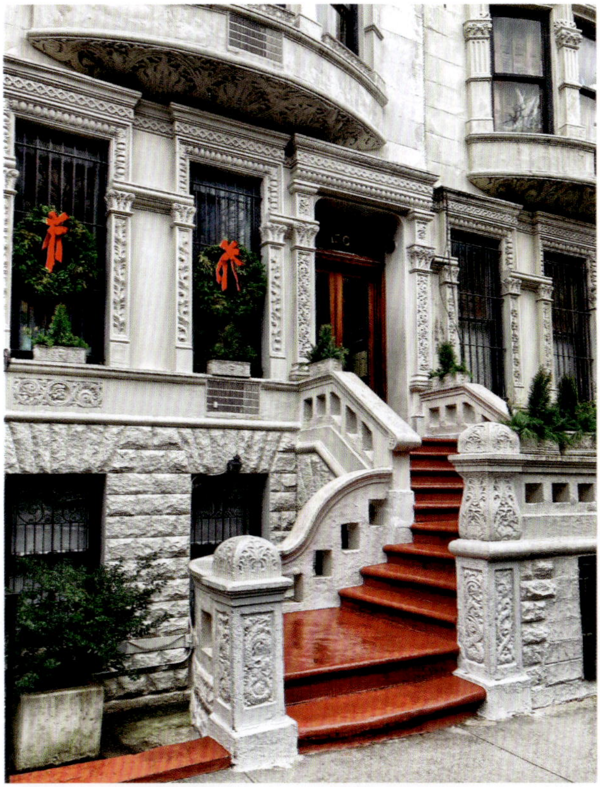

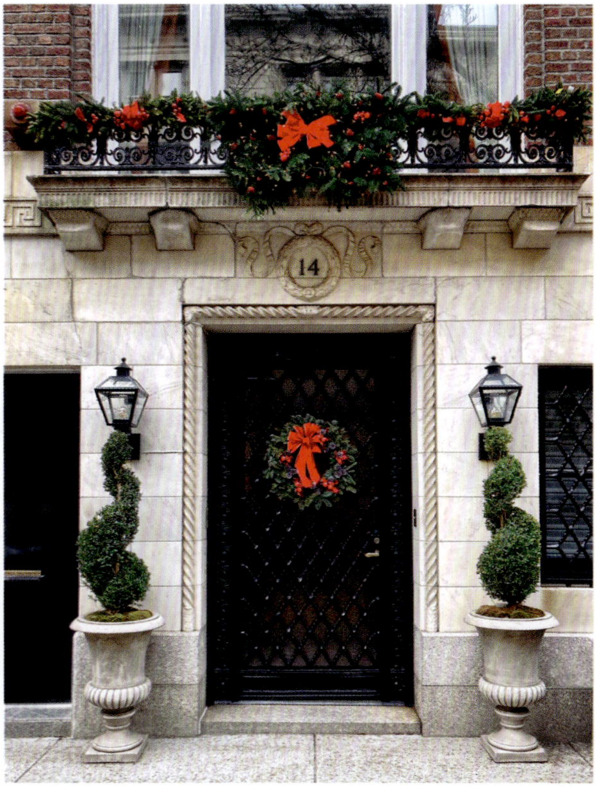
14

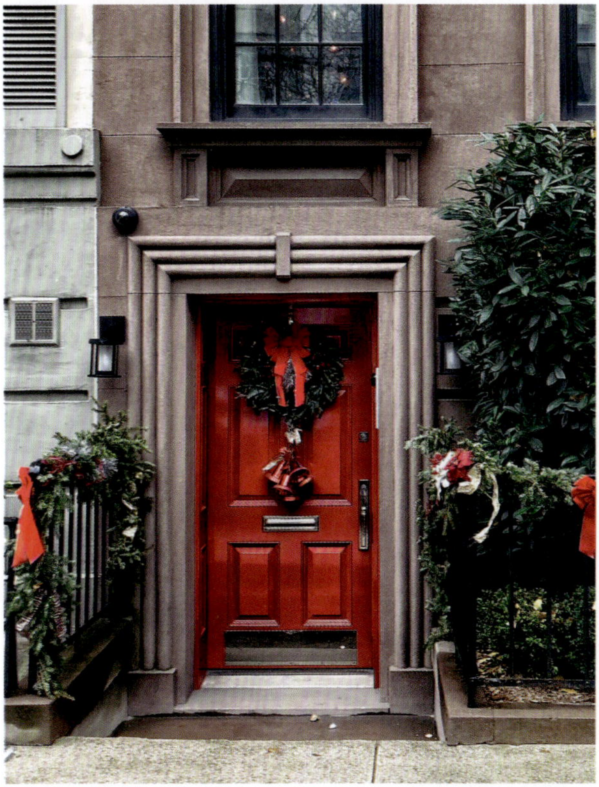

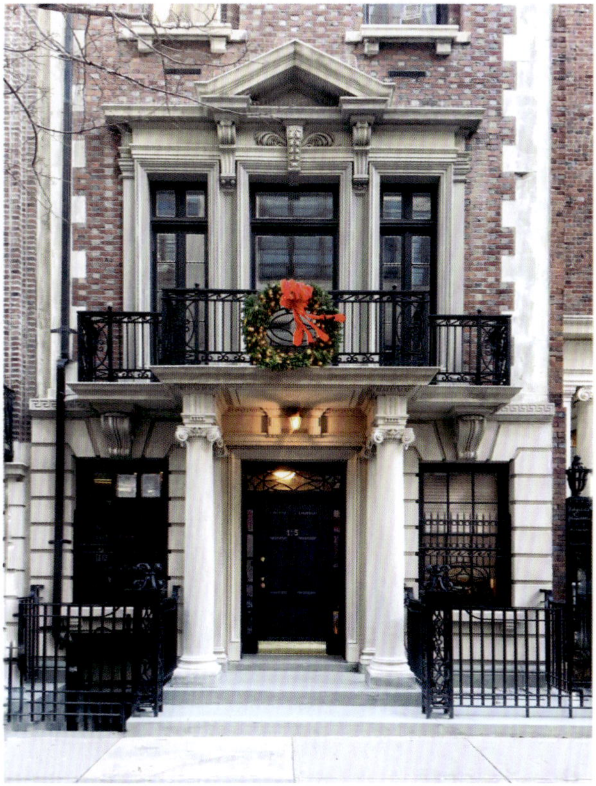

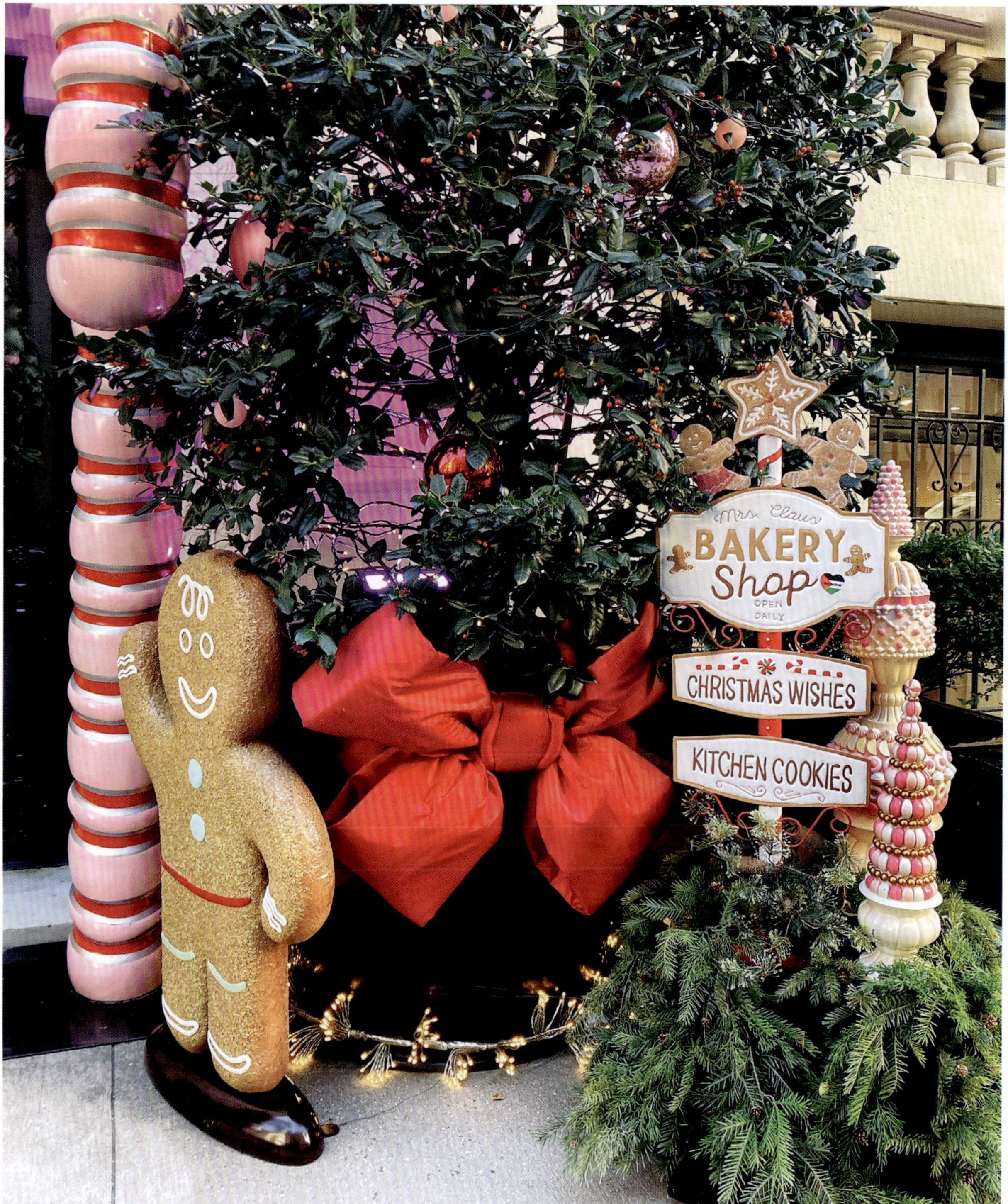

ABOVE: A sweet sidewalk display on East 64th Street between Fifth and Madison Avenues

Uptown *Holiday* favorites

1. **East 61st and 62nd Streets between Second and Third Avenues:** Showstopping blocks with many decorated townhouses, including the iconic blue door.

2. **East 64th Street between Madison and Fifth Avenues:** A fabulous townhouse whose owners always have creative and fun themes.

3. **Birley Bakery, East 69th Street between Madison and Fifth Avenues:** A festively decorated bakery and chocolate shop with a cozy café upstairs.

4. **Ralph Lauren, East 72nd Street and Madison Avenue:** Eye-catching window and interior displays, plus the charming Ralph's Coffee.

5. **East 76th Street between Madison and Fifth Avenues:** The Surrey Hotel, multiple decorated homes, and one of Uptown's most photographed stoops.

6. **East 78th Street between Second and Park Avenues:** Some of the most festively decorated townhouses on the Upper East Side.

7. **The Metropolitan Museum of Art, East 82nd Street and Fifth Avenue:** A stunning Christmas tree and Neapolitan crèche in the Medieval Sculpture Hall.

8. **East 83rd Street between Madison and Park Avenues:** More stunning townhouses with over-the-top decorations.

9. **West 82nd Street between Columbus and Amsterdam Avenues:** Designer Hillary Simon Wallace's Upper West Side brownstone is always a showstopper.

10. **East 91st to East 95th Streets between Park and Fifth Avenues:** Stroll the Carnegie Hill neighborhood to see classic decorations and lovely facades.

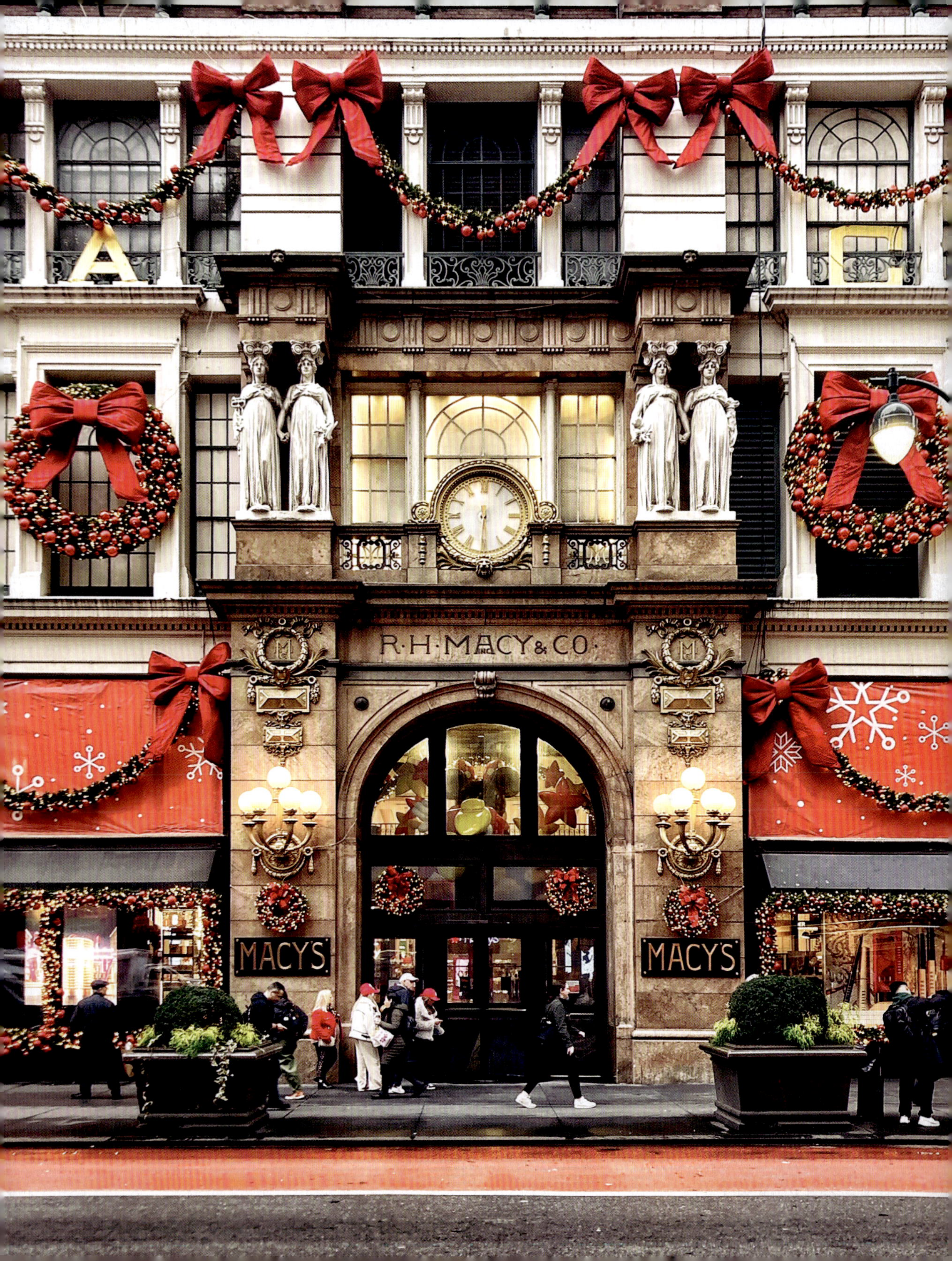
R·H·MACY & CO.
MACY'S
MACY'S

Midtown

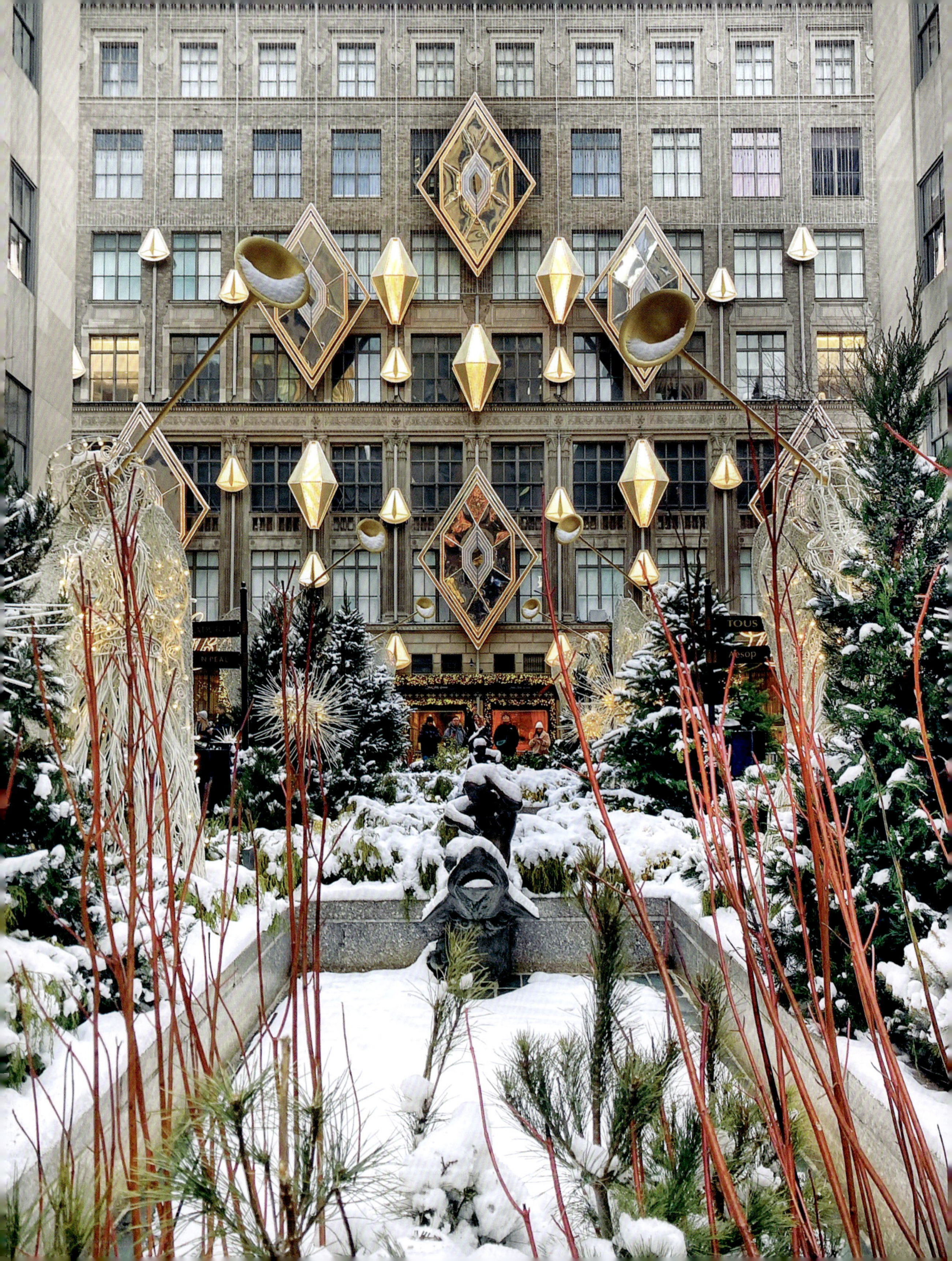
TOUS

Midtown

For many years I worked in the heart of Midtown Manhattan. Radio City Music Hall was directly across the street from my office, and every holiday season I could look out my window at the crowds lining up to see the Radio City Rockettes. Even on the thirtieth floor, I could feel the energy on the street below me.

But I was a bit of a Grinch back then. As a fast-walking New Yorker, I was constantly frustrated by the throngs of slow-moving tourists blocking my way. While they were enjoying the iconic sights in my work neighborhood, I was too busy to notice or appreciate the fantastic seasonal displays all around me. Now, I'm happy to say, I see things differently.

For pure, unadulterated holiday magic, there's nowhere like Midtown—it's almost like a fabulous movie set where everything is bigger, brighter, and more dramatic than anywhere else in town. The Rockefeller Center Christmas tree! The Plaza hotel! Bergdorf Goodman's windows! The Saks Fifth Avenue light show! Every block between 49th and 59th Streets has something to marvel at: the gigantic red ornaments, candy canes, and Nutcrackers along Sixth Avenue; St. Patrick's Cathedral, the glittering thirty-foot-tall snowflake suspended above 57th Street, and the dazzling storefronts on Fifth Avenue.

One of my favorite spots to visit and shoot, just a little farther down Fifth Avenue, is the Winter Village at Bryant Park, which includes an ice-skating rink, igloos for dining, and a European-style holiday market for shopping and snacking. What could be more festive than that!

I'm not sure what town the composers of "Silver Bells" had in mind when they wrote "City sidewalks, busy sidewalks. Dressed in holiday style," but I think they described Midtown perfectly.

PREVIOUS: Macy's Herald Square's beautiful Beaux-Arts building's facade on West 34th Street is festively decked out before their annual Thanksgiving Day Parade. Built in 1902, it takes up a full city block. **OPPOSITE:** A view of Saks Fifth Avenue's dazzling diamond-themed exterior, seen from Rockefeller Center's snow-covered Channel Gardens on Fifth Avenue between 49th and 50th Streets. In the evening it becomes a spectacular light and music extravaganza.

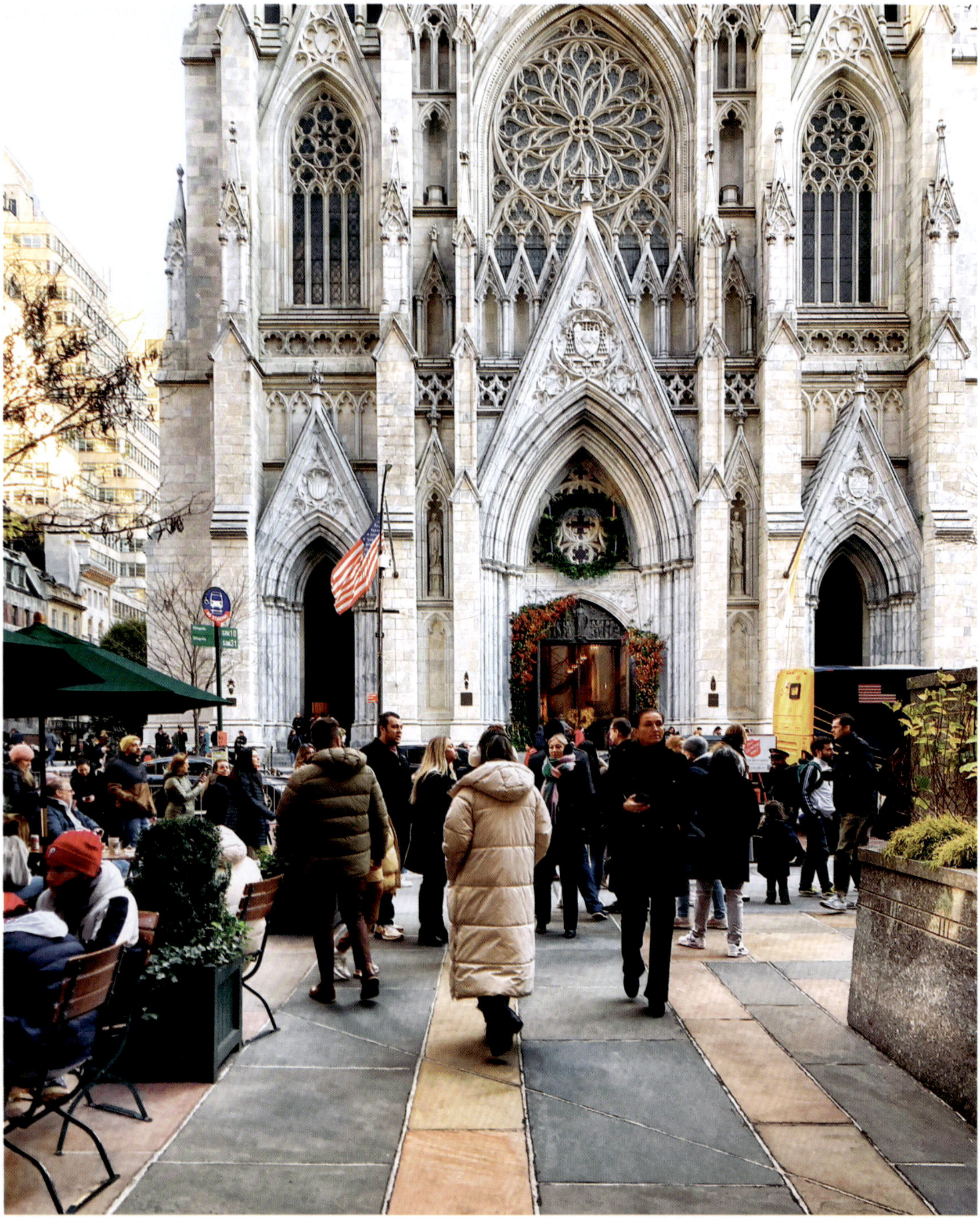

ABOVE: Crowds milling opposite St. Patrick's Cathedral, the largest Gothic Revival Catholic church in North America (completed in 1879) on Fifth Avenue and 50th Street. **OPPOSITE:** The New York Public Library's striking nature-themed tree in Astor Hall on Fifth Avenue and 41st Street is decorated with birds, owls, nests, pine cones, and a dusting of snow.

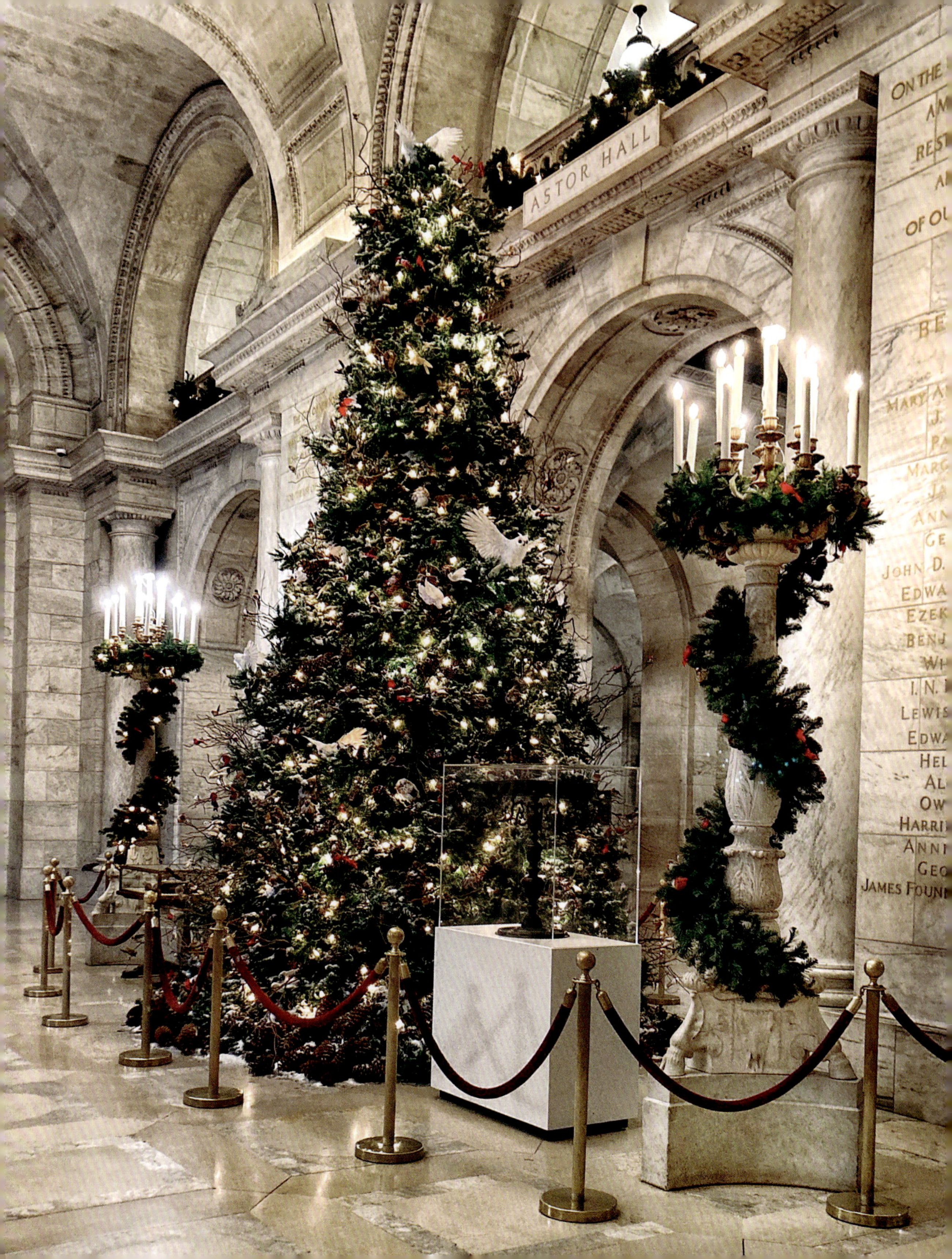
ASTOR HALL
ON THE

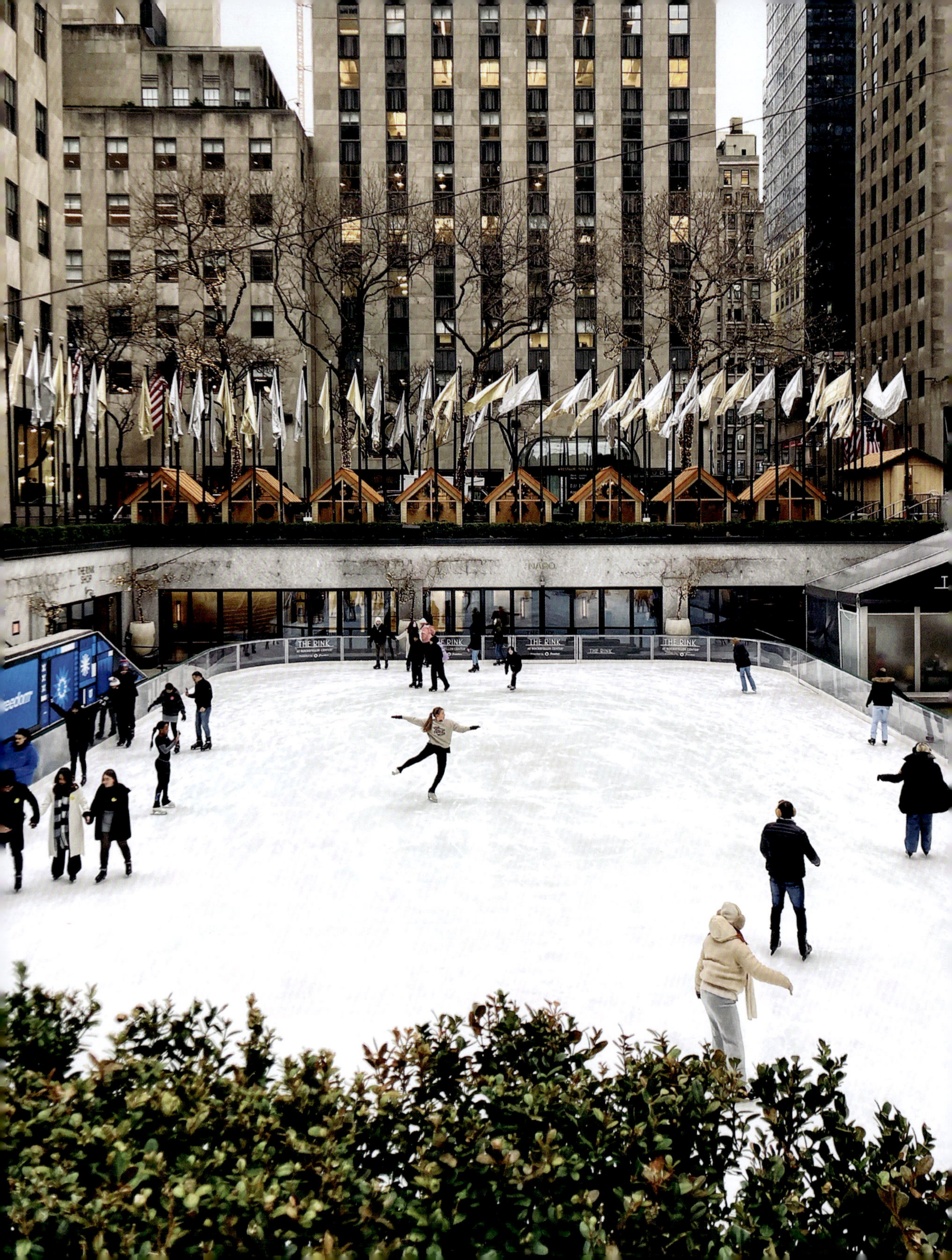
THE RINK

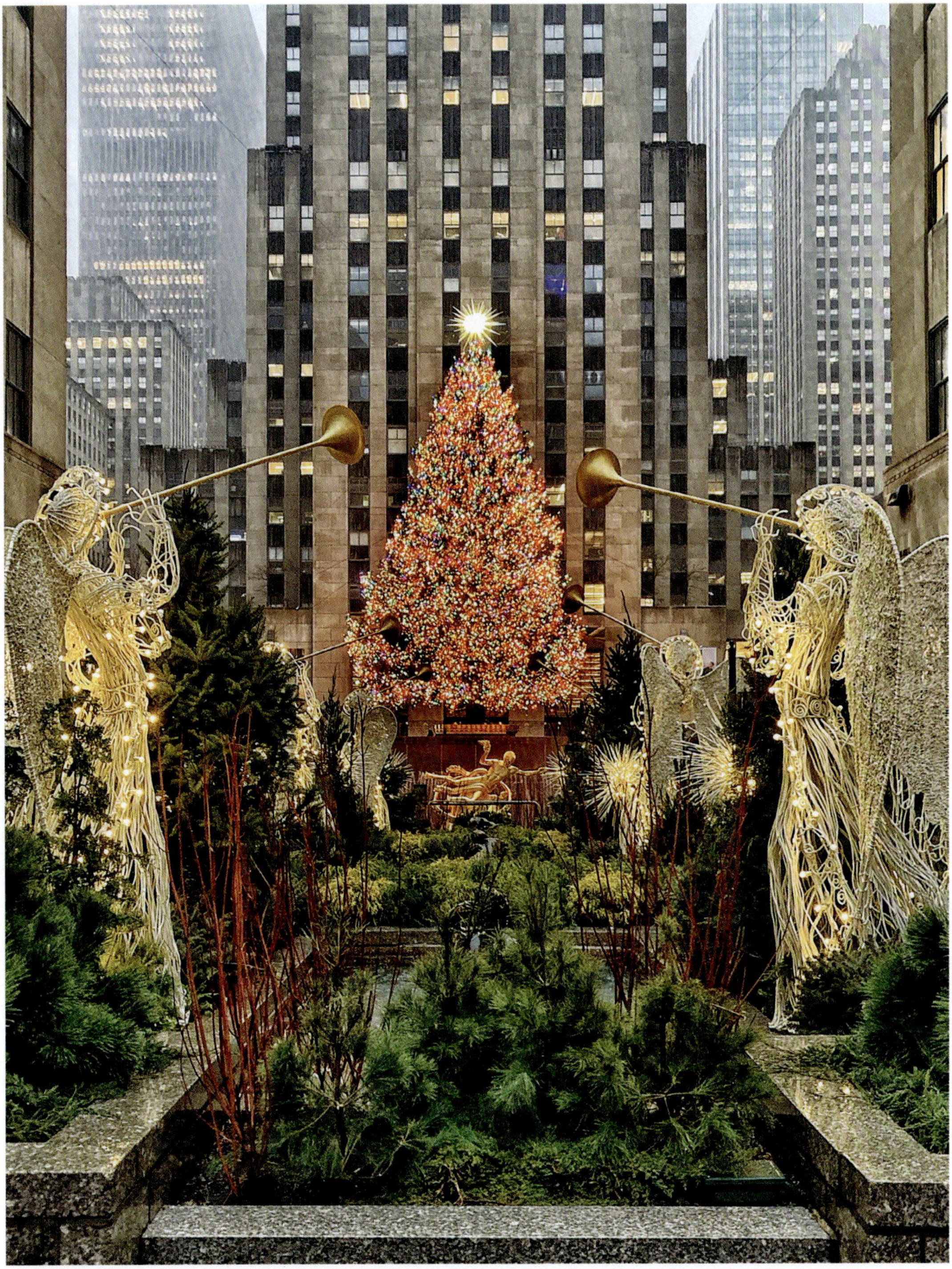

OPPOSITE: Ice skaters enjoying the Rink at Rockefeller Center. **ABOVE:** The world-famous Rockefeller Center Christmas tree is a seventy-five-foot Norway Spruce covered in more than fifty thousand LED lights and topped with a giant nine-hundred-pound Swarovski crystal star.

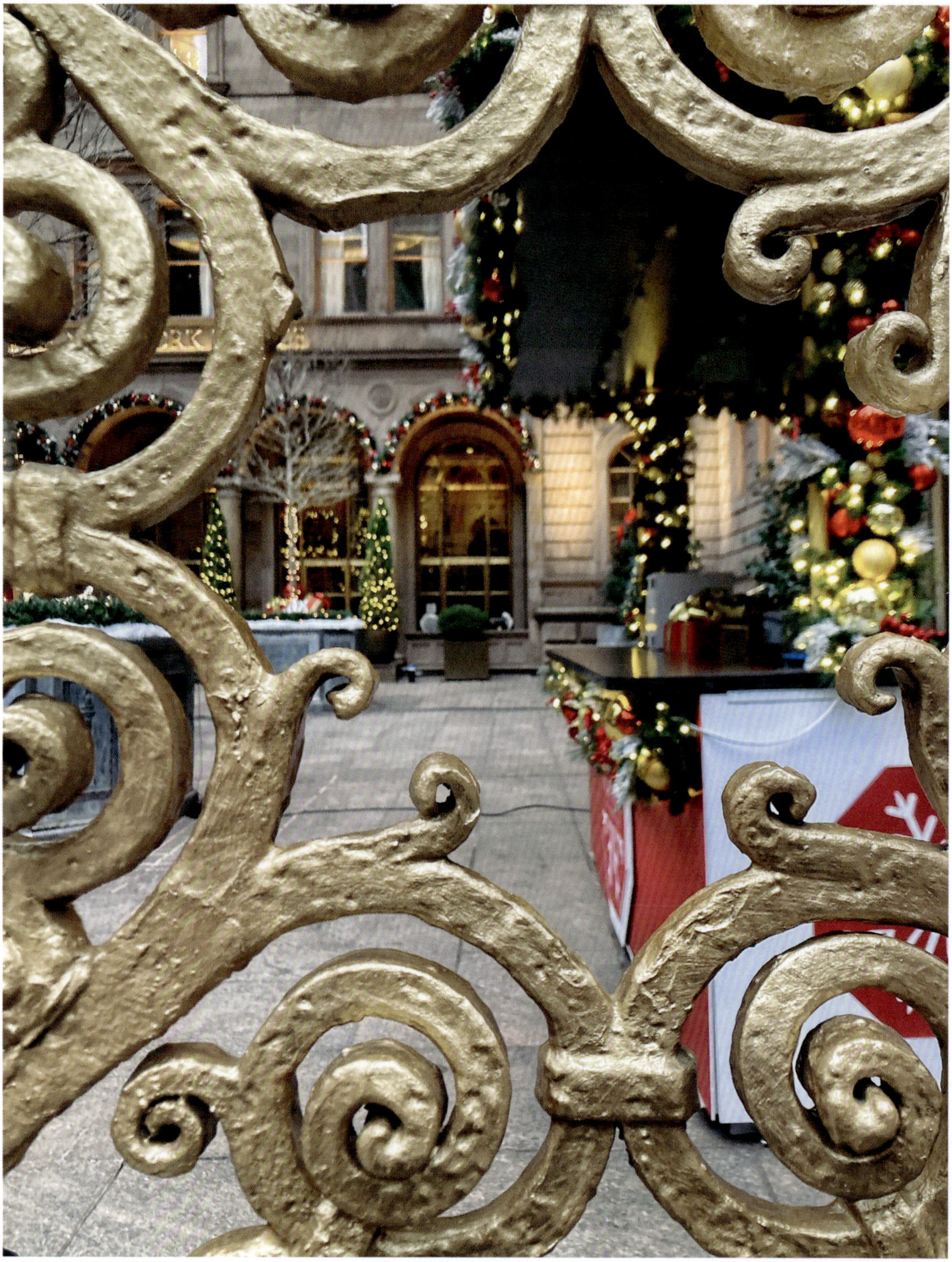

ABOVE: The Lotte New York Palace hotel's courtyard on Madison Avenue and 50th Street, seen through its fanciful gold fence section. **OPPOSITE:** The Cartier mansion on Fifth Avenue and 52nd Street is wrapped in a crimson red ribbon (its signature color) and draped in shimmering gold.

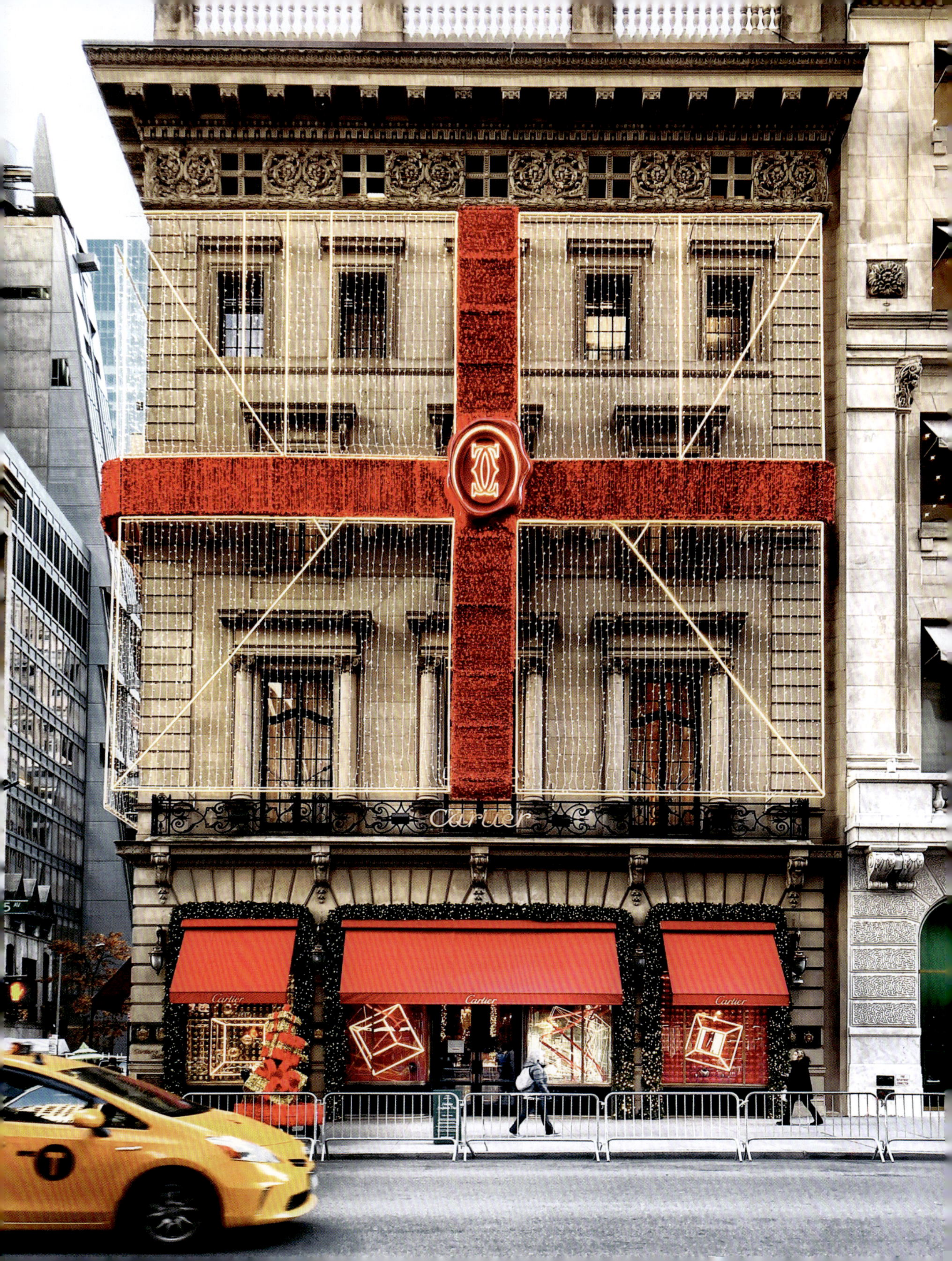
Cartier
Cartier
Cartier
Cartier

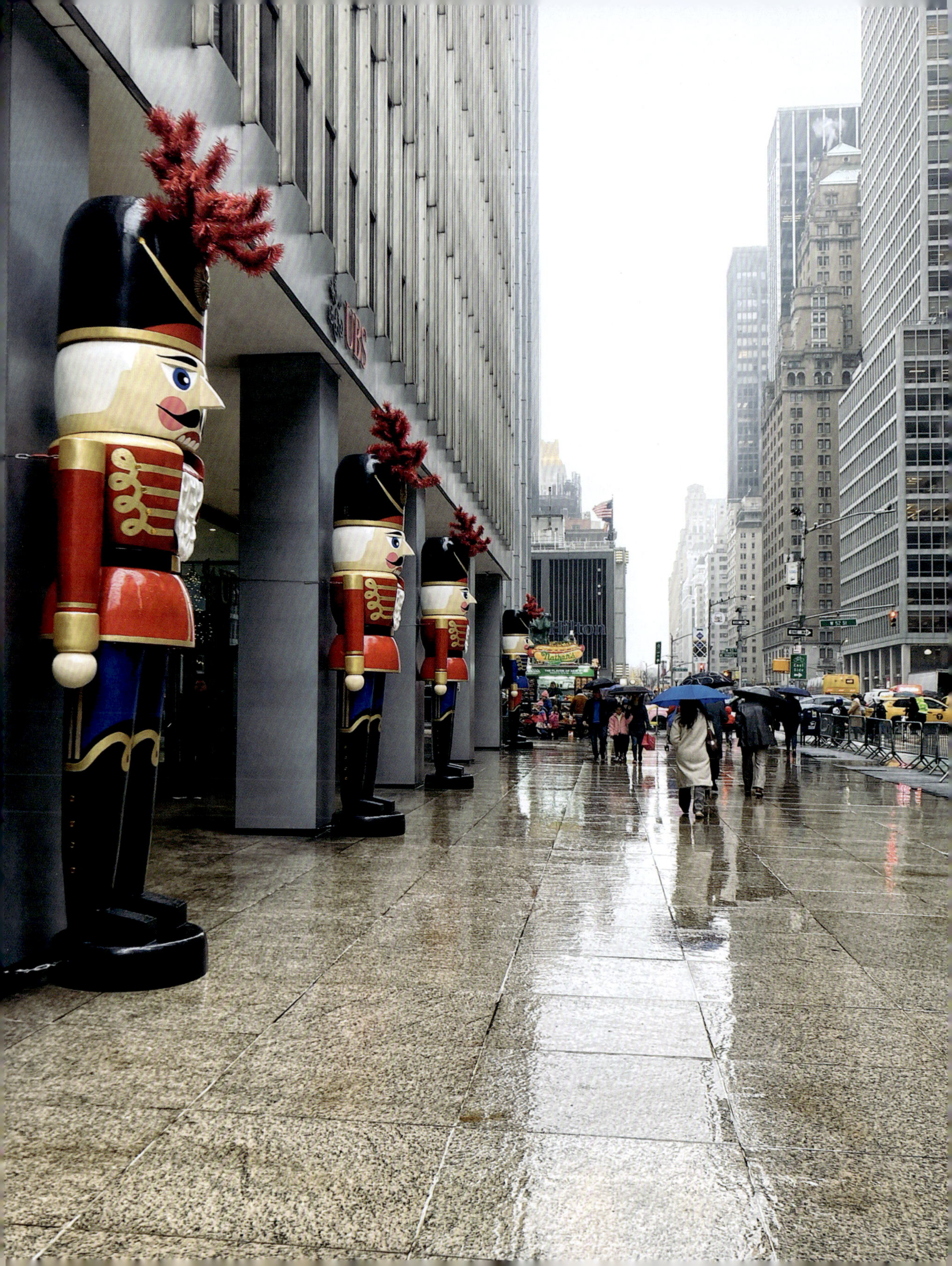
UBS
Hilton
Nathan's

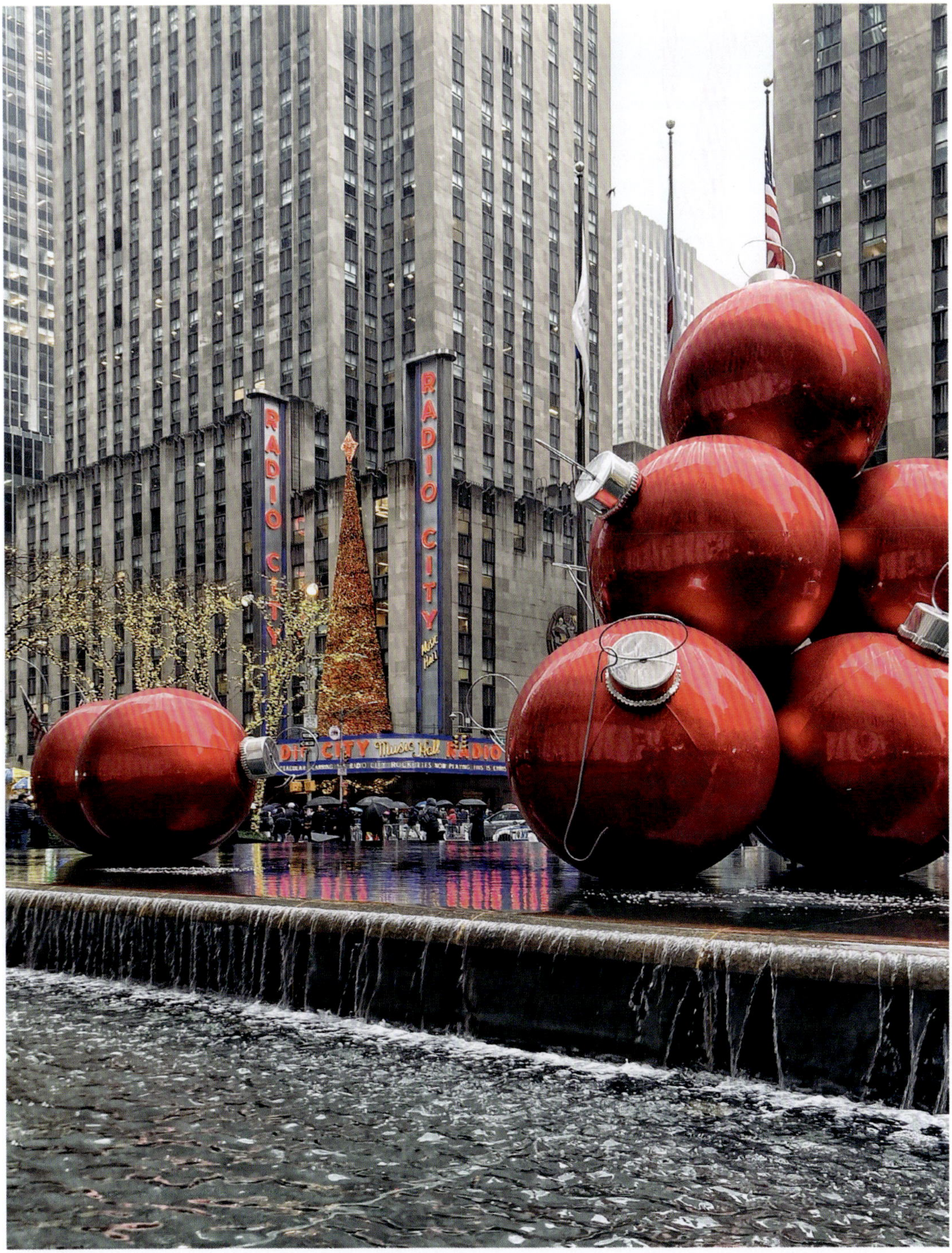

OPPOSITE: Classic Nutcrackers stand at attention along Sixth Avenue between 51st and 52nd Streets.
ABOVE: A view of Radio City Music Hall (home of the Rockettes), through the giant red ornaments displayed on Sixth Avenue between 49th and 50th Streets.

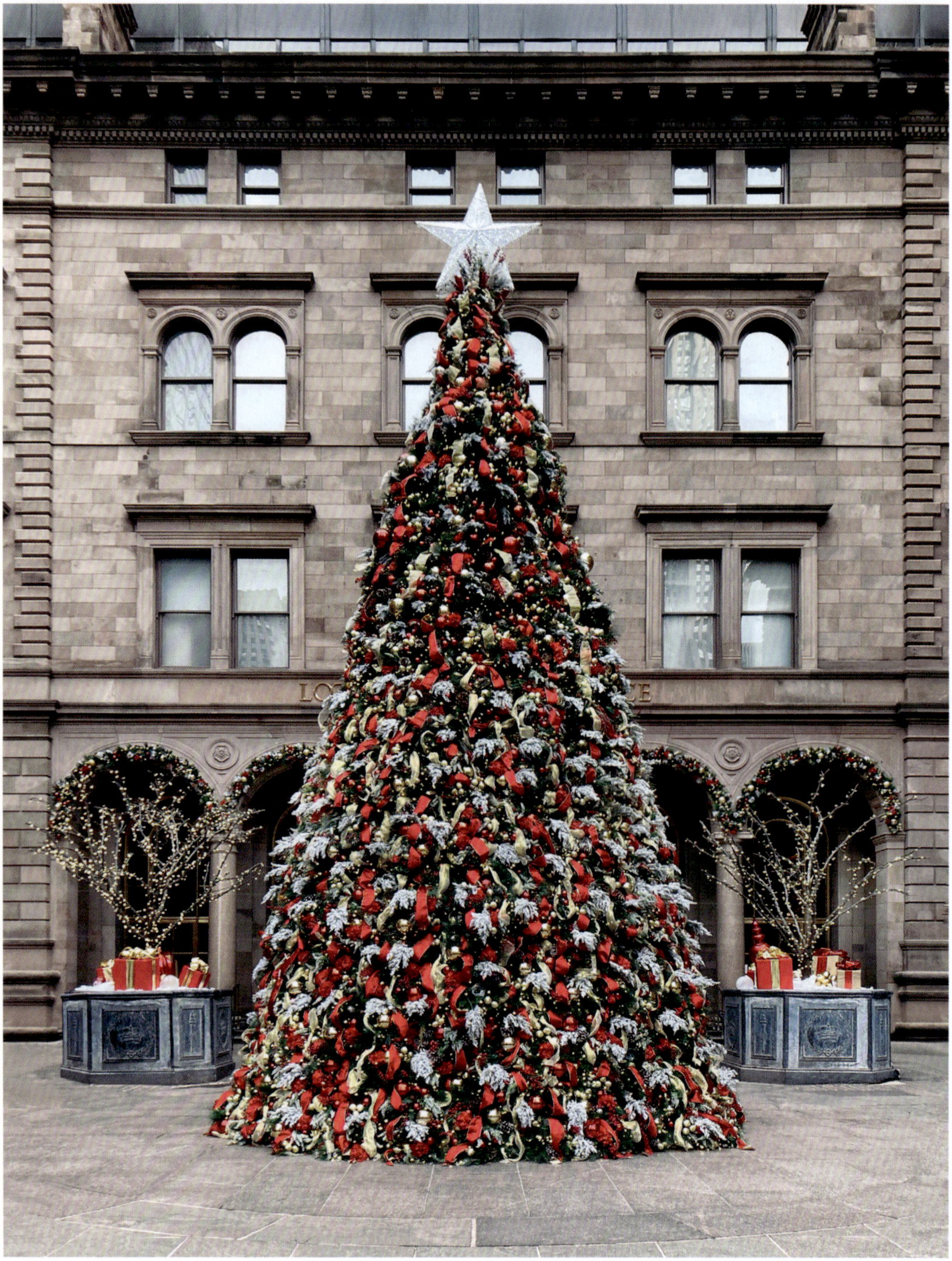

ABOVE AND OPPOSITE: The gorgeous thirty-foot-tall Christmas tree in the courtyard of the luxurious Gilded Age hotel the Lotte New York Palace on Madison Avenue and 50th Street is always a crowd favorite. A toy soldier stands at attention with St. Patrick's Cathedral in the background at the Lotte New York Palace hotel.

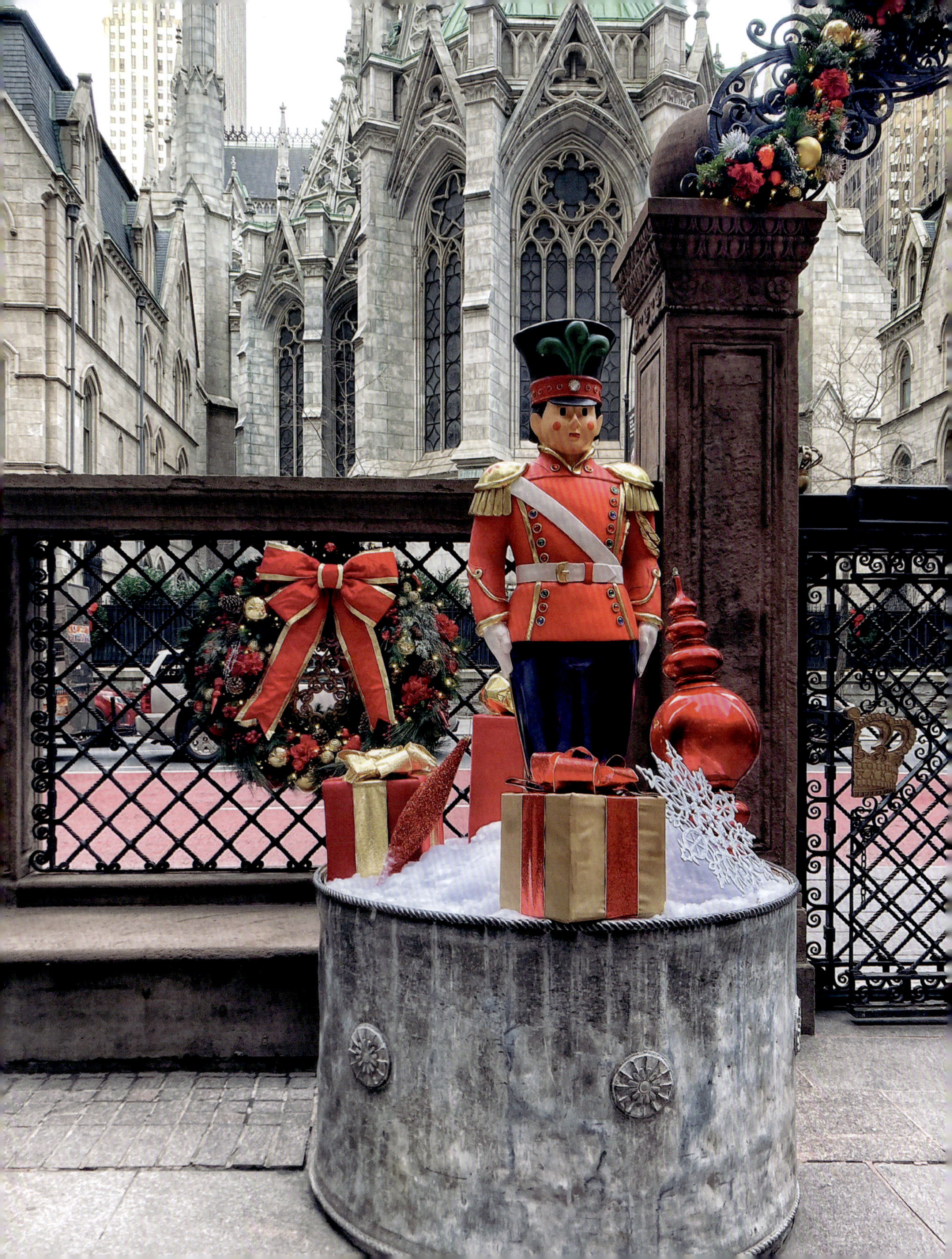

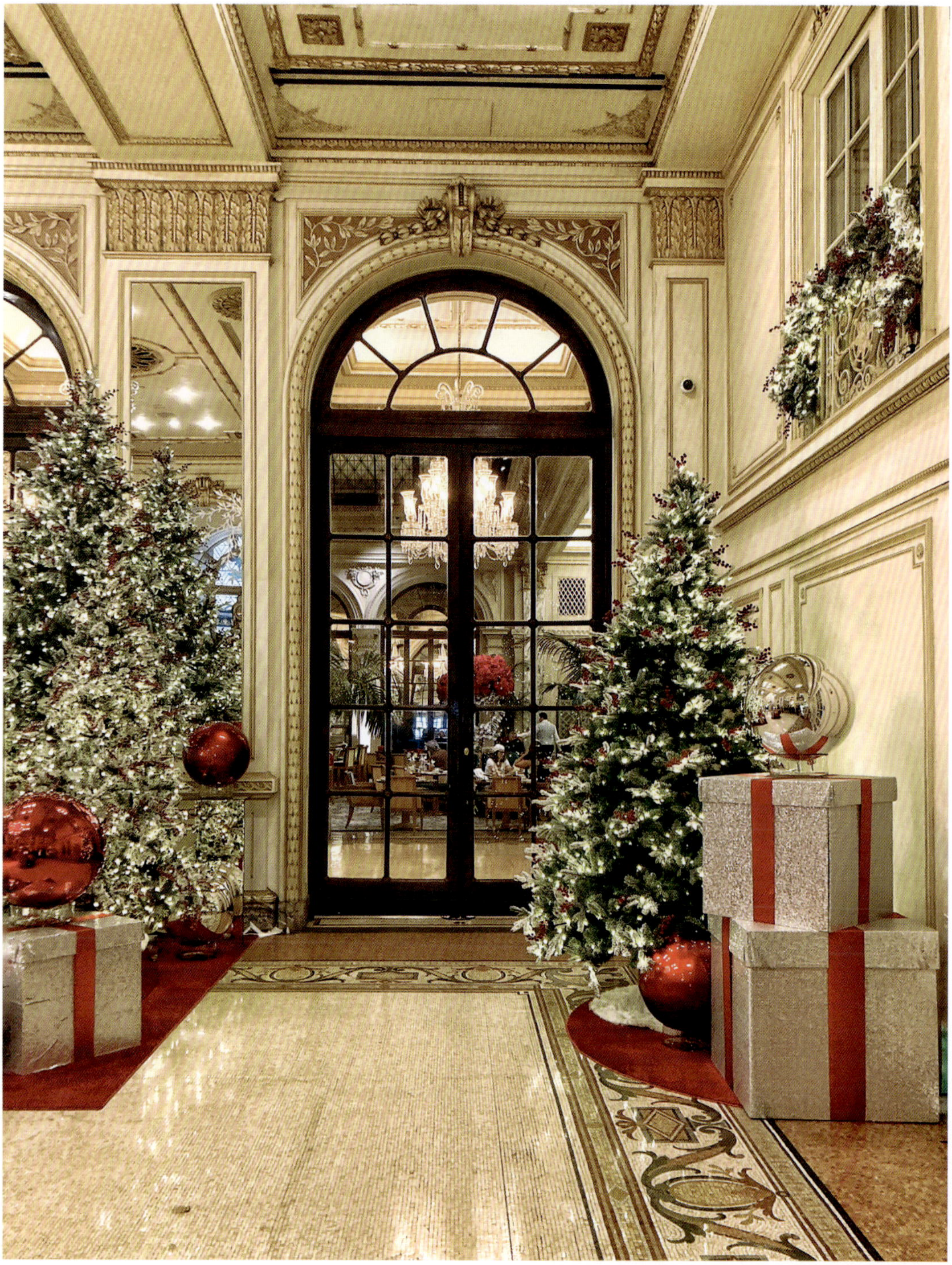

ABOVE: The opulent lobby of the legendary Plaza Hotel is filled with sparkling Christmas trees, presents, and oversized ornaments. **OPPOSITE, CLOCKWISE FROM TOP LEFT:** Details from the Plaza hotel: a silver ornament and gift; the Palm Court's candy-themed decor; a glamorous chandelier and shimmering trees; the Palm Court's sweetly decorated bar

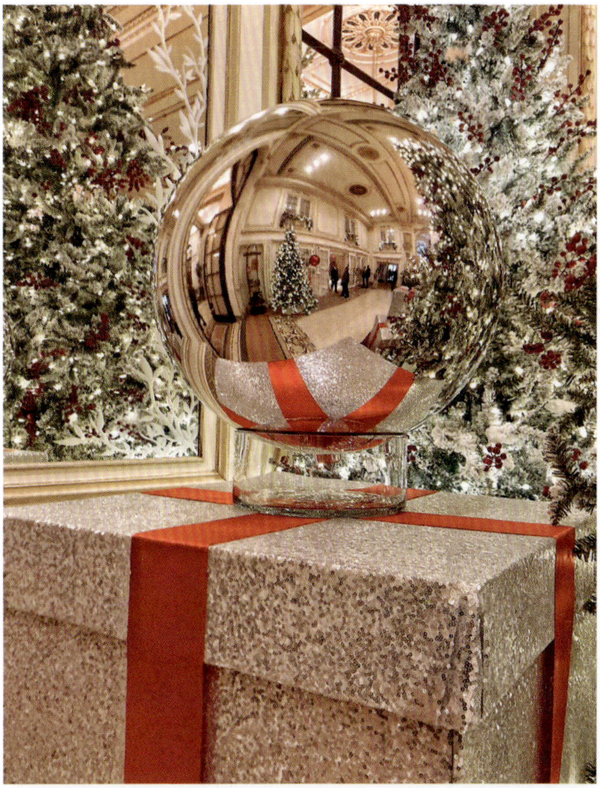

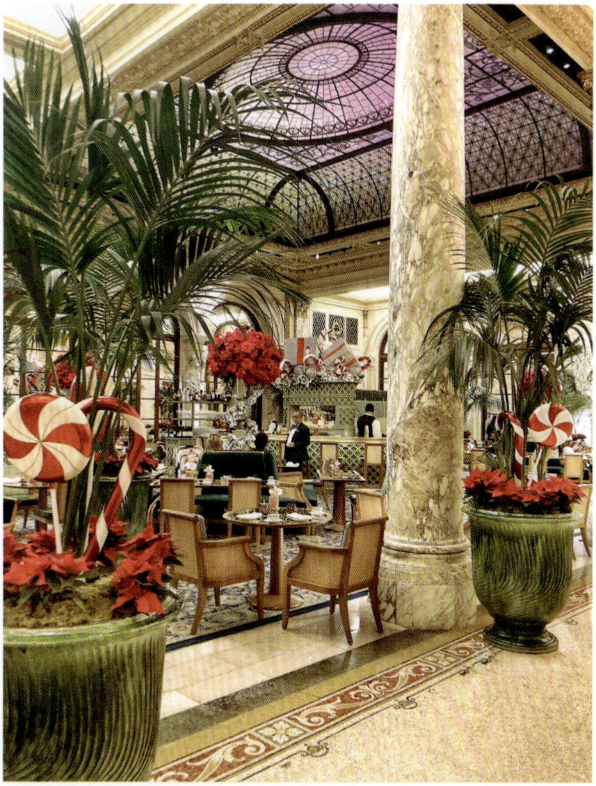

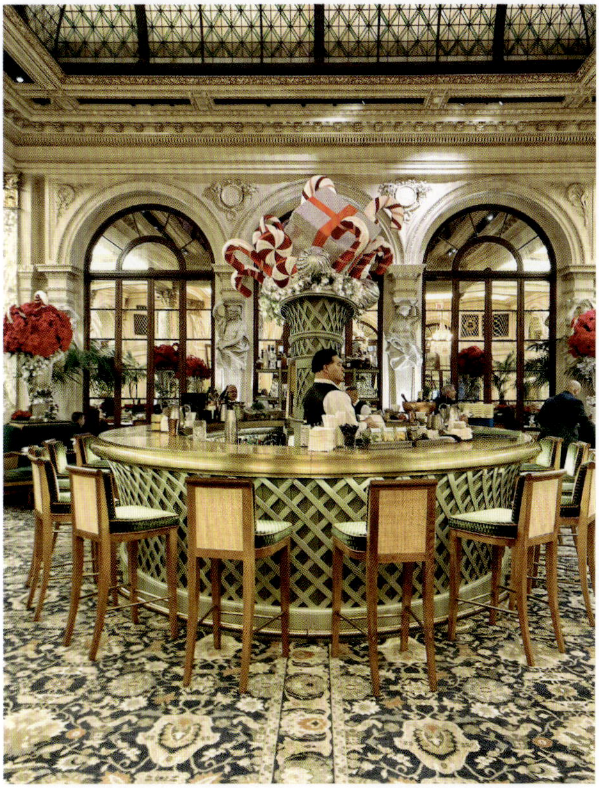

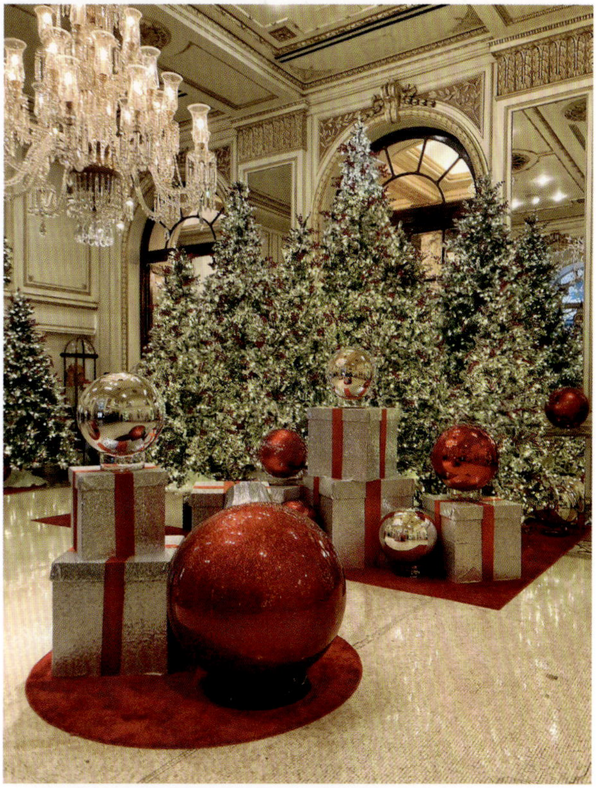

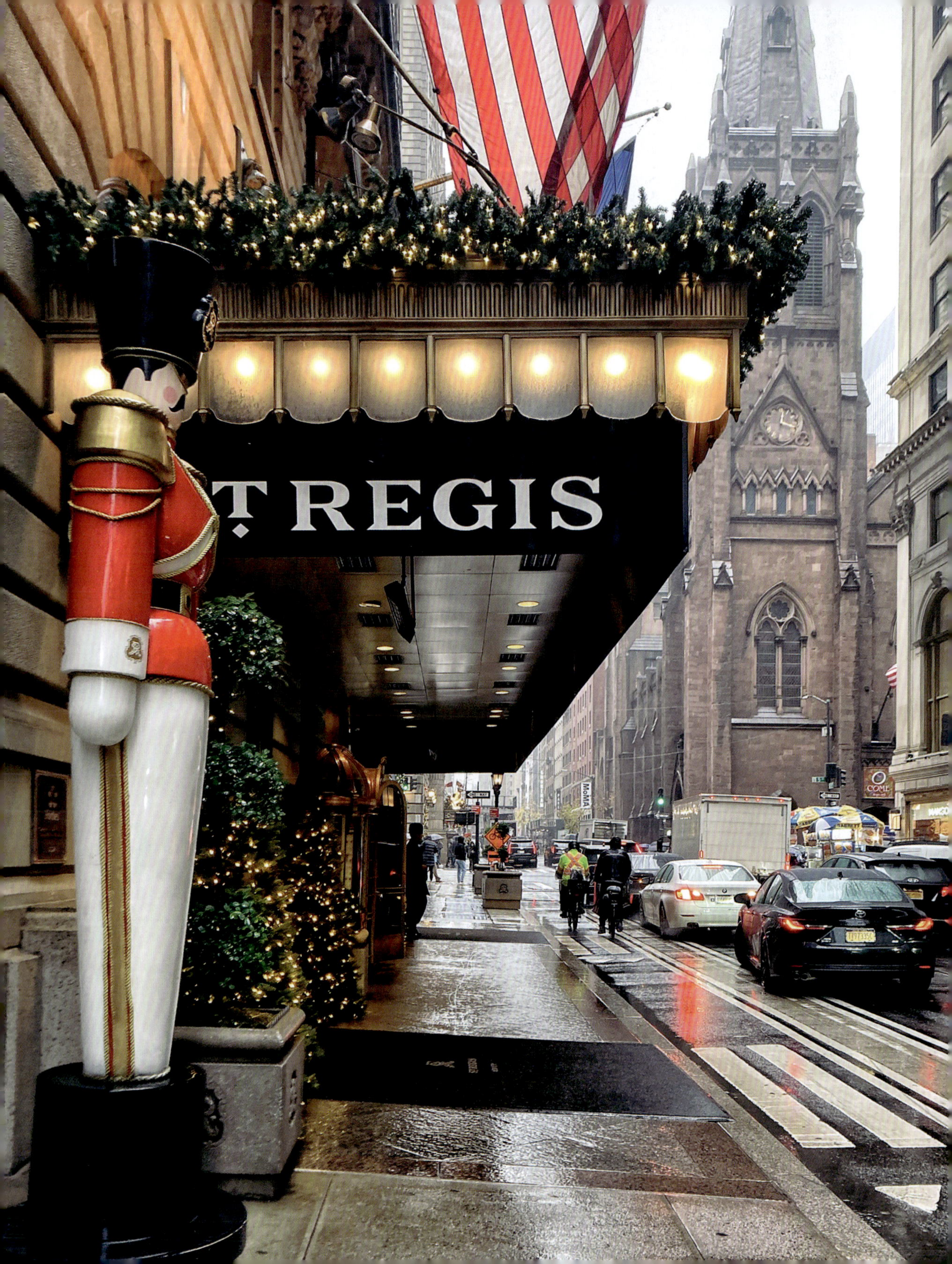
REGIS
MoMA

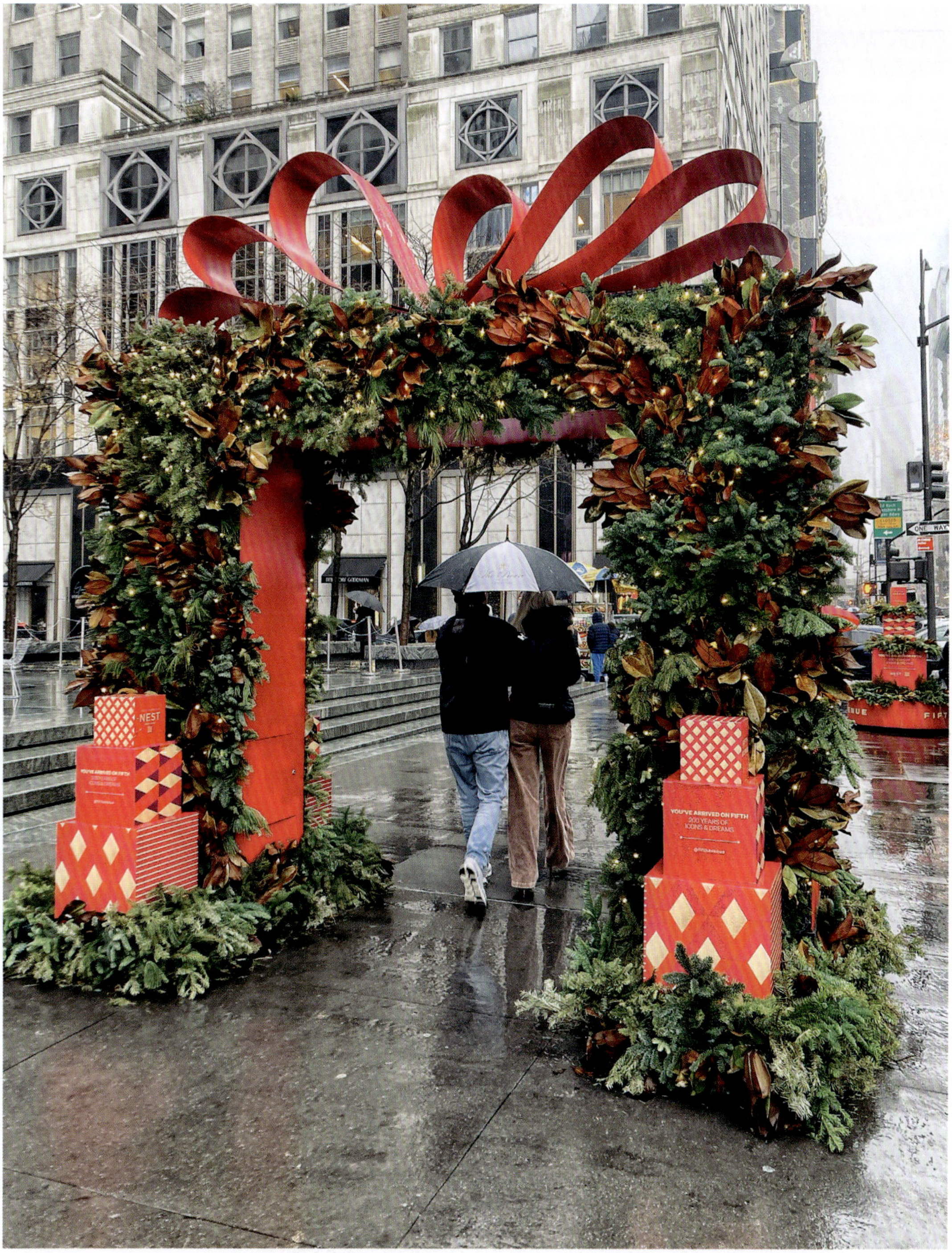

OPPOSITE: A rainy-day view of the elegant St. Regis hotel entrance on East 55th Street between Fifth and Madison Avenues. **ABOVE:** A couple stroll through Nest New York's fragrant and festive arch. Their installations on Fifth Avenue sidewalks diffuse a wonderful seasonal scent of pomegranate, pine, and spices from 47th to 59th Streets.

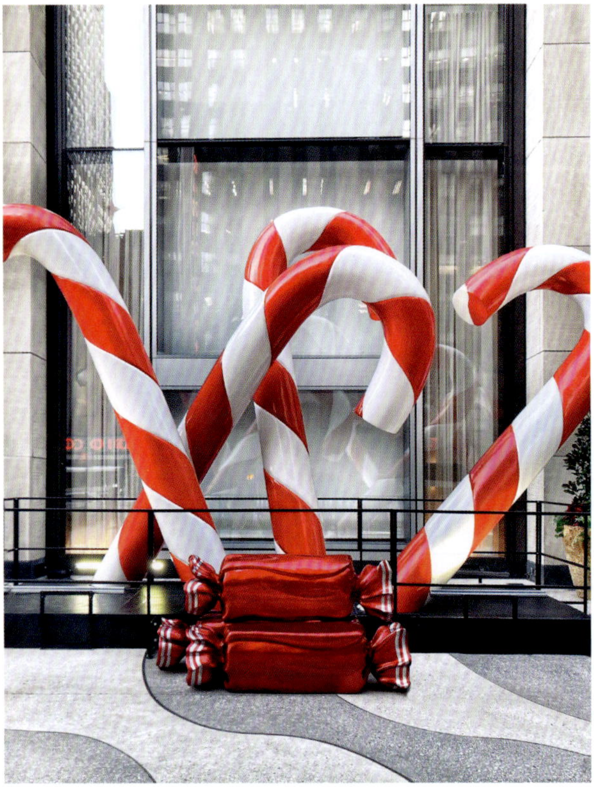

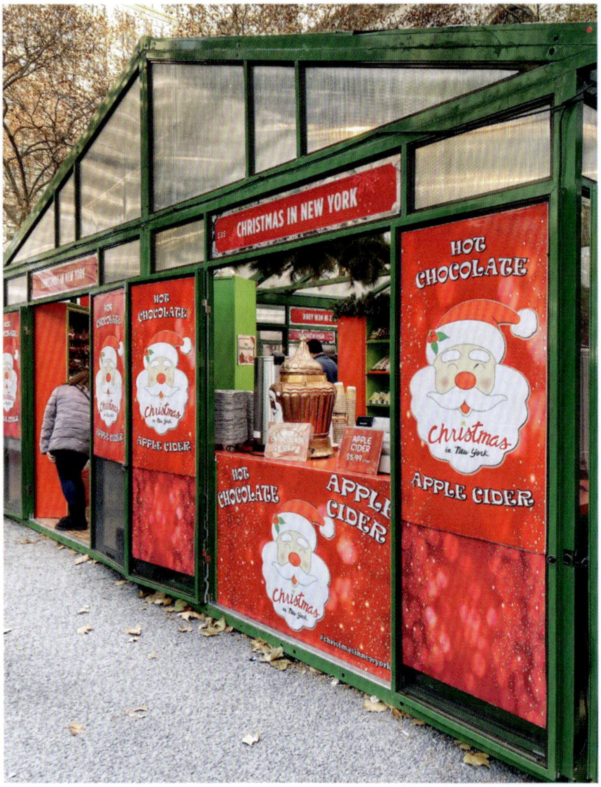
CHRISTMAS IN NEW YORK
HOT CHOCOLATE
Christmas in New York
APPLE CIDER
HOT CHOCOLATE
APPLE CIDER

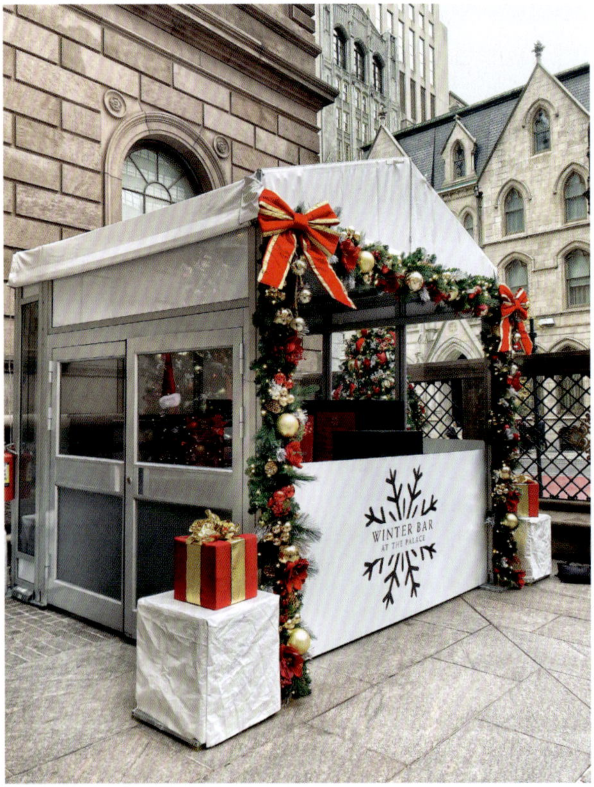
WINTER BAR
AT THE PALACE

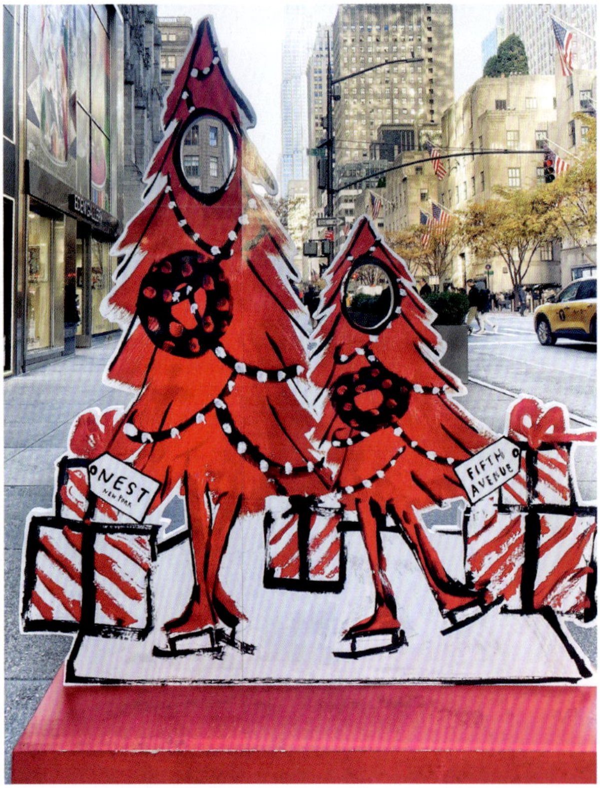
NEST
NEW YORK
FIFTH AVENUE

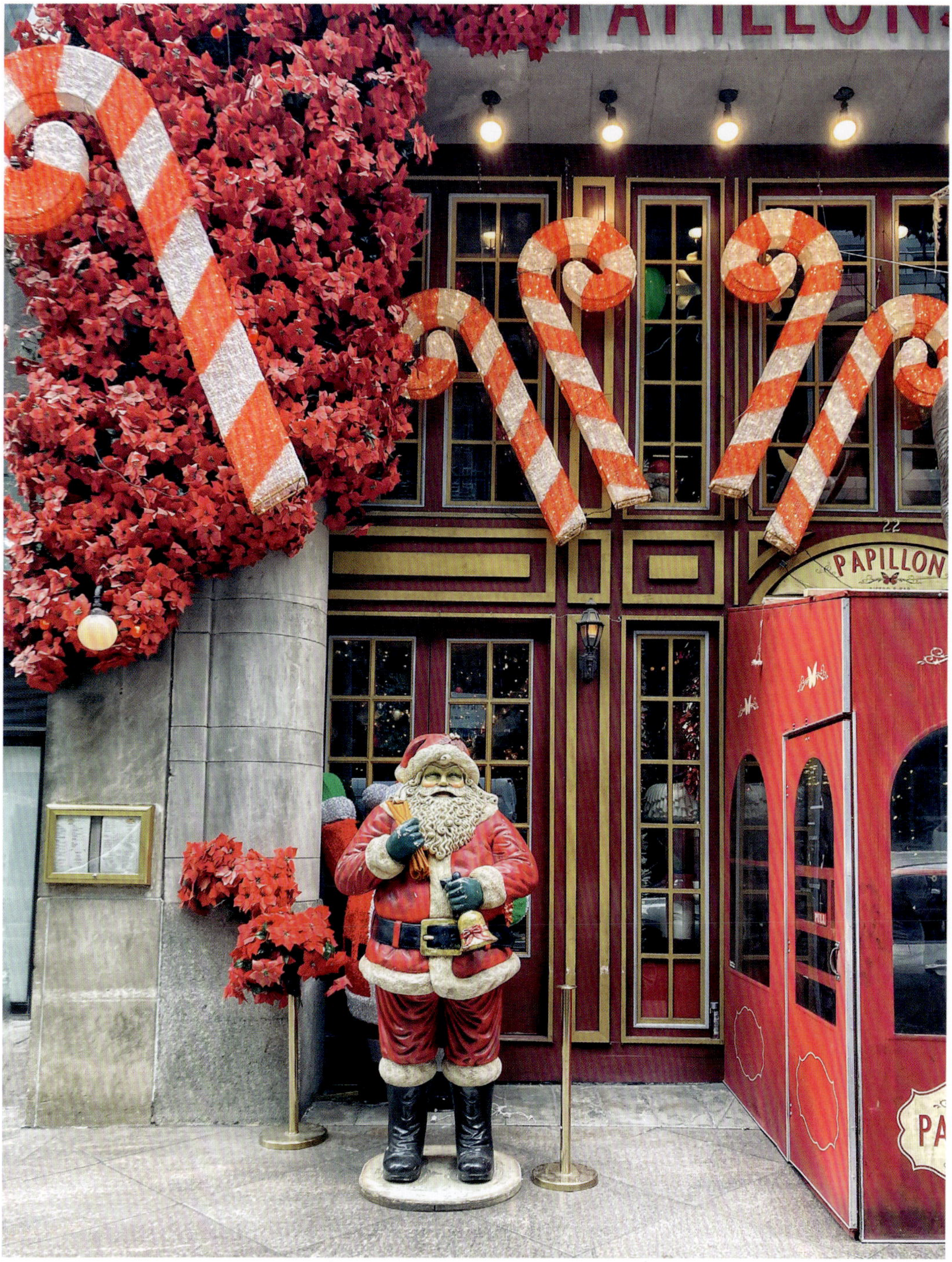

OPPOSITE, CLOCKWISE FROM TOP LEFT: Towering fifteen-foot candy canes on Sixth Avenue and 50th Street; one of 180 vendors at the Bryant Park holiday market; a cute cutout by artist Donald Robertson for Nest fragrances on Fifth Avenue; the Winter Bar at the Lotte New York Palace hotel on Madison Avenue. **ABOVE:** Santa Claus ringing a bell at Papillon Bistro & Bar, an over-the-top Christmas-decorated eatery on East 54th Street between Madison and 5th Avenues

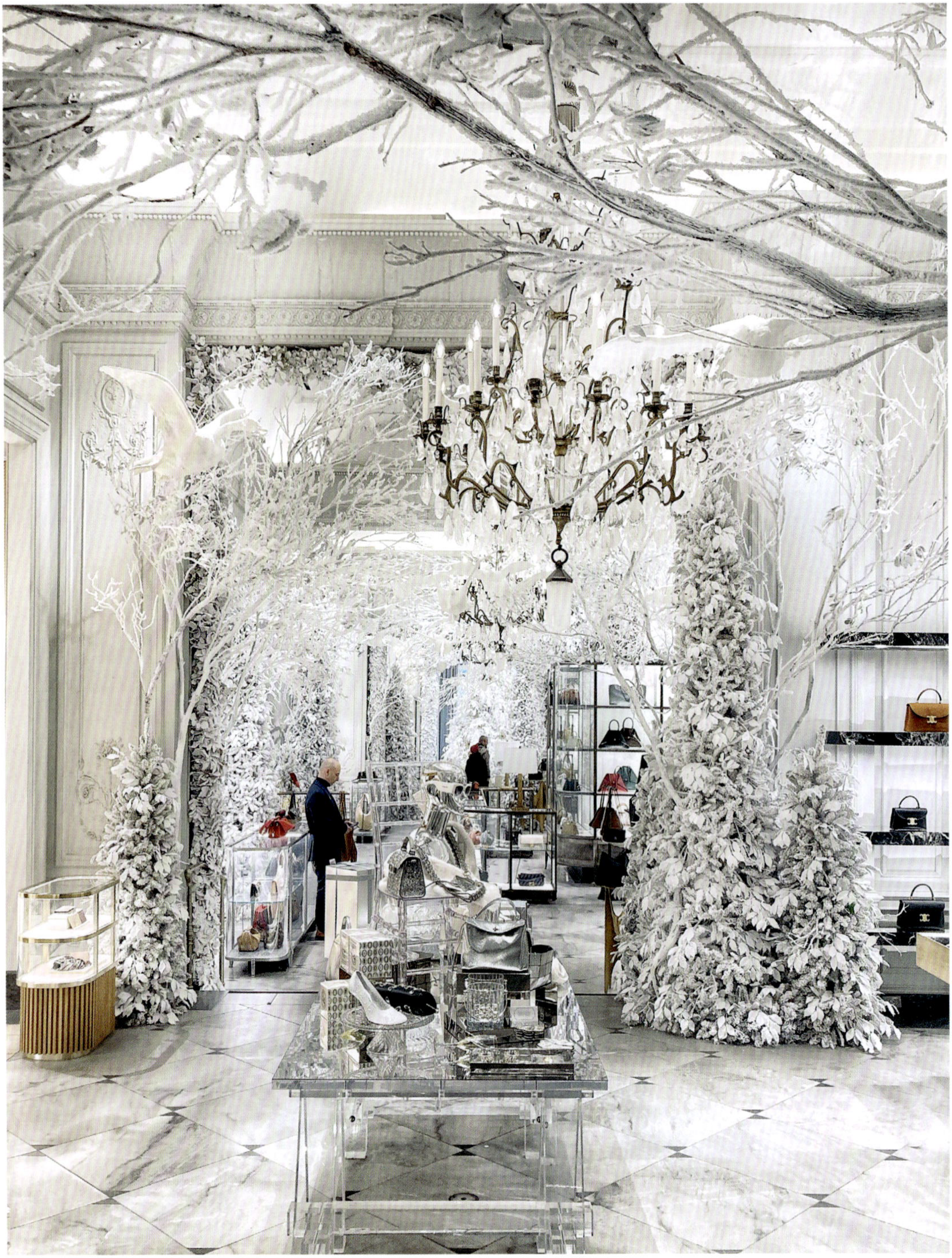

ABOVE AND OPPOSITE: Luxury department store Bergdorf Goodman's all-white winter wonderland interior by designer David Monn, featuring flying white plaster geese overhead, white branches, and snow-covered trees and garlands, is nothing short of magical.

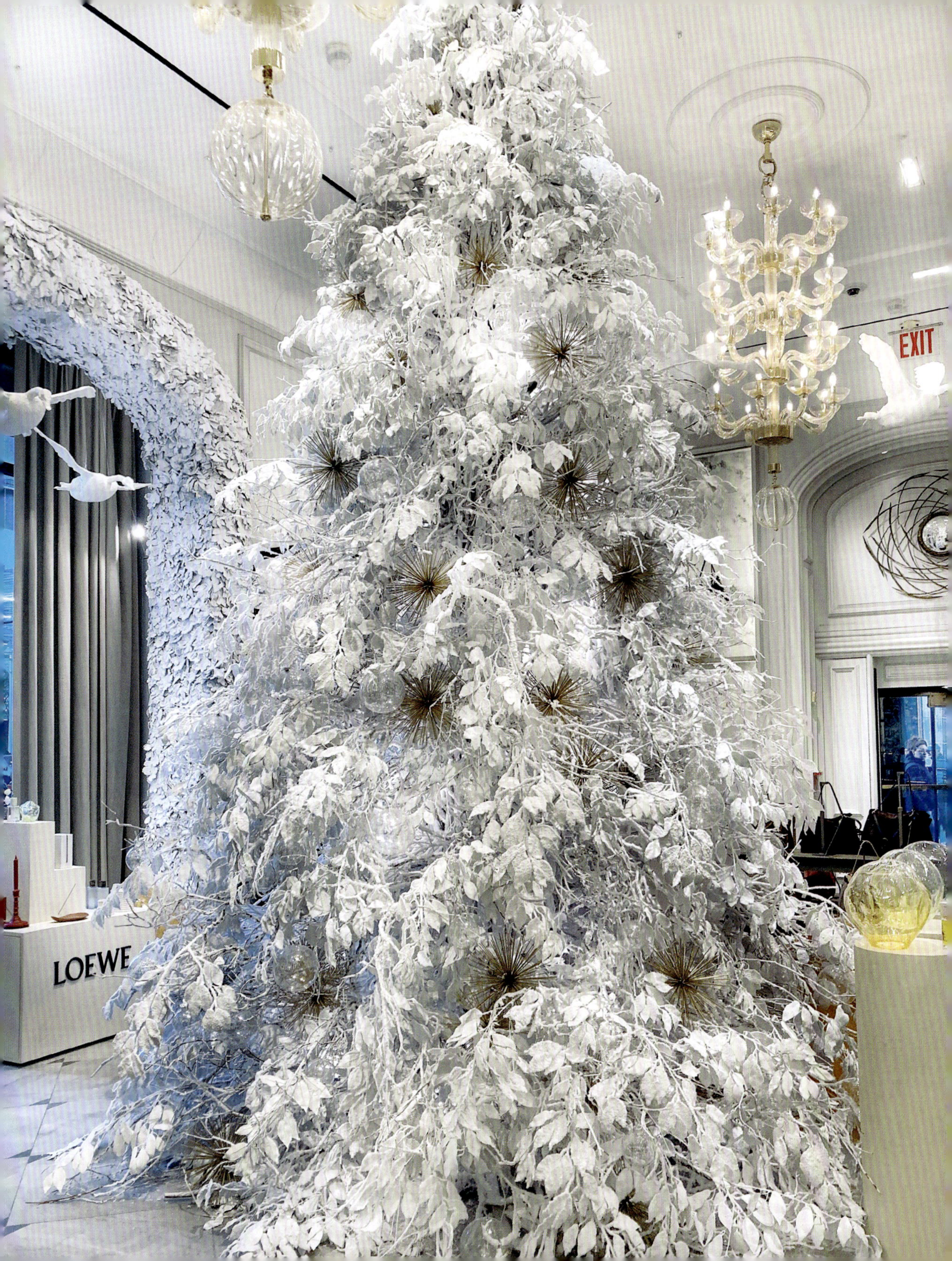
EXIT
LOEWE

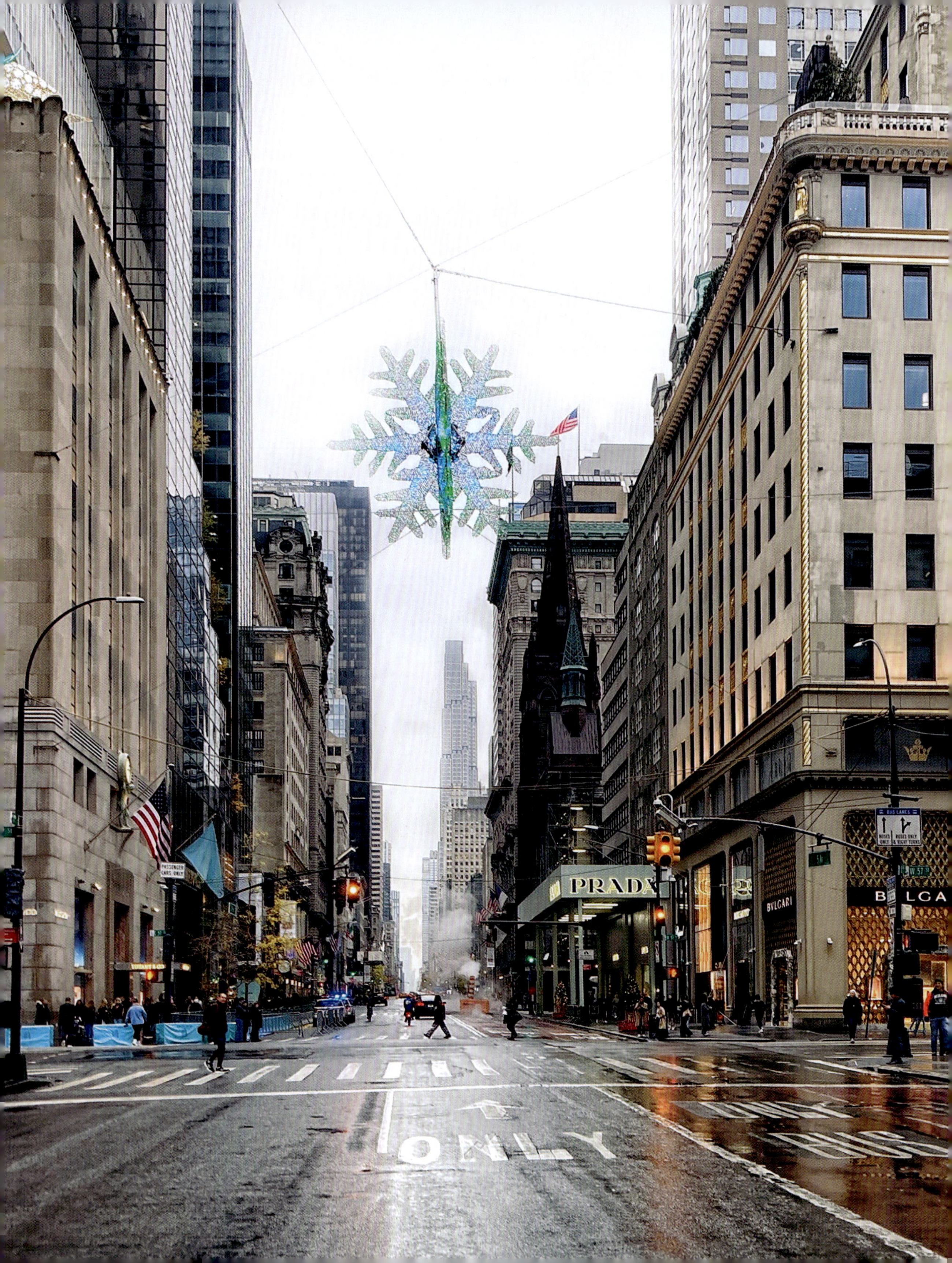
PRADA
BVLGARI
ONLY

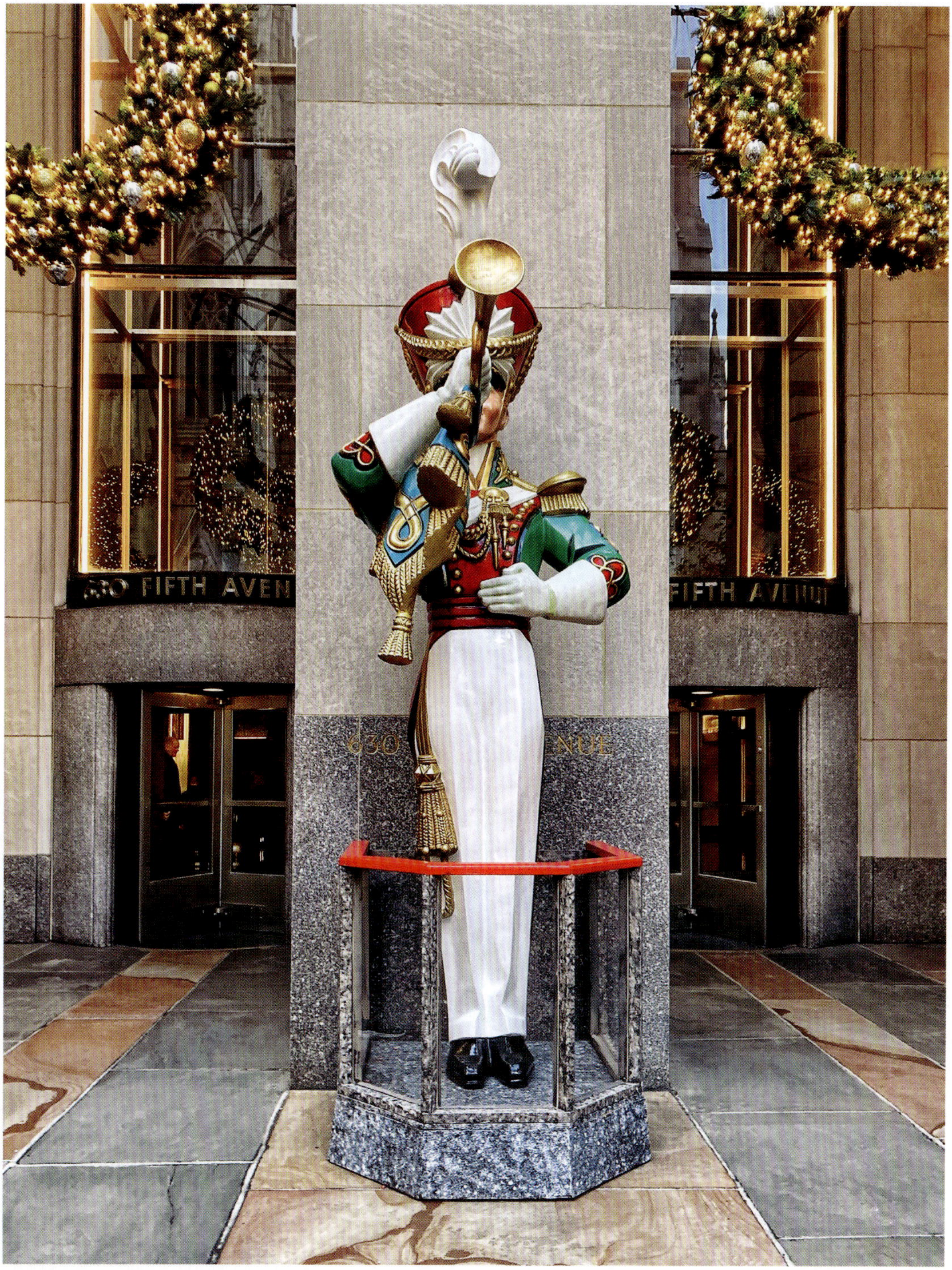

OPPOSITE: The Fifth Avenue Snowflake, suspended fifty feet above 57th Street on Fifth Avenue, is thirty feet wide and has more than sixteen thousand Baccarat crystals and LED lights, creating a sparkling light show of changing colors. **ABOVE:** A giant wooden toy soldier blows his horn at Rockefeller Center.

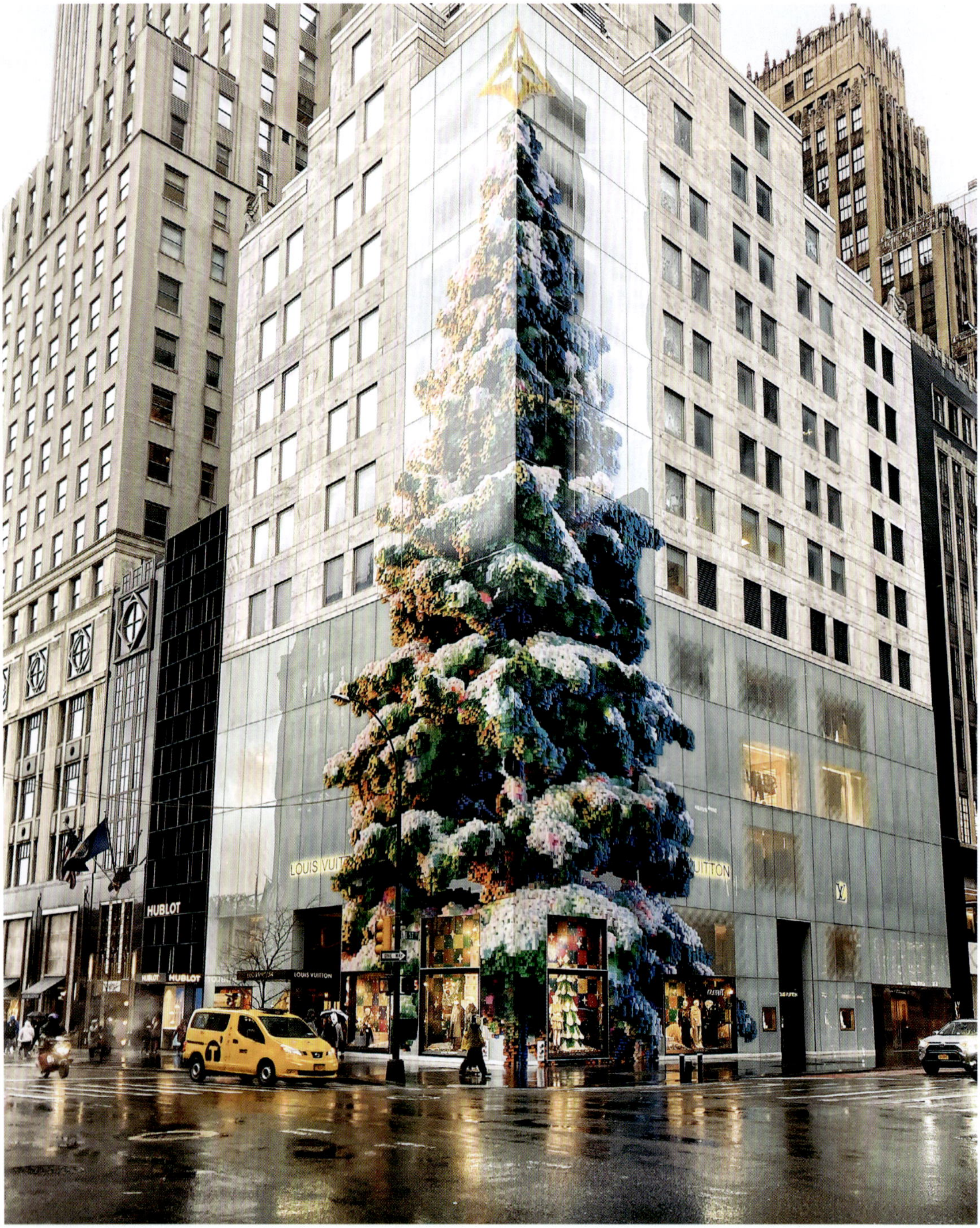

ABOVE: A fabulous twelve-story 2-D Christmas tree is displayed on the Louis Vuitton flagship store on the corner of 57th Street and Fifth Avenue. **OPPOSITE:** Ralph's Coffee's forest green coffee truck is decked out with all the classic holiday trimmings in Rockefeller Center.

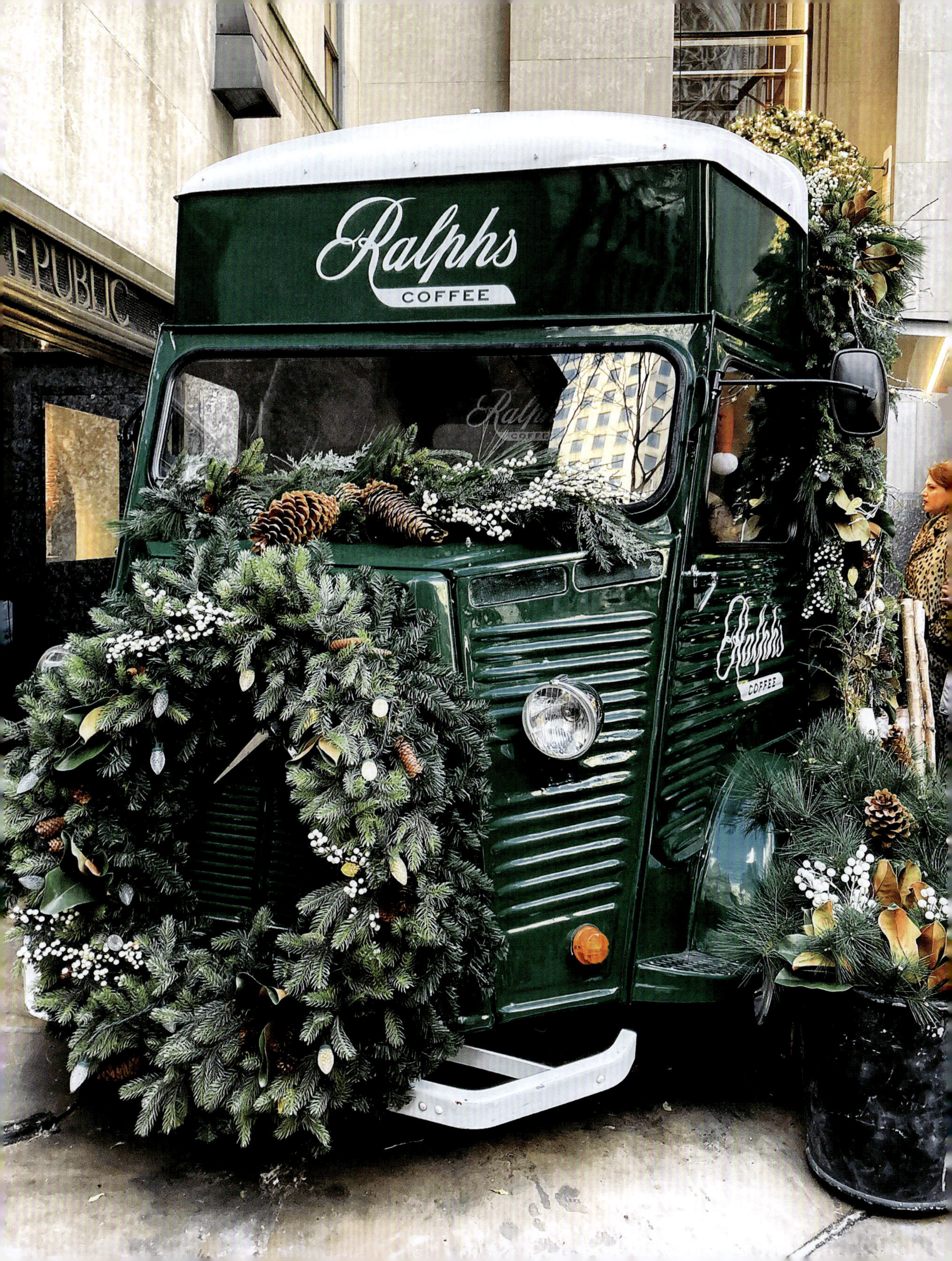
EPUBLIC
Ralphs
COFFEE
Ralphs
COFFEE

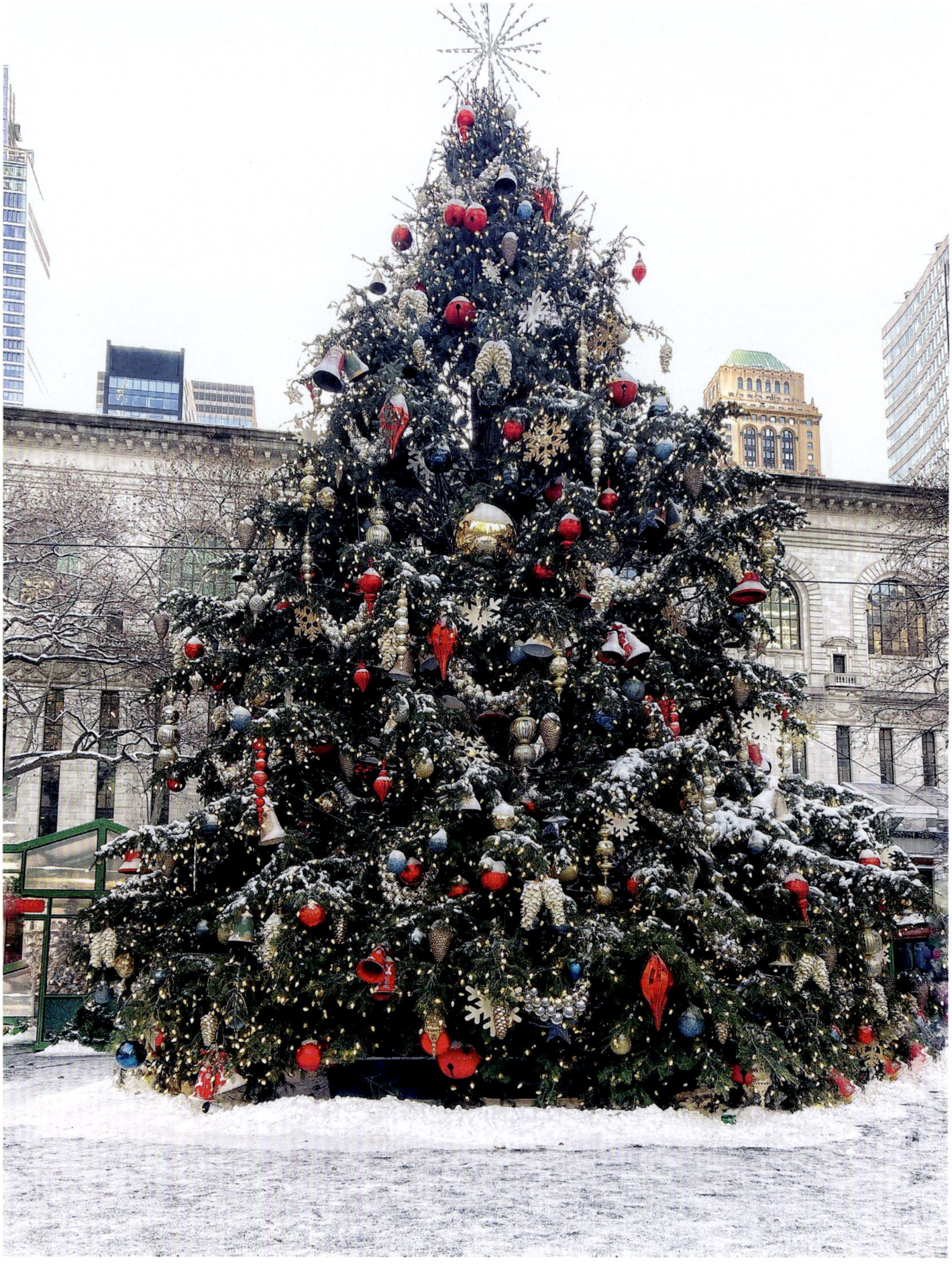

ABOVE: The forty-five-foot-tall, picture-perfect Bryant Park Christmas tree is trimmed with twelve hundred classic (and oversized) ornaments. **OPPOSITE, CLOCKWISE FROM TOP LEFT:** "Patience" the lion is accessorized for the holidays at the New York Public Library; snow-covered Bryant Park Grill; igloos for dining at the Bank of America Winter Village at Bryant Park; ice-skating in Bryant Park

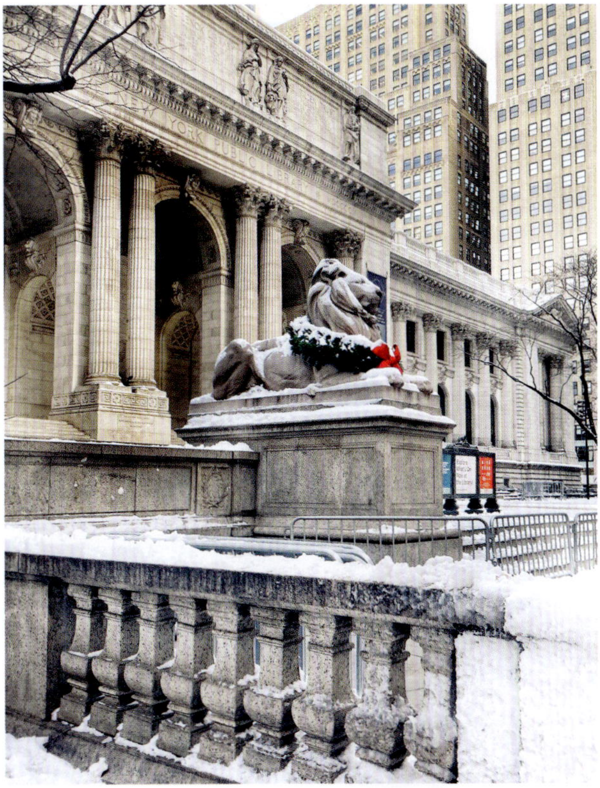

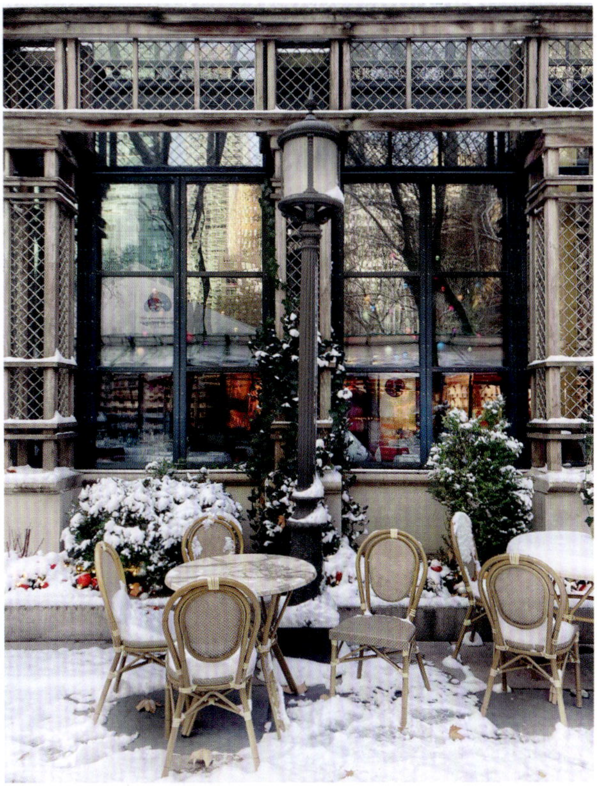

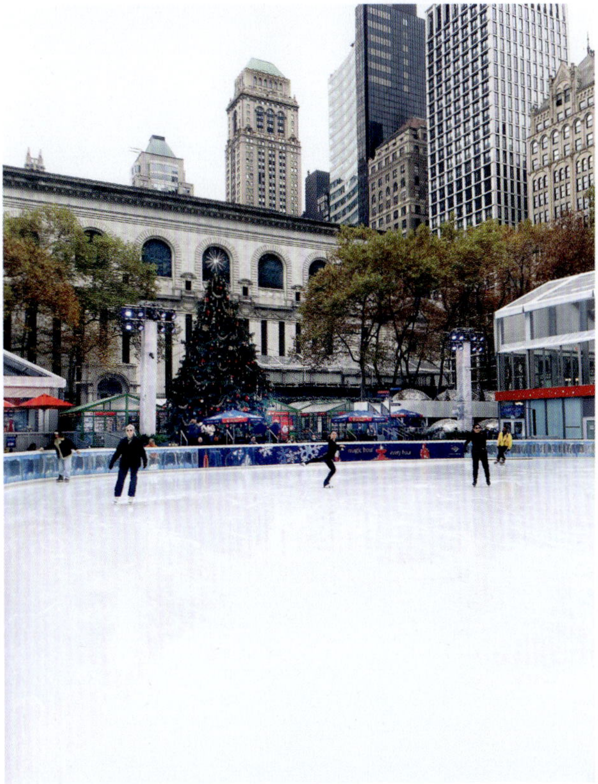

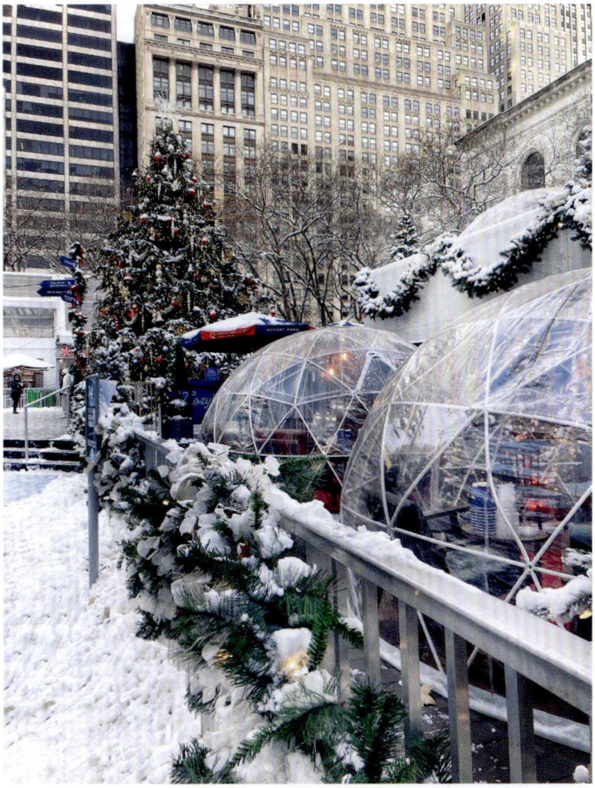

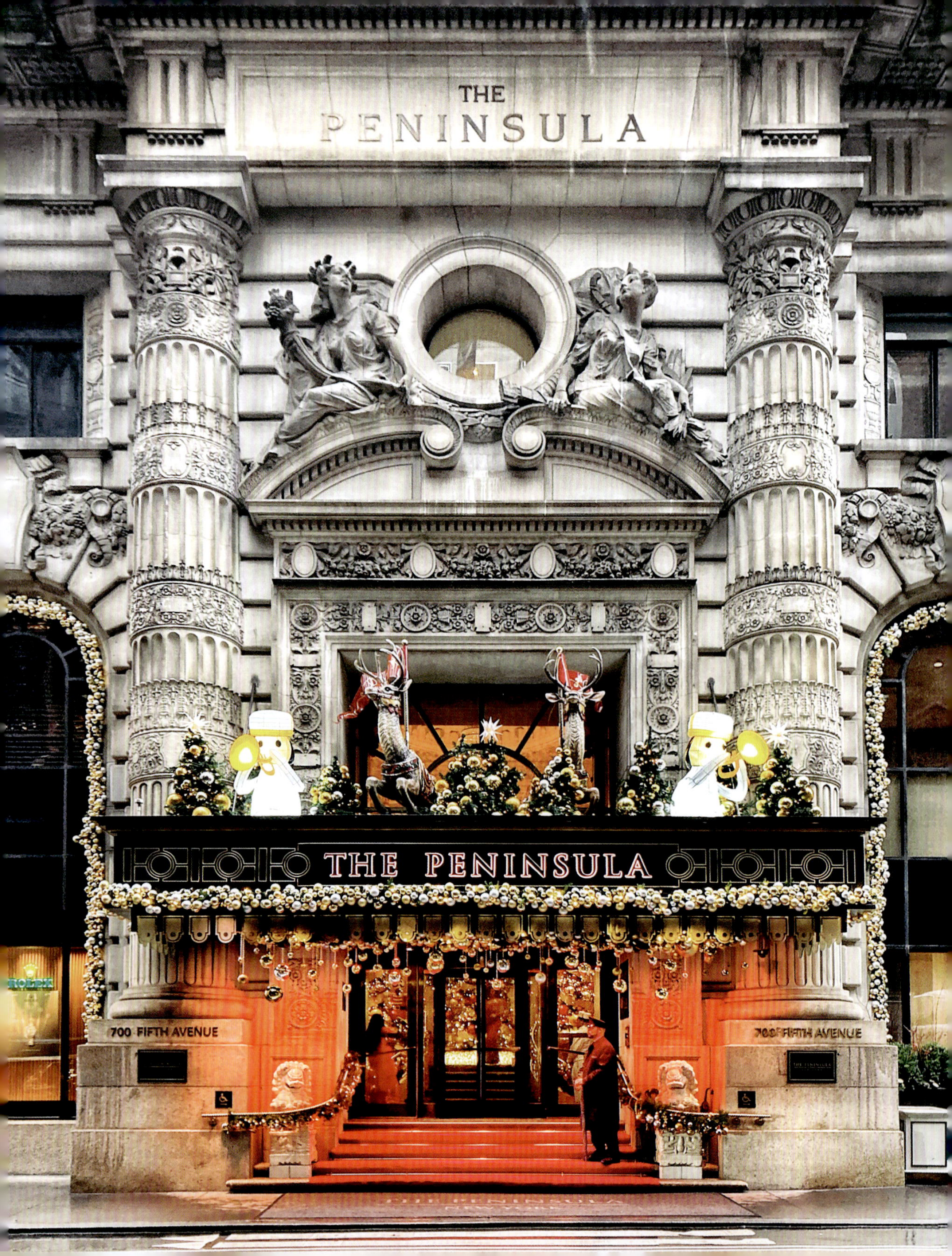
THE
PENINSULA
THE PENINSULA
700 FIFTH AVENUE
700 FIFTH AVENUE
ROLEX

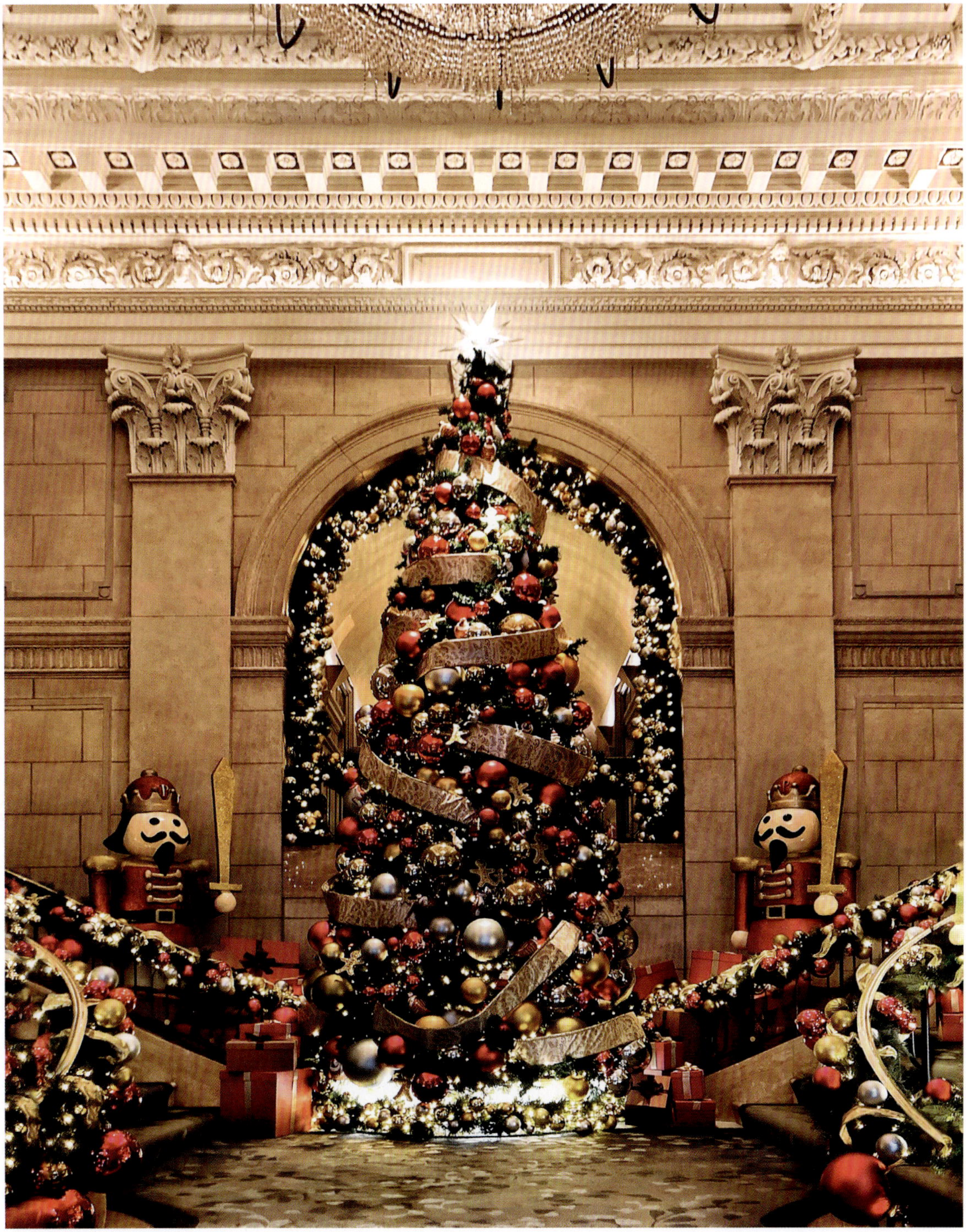

OPPOSITE AND ABOVE: The fabulous Peninsula Hotel on West 55th Street between Fifth and Sixth Avenues really gets into the spirit of the season with an ornate Christmas tree and Nutcrackers inside, and reindeer, snowmen, and baubles outside.

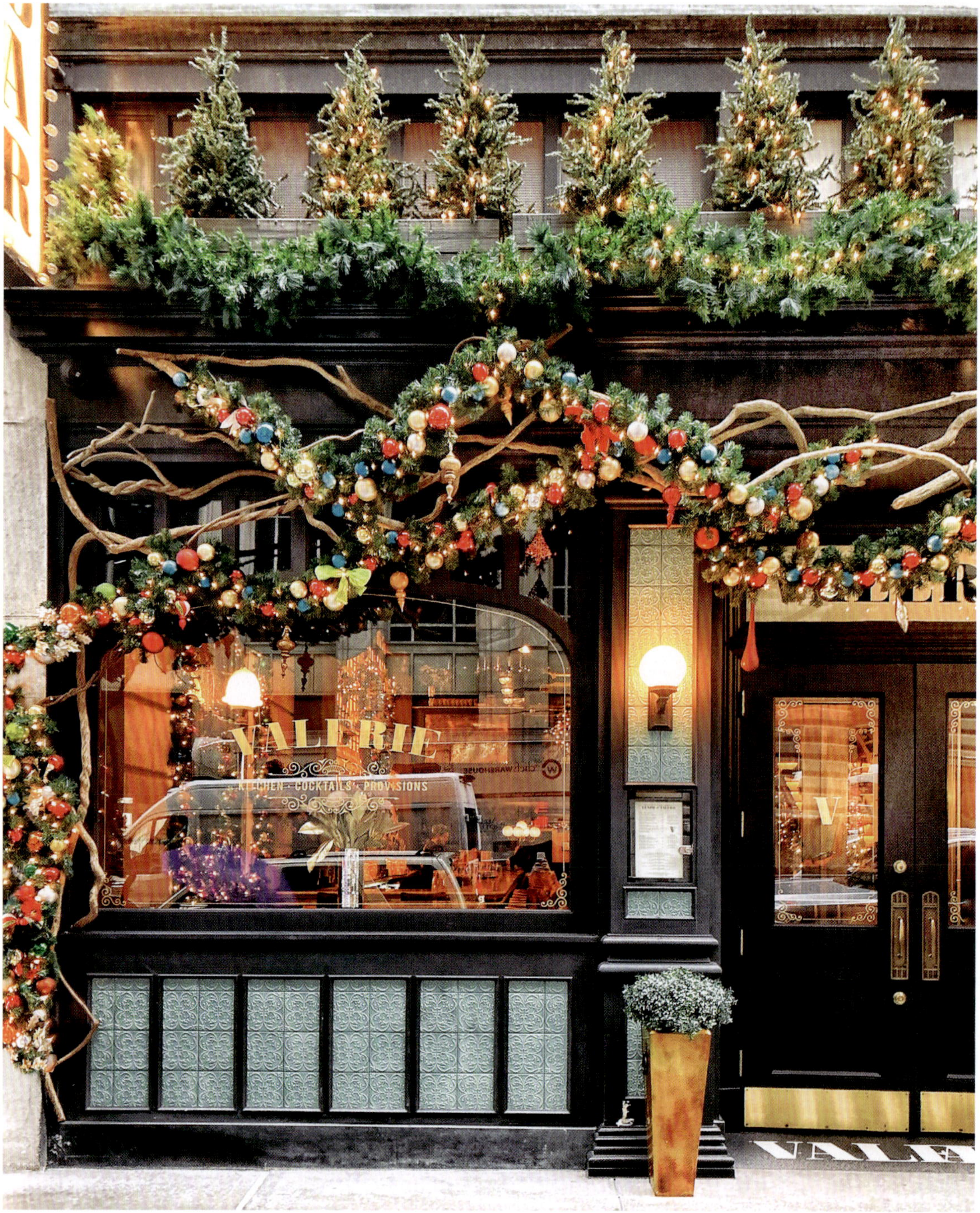

ABOVE: A warm glow emanates from the window of Valerie, a cocktail bar on West 45th Street between Fifth and Sixth Avenues. The fun holiday decor continues inside. **OPPOSITE:** Festive planters line the sidewalk on West 55th Street between Fifth and Sixth Avenues.

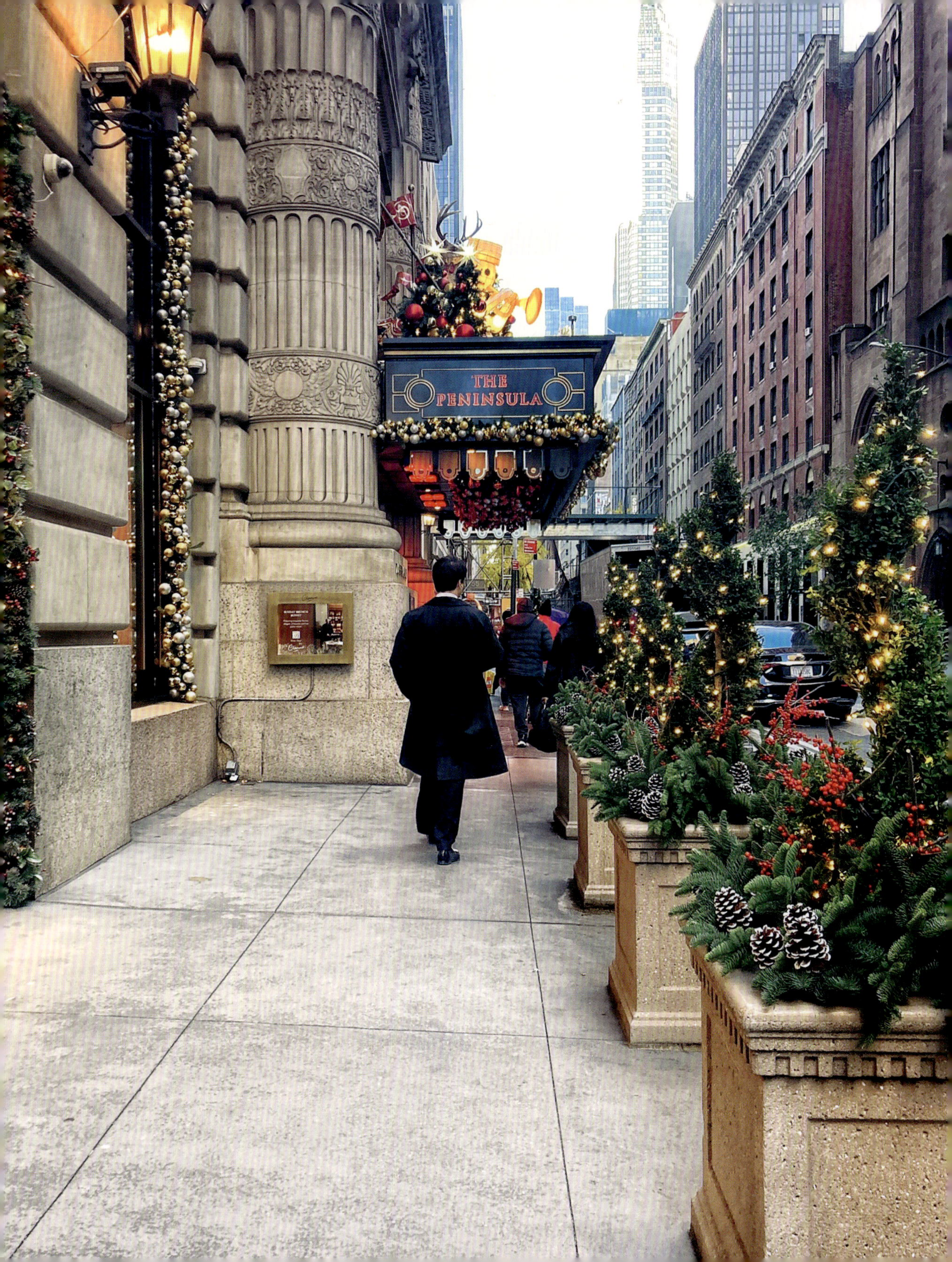
THE
PENINSULA

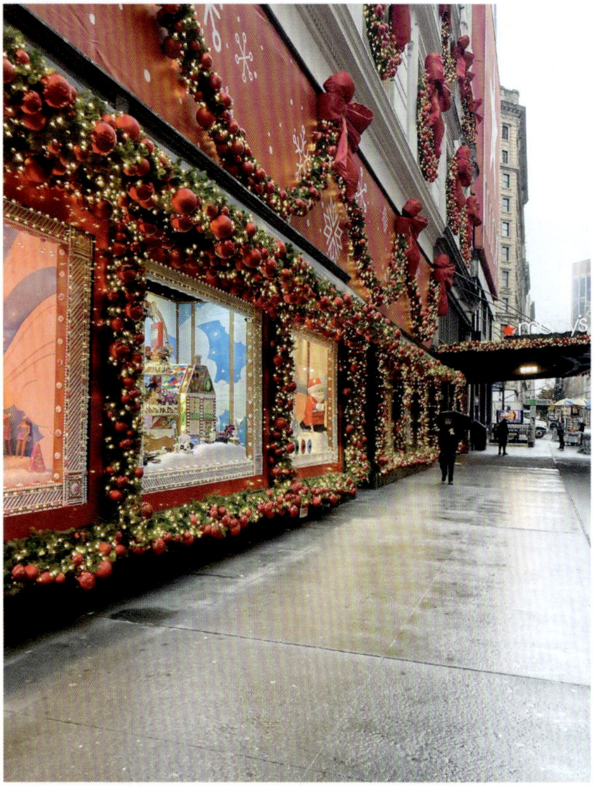

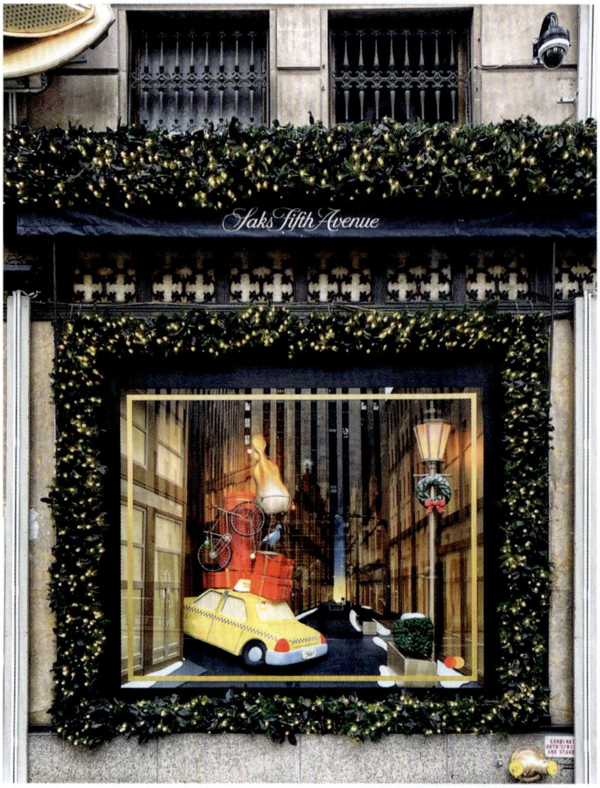
Saks Fifth Avenue

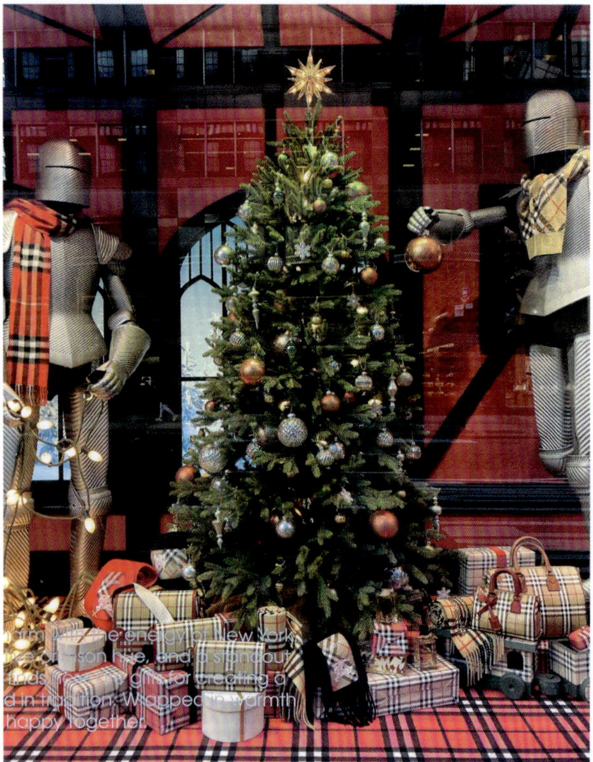
energy New York
and a standout
for creating a
Wrapped in warmth
happy together.

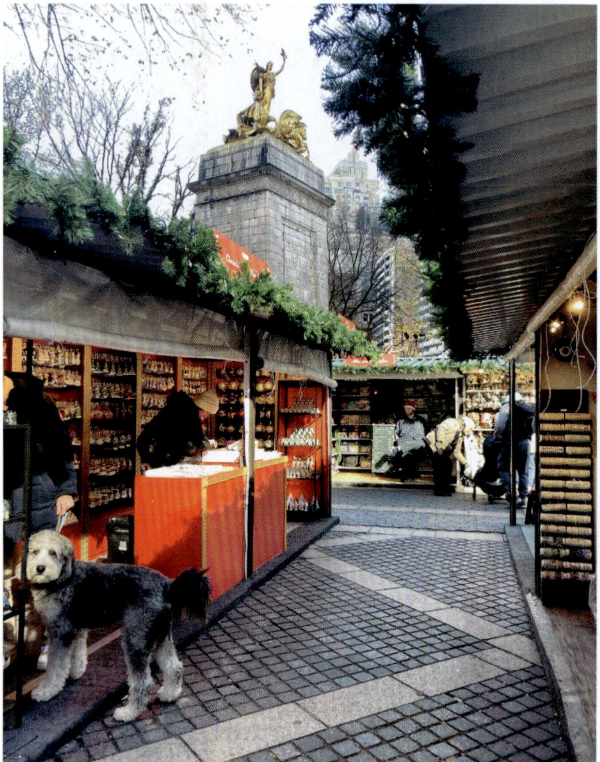

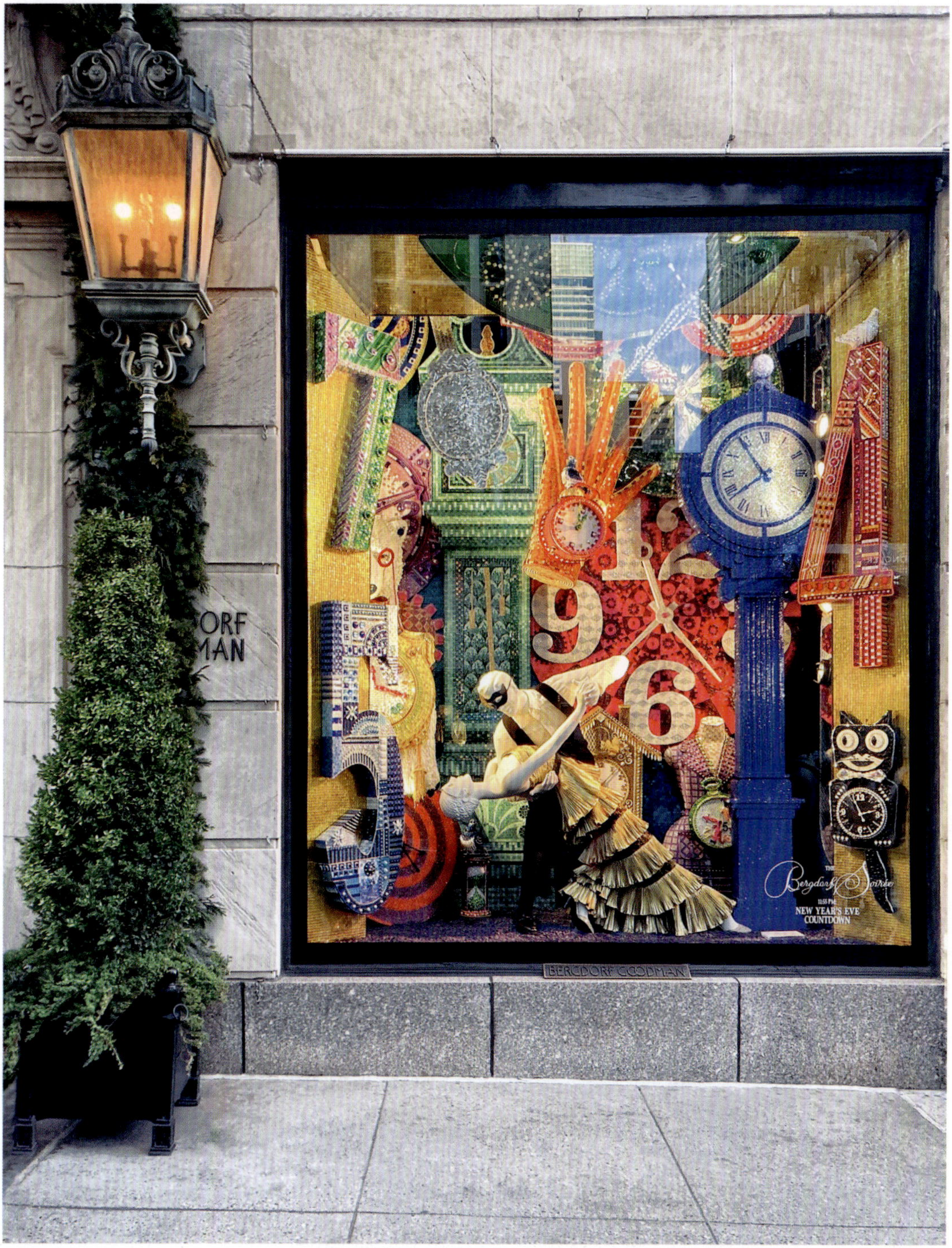

OPPOSITE, CLOCKWISE FROM TOP LEFT: Macy's fun and interactive window displays along West 34th Street; Saks Fifth Avenue's NYC-themed window; open-air stalls at the Columbus Circle Holiday Market on West 59th Street; Burberry's plaid accessories and armored knights in Bloomingdale's windows on Lexington Avenue and East 59th Street. **ABOVE:** Bergdorf Goodman's glamorous "Countdown to New Year's Eve"–themed window on Fifth Avenue and 58th Street

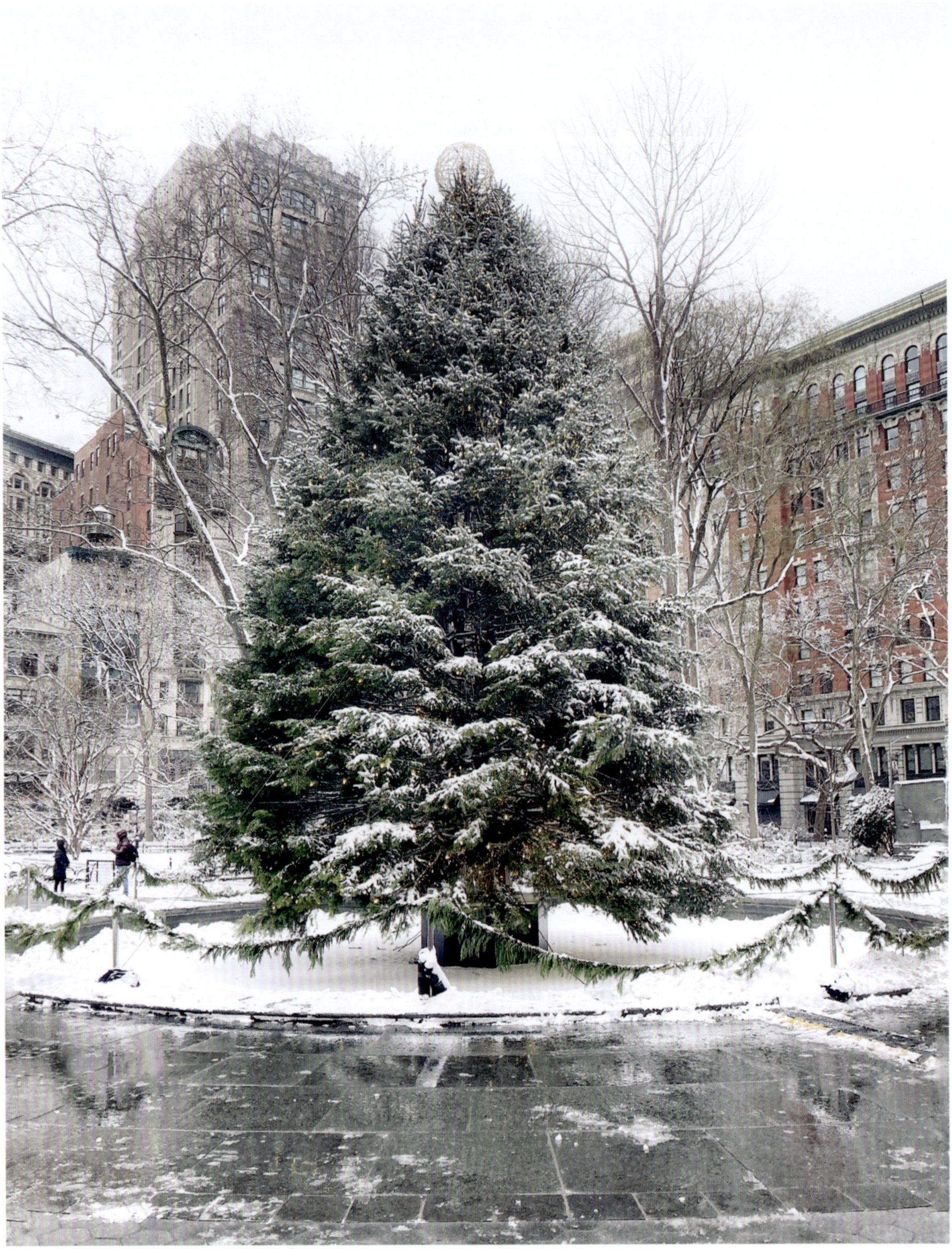

ABOVE: The snow-covered Madison Square Park Christmas tree off Fifth Avenue and East 26th Street. The first-ever public Christmas tree lighting took place here in 1912. **OPPOSITE:** A close-up of Dolce & Gabbana's playful ornaments and festive banner in the store's window on Fifth Avenue and 55th Street

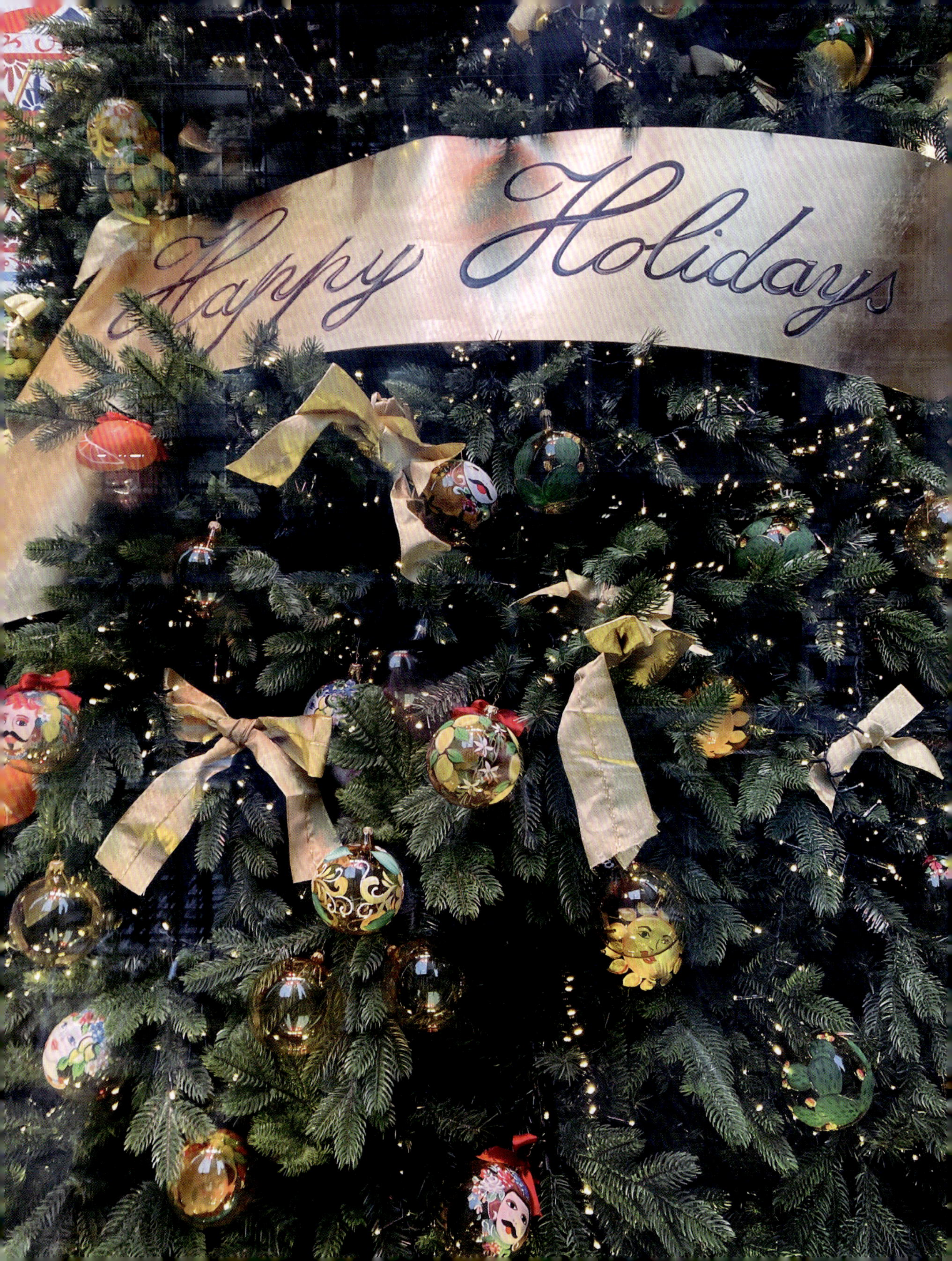
Happy Holidays

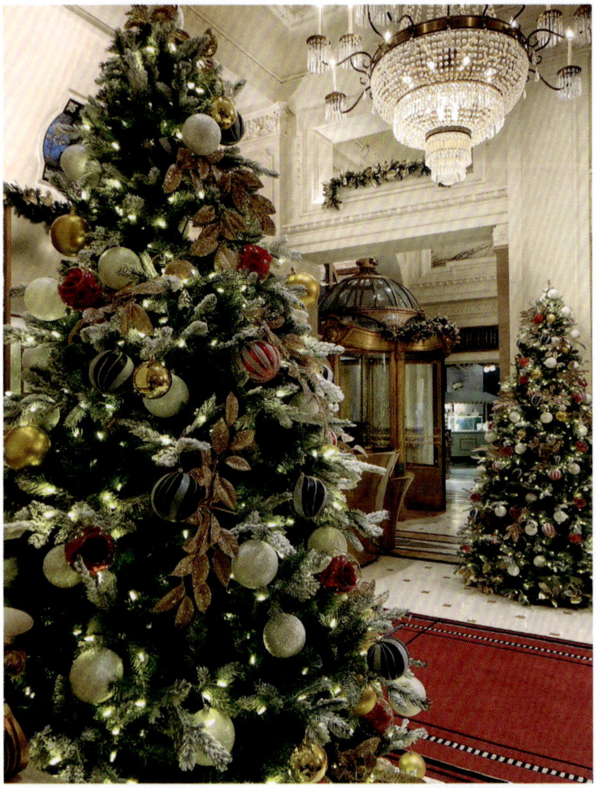

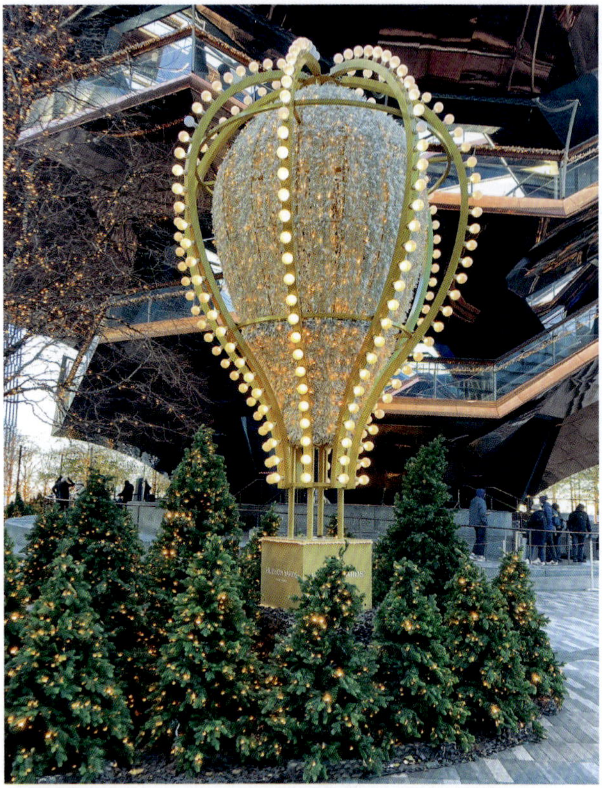

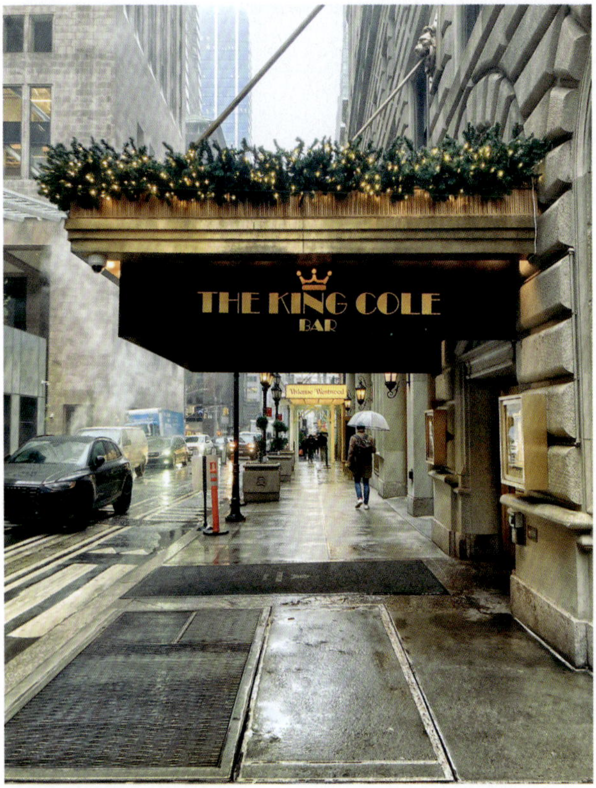
THE KING COLE
BAR

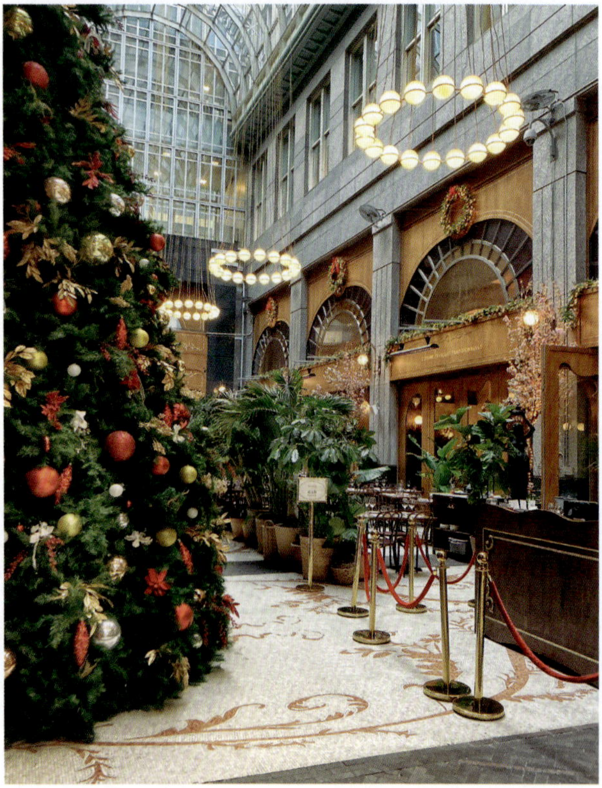

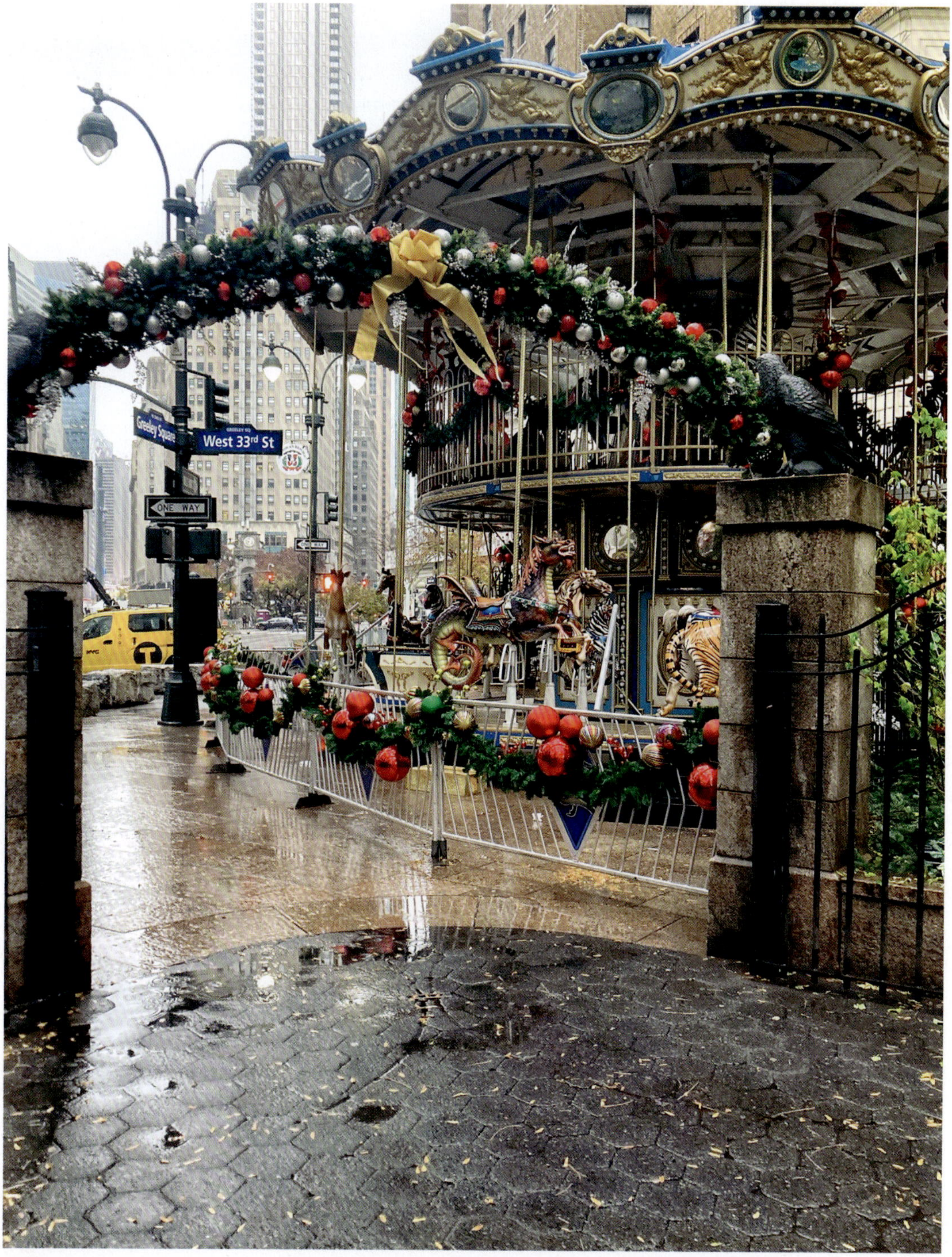

OPPOSITE, CLOCKWISE FROM TOP LEFT: Christmas trees in the elegant St. Regis hotel lobby; the "Shine Bright in Hudson Yards" glittering hot air balloon; French restaurant La Grand Boucherie on West 53rd between Sixth and Seventh Avenues; the St. Regis hotel's cozy Nat King Cole Bar. **ABOVE:** A fanciful double-decker Christmas carousel made its debut in Greeley Square, 33rd Street and Broadway, in 2025.

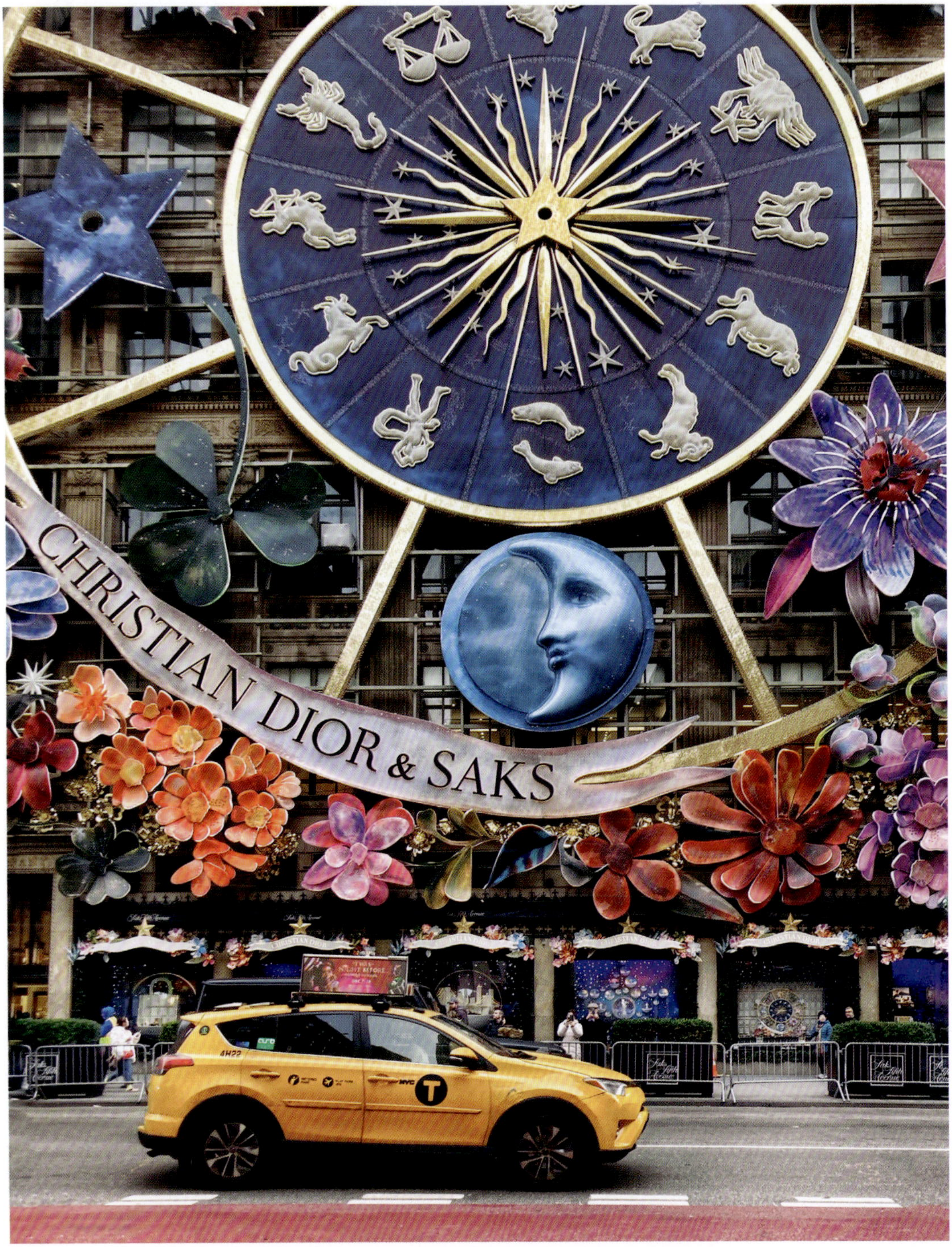

ABOVE: A taxi passes by "Dior's Carousel of Dreams," Saks Fifth Avenue's striking holiday installation created in collaboration with luxury brand Christian Dior, at Fifth Avenue between 49th and 50th Streets. **OPPOSITE:** Sparkling ornaments and gold baubles adorn the Pulitzer Fountain in Grand Army Plaza, near 59th Street and Fifth Avenue.

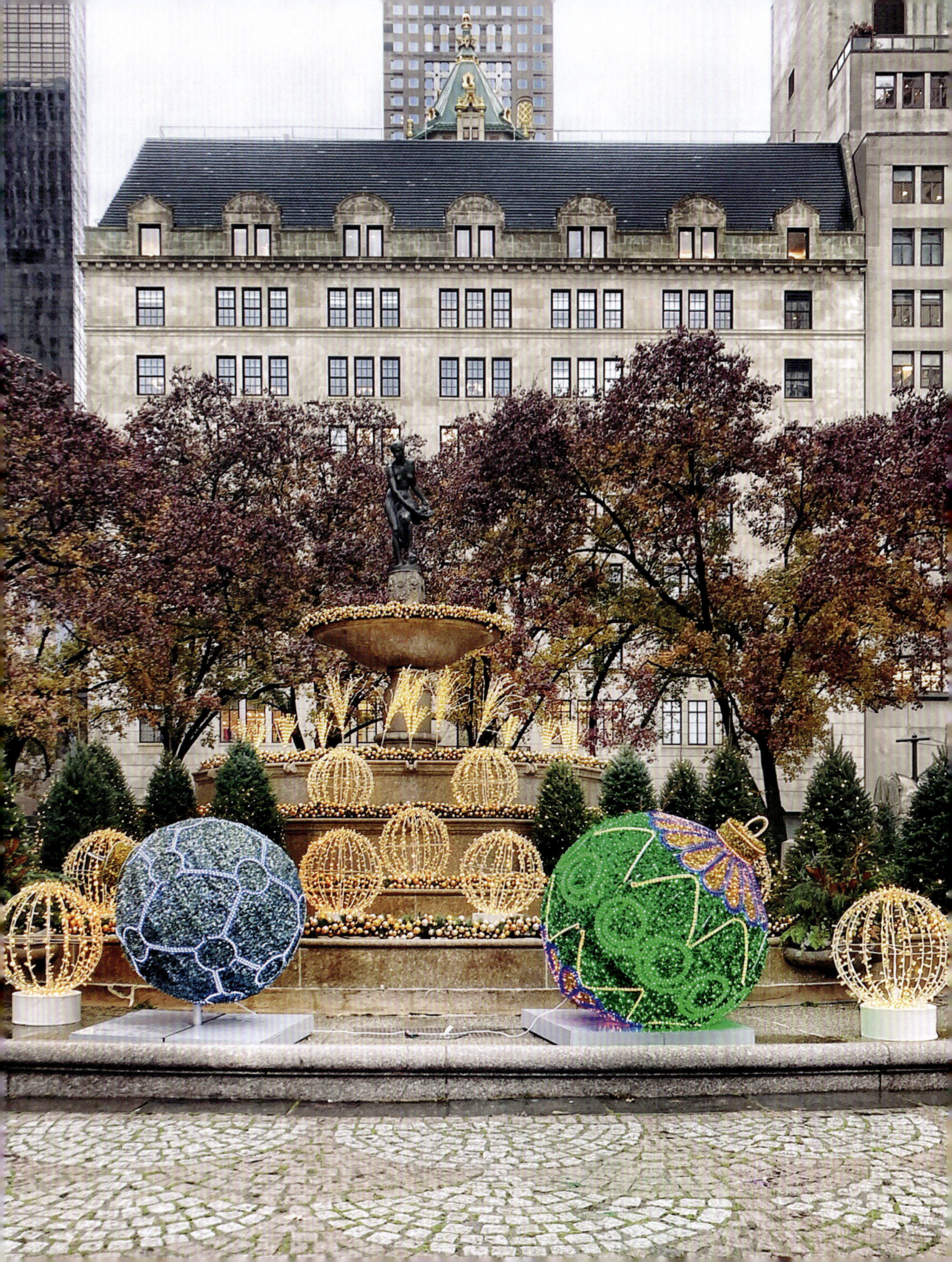

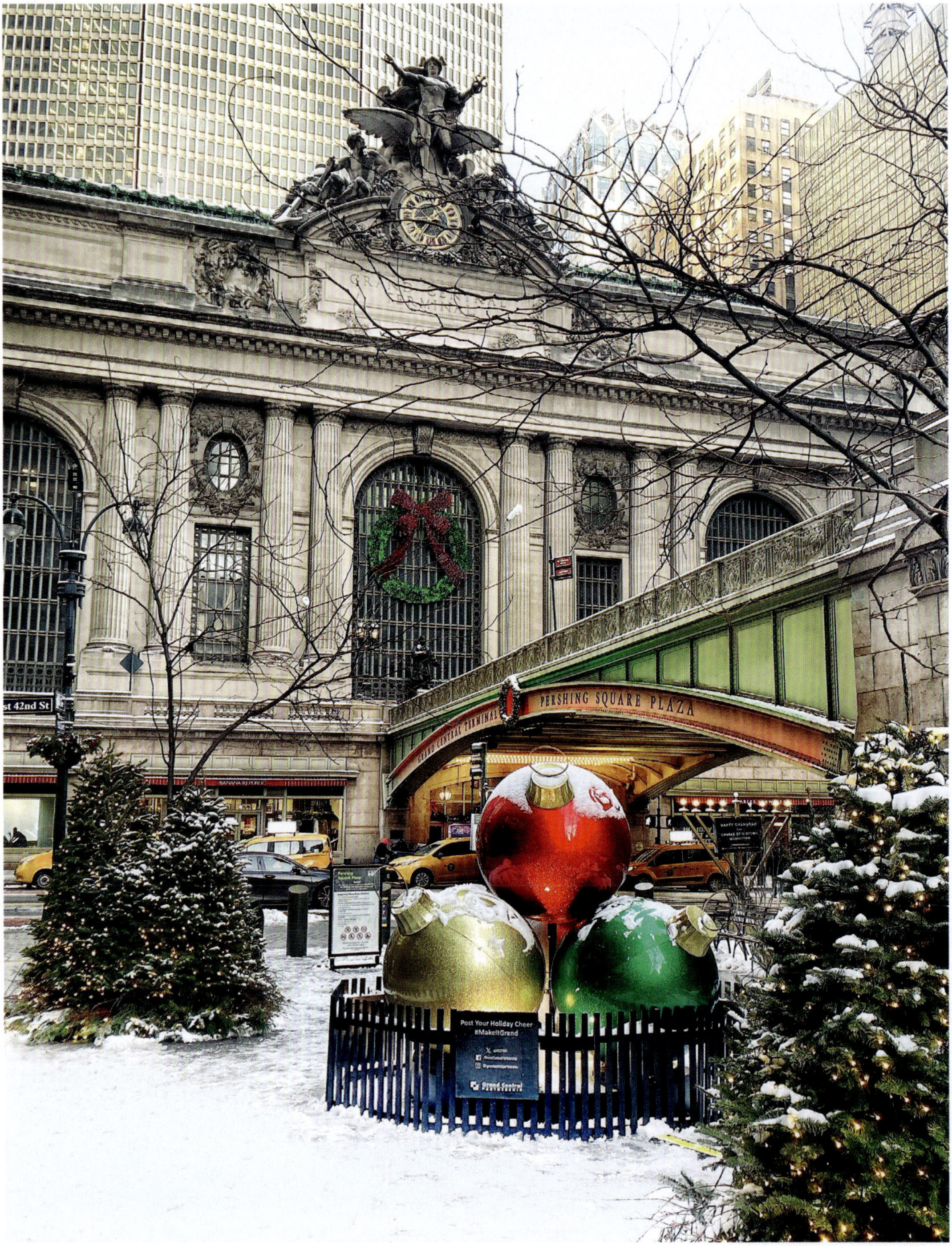

ABOVE: Grand Central Terminal's festive wreath and playful oversized ornaments and a menorah in Pershing Square brighten up 42nd Street. **OPPOSITE, CLOCKWISE FROM TOP LEFT:** Holiday scenes in Grand Central Terminal: Grand Brasserie restaurant in Vanderbilt Hall; Holiday Fair signs in Vanderbilt Hall; Palladino's steak and seafood restaurant on the West Balcony; festive garlands and crowds in the main terminal

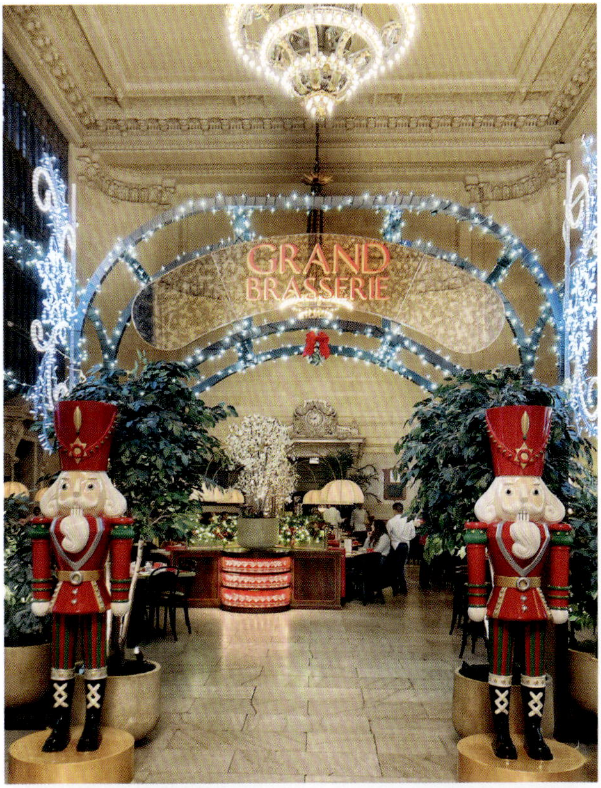
GRAND
BRASSERIE

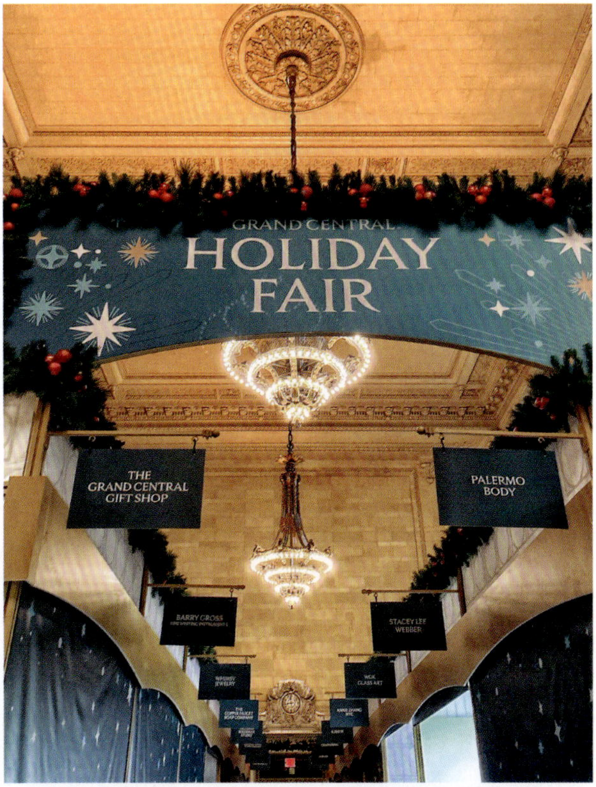
GRAND CENTRAL
HOLIDAY
FAIR
THE
GRAND CENTRAL
GIFT SHOP
PALERMO
BODY
BARRY CROSS
STACEY LEE
WEBBER

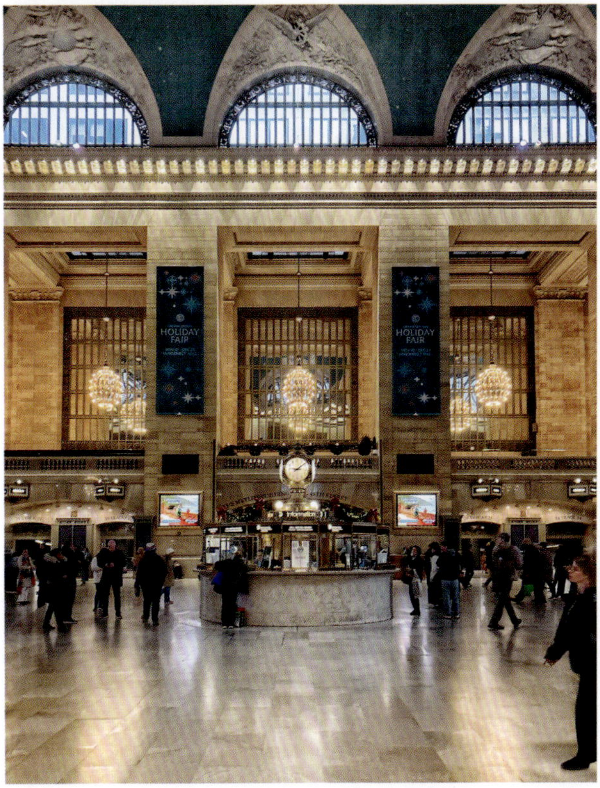
HOLIDAY
FAIR
HOLIDAY
FAIR

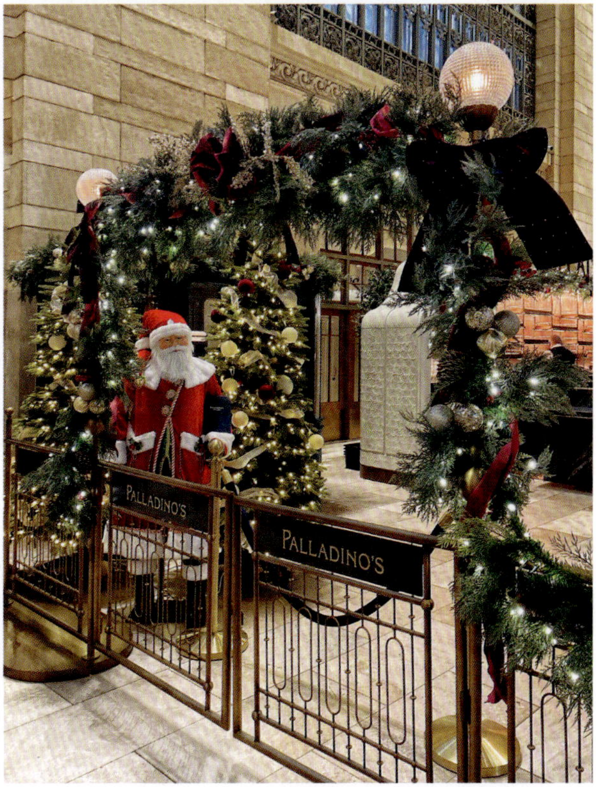
PALLADINO'S
PALLADINO'S

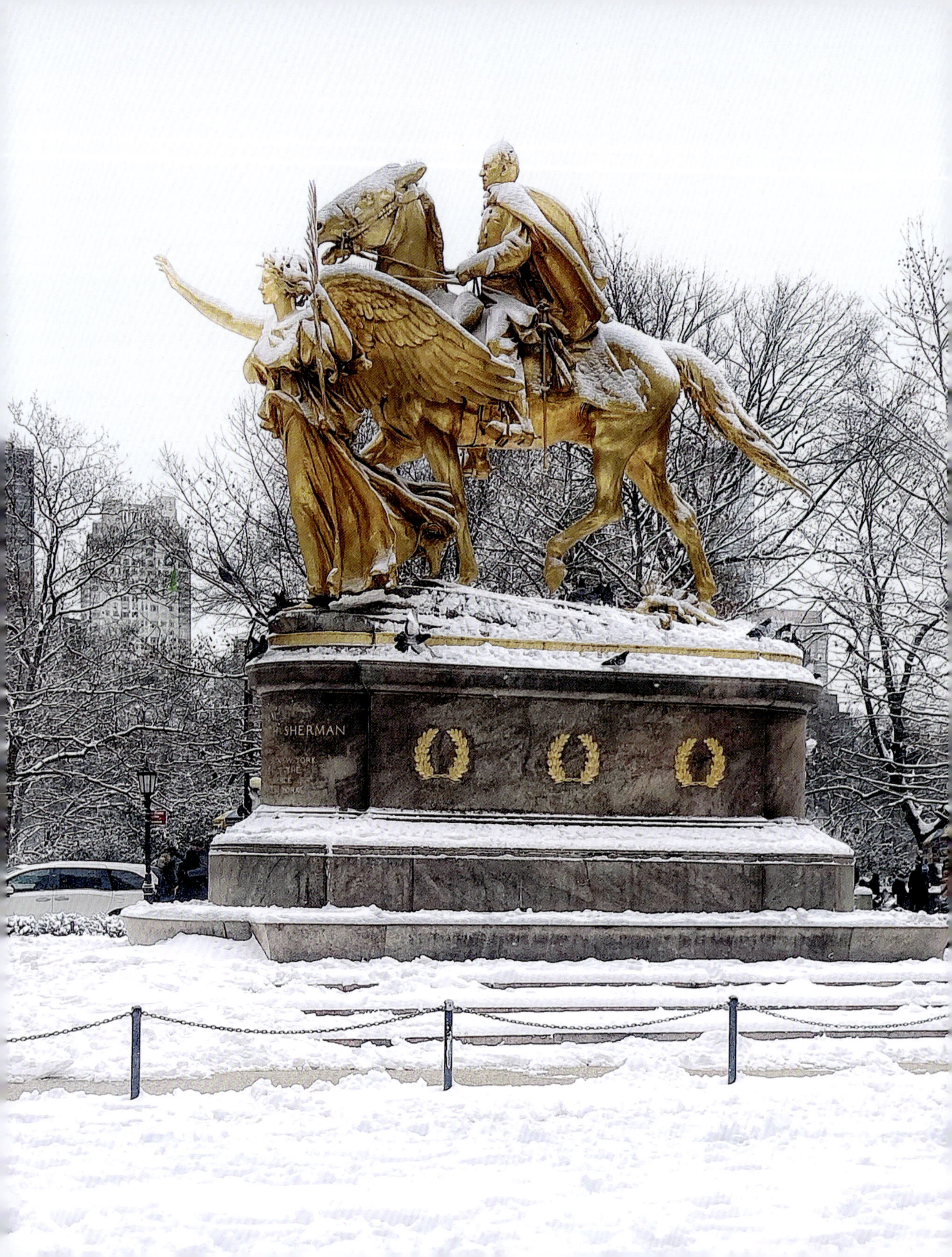
SHERMAN

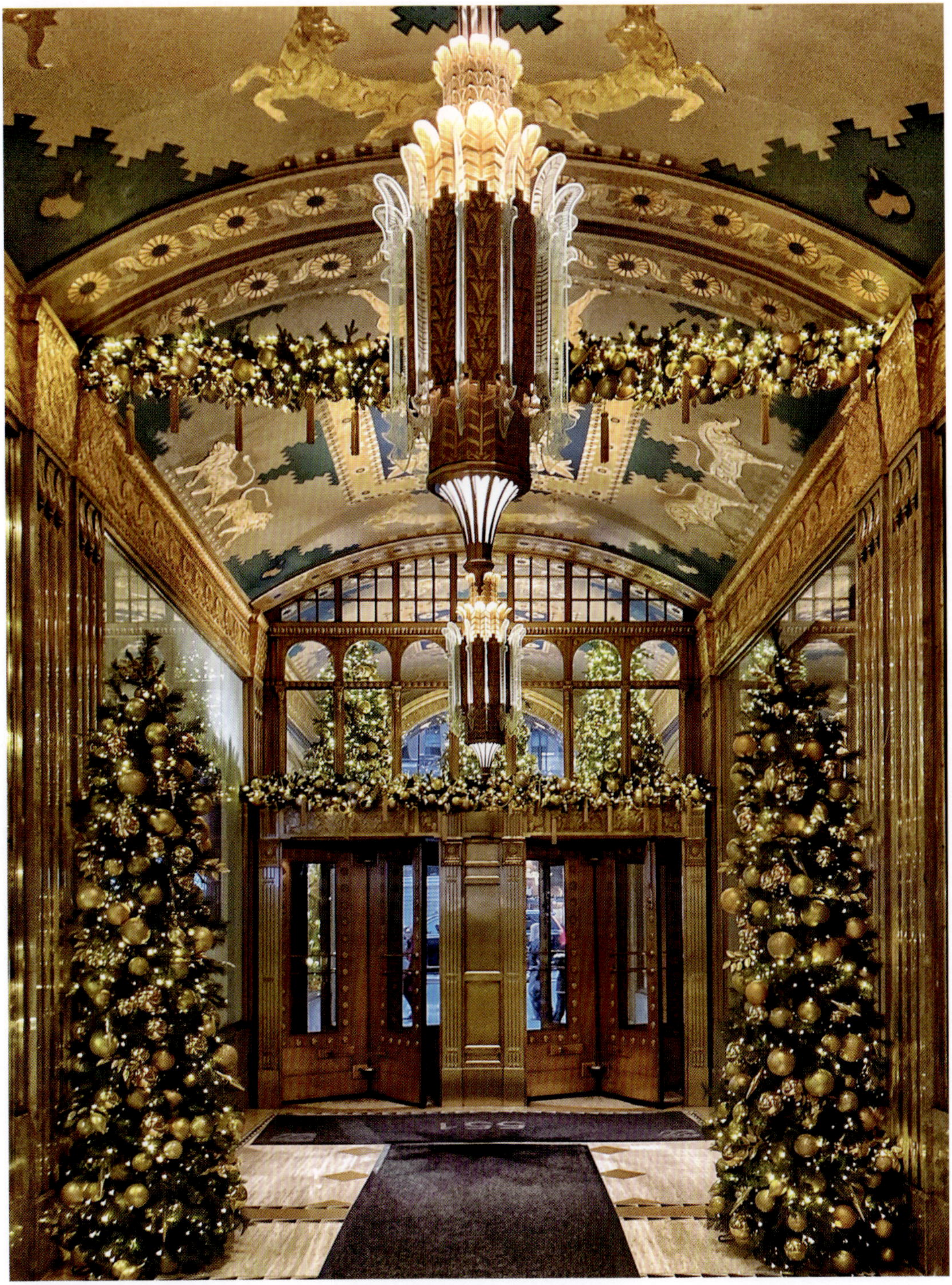

OPPOSITE: A snow-covered gilded-bronze monument of General William Tecumseh Sherman by Augustus Saint-Gaudens sits in Grand Army Plaza at 60th Street and Fifth Avenue. **ABOVE:** The Fred R. French Building's opulent lobby is a designated landmark (ca. 1926–27) on Fifth Avenue and 45th Street. The holiday decorations make it even more stunningly beautiful.

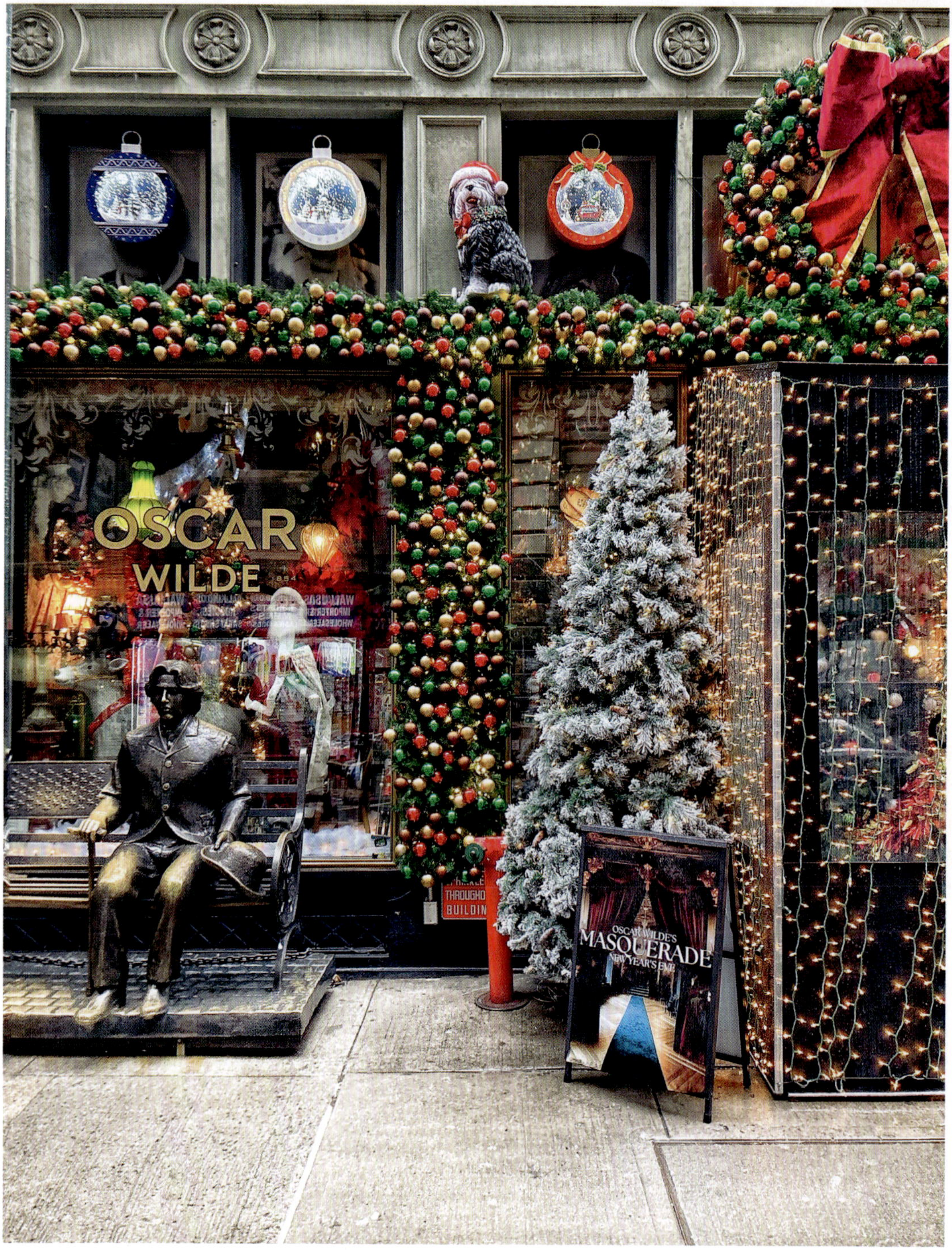

ABOVE AND OPPOSITE: Oscar Wilde's Victorian bar and restaurant on West 27th Street between Fifth and Sixth Avenues is known for its extravagant Christmas decorations. Polar bears and sparkling trees surround a red velvet Victorian chair—a perfect spot for a fun holiday photo-op.

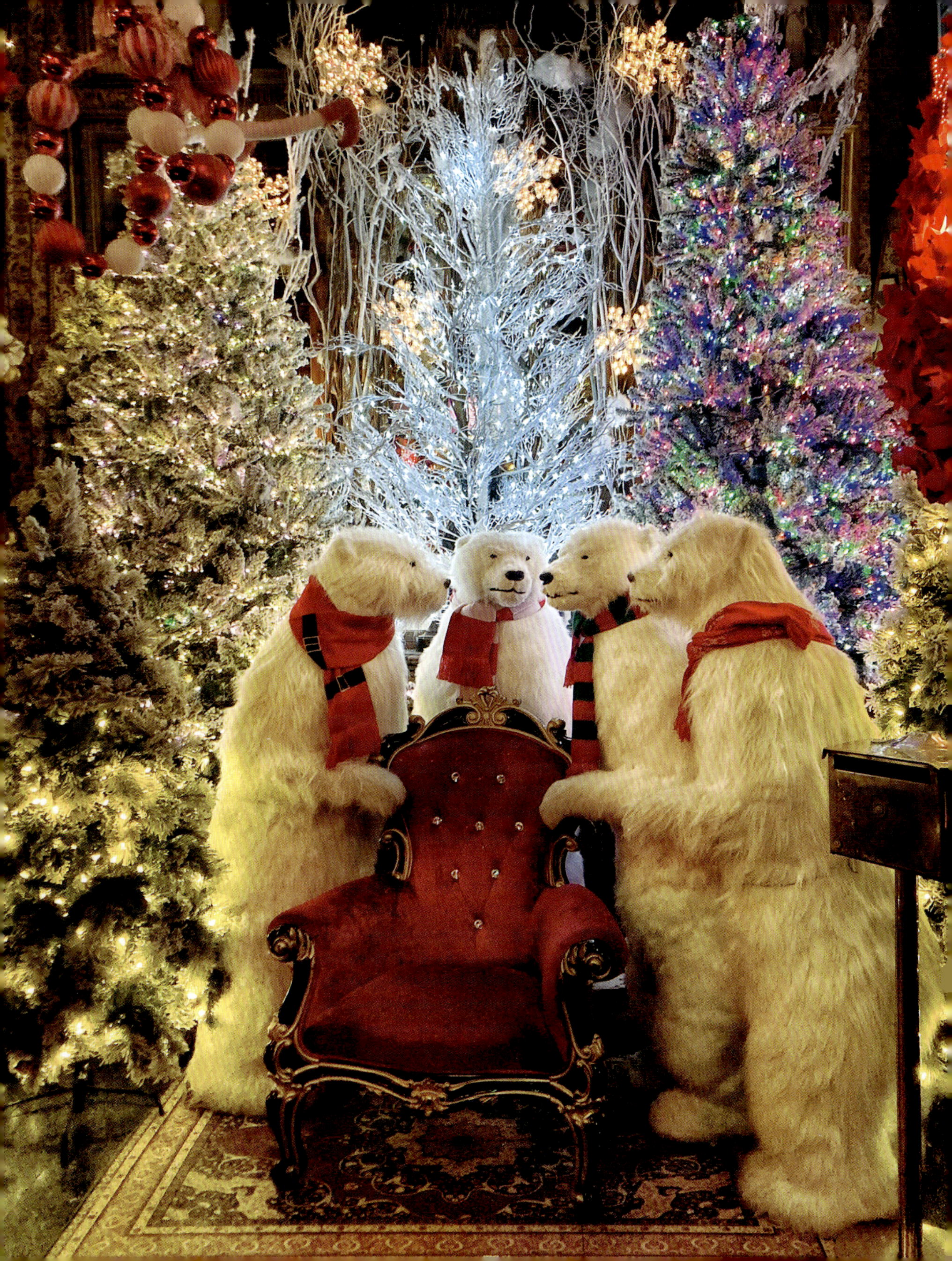

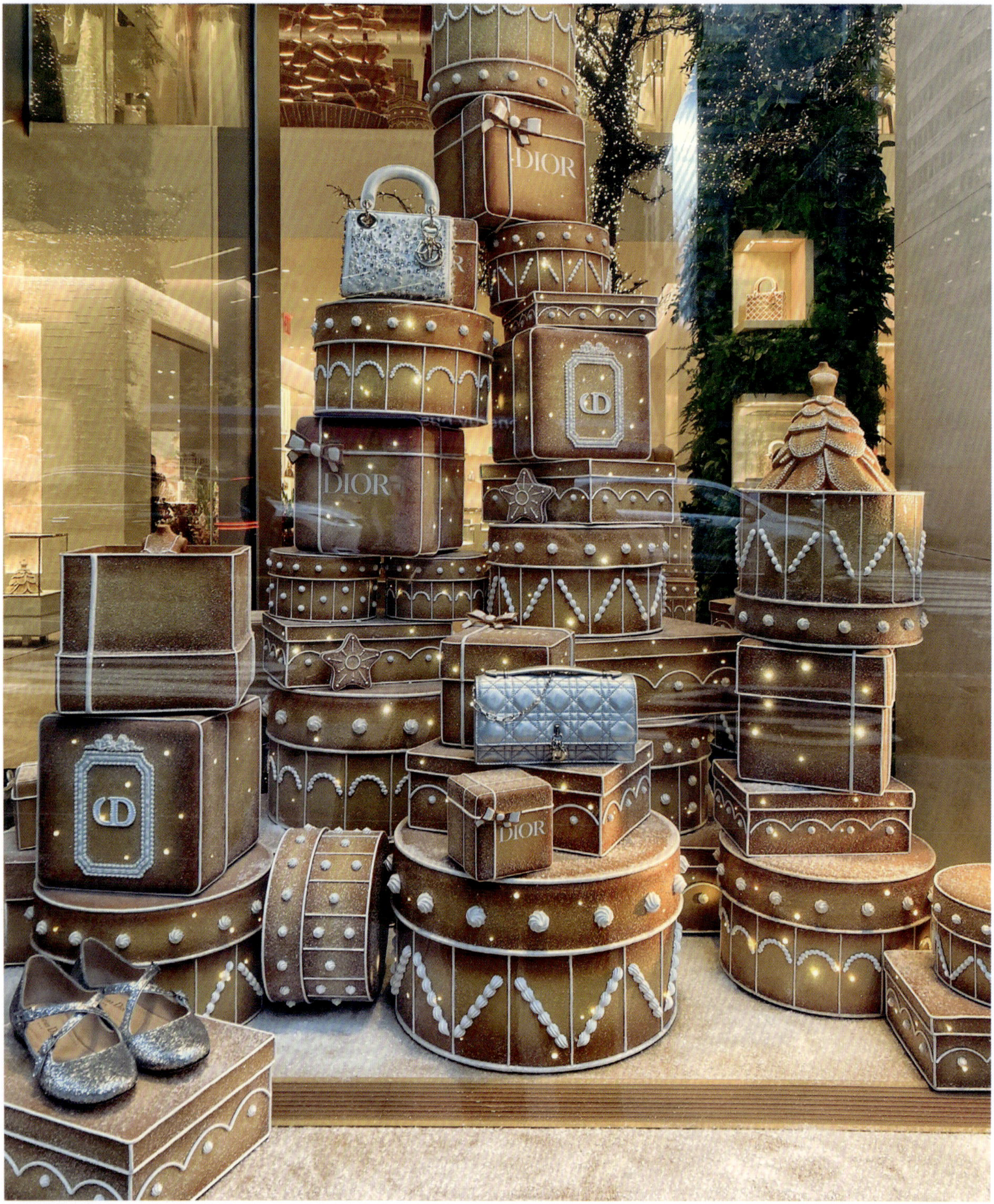

ABOVE: A stylish gingerbread-themed window at Christian Dior's flagship store on East 57th Street between Madison and Fifth Avenues

Midtown *Holiday* favorites

1. **Macy's Herald Square, West 34th Street and Broadway:** A gorgeous facade and fun interactive windows, plus a special holiday shop inside.

2. **Bryant Park Winter Village, between 40th and 42nd Street and Fifth and Sixth Avenues:** A magnificent tree, an ice-skating rink, and a holiday market. So much fun in one beautiful park. Just go early to avoid crowds!

3. **New York Public Library, 41st Street and Fifth Avenue:** The library's grand marble lions, Fortitude and Patience, greet you outside, and the artistic Christmas tree awaits you inside.

4. **French Building, Fifth Avenue and 45th Street:** The beautiful lobby of this historic building is even more stunning when decorated for the holidays. It's closed on weekends.

5. **Avenue of the Americas between 48th and 52nd Streets:** Many whimsical decorations along this stretch: gigantic candy canes, Nutcrackers, and ornaments, plus two spectacular Christmas trees and Radio City Music Hall.

6. **La Grande Boucherie, West 53rd Street between Sixth and Seventh Avenues:** A French restaurant with a glorious Christmas tree in a beautiful Art Nouveau–style space.

7. **Fifth Avenue between 49th and 59th Streets:** All the major dazzling attractions, from the Rockefeller Center Christmas tree and Saks Fifth Avenue to St. Patrick's Cathedral and all the decorated stores and window displays.

8. **Grand Central Terminal and Pershing Square,** East 42nd Street between Lexington and Vanderbilt: Check out the fun decorations in Pershing Square and the view of Grand Central. Inside the terminal you'll find the Holiday Fair and many festive restaurants.

9. **Lotte New York Palace, Madison Avenue between 50th and 51st Streets:** A magnificent tree in the luxury hotel's courtyard.

10. **The Plaza, Fifth Avenue between 58th and 59th Streets:** Spectacular lobby decorations, but you'll need a room or Palm Court reservation to enter this iconic hotel.

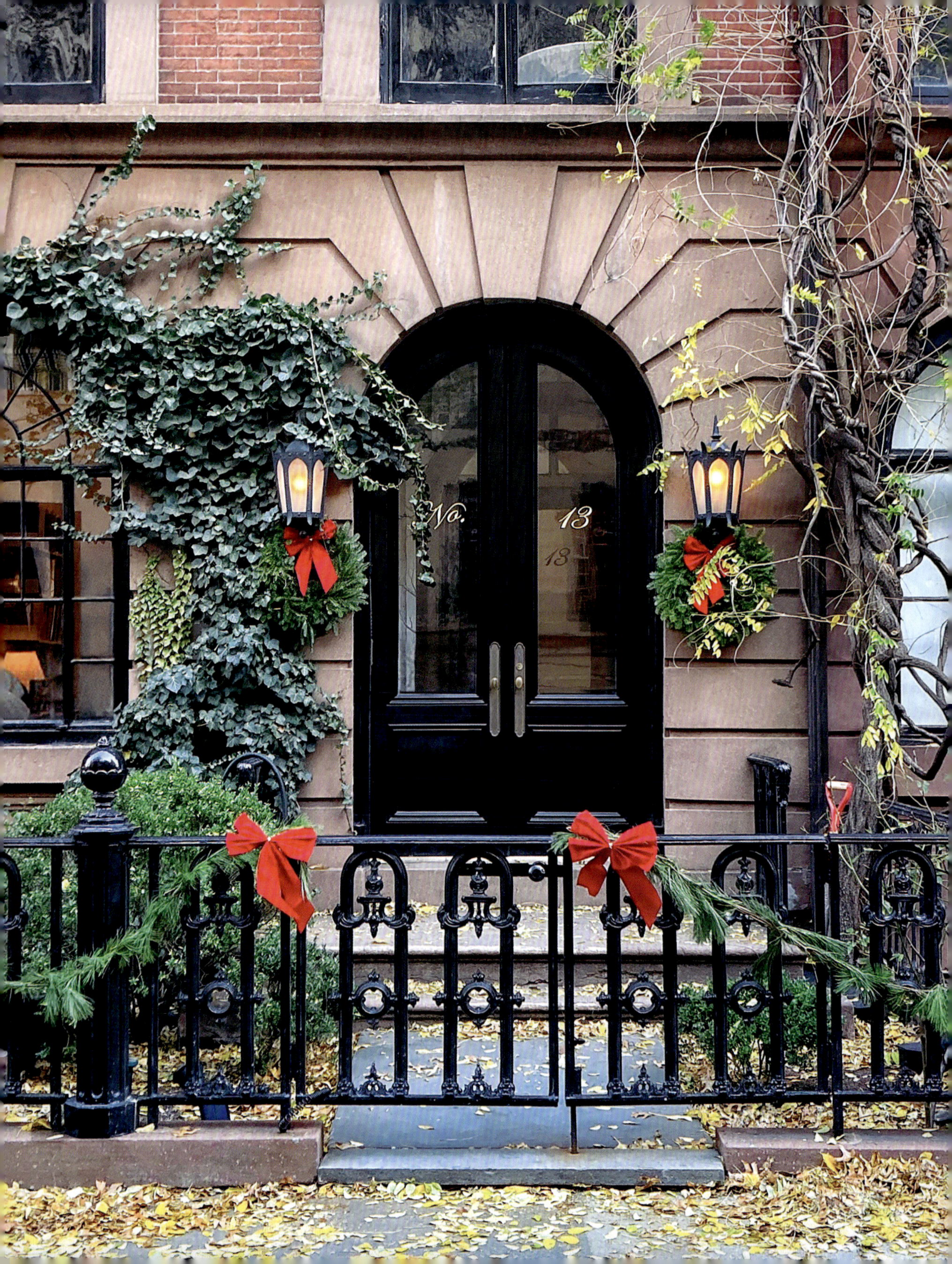
No. 13
13

Downtown

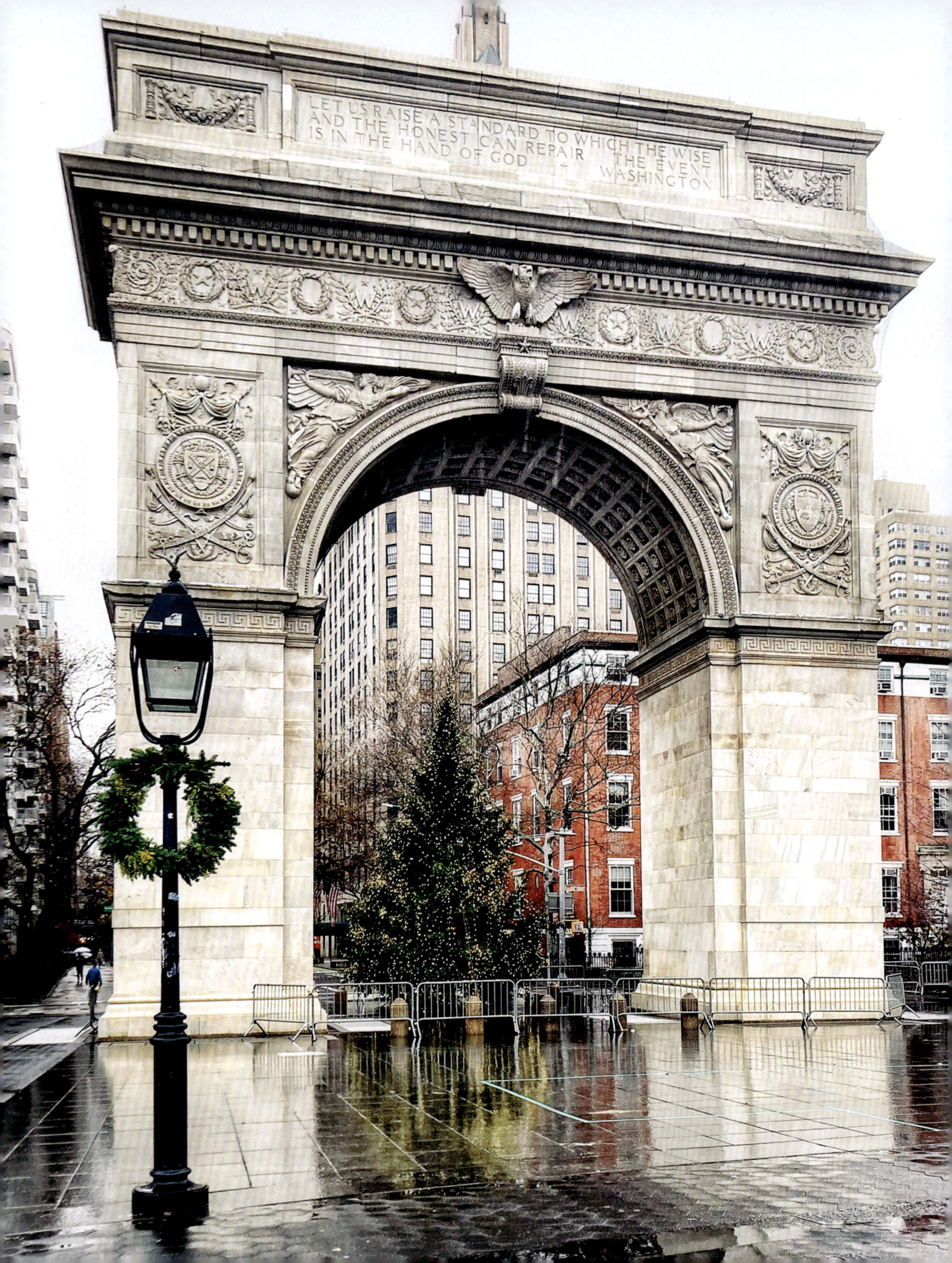
LET US RAISE A STANDARD TO WHICH THE WISE
AND THE HONEST CAN REPAIR THE EVENT
IS IN THE HAND OF GOD ★ WASHINGTON

Downtown

Below 23rd Street, everything feels a bit more laid-back. Downtown still buzzes with holiday cheer, but it's not quite as flashy and frenetic as Midtown. And you actually have room to walk on the sidewalks! As much as I enjoy the hustle and bustle and dazzling sights of Midtown, and appreciate the extravagantly decorated townhouses of Uptown, I'm happiest when I'm wandering my own charming but equally festive Greenwich Village neighborhood.

And lucky me, many of my favorite places to shoot, shop, and dine during the holiday season are within walking distance of my apartment: The iconic Washington Square Park Christmas tree; the warm and sparkling Balthazar restaurant in SoHo; the Union Square Holiday Market, with its maze of open-air stalls—about one hundred and fifty of them; and John Derian's charming East Village Christmas shop, a jewel box bursting with more than thirty thousand ornaments. (It's also bursting with shoppers, so I do my gift buying there in October, before the December crowds arrive.)

It's no surprise that Union Square, the West Village, and SoHo are the most popular areas for tourists and locals alike. They come to sip hot cocoa at the many charming cafés, meet for drinks at holiday-decorated bars, shop at indie boutiques, and take in the stylishly decorated homes in the West Village. There's a real party atmosphere in these neighborhoods, especially on the weekends. It can be a lot of fun, and the excitement in the air is contagious. But if you're like me, and sometimes you need a little quiet time to wander, window-shop, and snap photos, then make sure to visit on weekdays or early in the morning, which happily is my favorite time of day to take pictures.

PREVIOUS: Traditional wreaths, red bows, and old-fashioned lanterns give this entrance on West 9th Street between Fifth and Sixth Avenues a timeless feeling. **OPPOSITE:** The historic Stanford White-designed Washington Square Arch and sparkling Christmas tree on a rainy day

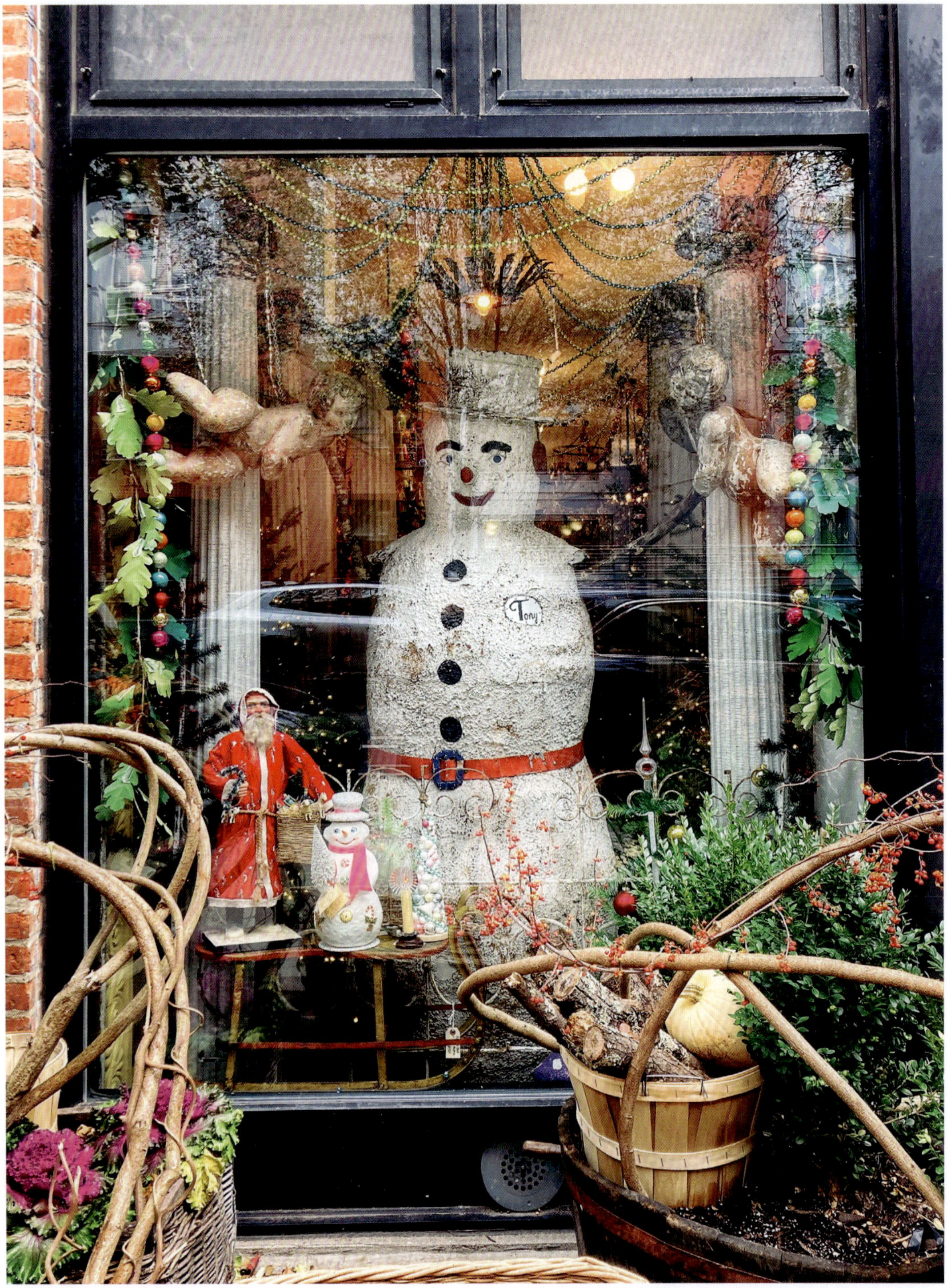

ABOVE AND OPPOSITE: A cute snowman in the window of John Derian's Christmas shop on East 2nd Street between Bowery and Second Avenue. His dazzling shop is filled with every kind of ornament and Christmas-themed object imaginable—perfect for gift buying or treating yourself.

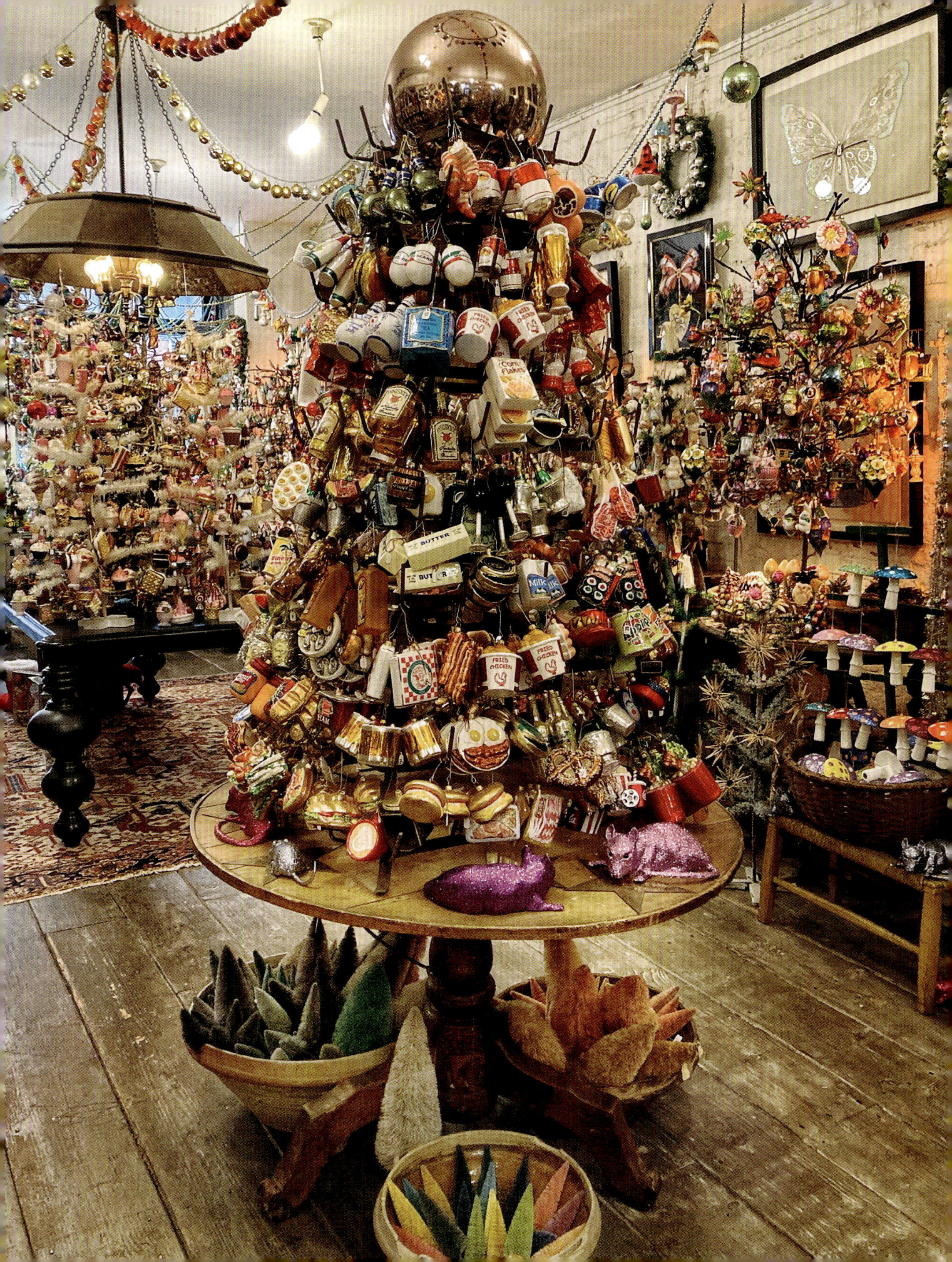
FRIED CHICKEN
Corn Flakes
WHISKEY
BUTTER
Milk
HAM

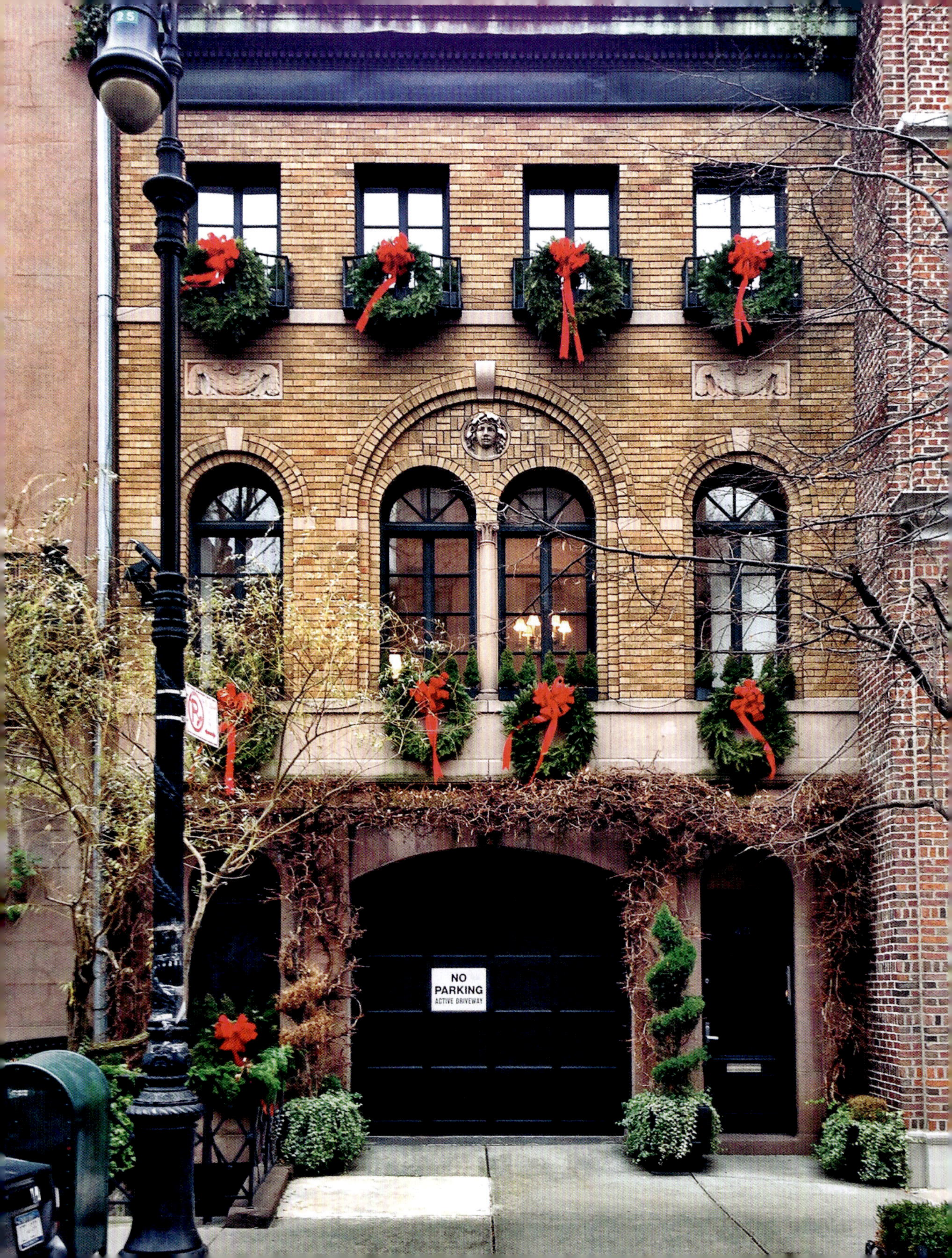
NO
PARKING
ACTIVE DRIVEWAY

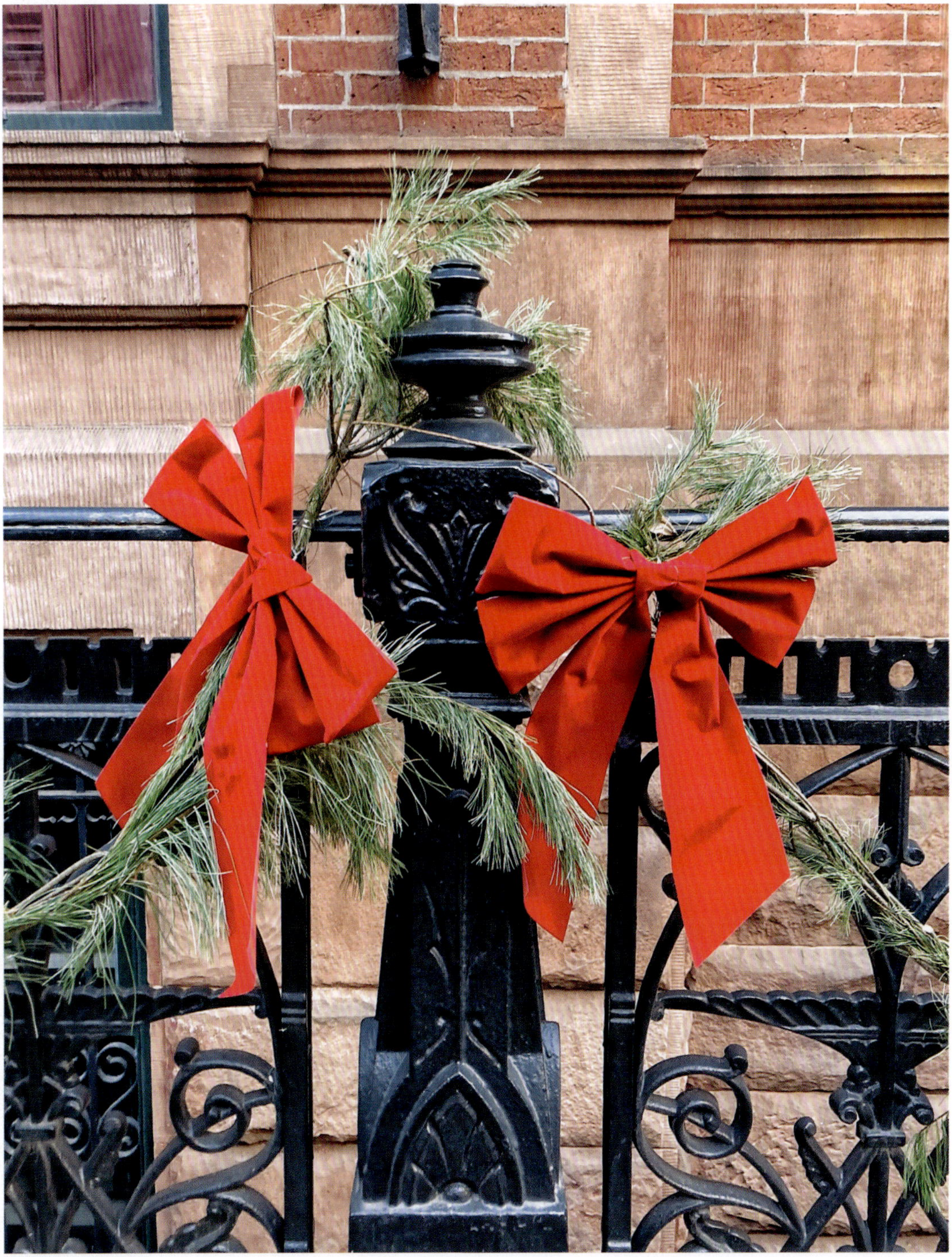

OPPOSITE: Festive wreaths in every window of this historic carriage house (ca. 1863) on West 10th Street between Fifth and Sixth Avenues. **ABOVE:** A simple garland and red bows dress up a lovely iron fence on West 9th Street between Fifth and Sixth Avenues.

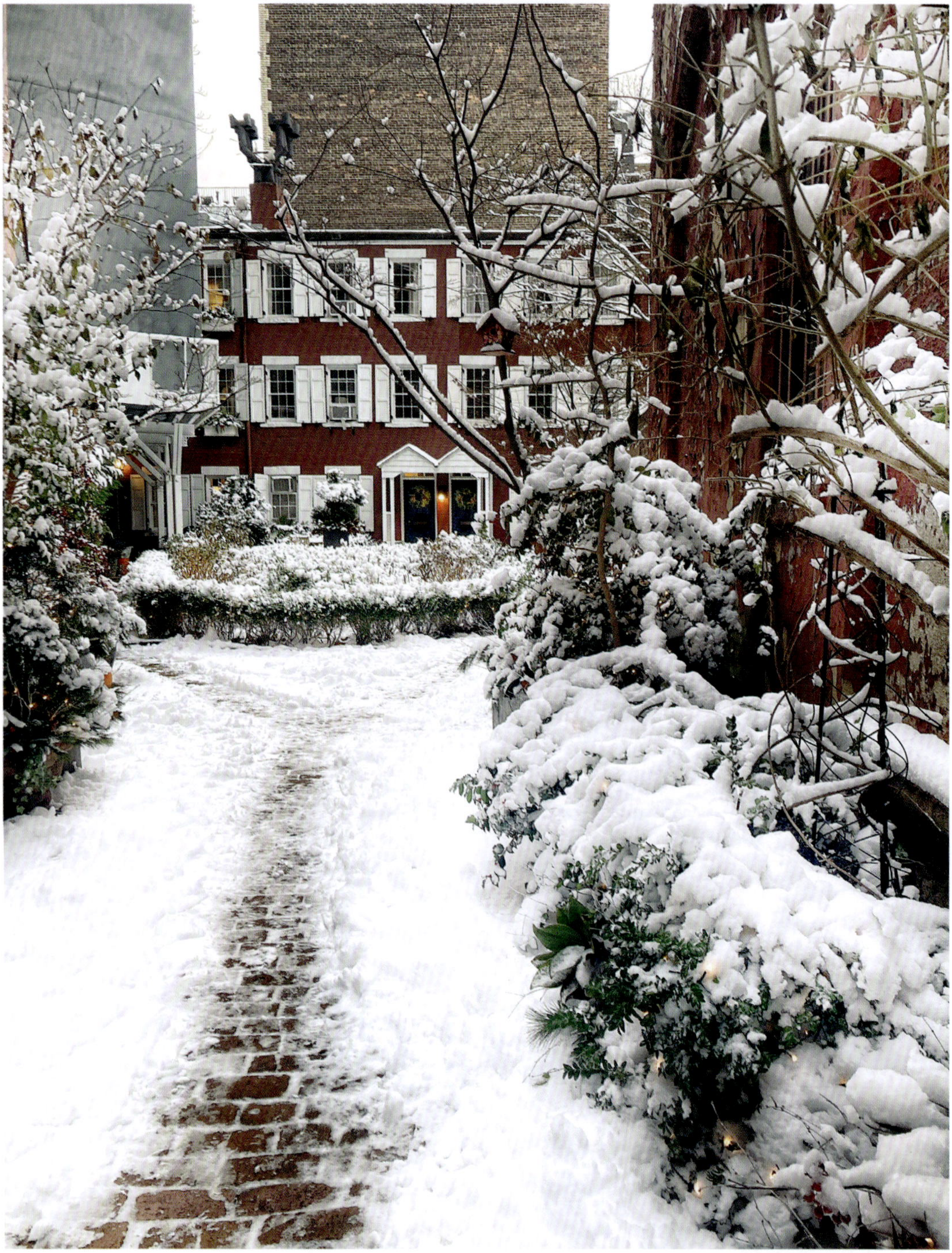

ABOVE: Lights twinkle through the snow at Grove Court, a hidden treasure on Grove Street between Hudson and Bedford Streets. **OPPOSITE, CLOCKWISE FROM TOP LEFT:** Snow scenes: a charming brick townhouse on Gay Street; Grove Street between Bedford and Hudson Streets; Freemans Restaurant in Freeman Alley; the Cherry Lane Theatre and the Commerce Inn on Commerce Street

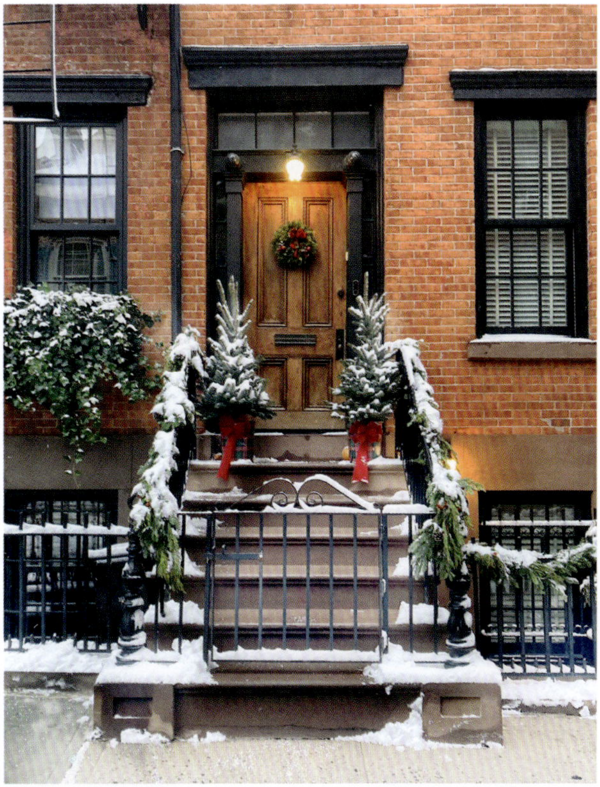

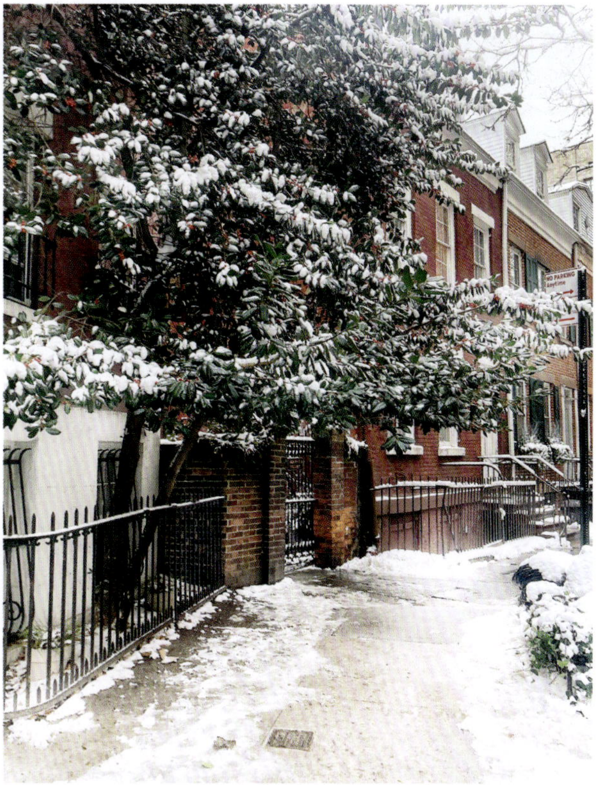

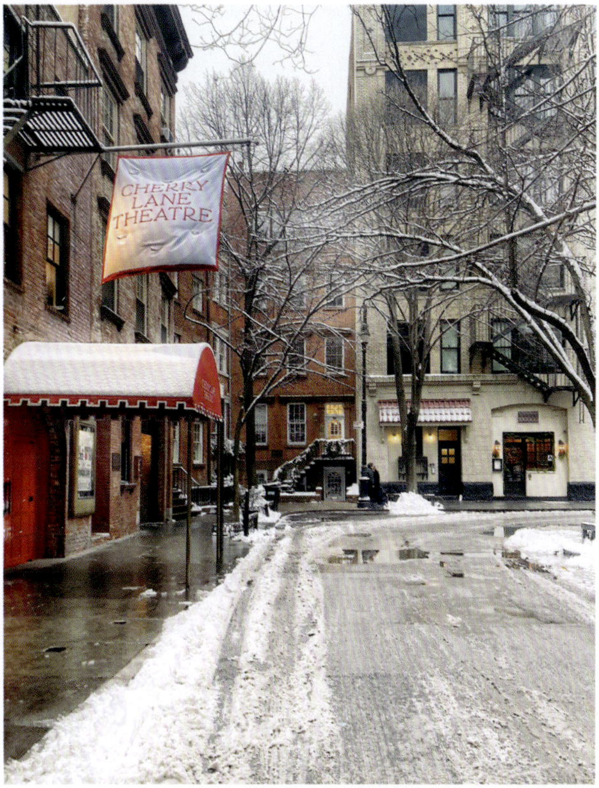
CHERRY LANE THEATRE

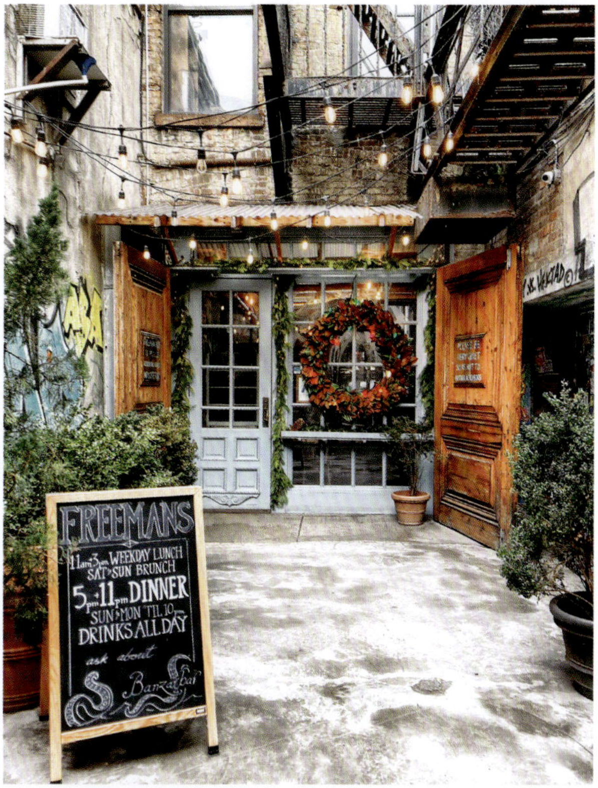
FREEMANS
11am-3pm WEEKDAY LUNCH
SAT-SUN BRUNCH
5pm-11pm DINNER
SUN-MON TIL 10pm
DRINKS ALL DAY
ask about
Banzaibar

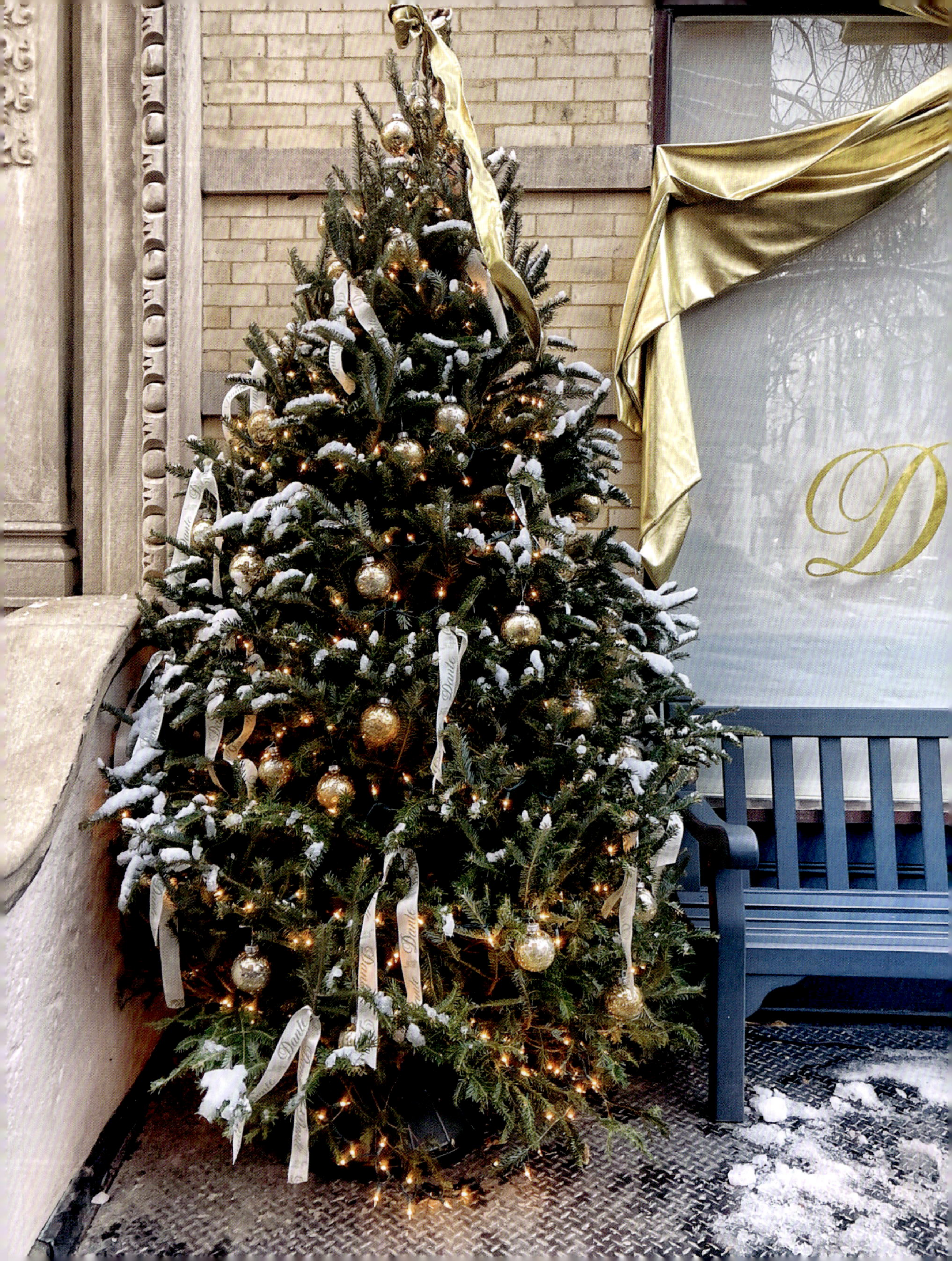
D

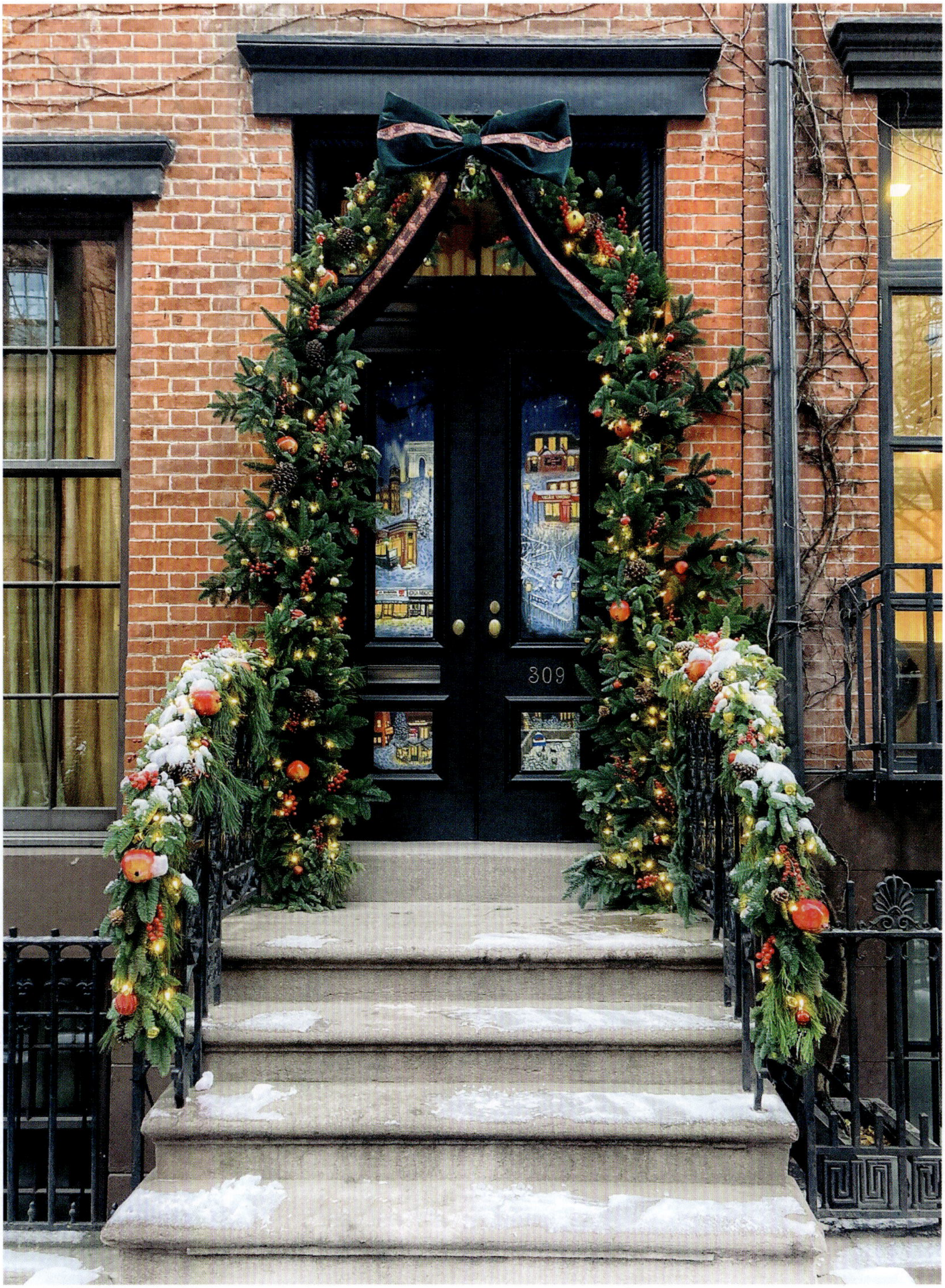

OPPOSITE: Dante Aperitivo Bar's stylish gold-trimmed tree on the corner of West 4th and Bank Streets.
ABOVE: An artistic take on holiday decorating—artist Madeline Goddard hand-painted classic West Village spots on the door of this townhouse on West 4th Street between Bank and West 12th Streets.

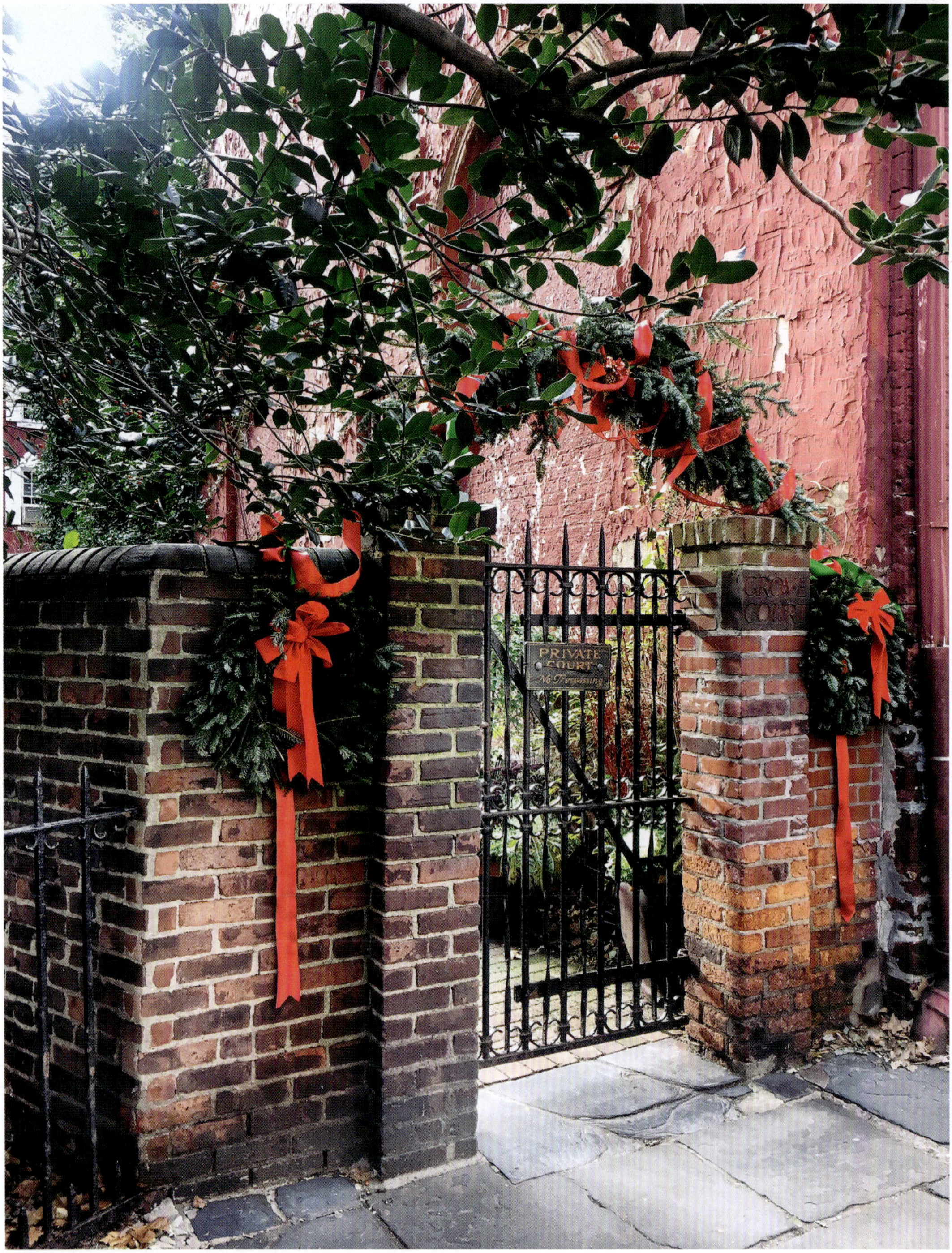

ABOVE: Grove Court's gated arch is wrapped in an evergreen garland and red ribbons on Grove Street. **OPPOSITE:** Elegant magnolia wreaths hang in the windows of Buvette, a French eatery on Grove Street between Bleecker and Bedford Streets.

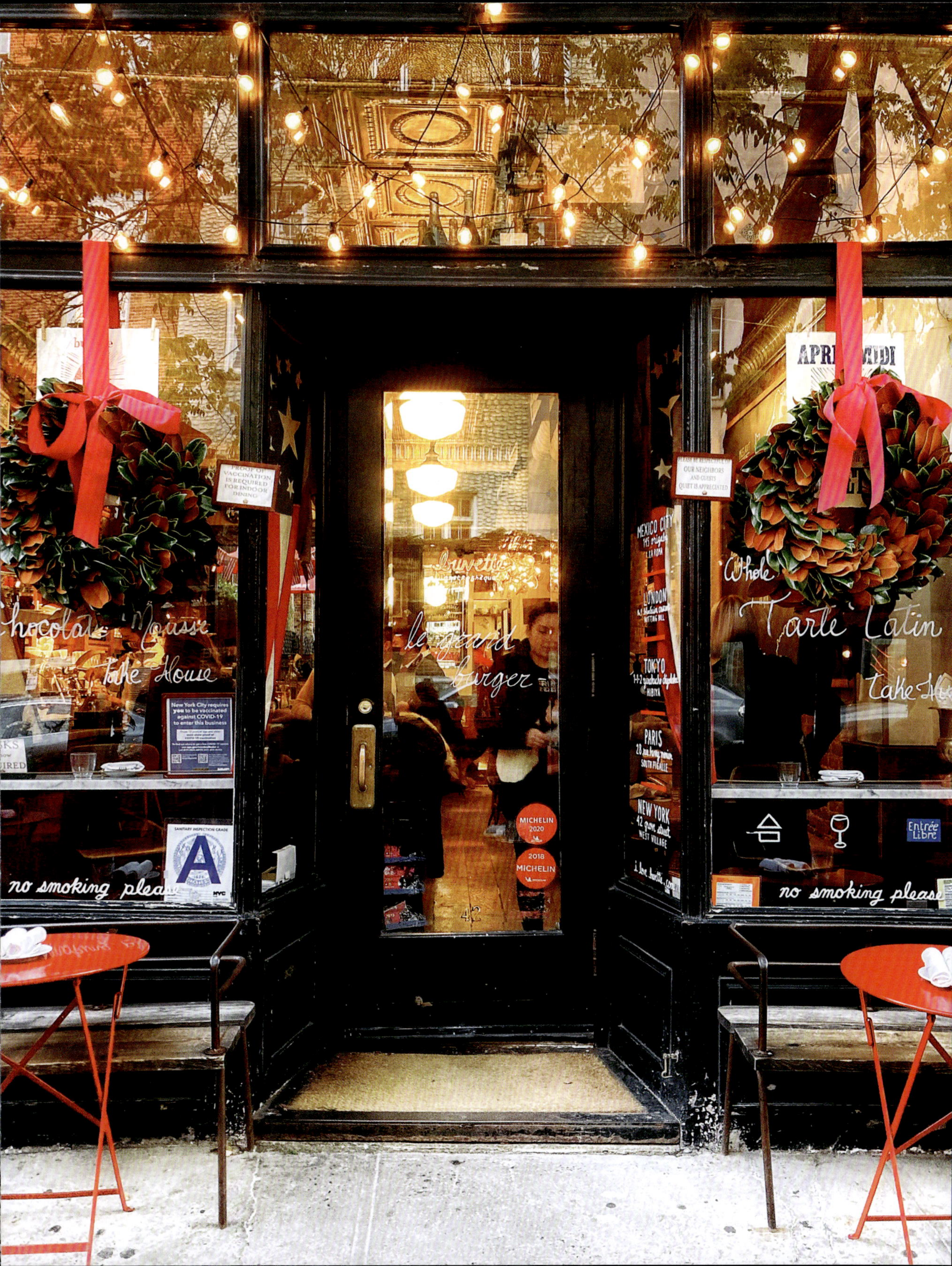

Whole
Tarte Latin
Take House
MEXICO CITY
LONDON
TOKYO
PARIS
NEW YORK
WEST VILLAGE
MICHELIN 2020
2018 MICHELIN
Entrée Libre
SANITARY INSPECTION GRADE
A
NYC
no smoking please

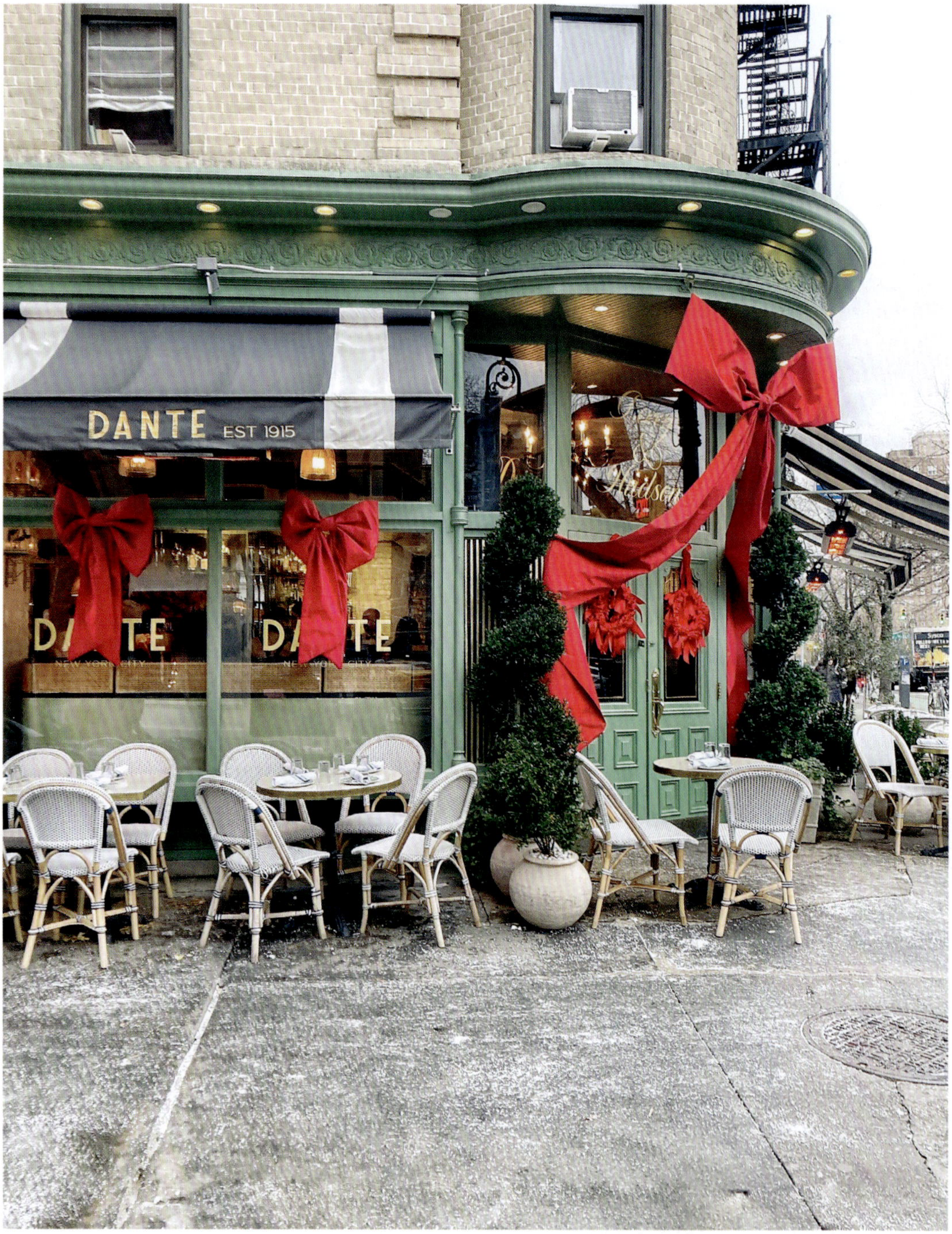

ABOVE: Dante West Village's graceful green facade on the corner of Perry and Hudson Streets is decked out with festive red bows. **OPPOSITE, CLOCKWISE FROM TOP LEFT:** Traditional red bows: on the Jackson Square Park fountain in the West Village; planters on Centre Street in SoHo; The C Cafe on Hudson Street; an East 11th Street townhouse's railings

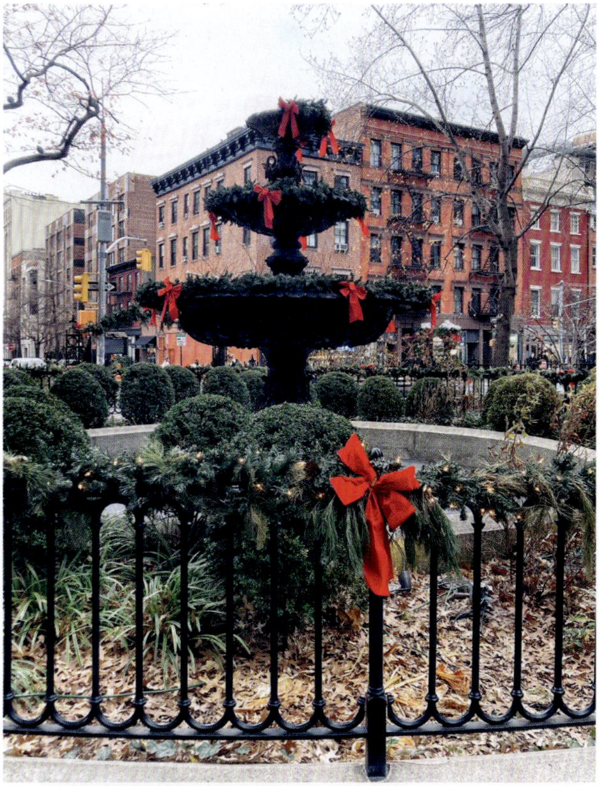

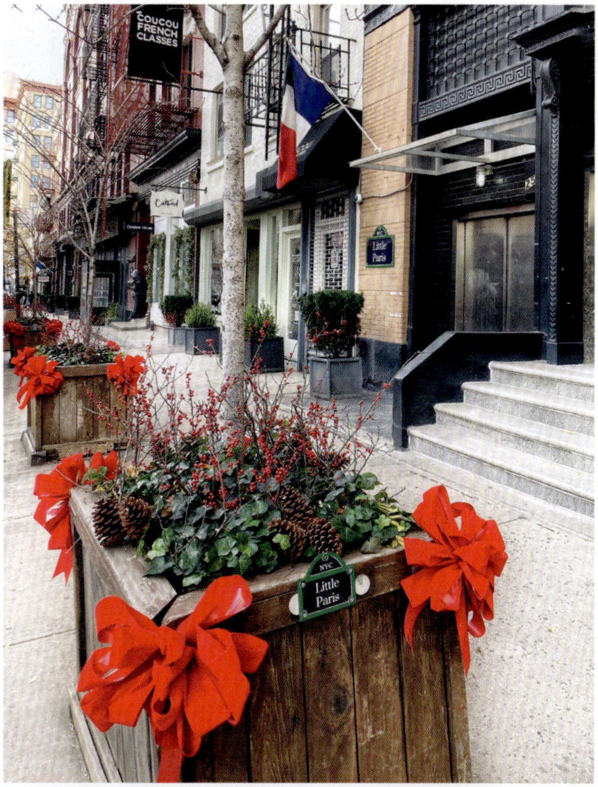
COUCOU
FRENCH
CLASSES
Little
Paris

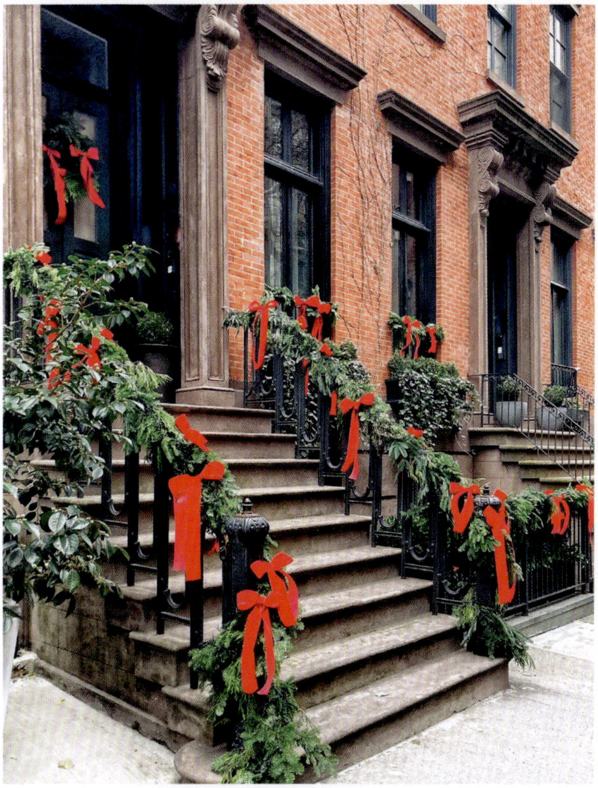

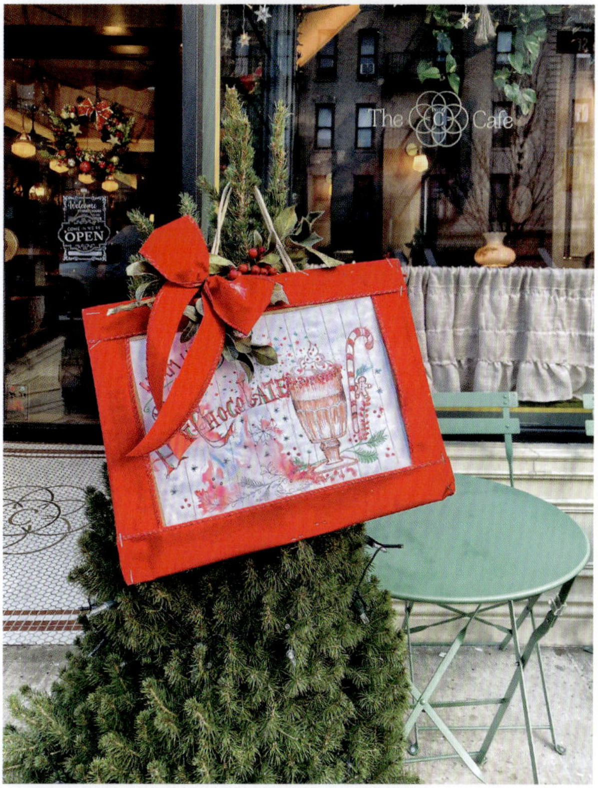
The
Cafe
OPEN

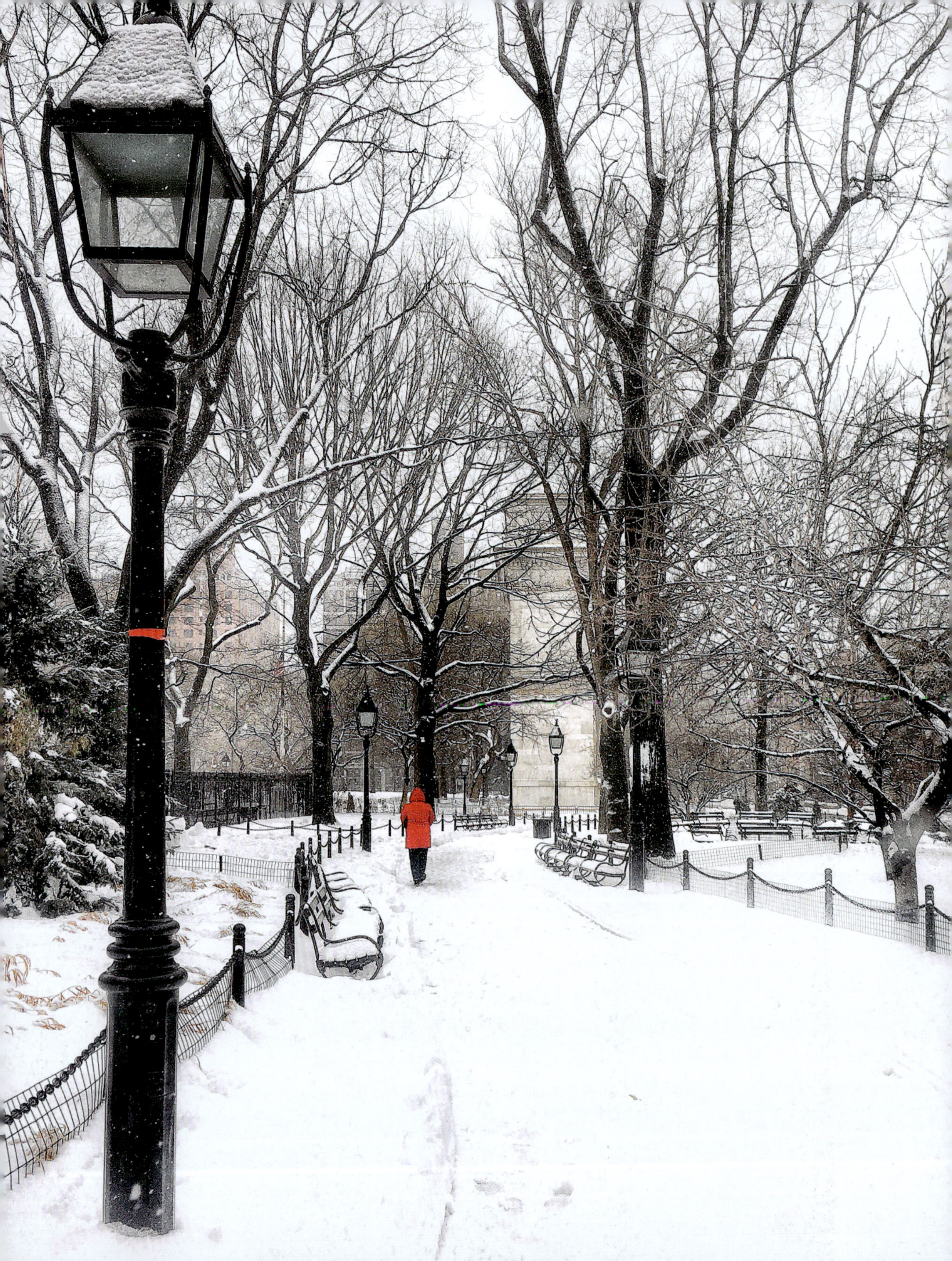

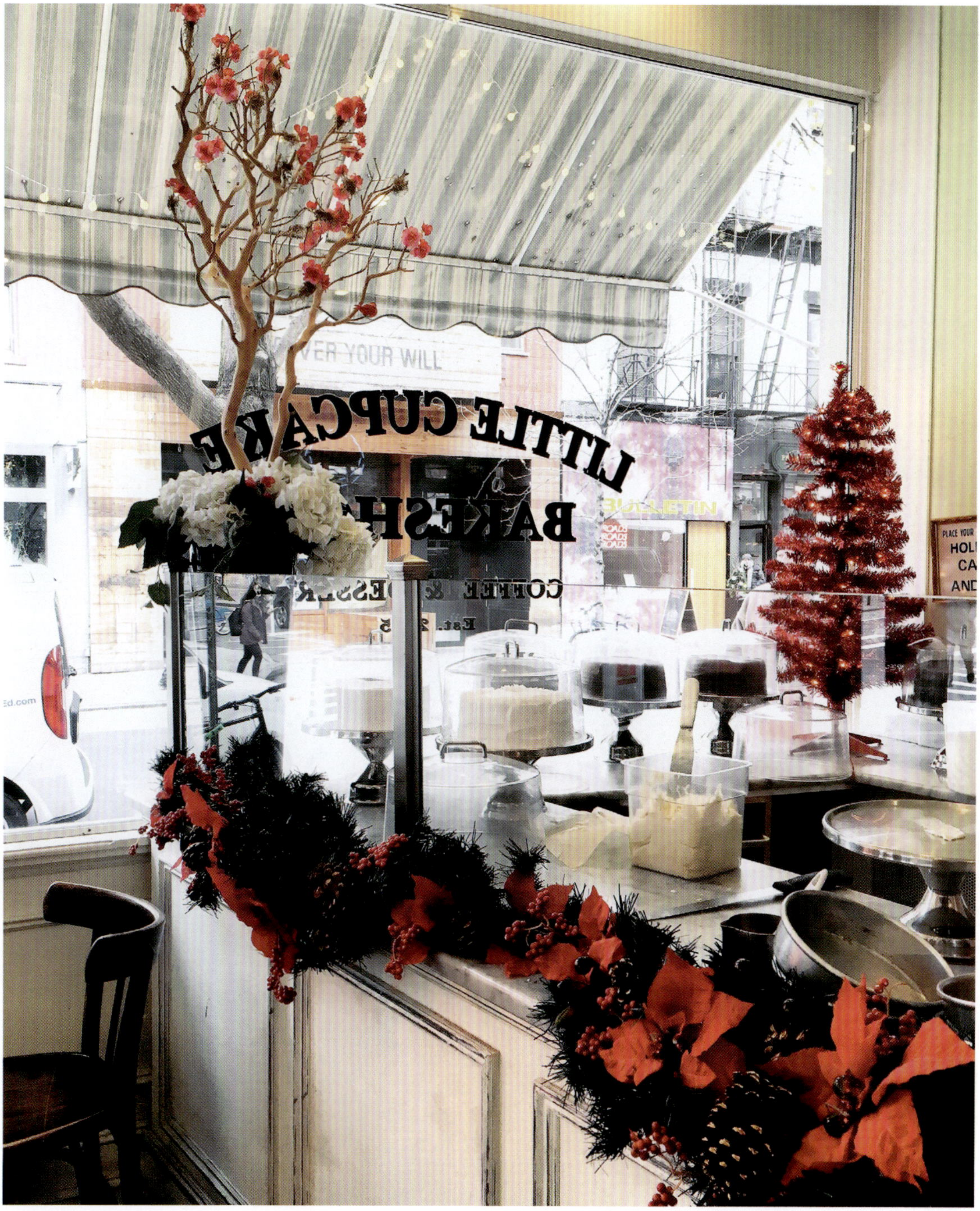

OPPOSITE: A red jacket pops against the white snow in Washington Square Park. **ABOVE:** Classic red poinsettia leaves and pine cones adorn the counter at the Little Cupcake Bakeshop on the corner of Prince and Mott Streets in SoHo.

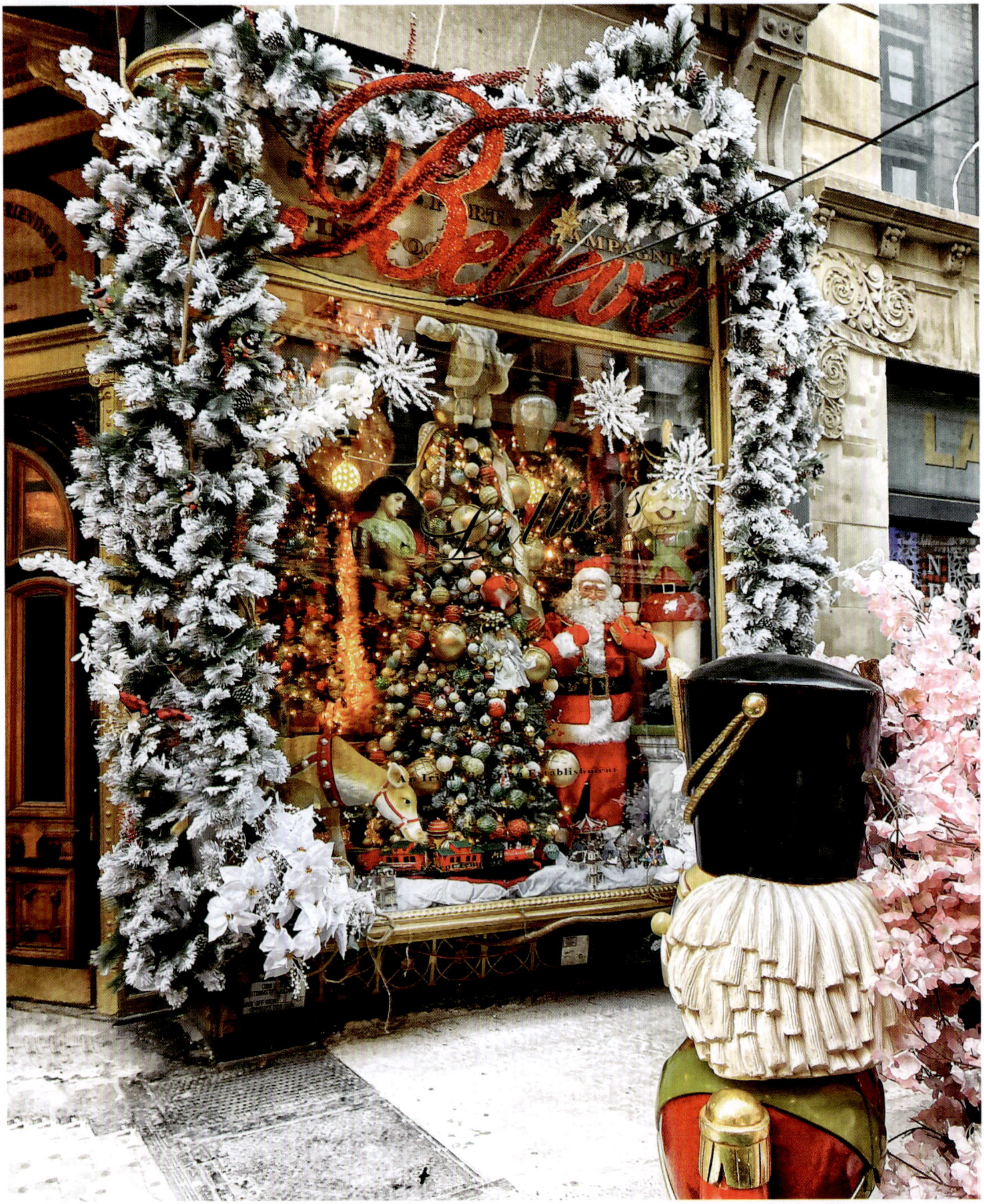

ABOVE AND OPPOSITE: Lillie's Victorian Establishment's old-fashioned holiday window decorations on East 17th Street in Union Square. The over-the-top Christmas decorations in Lillie's Victorian's restaurant and bar make it the perfect gathering spot for holiday celebrations.

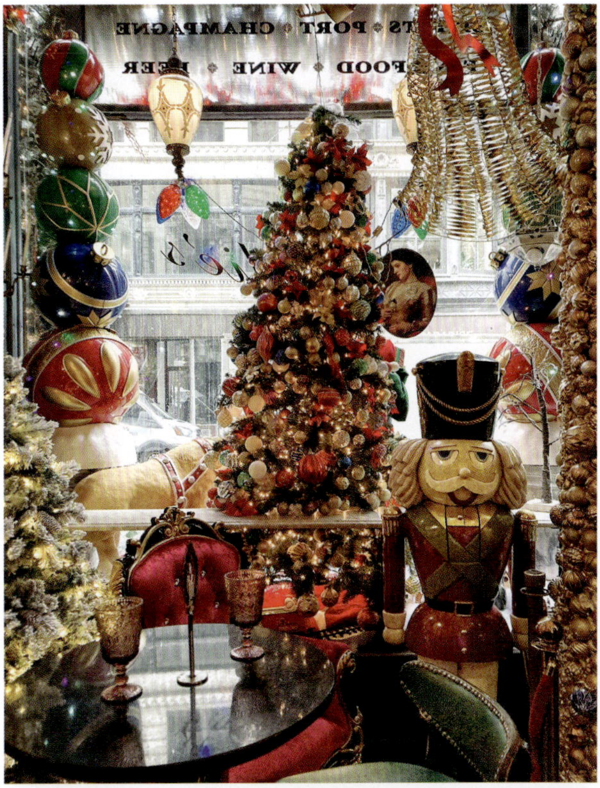

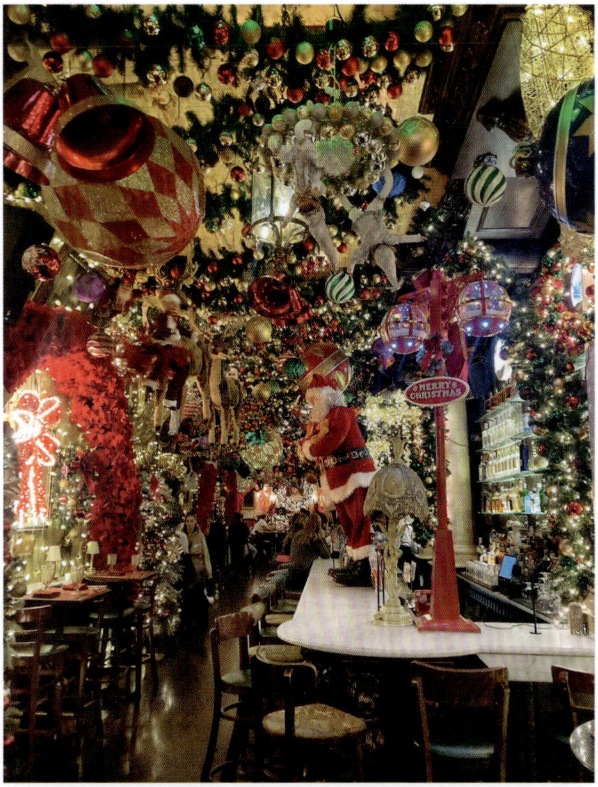
MERRY CHRISTMAS

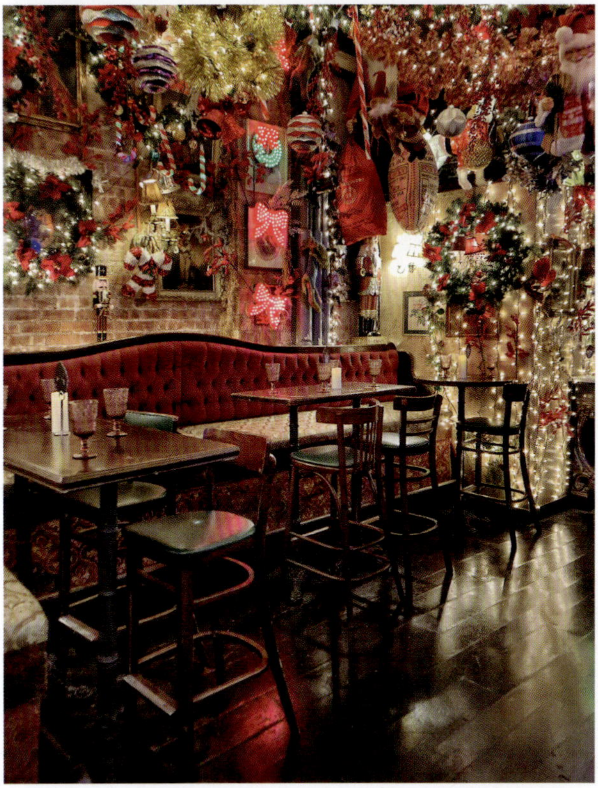

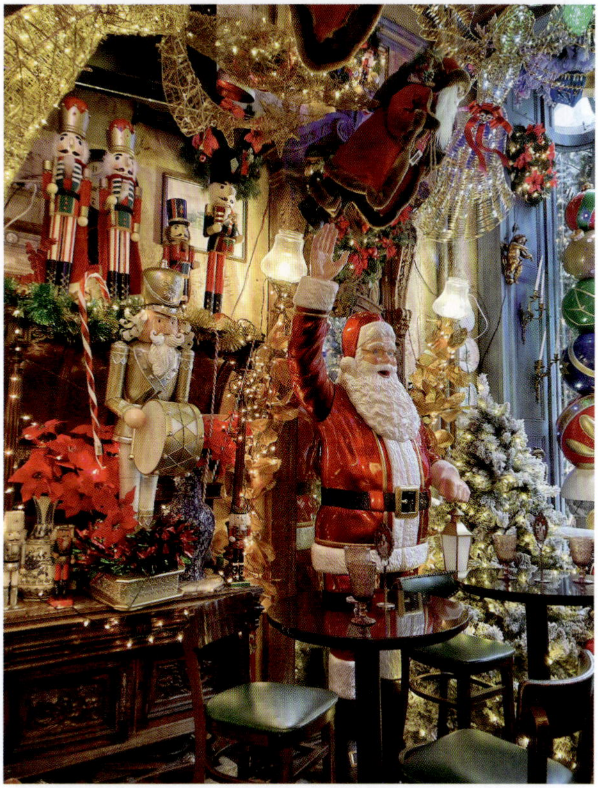

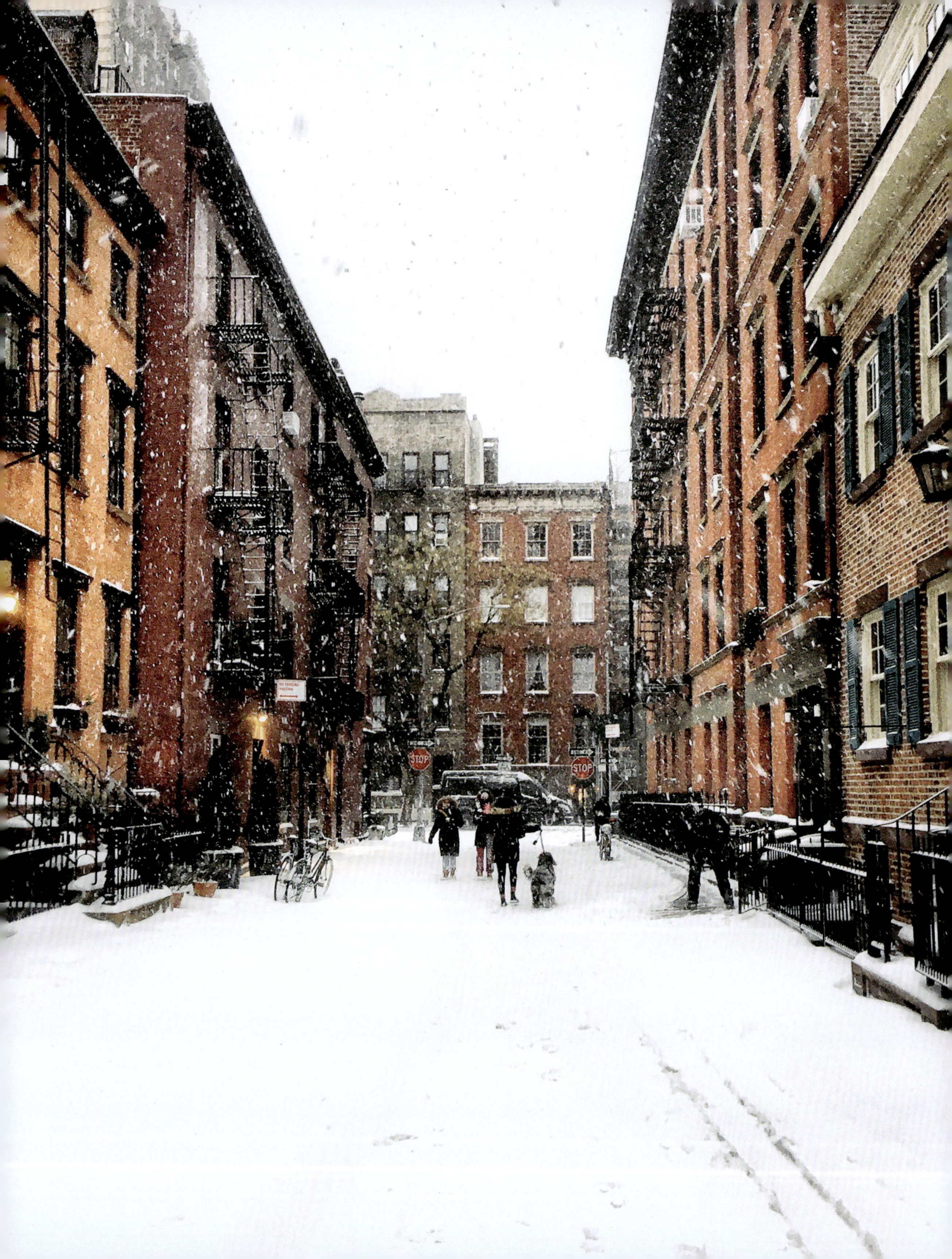
STOP
STOP

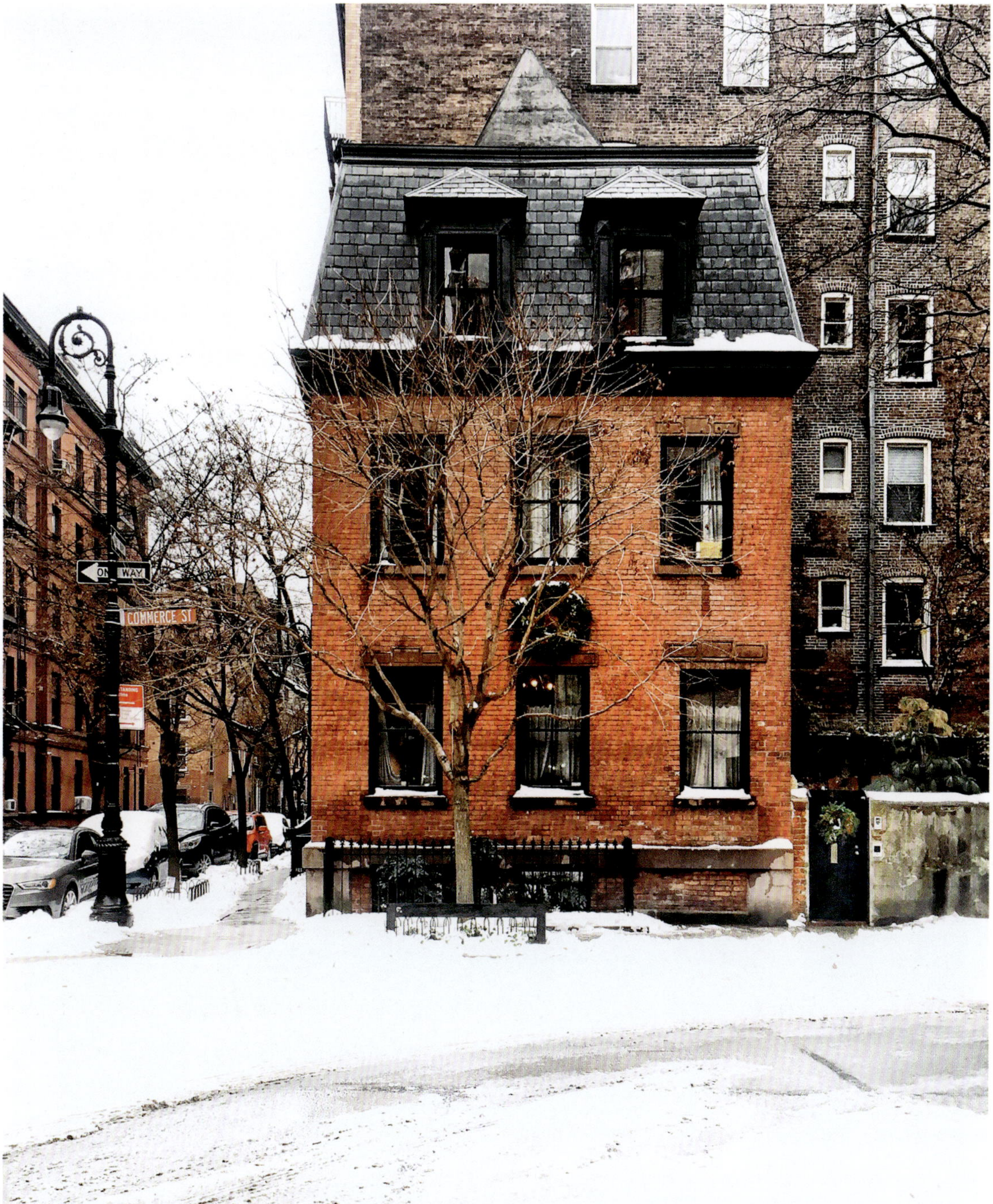

OPPOSITE: Snow falling on historic Gay Street in Greenwich Village. **ABOVE:** A simple wreath adorns a beautiful brick house (ca. 1831) on the corner of Commerce and Barrow Streets in the West Village.

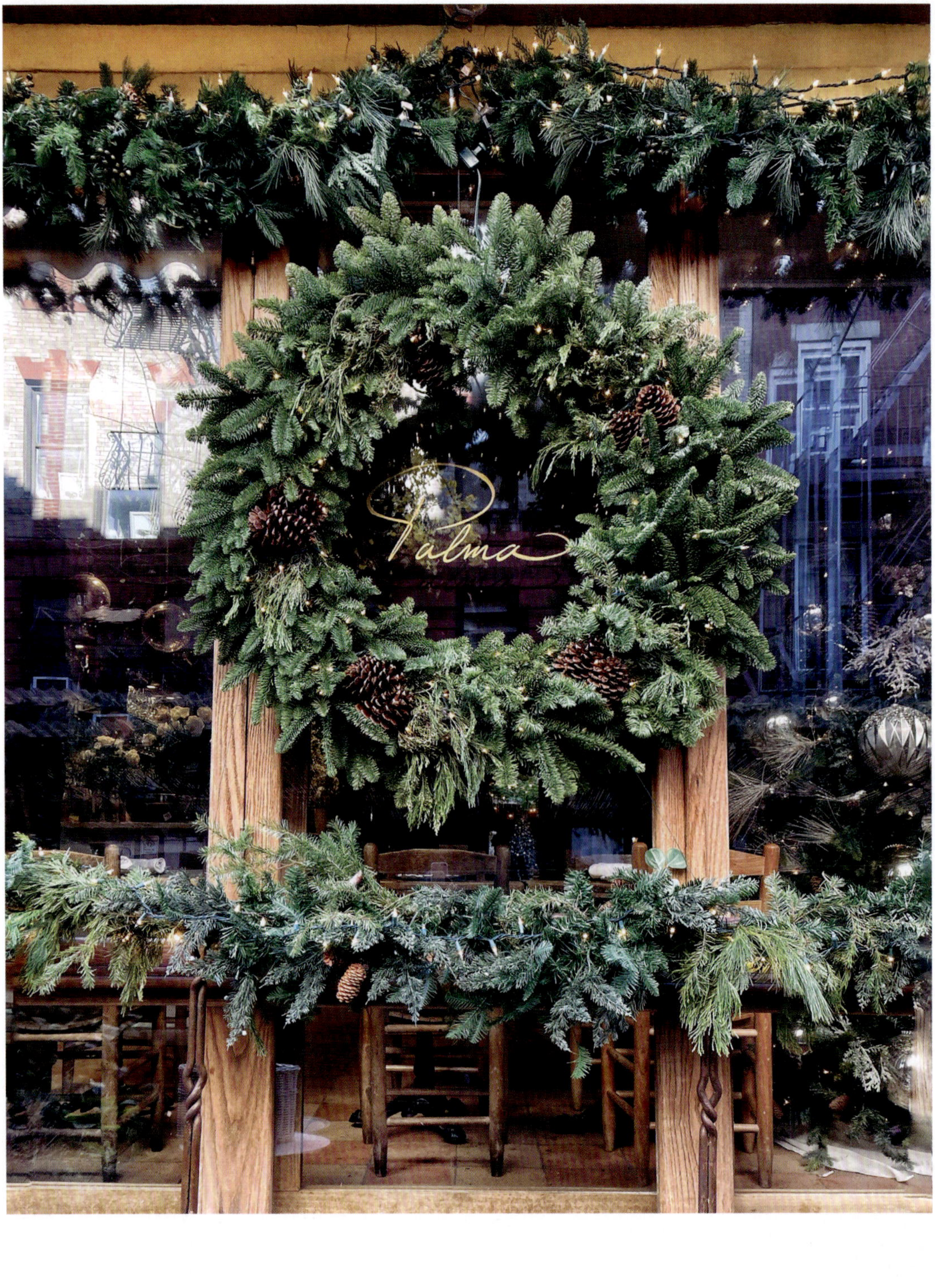

ABOVE AND OPPOSITE: A classic wreath and garlands adorn the facade of Palma, an organic Italian restaurant on Cornelia Street. A shimmering silver and white Christmas tree in Palma's rustic interior

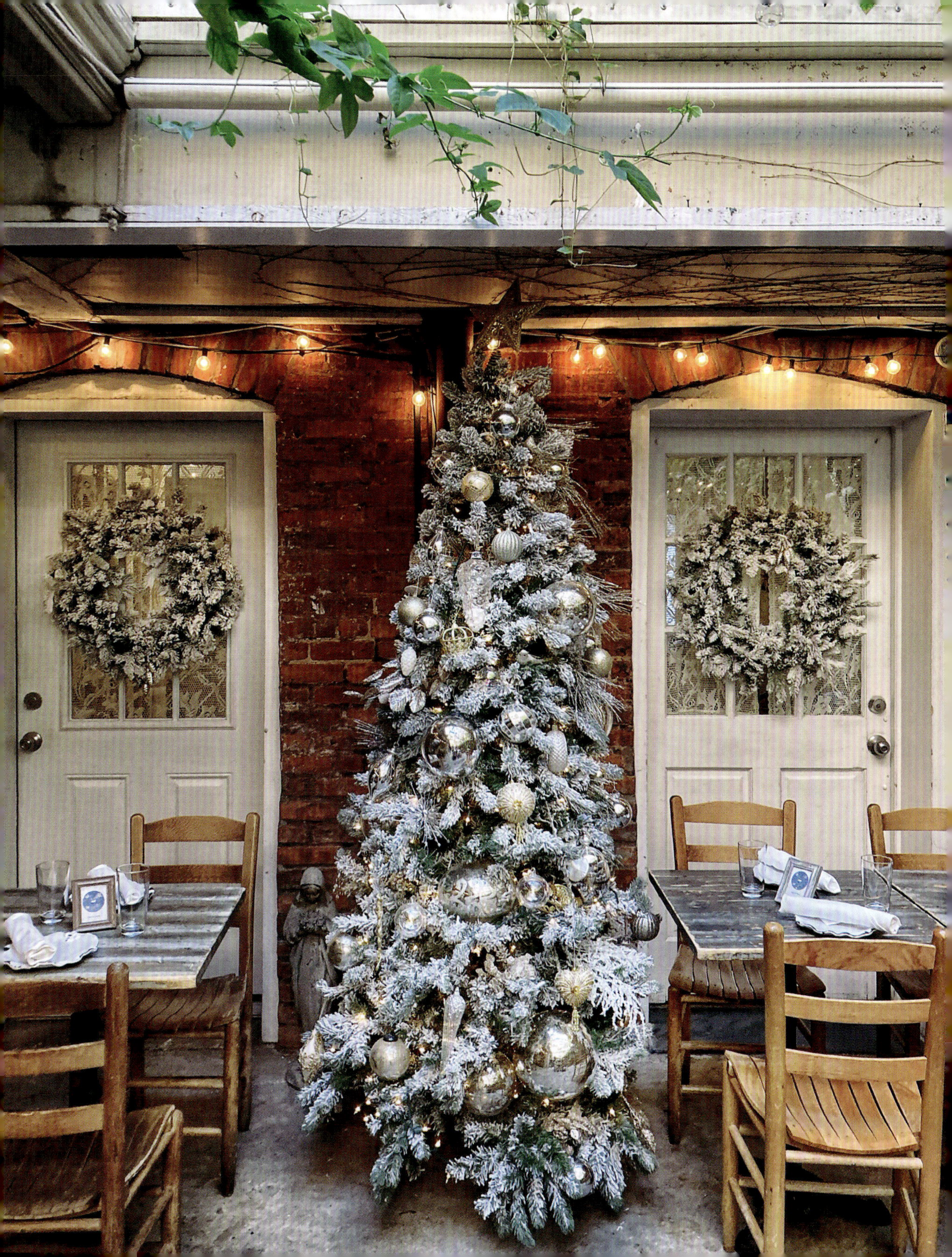

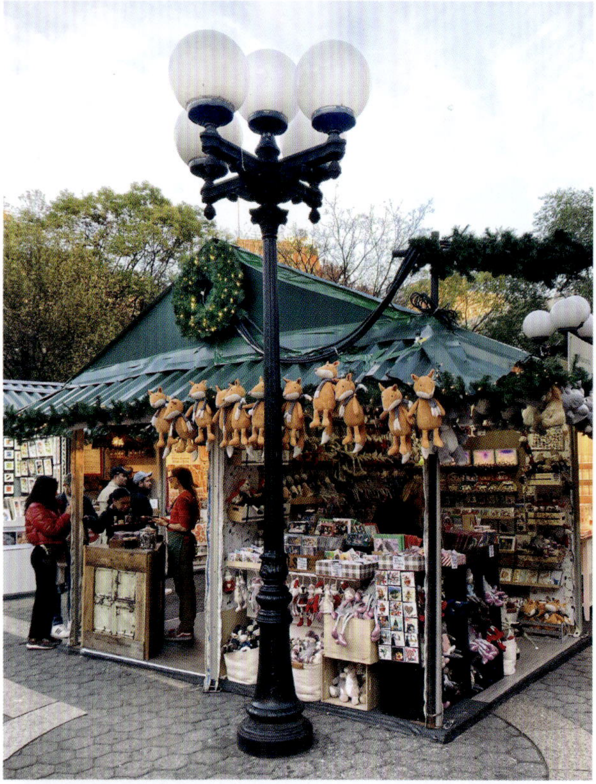

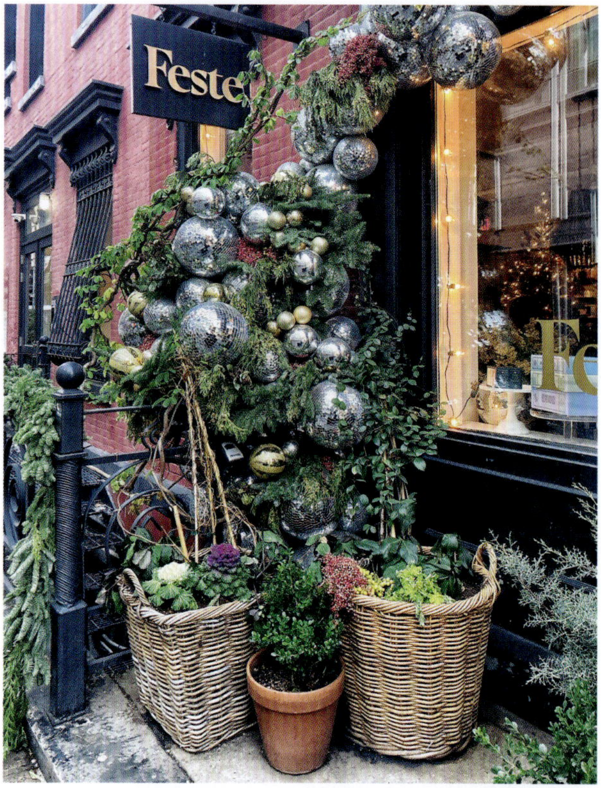
Feste

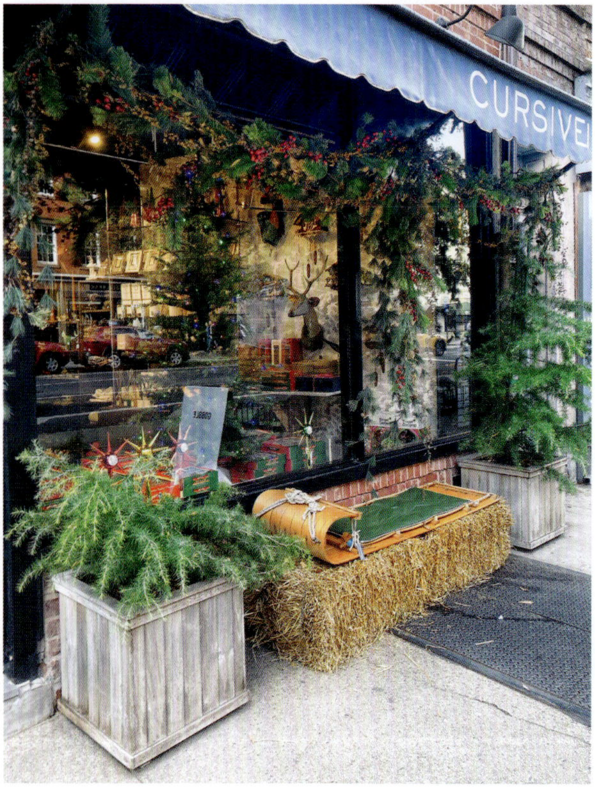
CURSIVE

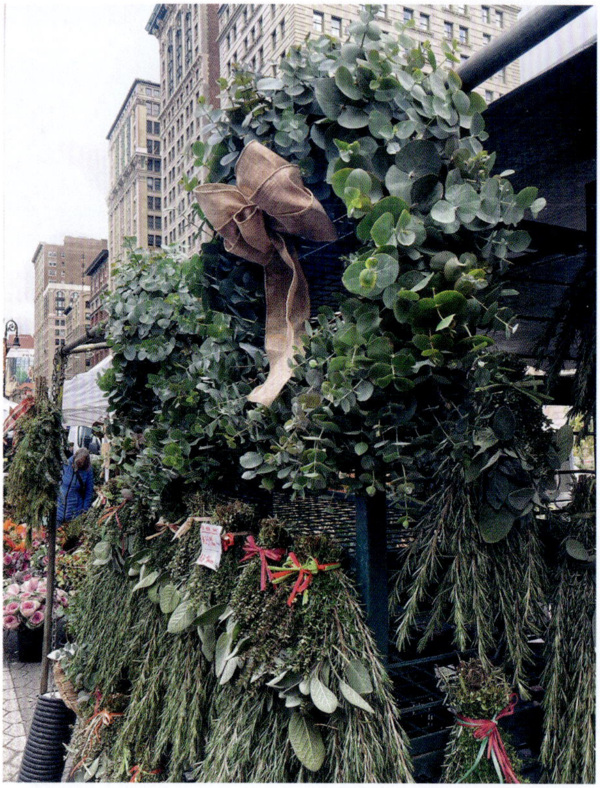

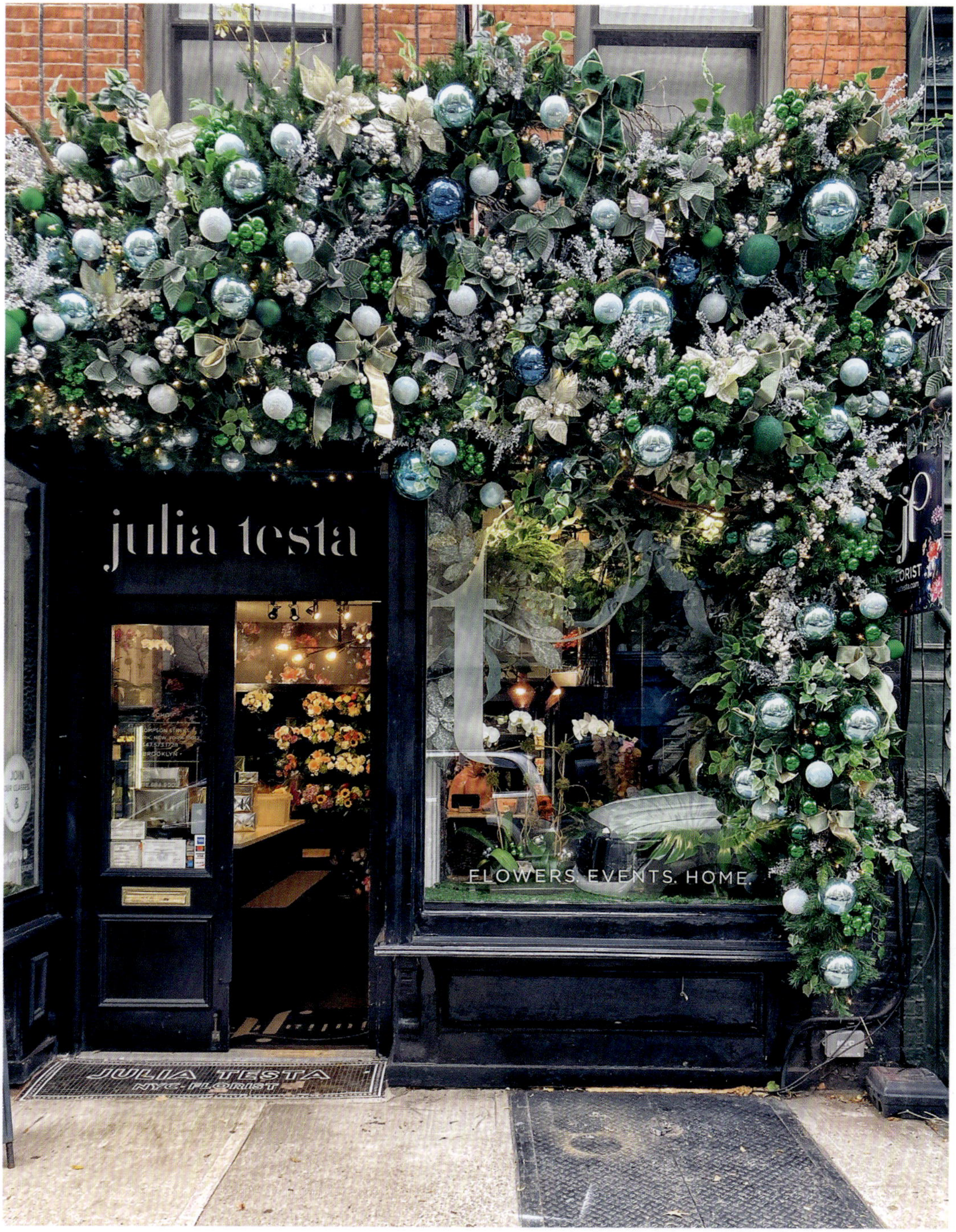

OPPOSITE, CLOCKWISE FROM TOP LEFT: An open-air gift stall at the Union Square Holiday Market by Urbanspace; Feste's festive party shop on Crosby Street in SoHo; wreaths and seasonal greenery for sale at the Union Square Greenmarket; an old-fashioned sled at Cursive's gift shop on Hudson Street in the West Village. **ABOVE:** Julia Testa's flower shop on Thompson Street in SoHo is all decked out in gorgeous green and blue baubles and silver ribbons.

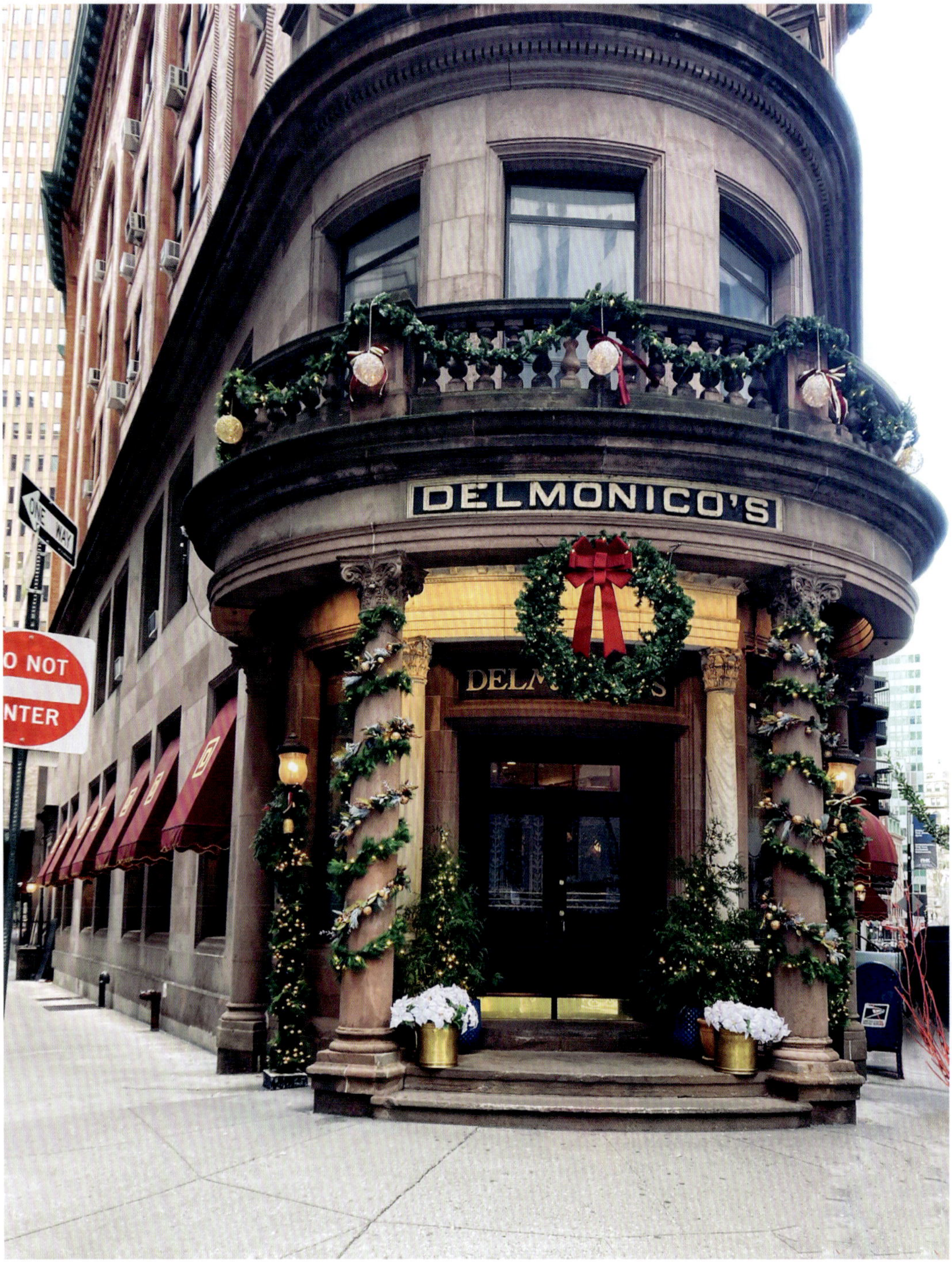

ABOVE: Delmonico's, a historic New York City steakhouse on Beaver Street in the Financial District, exudes old-world yuletide charm with classic decorations. **OPPOSITE:** A warm glow radiates from behind a rustic wood door on West 9th Street between Fifth and Sixth Avenues in Greenwich Village.

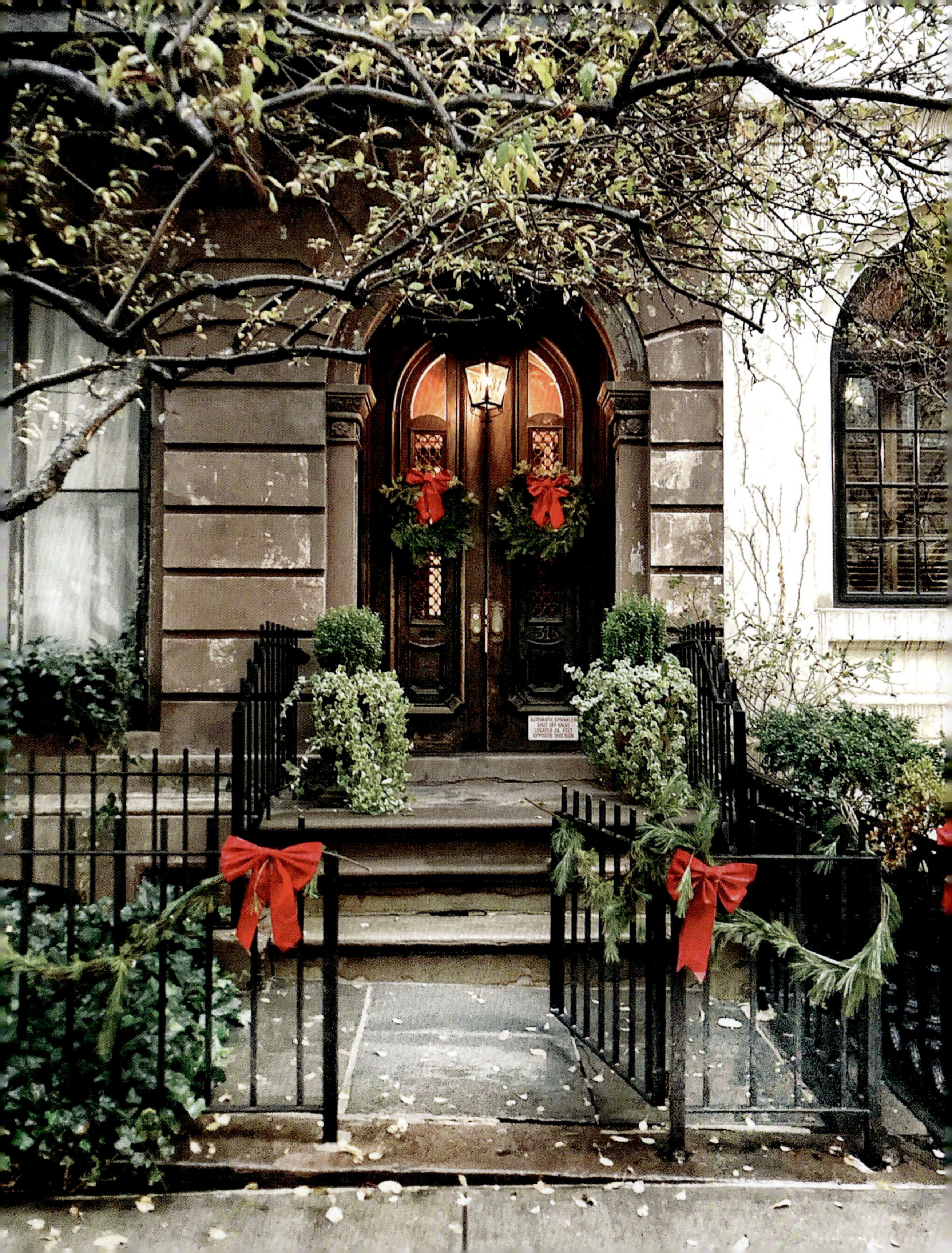
AUTOMATIC SPRINKLER
SHUT OFF VALVE
OPPOSITE THIS SIGN

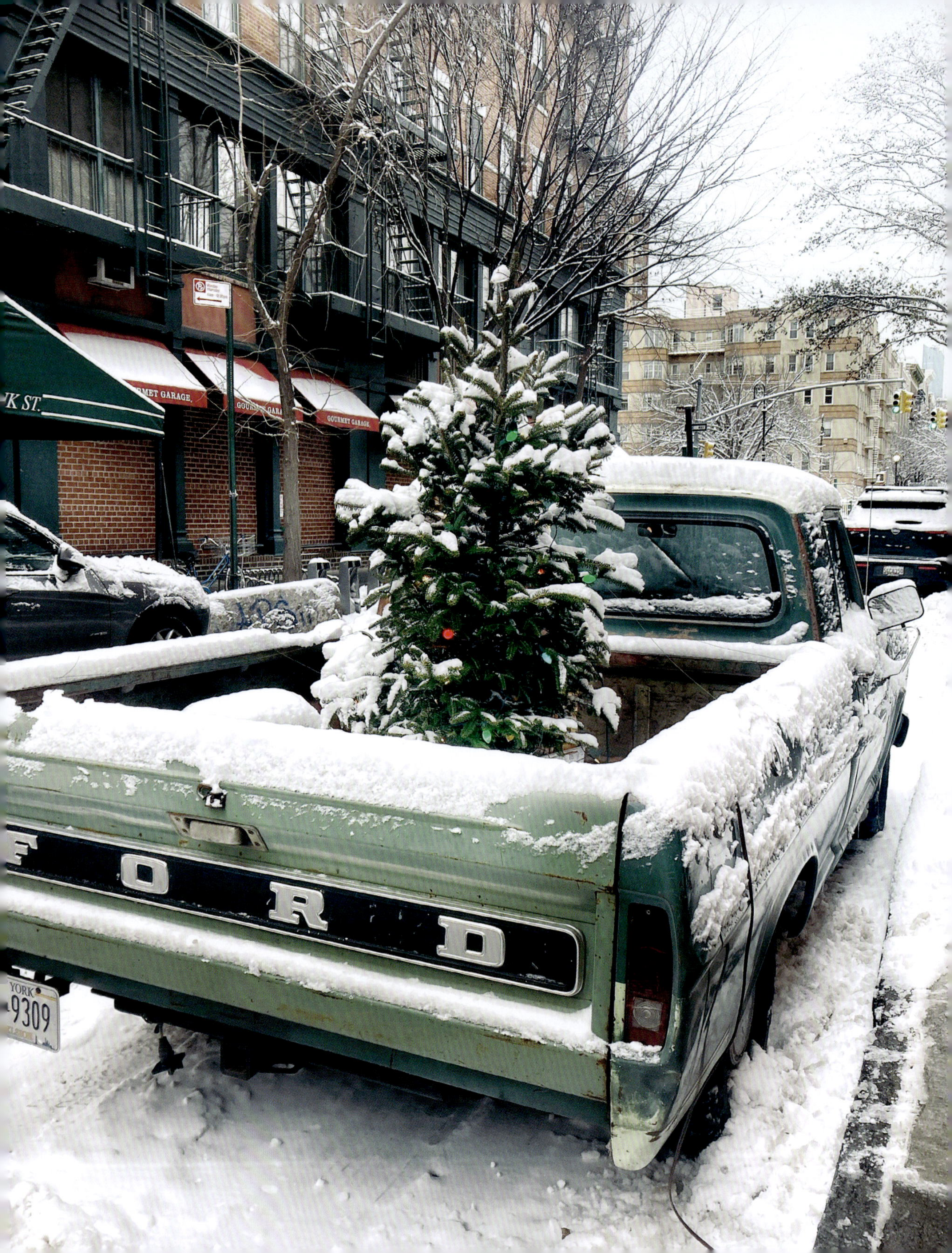
K ST.
GOURMET GARAGE
GOURMET GARAGE
FORD
YORK
9309

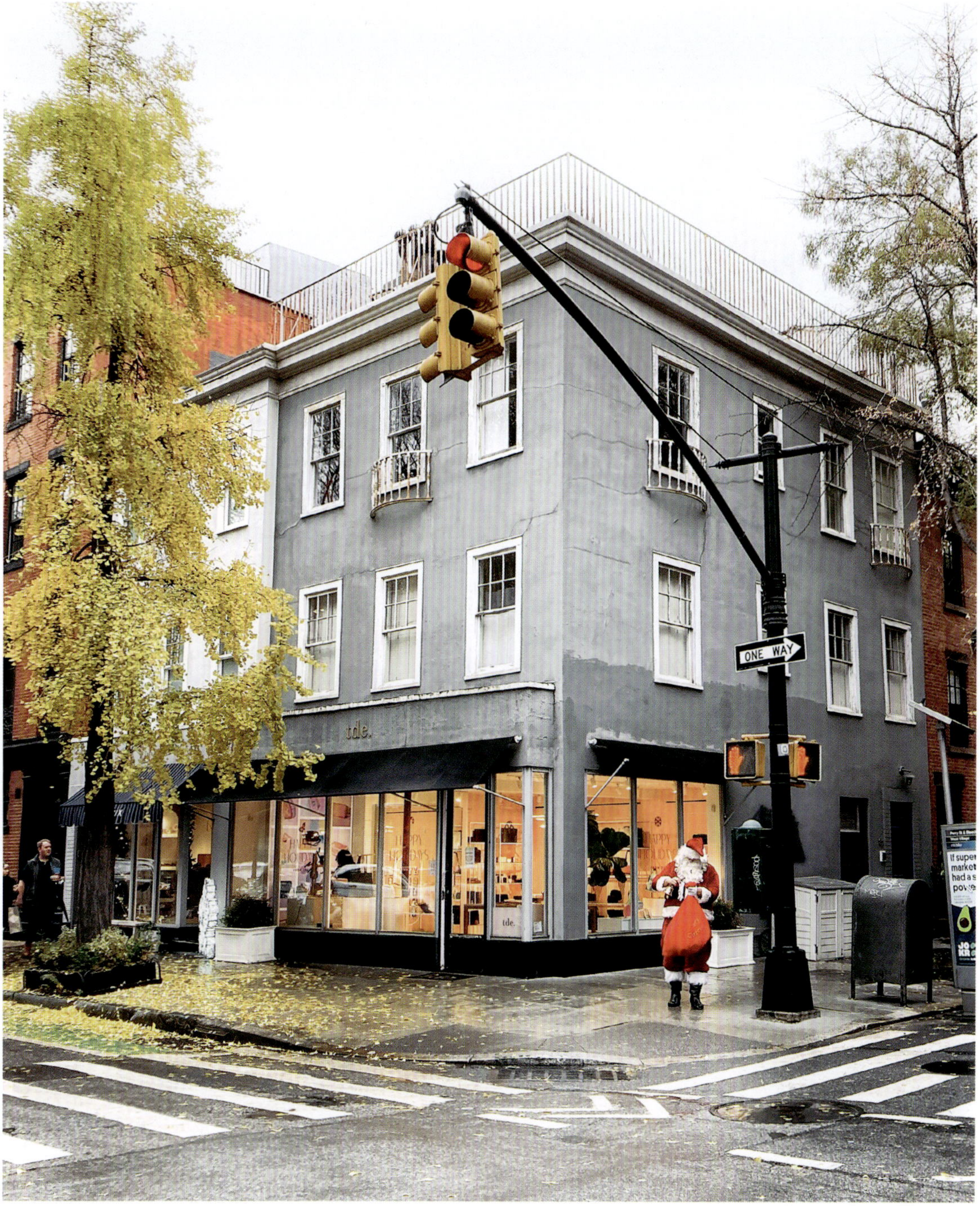

OPPOSITE: A snow-covered Christmas tree sits unexpectedly in the back of a vintage Ford pickup truck on Bank Street in the West Village. **ABOVE:** A lone Santa Claus spotted on a West Village corner during a mid-December "Santa Con" pub crawl.

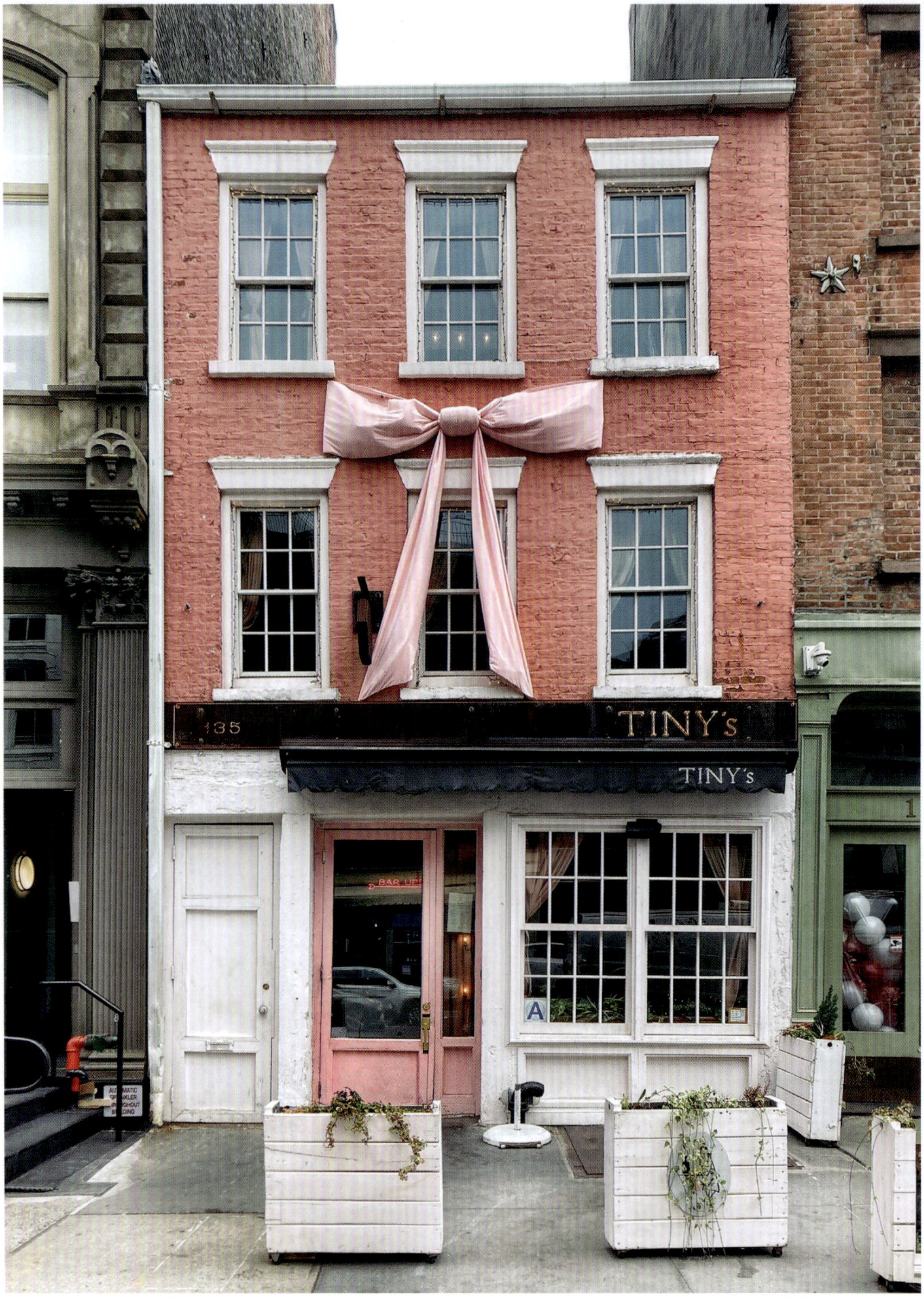

ABOVE: An oversized pink bow gives a sweet nod to the season on Tiny's & The Bar Upstairs' landmarked townhouse (ca. 1810) on West Broadway in Tribeca. **OPPOSITE:** Stoney Clover Lane's pretty holiday decor on Bleecker Street in the West Village is a vision in pink.

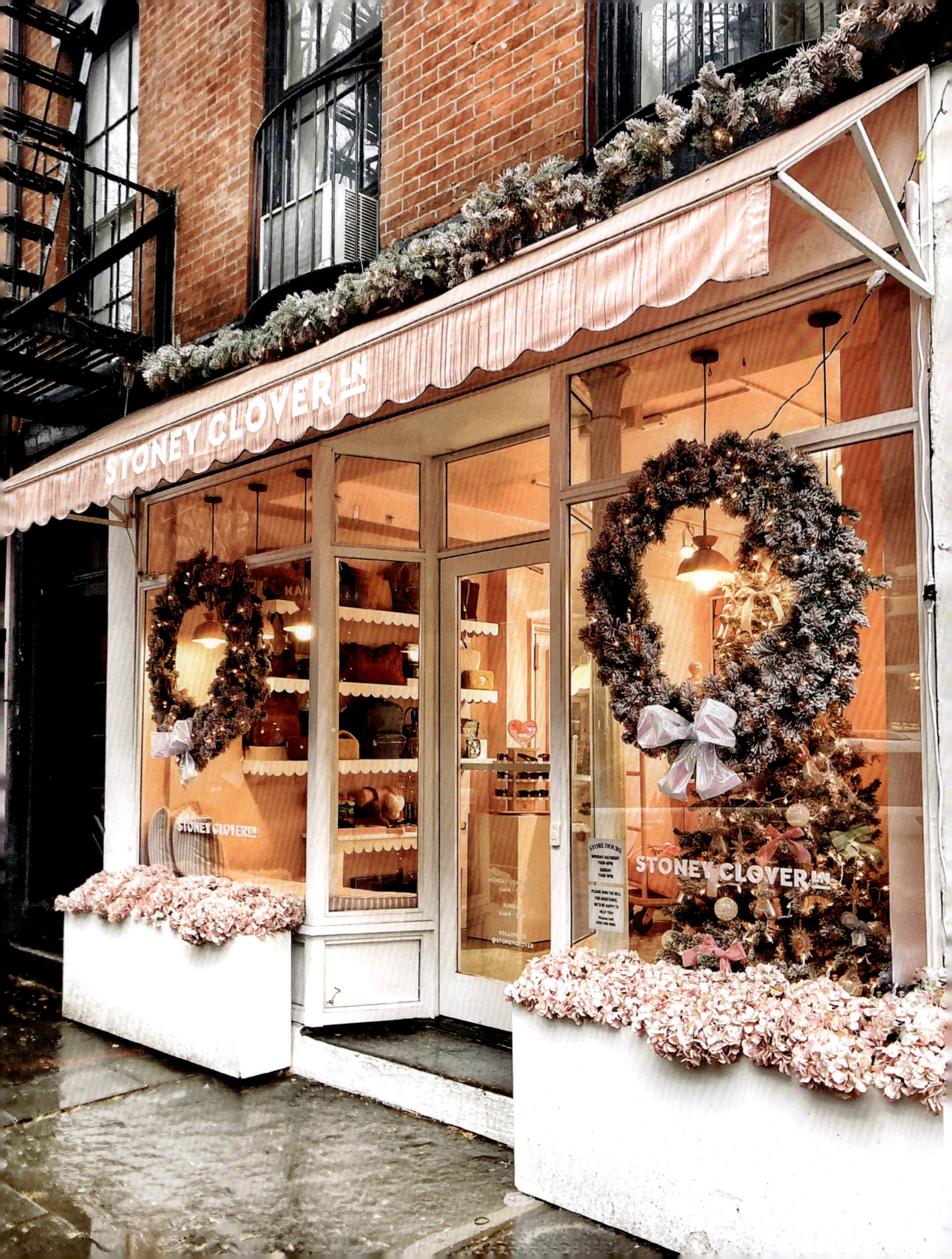
STONEY CLOVER LN
STONEY CLOVER LN
STONEY CLOVER LN

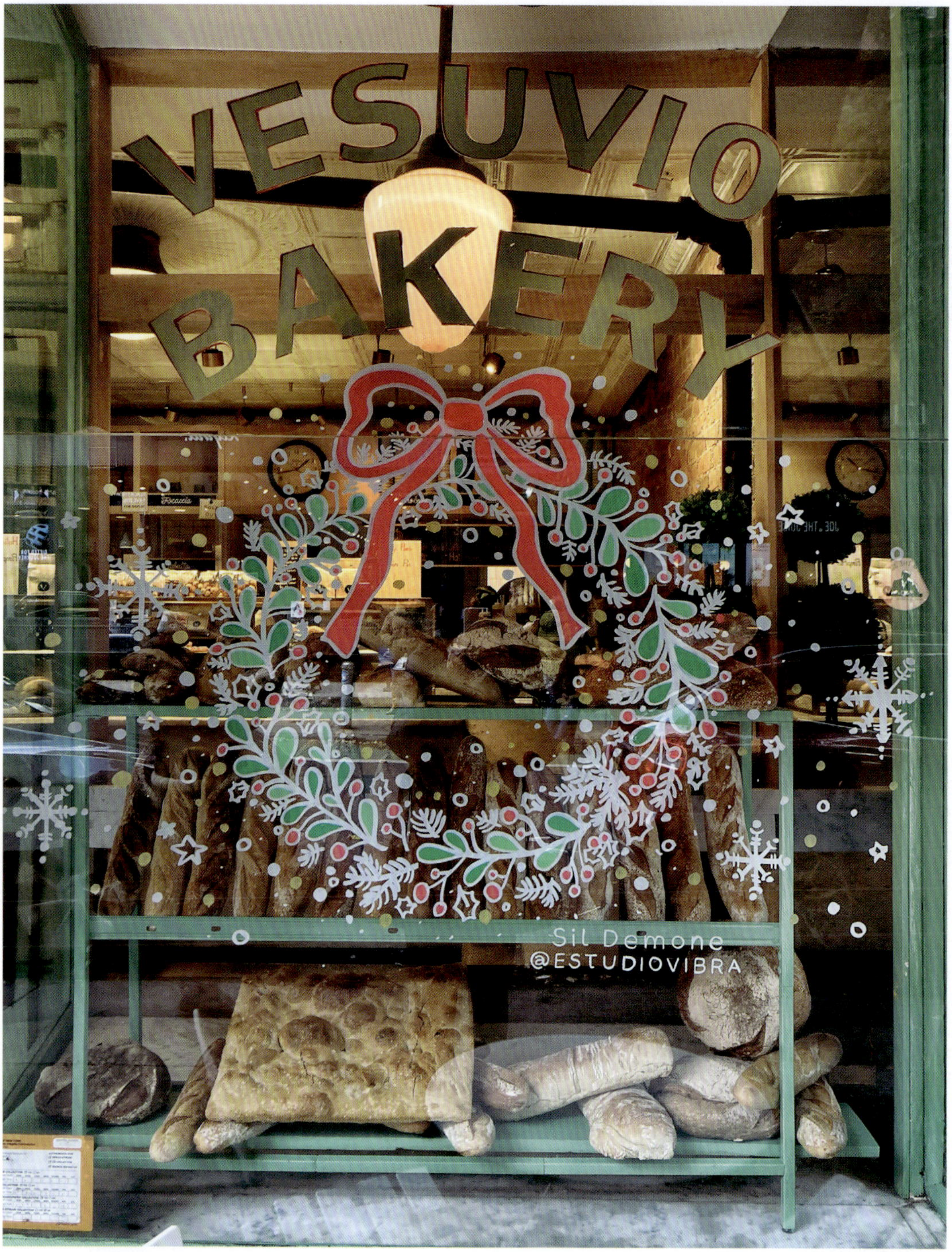

ABOVE: A delightful stenciled wreath by artist Sil Demone adds the perfect festive touch to Vesuvio Bakery's window on Prince Street in SoHo. **OPPOSITE, CLOCKWISE FROM TOP LEFT:** Candy cane stripes and flowers at Drip Drop Café on Thompson Street in SoHo; striped stockings at Abbode embroidery shop on Elizabeth Street in Nolita; a red sash on a blue West Village door; a fabulous red faux Christmas tree in Little Cupcake Bakeshop on Prince Street in SoHo

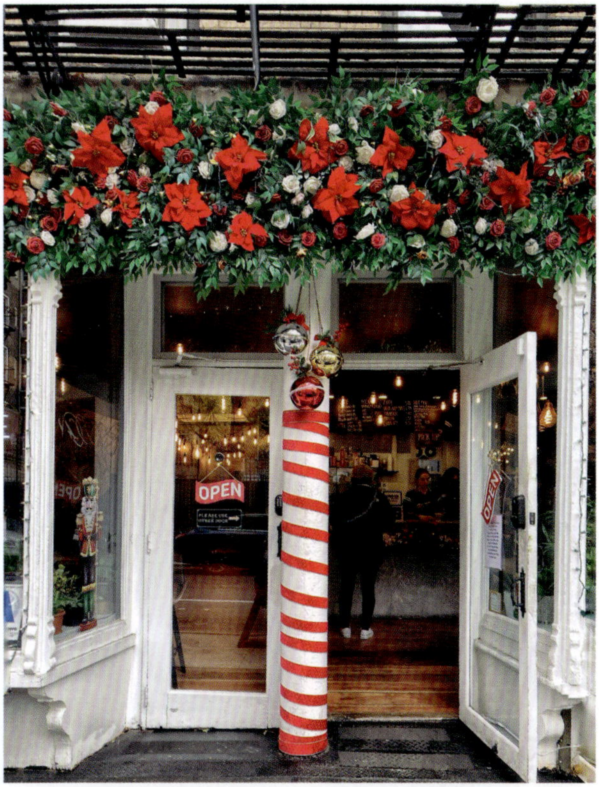
OPEN

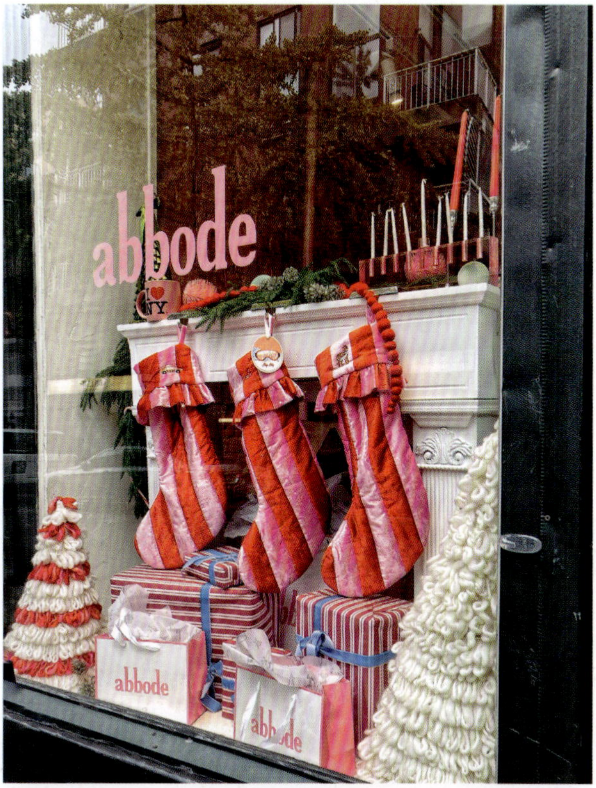
abbode
abbode
abbode

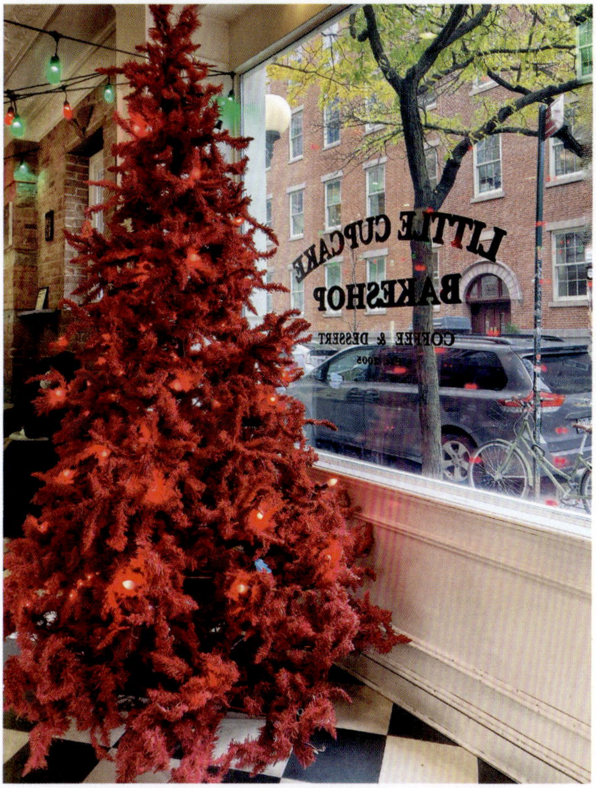
LITTLE CUPCAKE
BAKESHOP
COFFEE & DESSERT

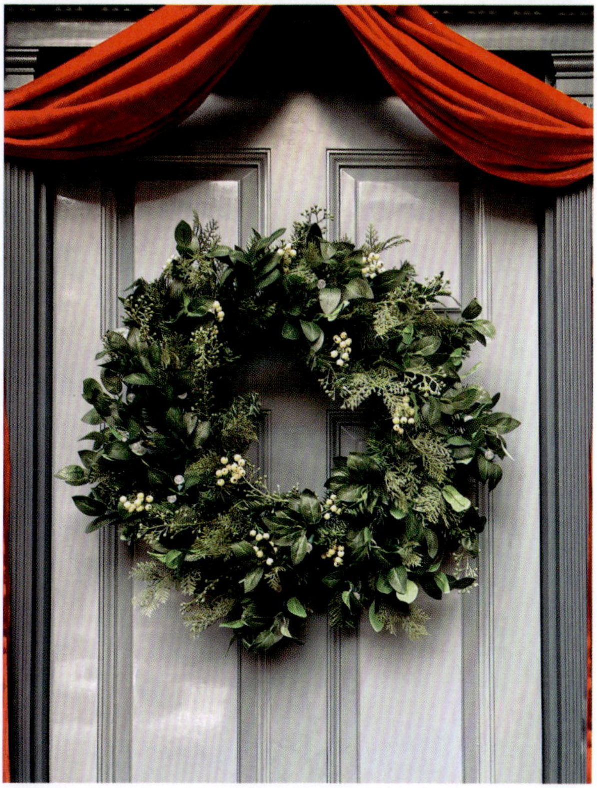

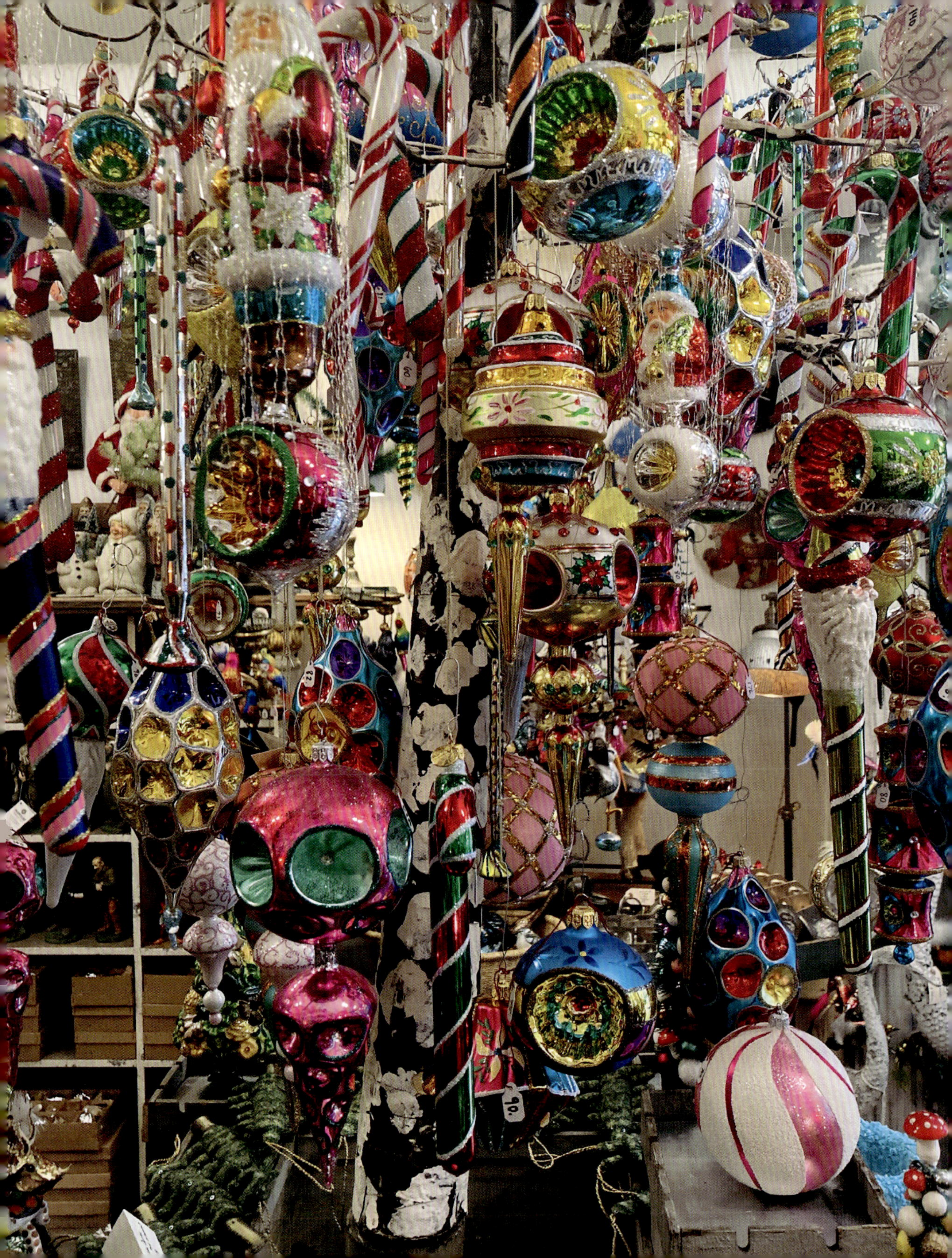

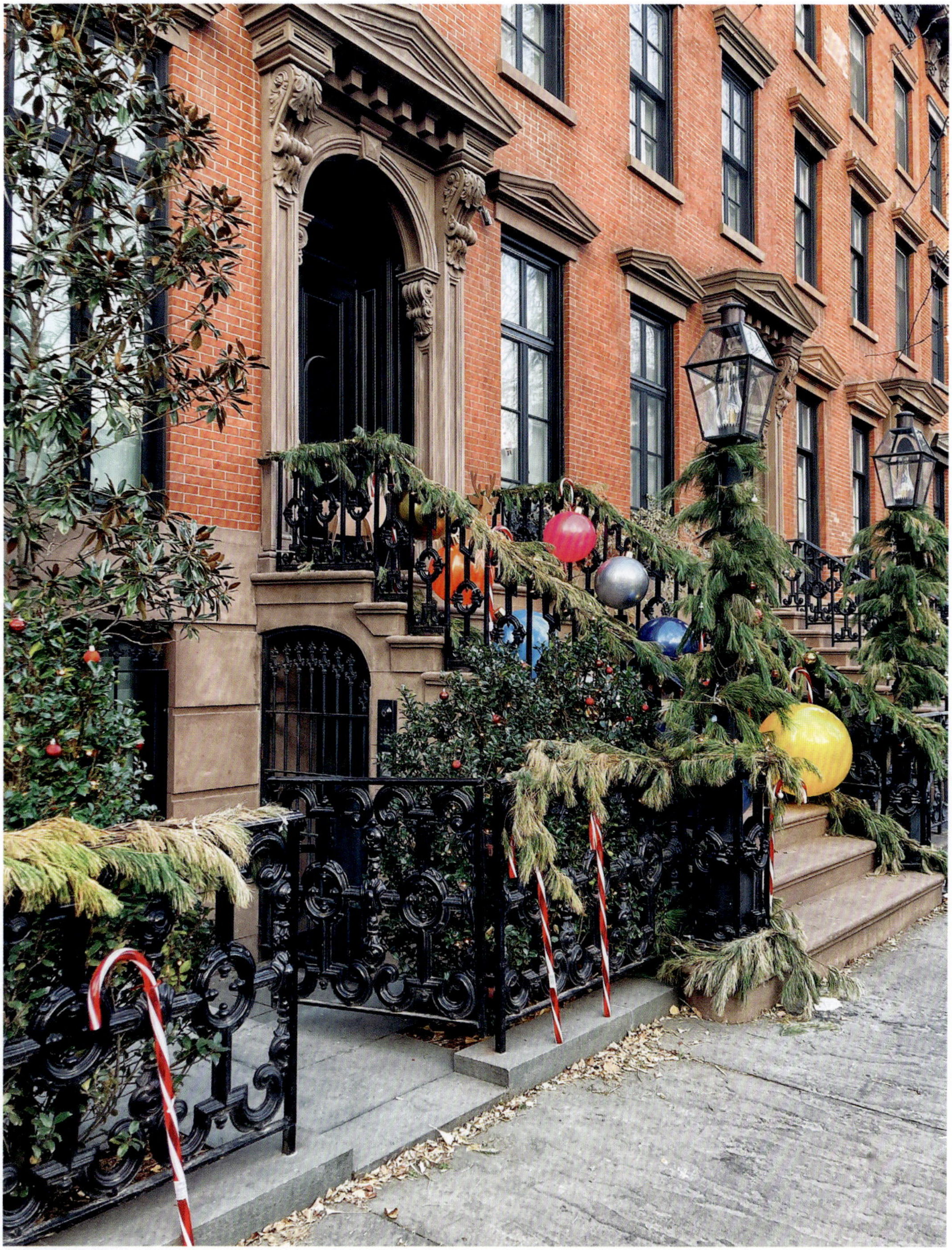

OPPOSITE: A fabulous assortment of multicolored vintage-inspired ornaments at John Derian's Christmas shop on East 2nd Street between Bowery and Second Avenue. **ABOVE:** Colorful oversized ornaments make a townhouse's stoop on Leroy Street in the West Village a jolly sight.

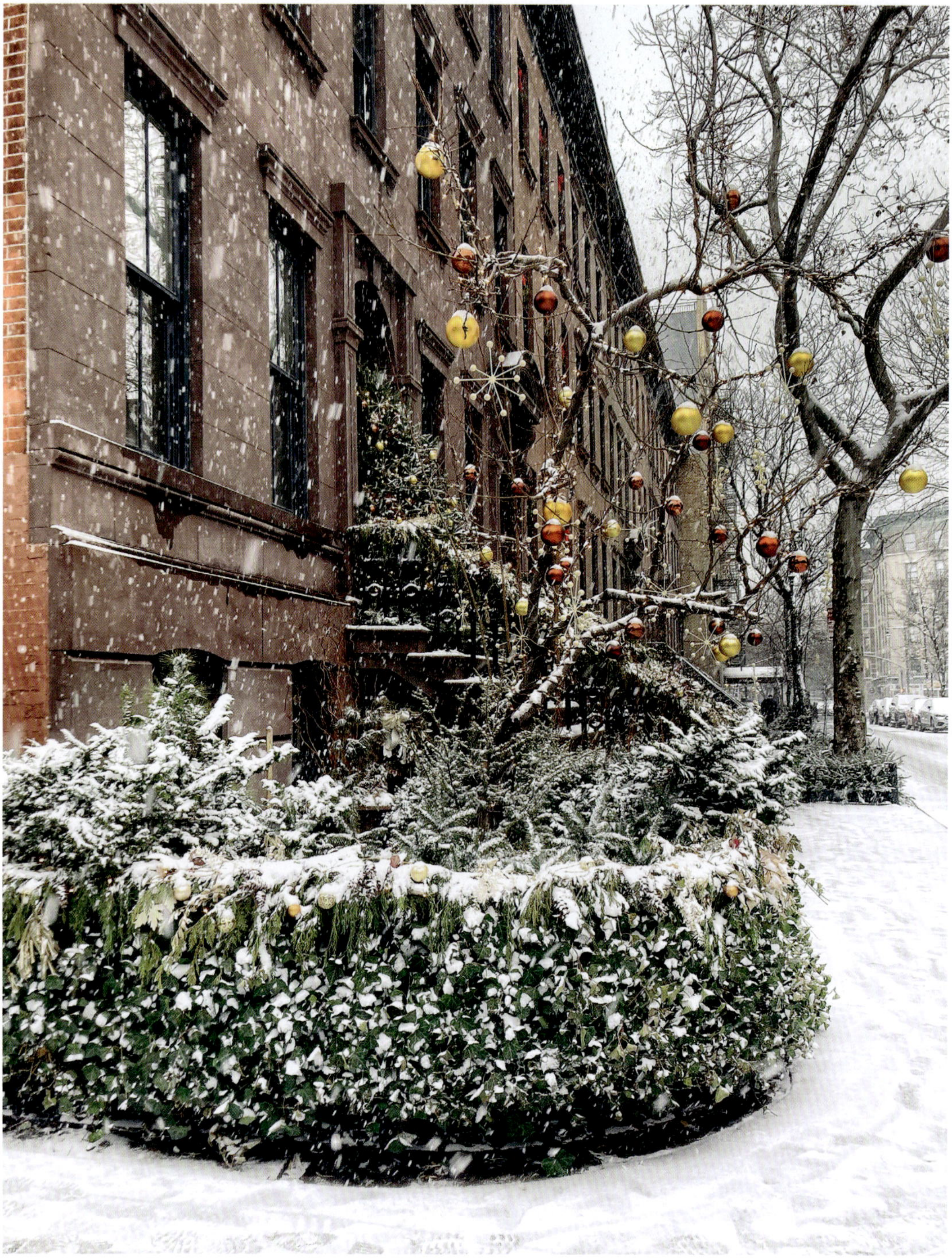

ABOVE AND OPPOSITE: The owners of this townhouse on Charles Street between West 4th Street and Seventh Avenue South always bring the holiday cheer to the block with their signature Christmas tree in the doorway. (They have a separate entrance.) They never repeat their decorations, so every holiday season there's something new and wonderful to see.

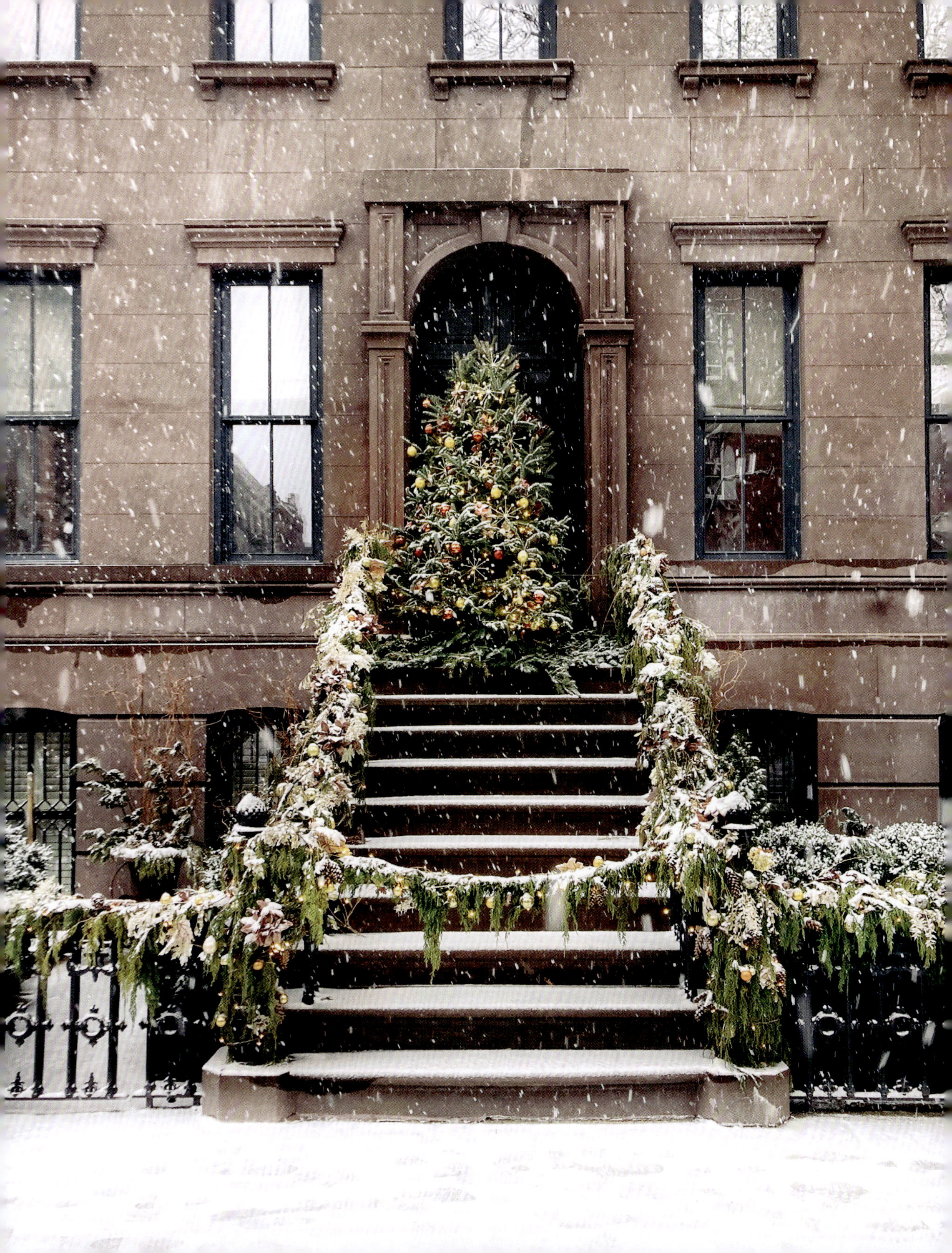

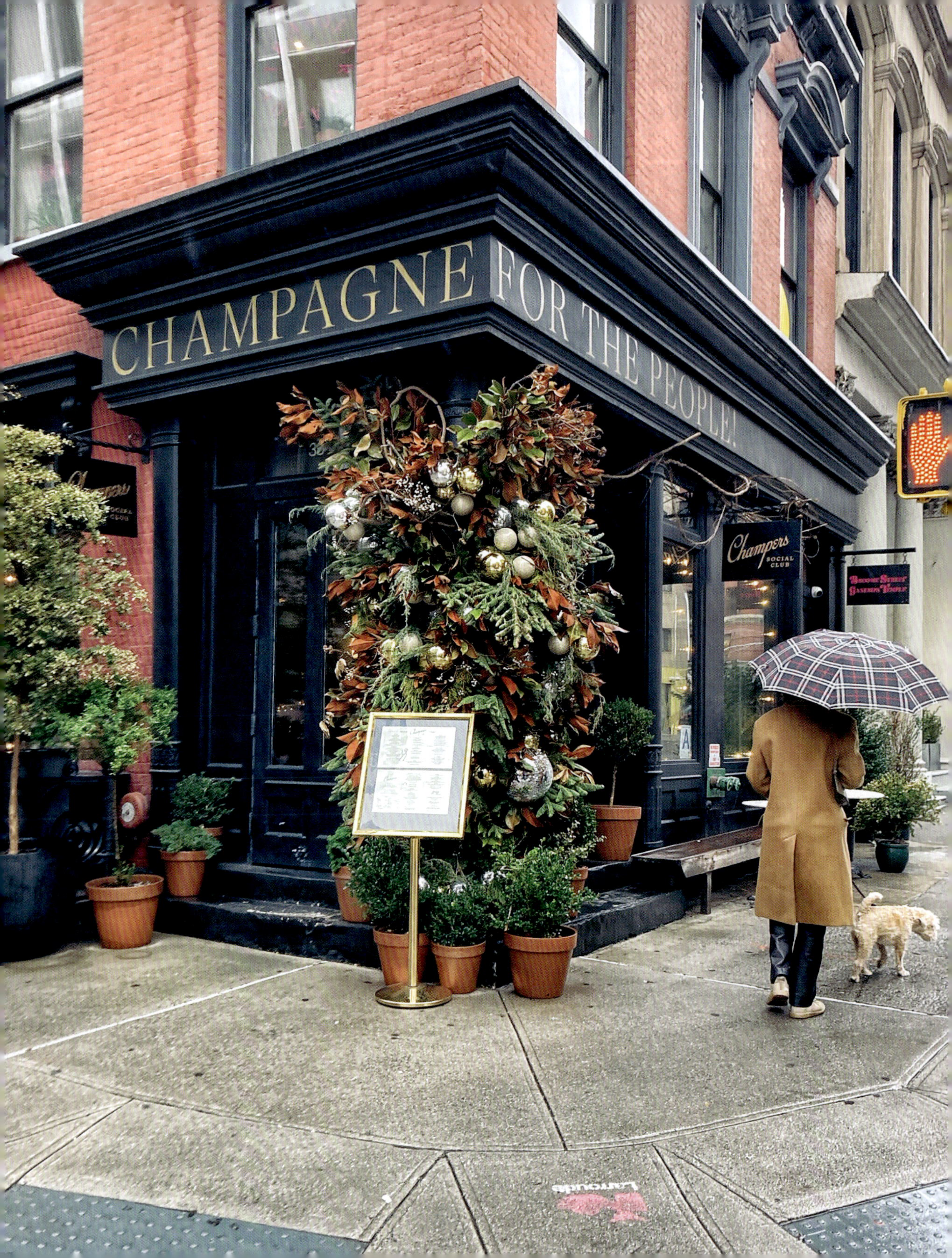
CHAMPAGNE FOR THE PEOPLE!
Champers
SOCIAL CLUB

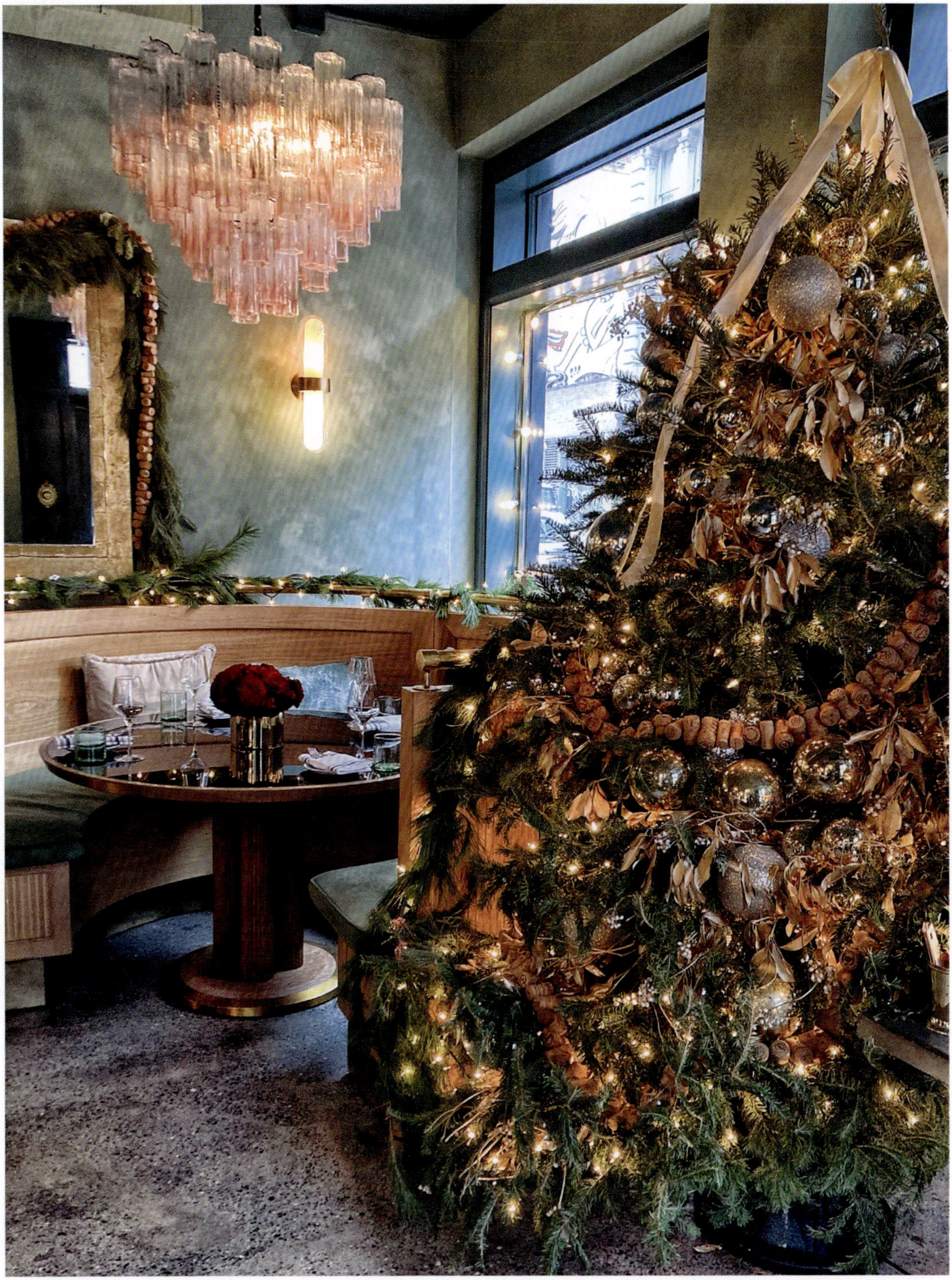

OPPOSITE AND ABOVE: Champers Social Club, a champagne bar and café on Crosby Street in SoHo, is decorated with magnolia blossoms and silver baubles on the outside. Inside, a rustic Christmas tree festooned with champagne corks sets a festive tone.

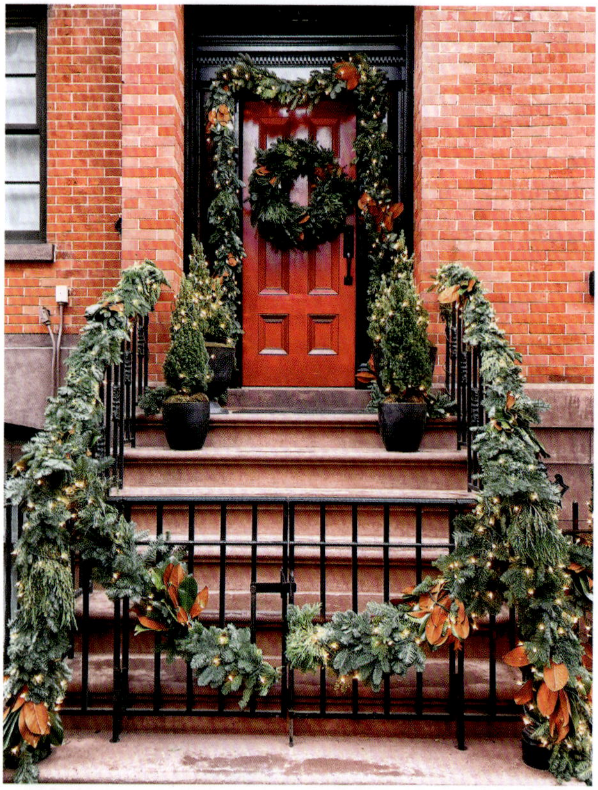

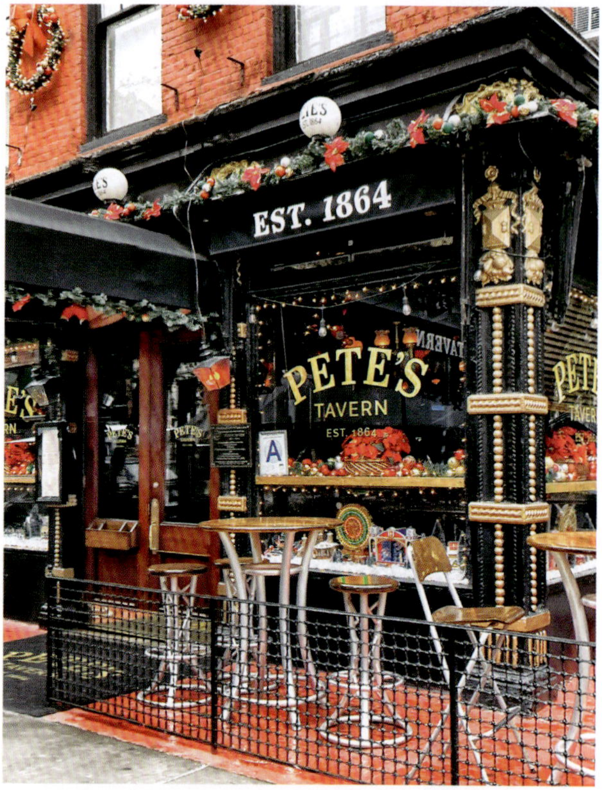
EST. 1864
PETE'S
TAVERN
EST. 1864

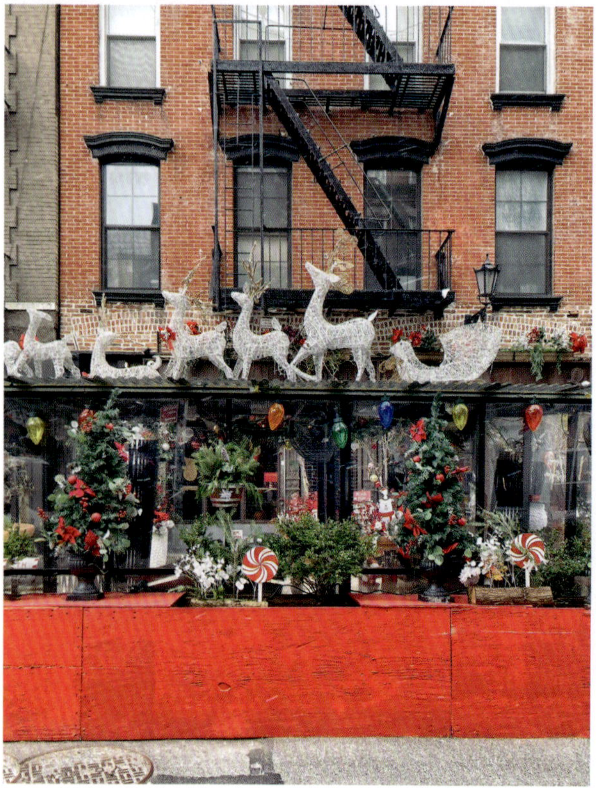

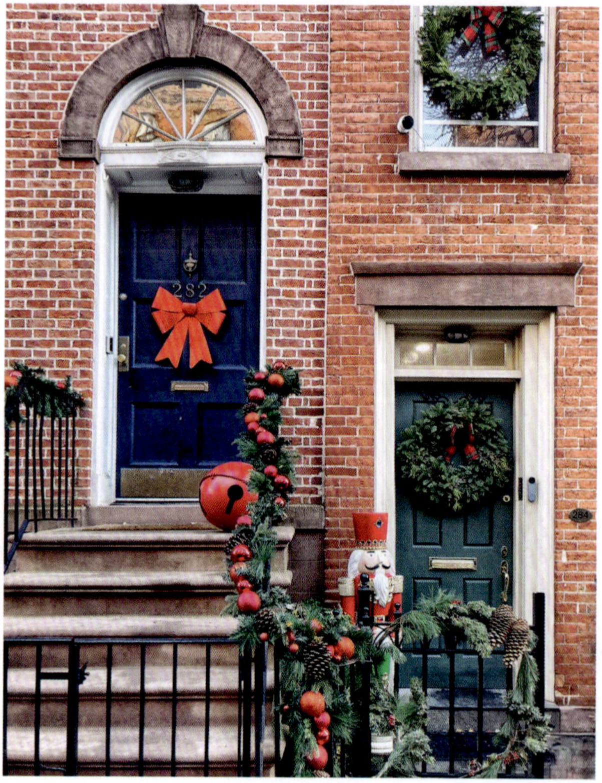
282

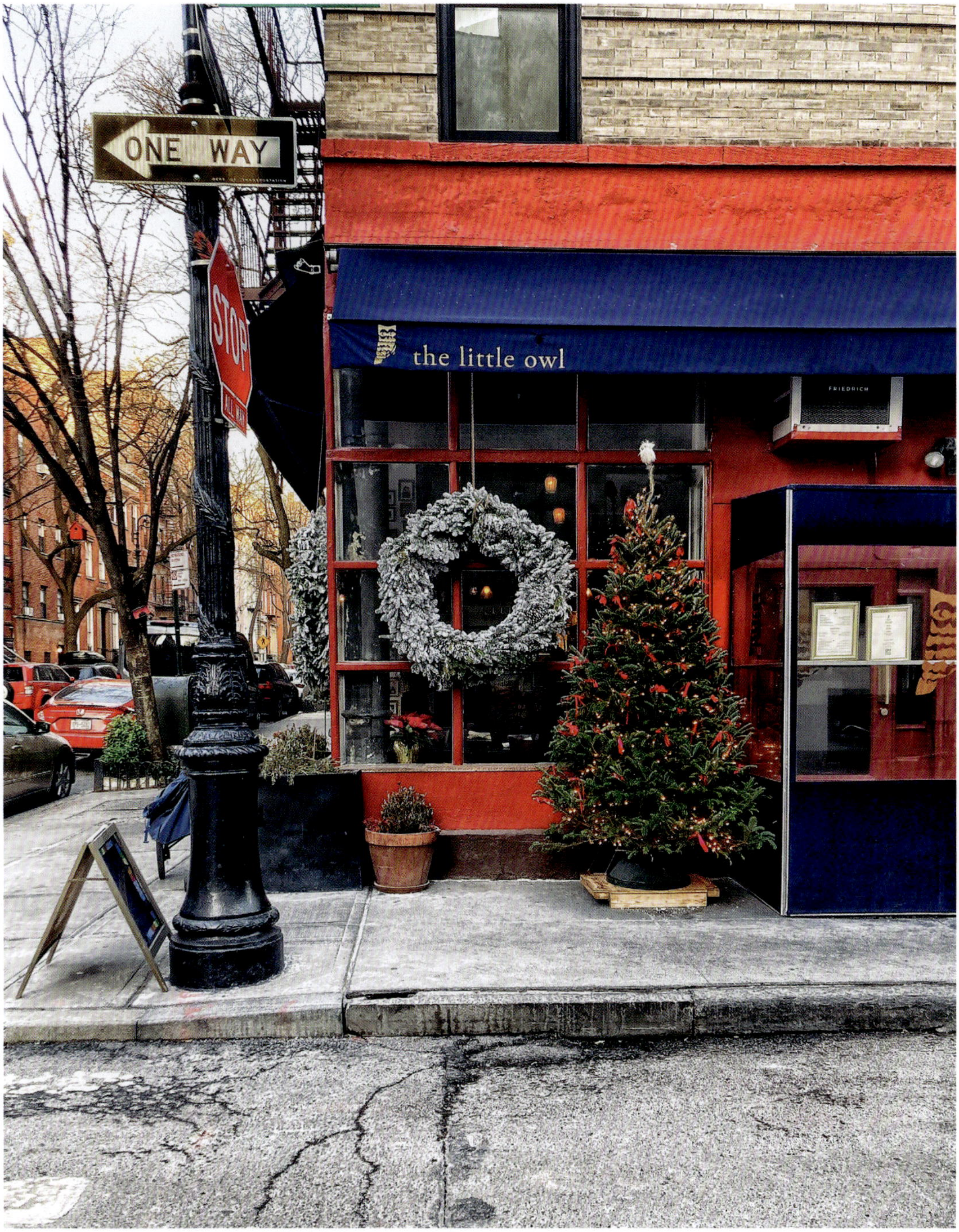

OPPOSITE, CLOCKWISE FROM TOP LEFT: Luxurious garlands frame a red door on West 10th Street; historic Pete's Tavern on Irving Place and East 18th Street is a perennial holiday favorite; two festive West Village doors on West 11th Street; prancing reindeer at the Loreley Beer Garden on Rivington Street on the Lower East Side. **ABOVE:** The Little Owl restaurant on the corner of the famous *Friends* apartment building on Bedford and Grove Streets is a popular West Village spot.

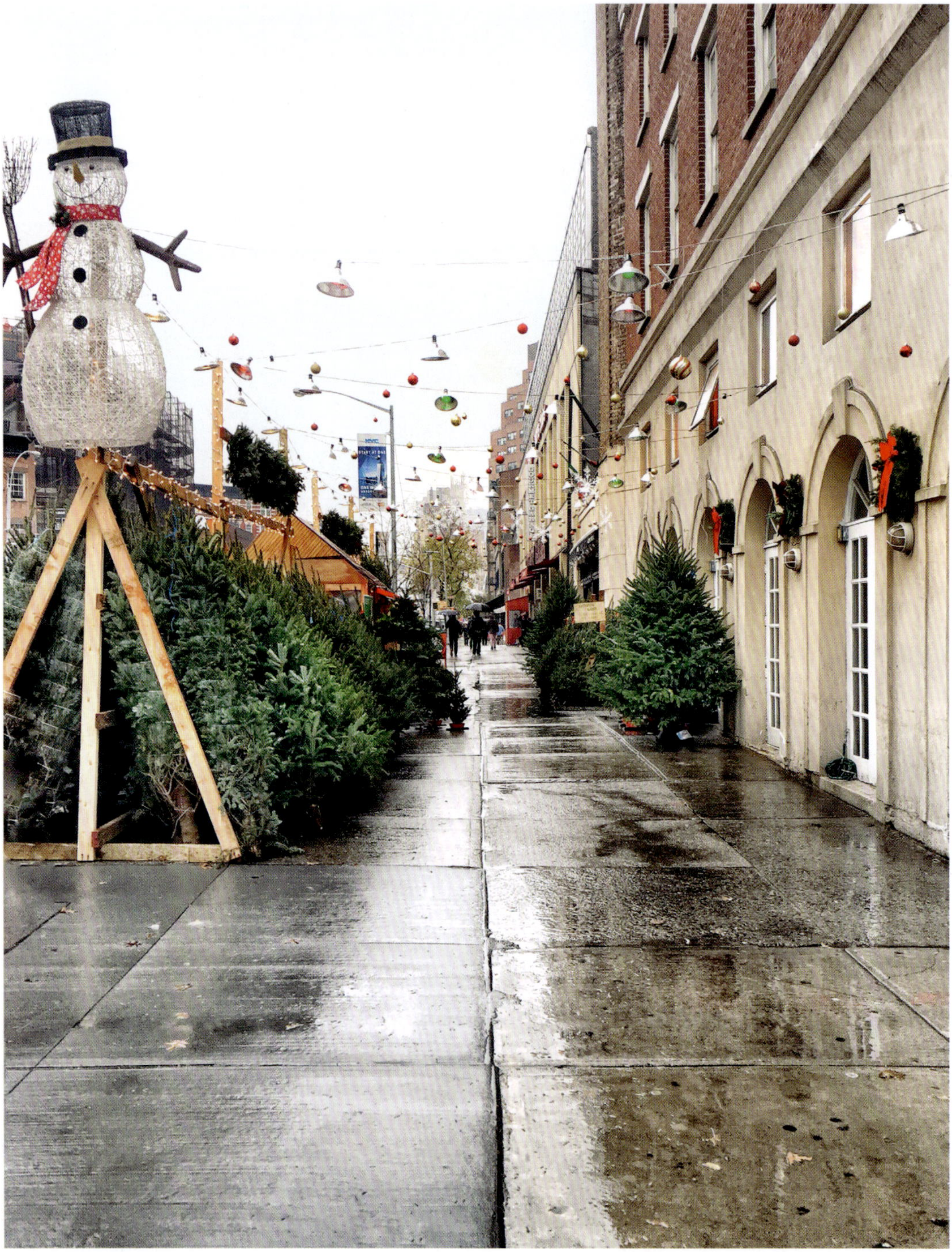

ABOVE: Christmas trees for sale along Seventh Avenue South in the West Village. A snowman and colorful lights and snowflakes strung above the sidewalk add a touch of festive fun on a rainy day. **OPPOSITE:** A classic little Christmas tree sits at the end of historic Patchin Place in Greenwich Village.

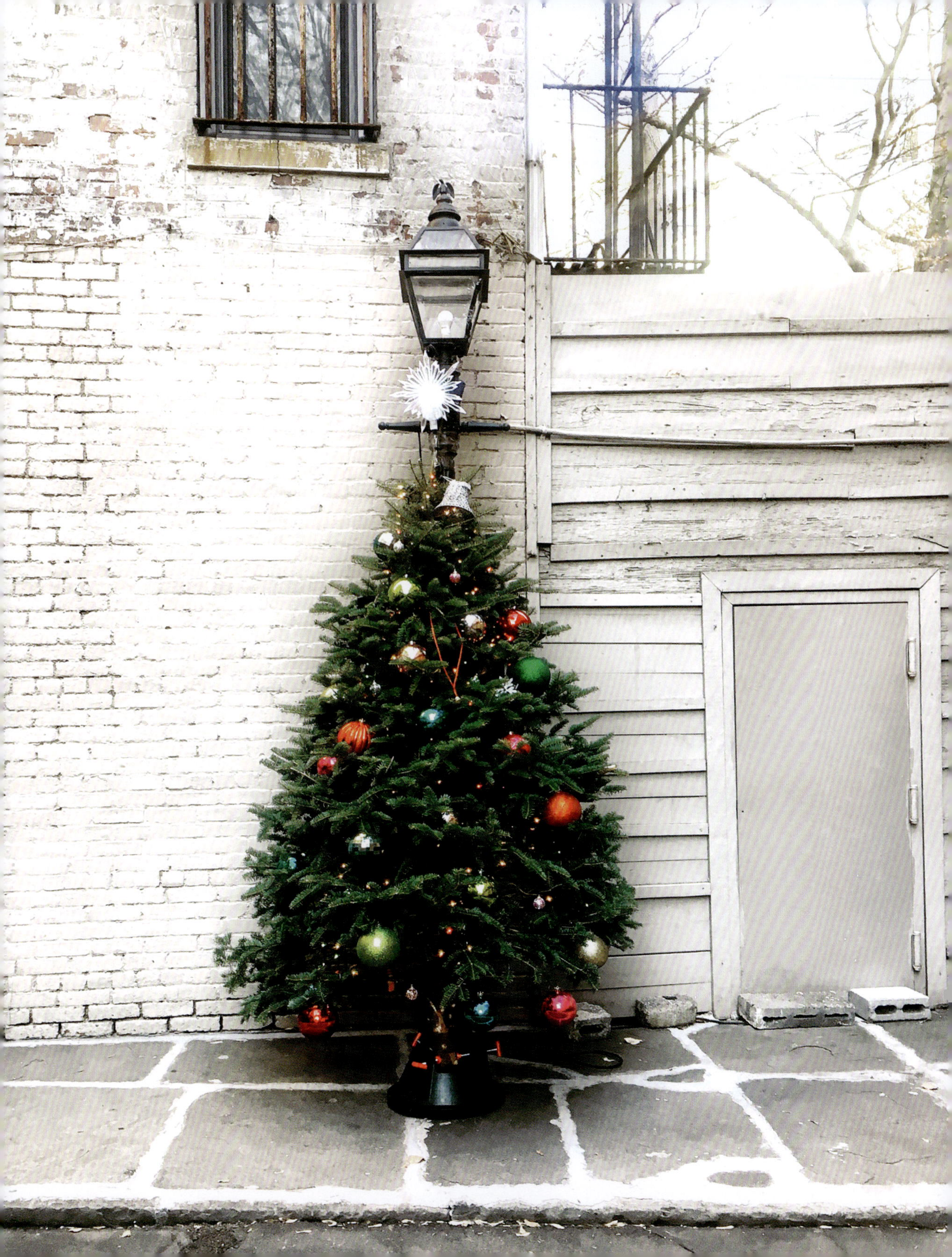

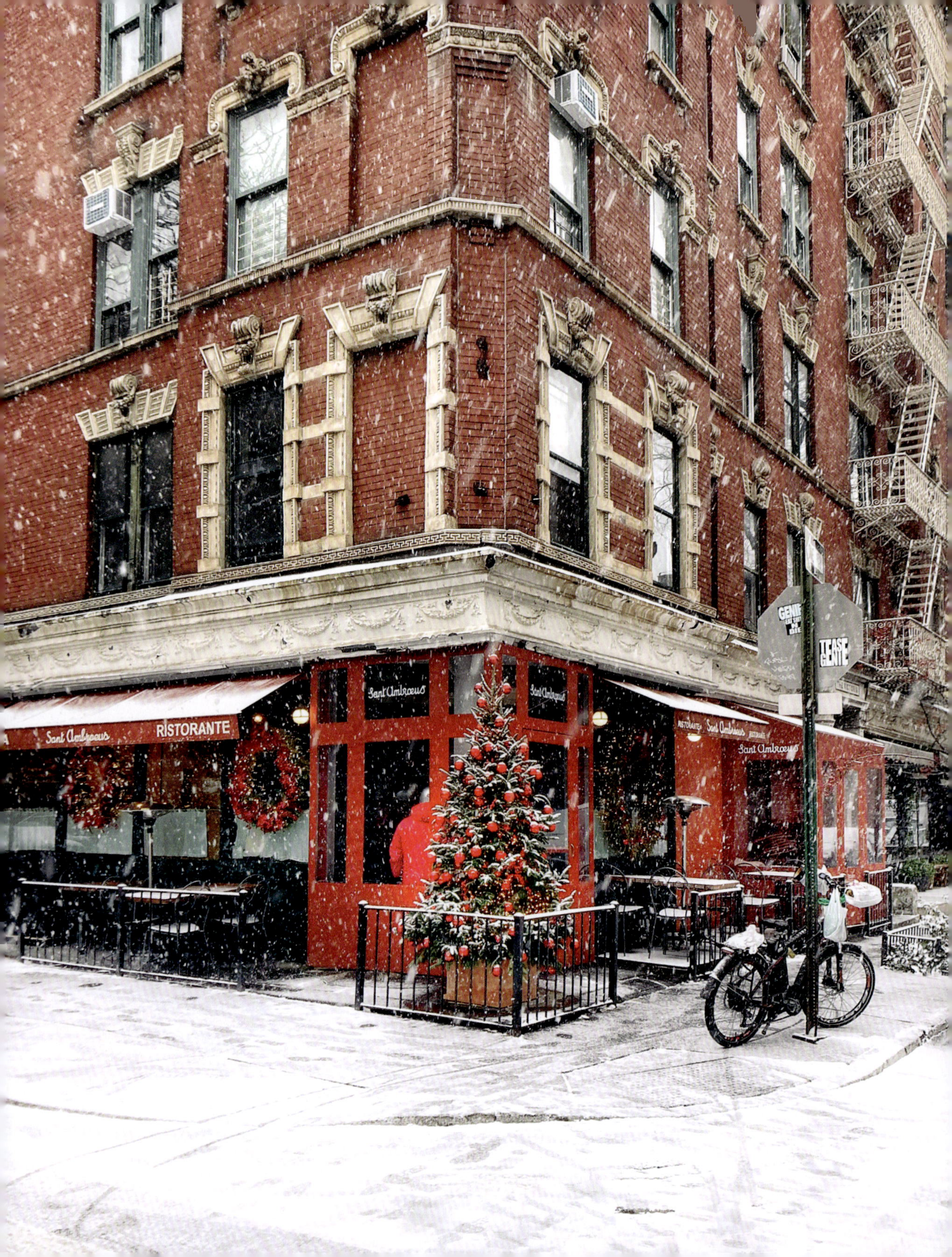
Sant Ambroeus
RISTORANTE
Sant Ambroeus
Sant Ambroeus
RISTORANTE
Sant Ambroeus
Sant Ambroeus

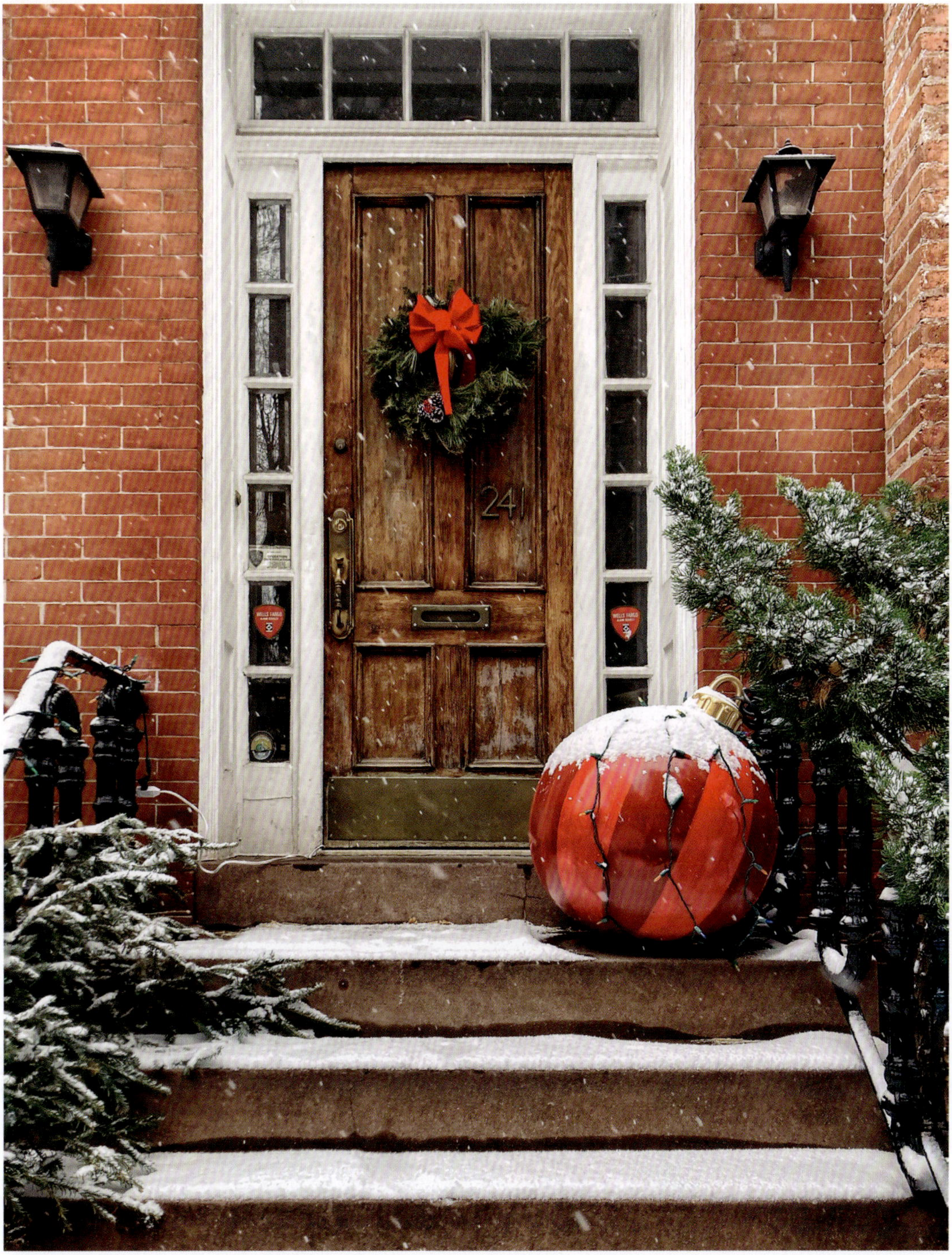

OPPOSITE: Fashionable Italian restaurant Sant Ambroeus brightens the corner of Perry and West 4th Streets with its charming Christmas tree and wreaths. **ABOVE:** A cute red ornament covered with a dusting of snow adds a touch of winter whimsy to this Waverly Place home in the West Village.

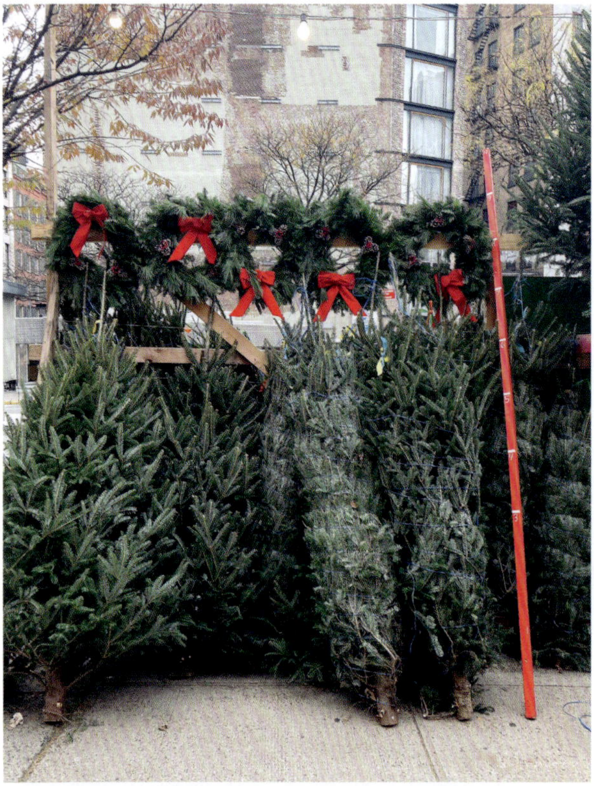

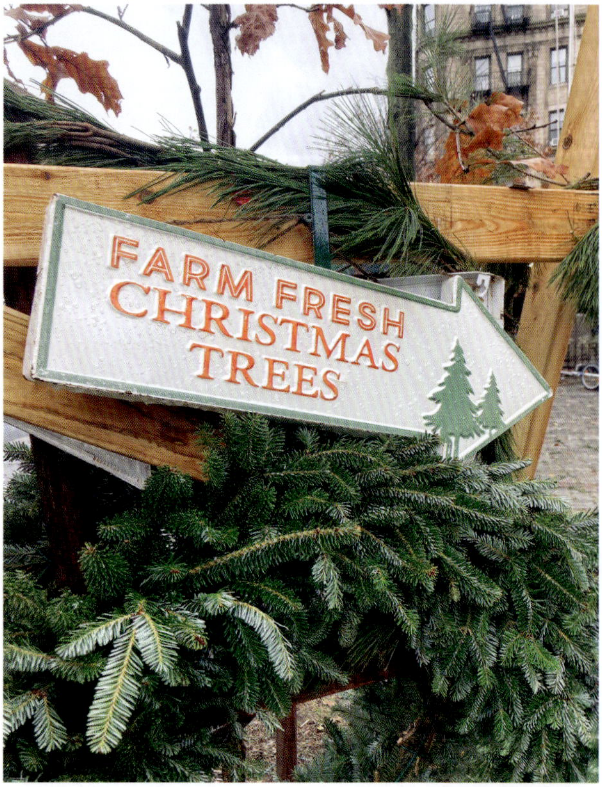
FARM FRESH
CHRISTMAS
TREES

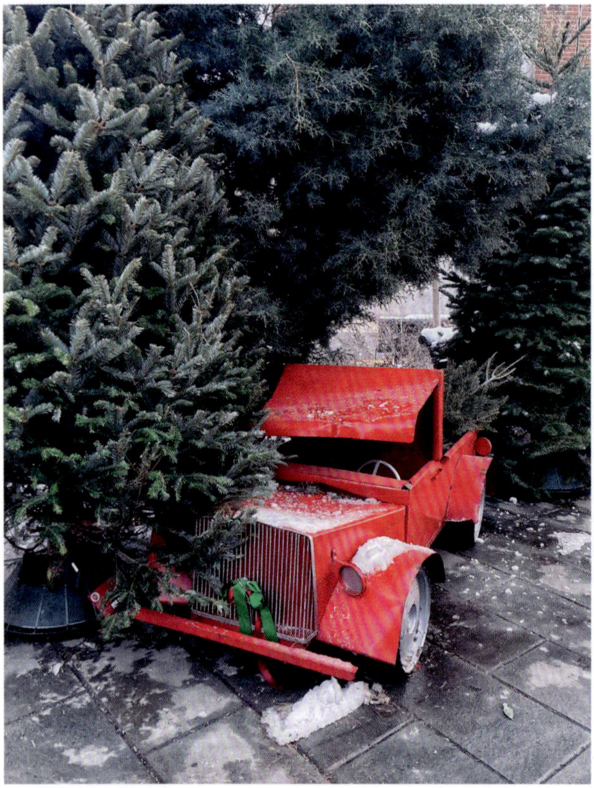

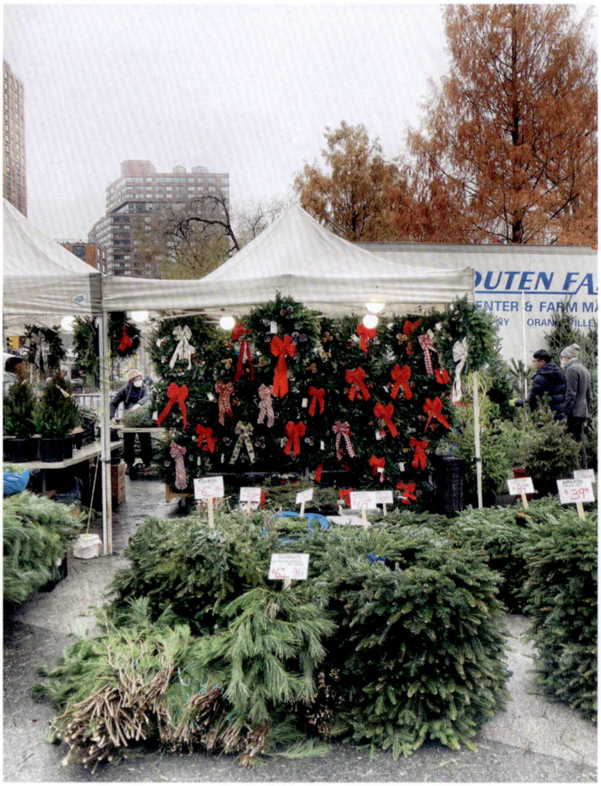

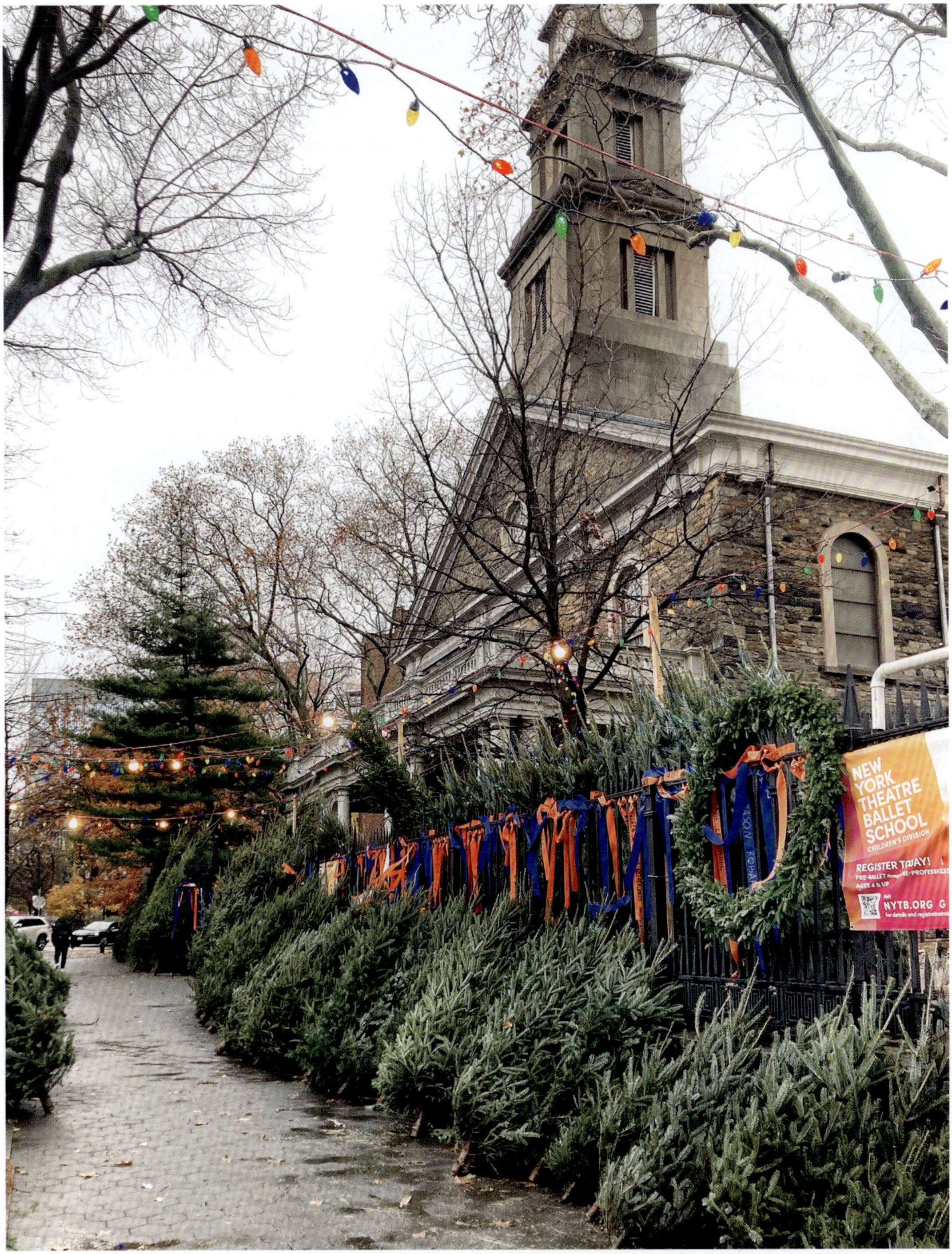

OPPOSITE, CLOCKWISE FROM TOP LEFT: Trees and wreaths for sale: on West Broadway in Tribeca; a sign pointing to St. Mark's trees in the East Village; at the Union Square Greenmarket; a cute red truck in the West Village. **ABOVE:** The St. Mark's Church in-the-Bowery's annual Christmas tree sale supports local charities. Fresh-cut trees line the sidewalk along Second Avenue between Ninth and Tenth Streets.

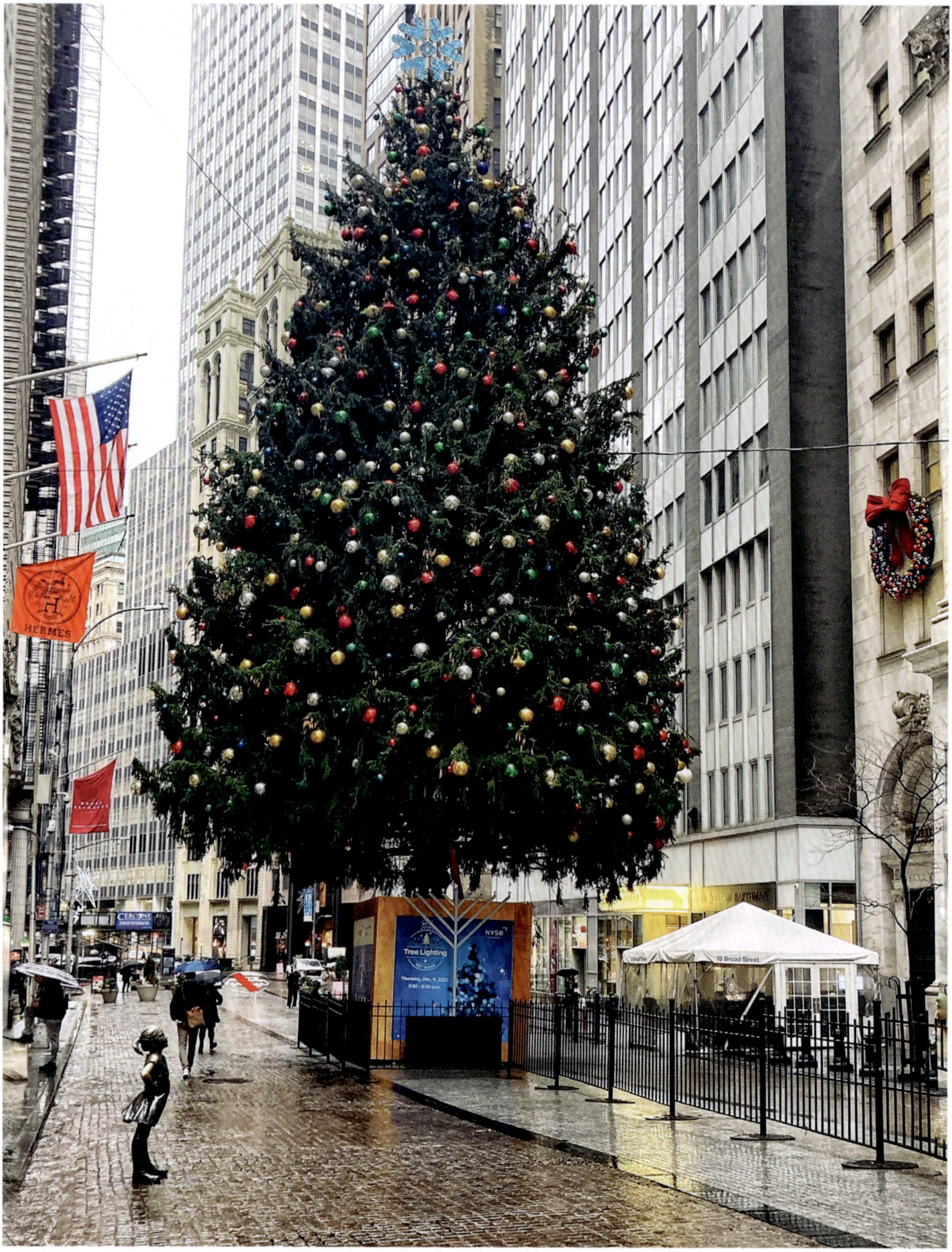

ABOVE: The New York Stock Exchange's stunning seventy-five-foot-tall Christmas tree on Wall and Broad Streets is Downtown's answer to Midtown's Rockefeller Center tree. It's been a Wall Street tradition since 1923. The *Fearless Girl* bronze statue by Kristen Visbal was added in 2017. **OPPOSITE:** The view of historic Trinity Church on Broadway from Wall Street's glistening rain-soaked cobblestones

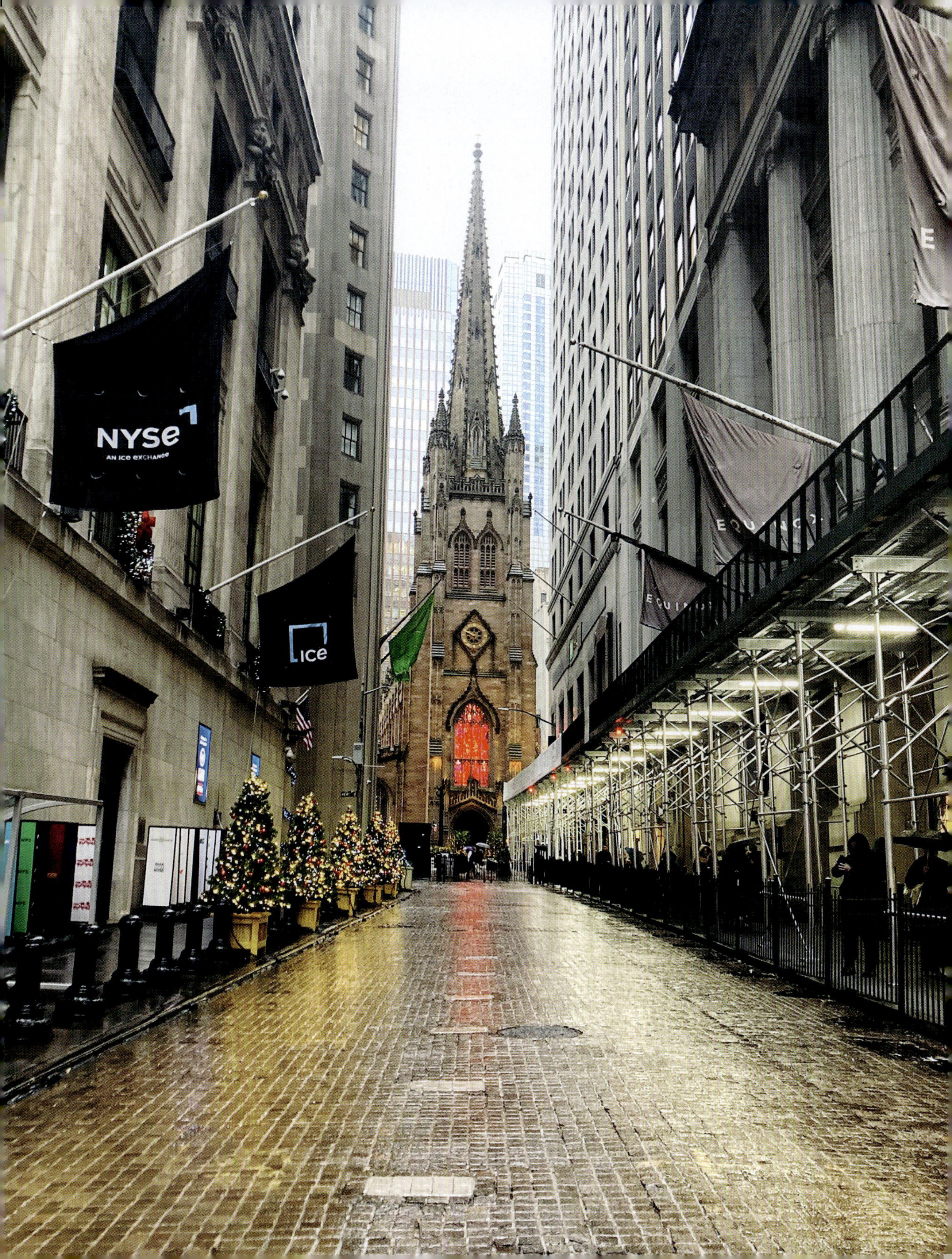
NYSE
AN ICE EXCHANGE
ICE

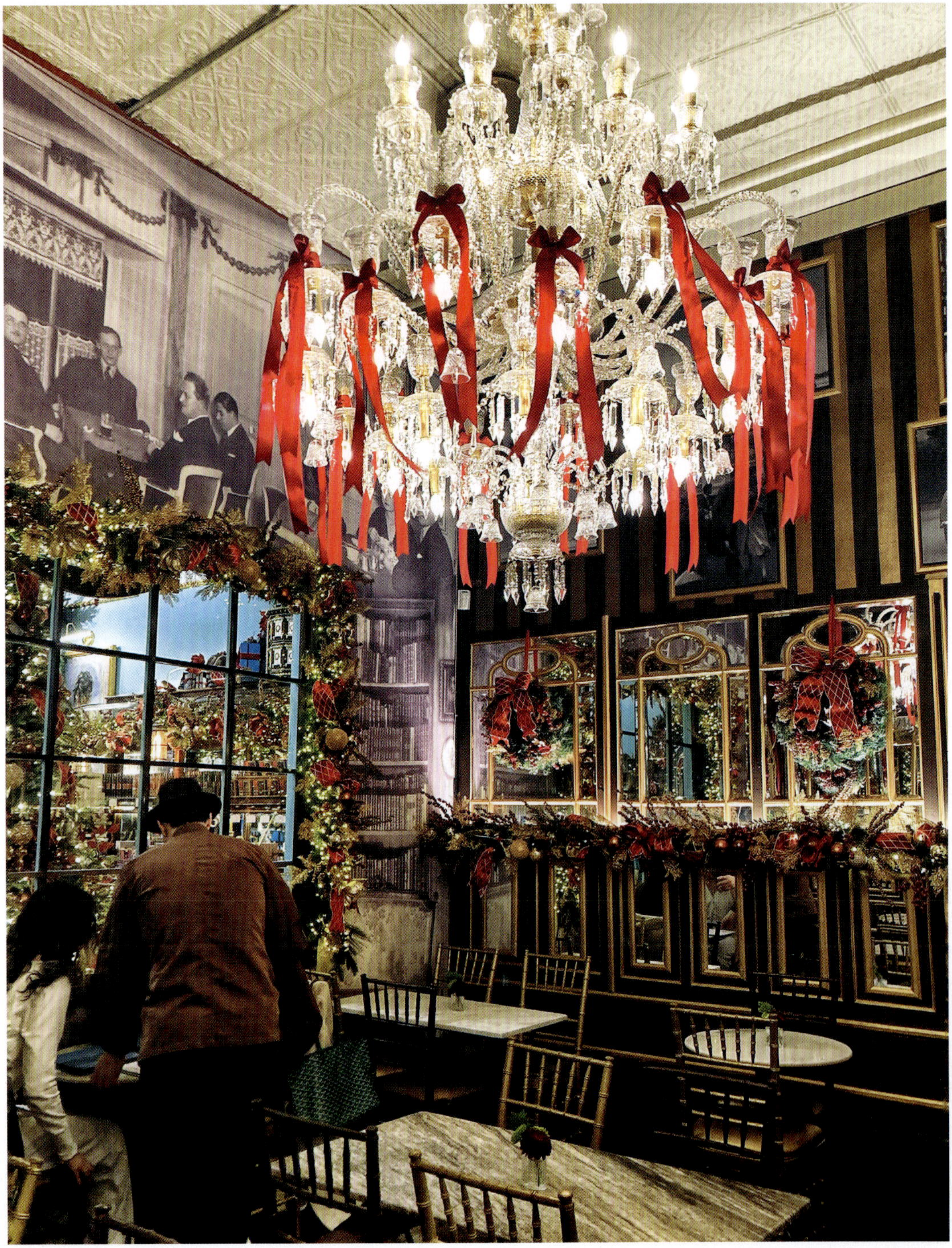

ABOVE: Red satin ribbons adorn an opulent chandelier in chocolatier MarieBelle's cozy cacao bar on Broome Street in SoHo. **OPPOSITE, CLOCKWISE FROM TOP LEFT:** French bistro Pastis on Gansevoort Street; the original Christmas-themed NYC restaurant, legendary Rolf's German Restaurant on Third Avenue, is decorated with thousands of ornaments; Balthazar's charming French bakery on Spring Street; a warm and inviting holiday glow at Balthazar, a classic French bistro on Spring Street in SoHo

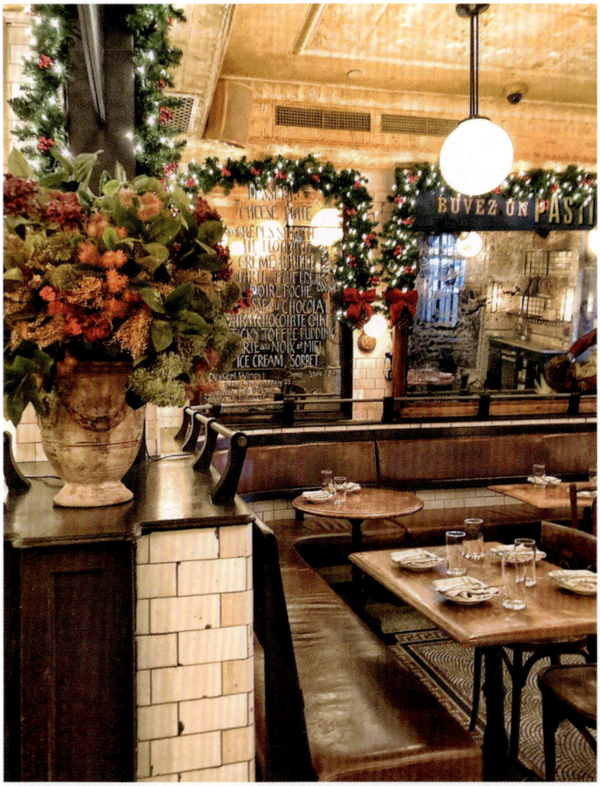
CHEESE PLATE
POIRE POCHE
ICE CREAM, SORBET

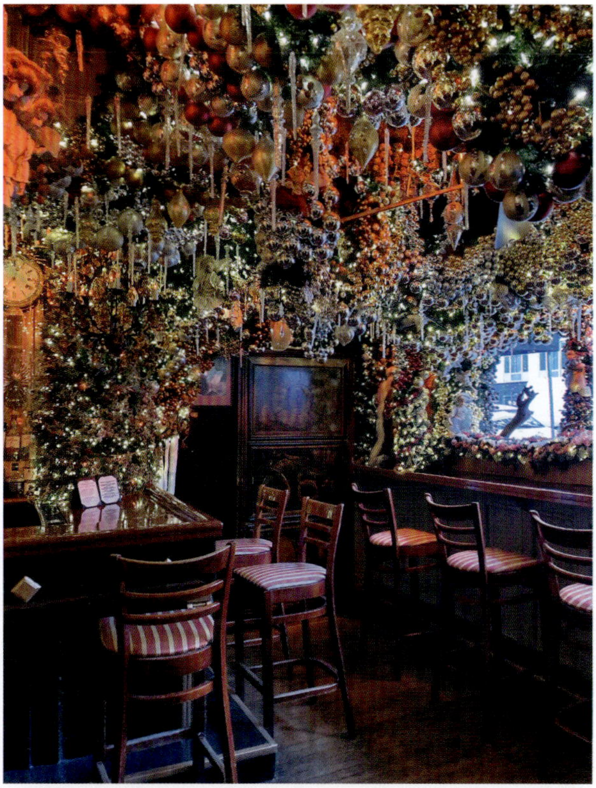

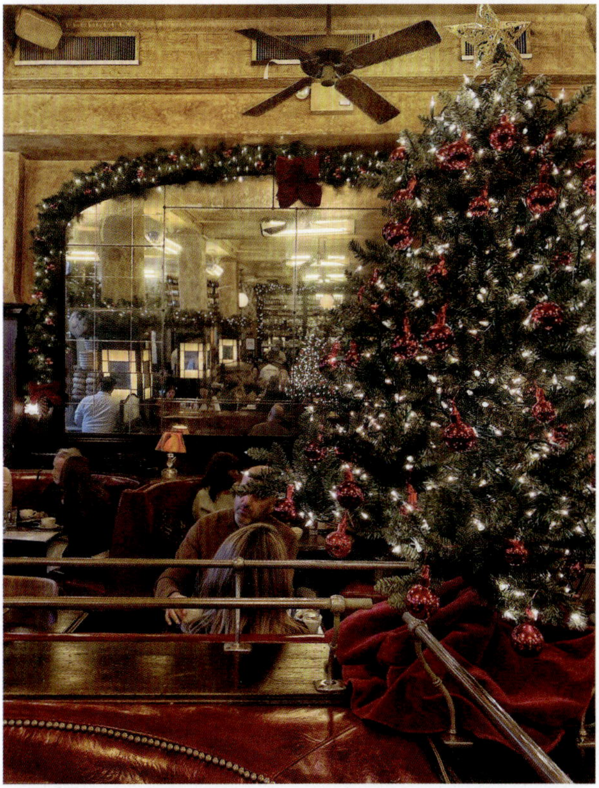

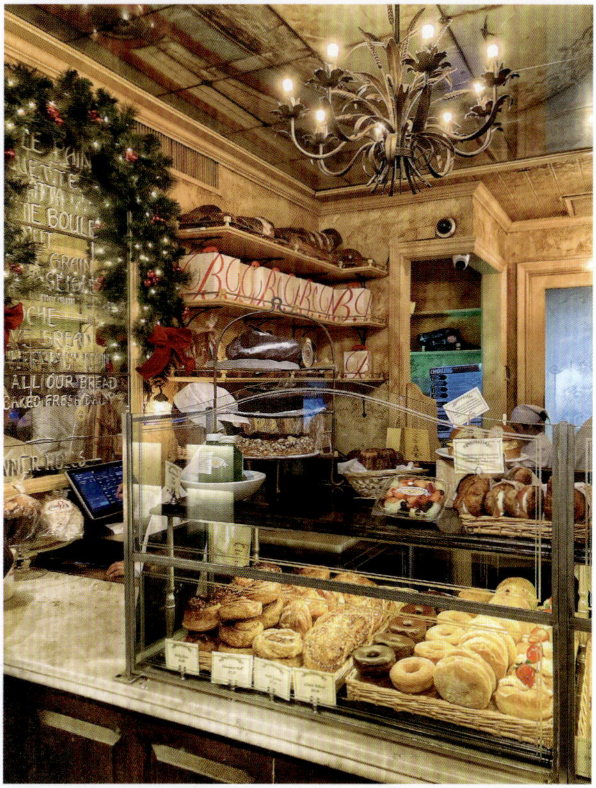
ALL OUR BREAD

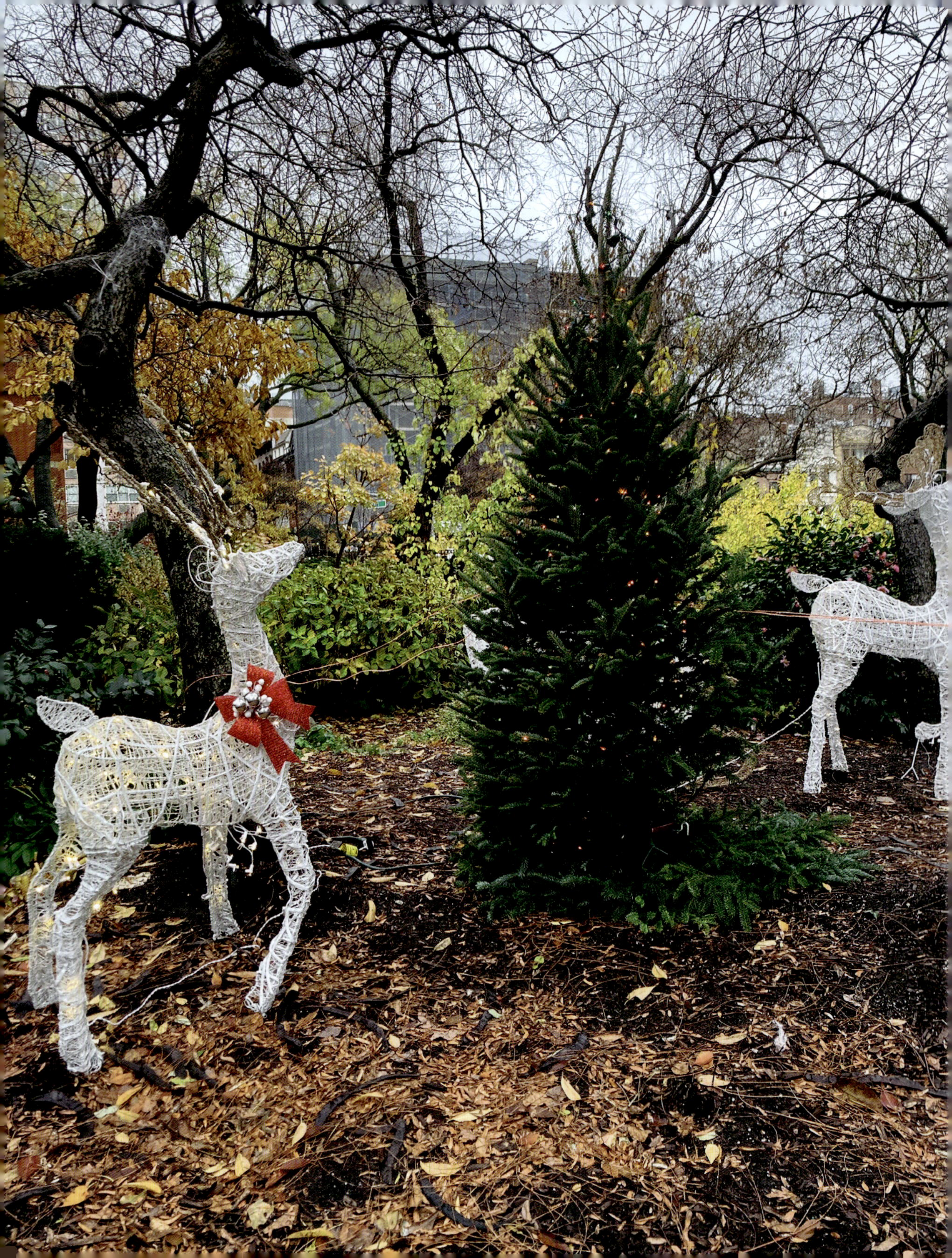

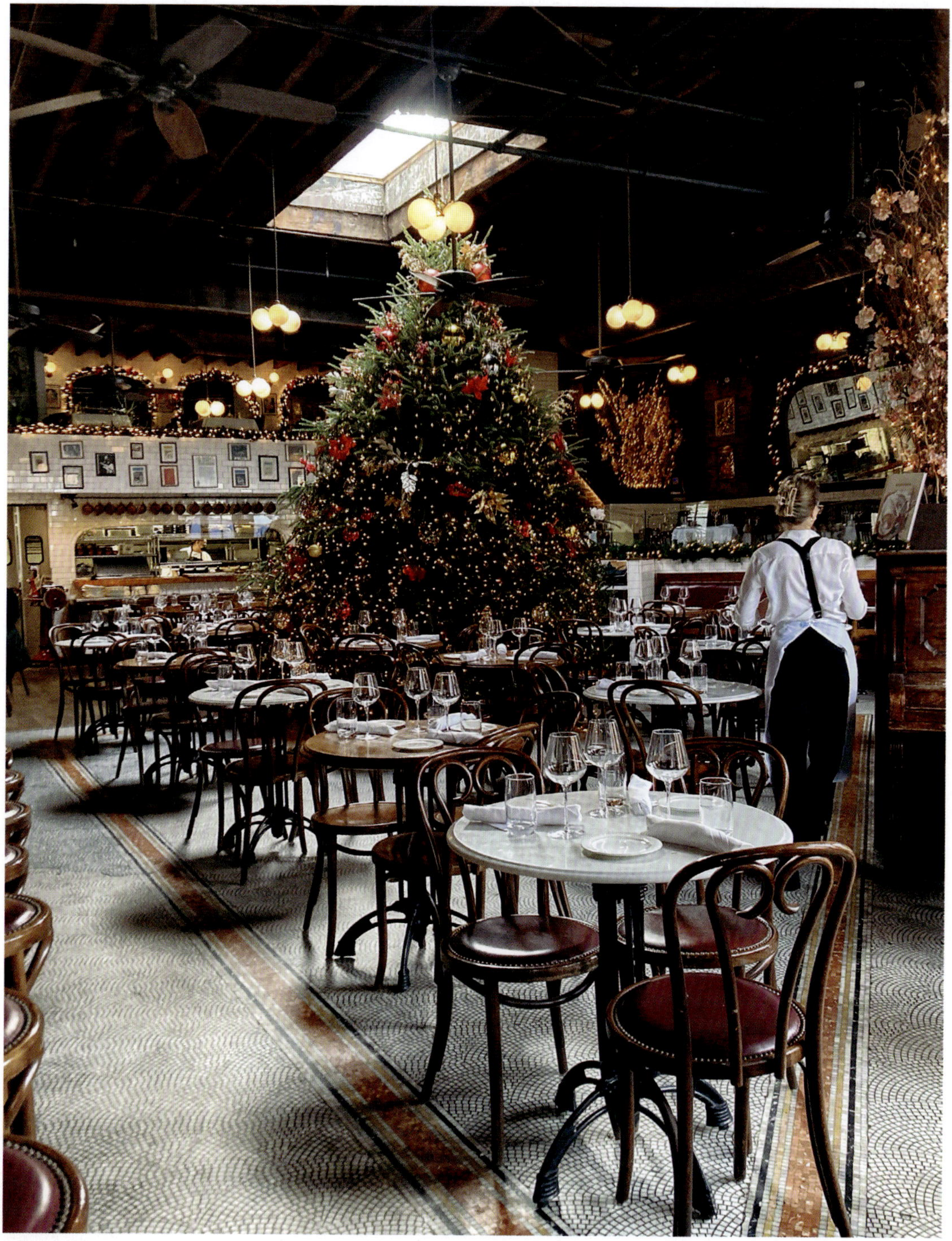

OPPOSITE: Reindeer frolic among the trees and bushes in the Jefferson Market Garden in Greenwich Village.
ABOVE: A picture-perfect Christmas tree sits in the middle of French bistro Boucherie on Seventh Avenue South in the West Village.

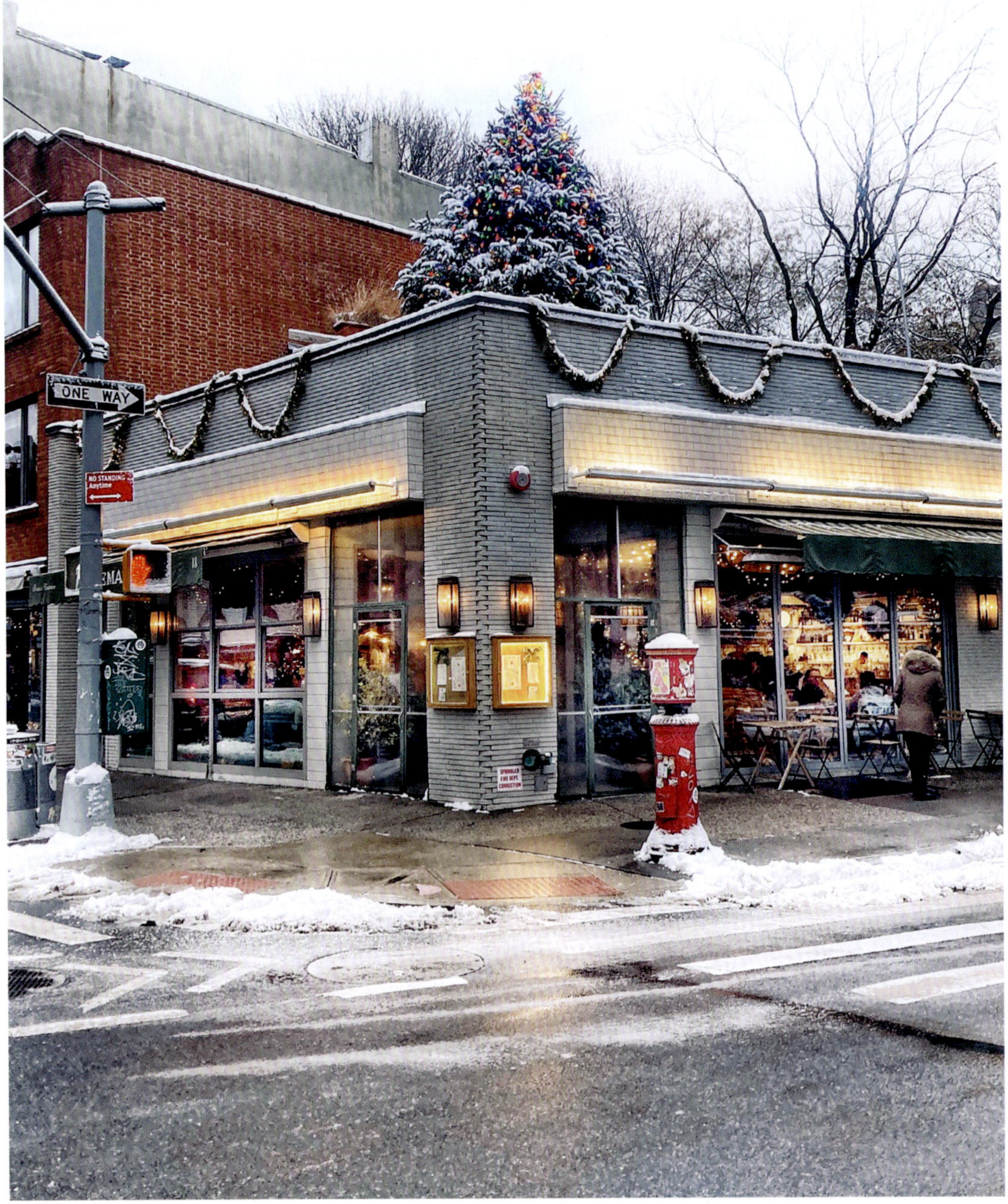

ABOVE: The lighting of the Christmas tree perched atop Italian restaurant Rosemary's on the corner of Greenwich Avenue and West 10th Street has become a West Village holiday tradition. **OPPOSITE:** Snow adds even more holiday magic to the scene in the Jefferson Market Garden on Greenwich Avenue.

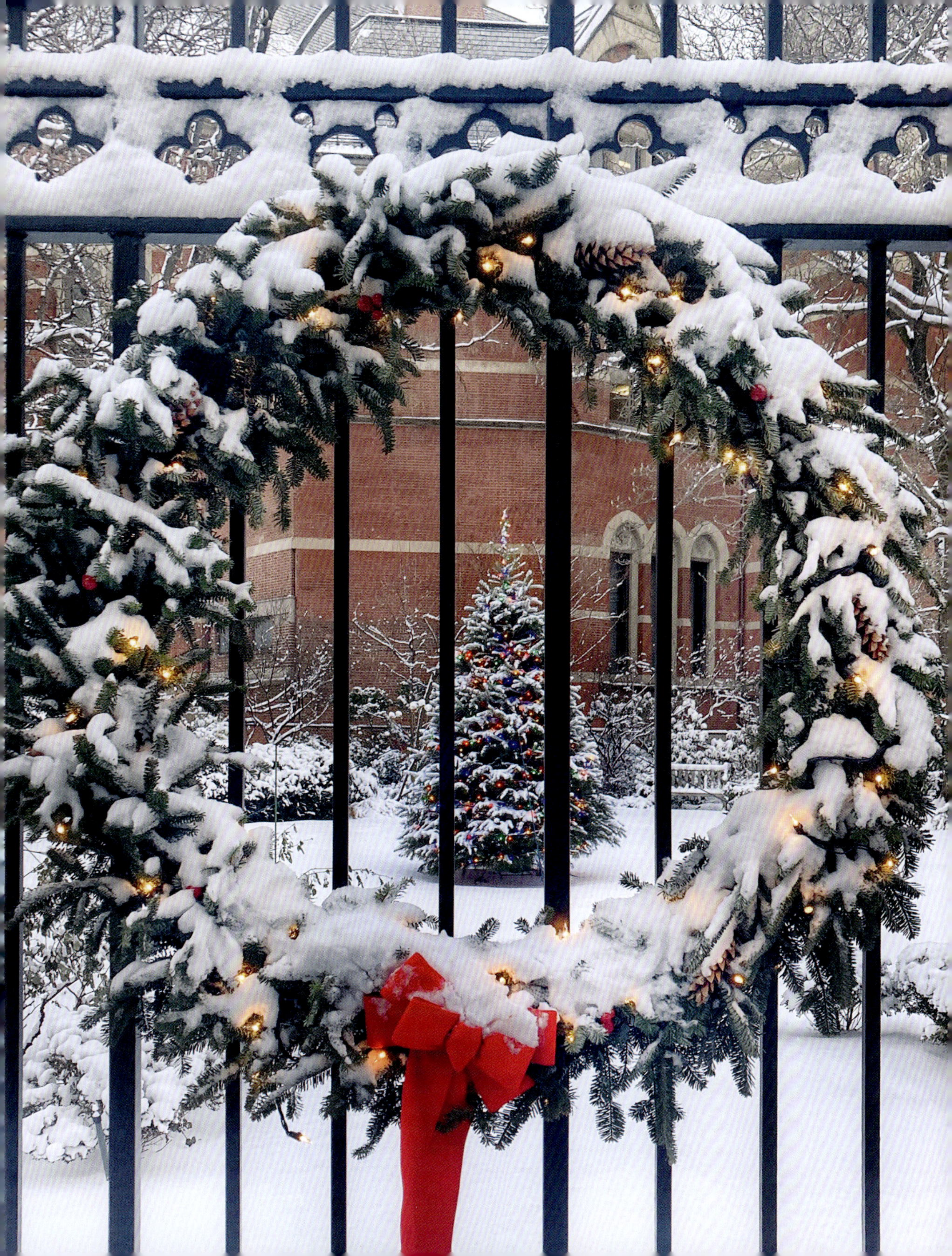

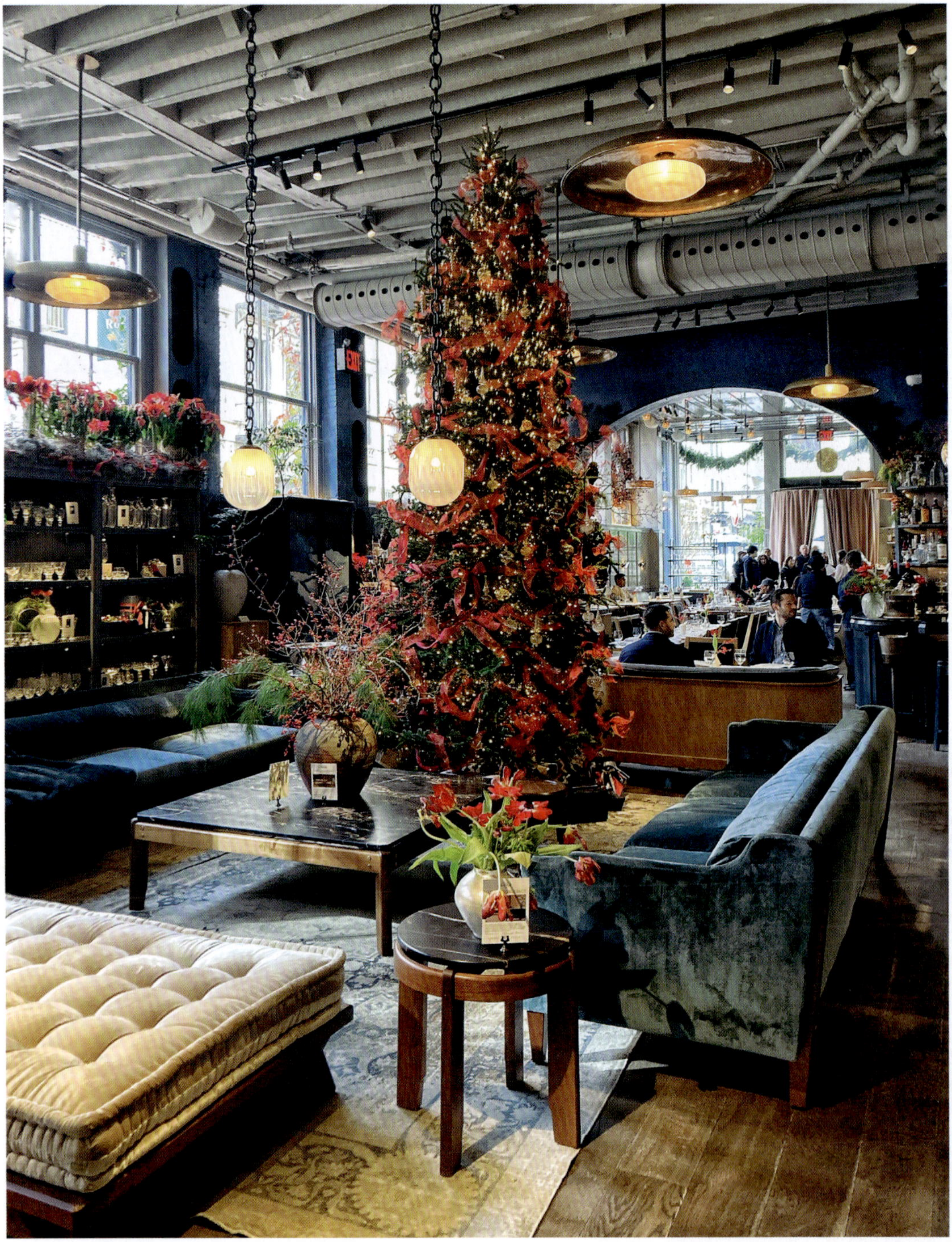

ABOVE: An elegant red-ribboned tree takes center stage at the Roman and Williams Guild shop and La Mercerie restaurant on Howard Street in SoHo. **OPPOSITE, CLOCKWISE FROM TOP LEFT:** McNally Jackson bookstore on Fulton Street in the South Street Seaport; the MUD café's giant peace sign with their signature orange coffee cup on East 9th Street; an evergreen peace sign with colorful lights at the Chelsea Hotel on West 23rd Street; Lafayette Grand Café & Bakery on Lafayette Street in Noho

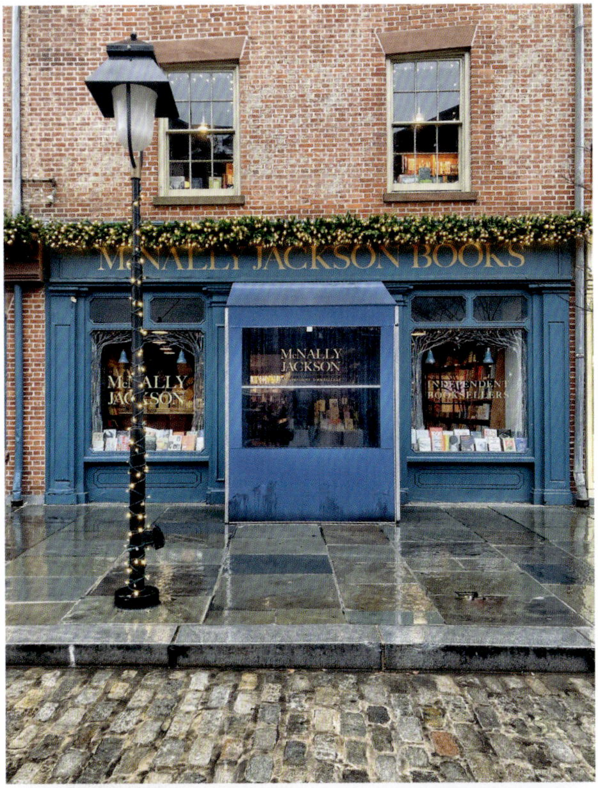
McNALLY JACKSON BOOKS
McNALLY
JACKSON
INDEPENDENT
BOOKSELLERS

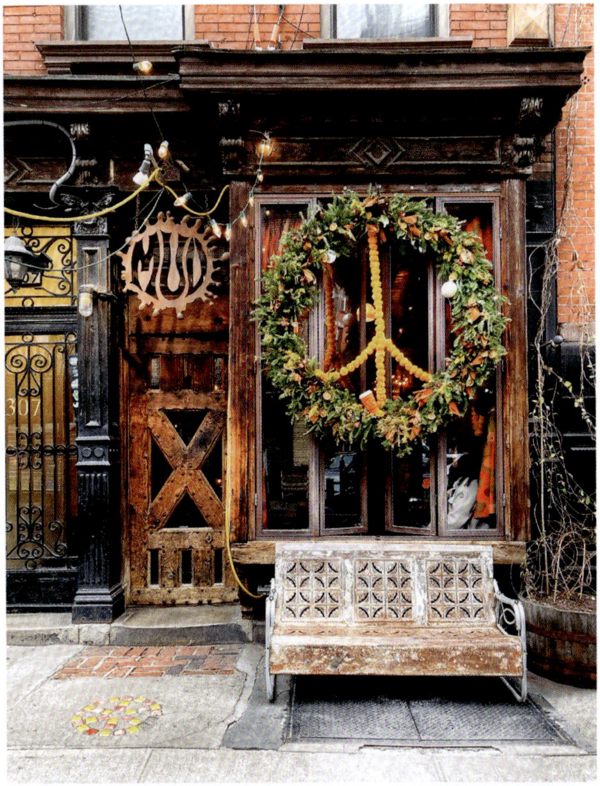

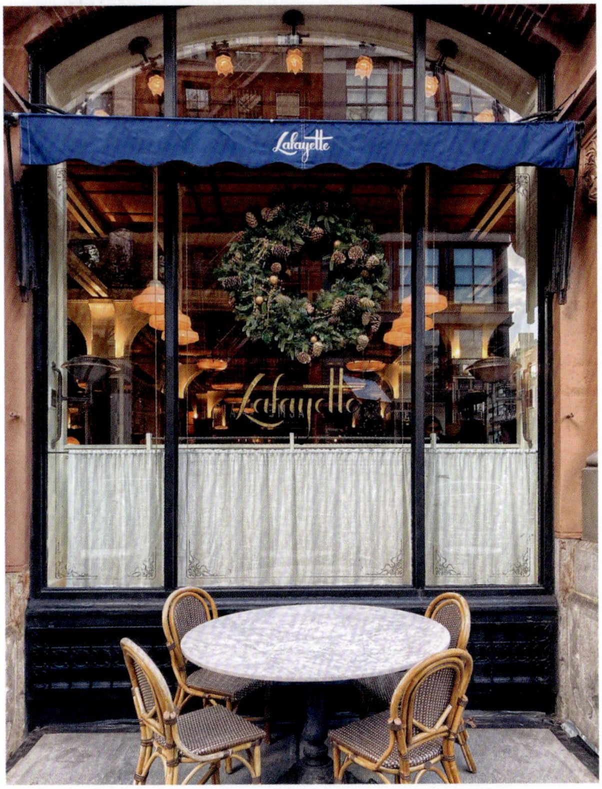
Lafayette

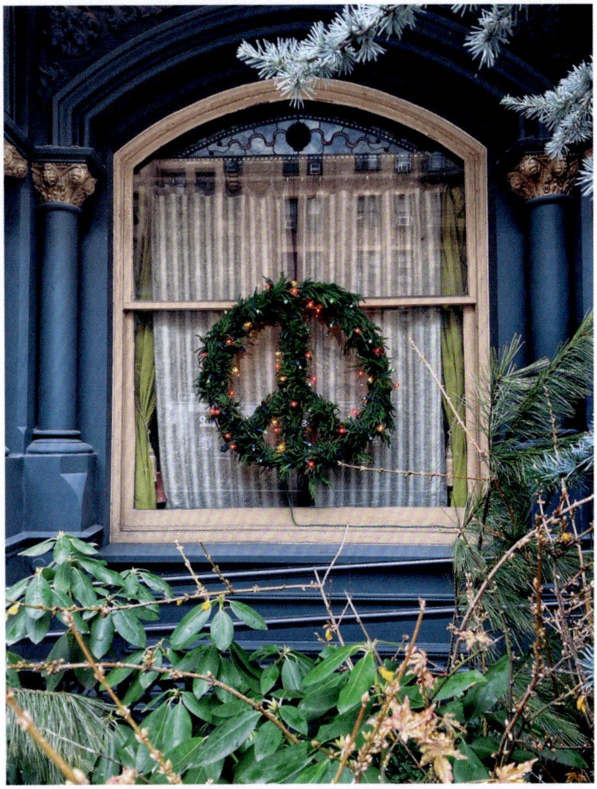

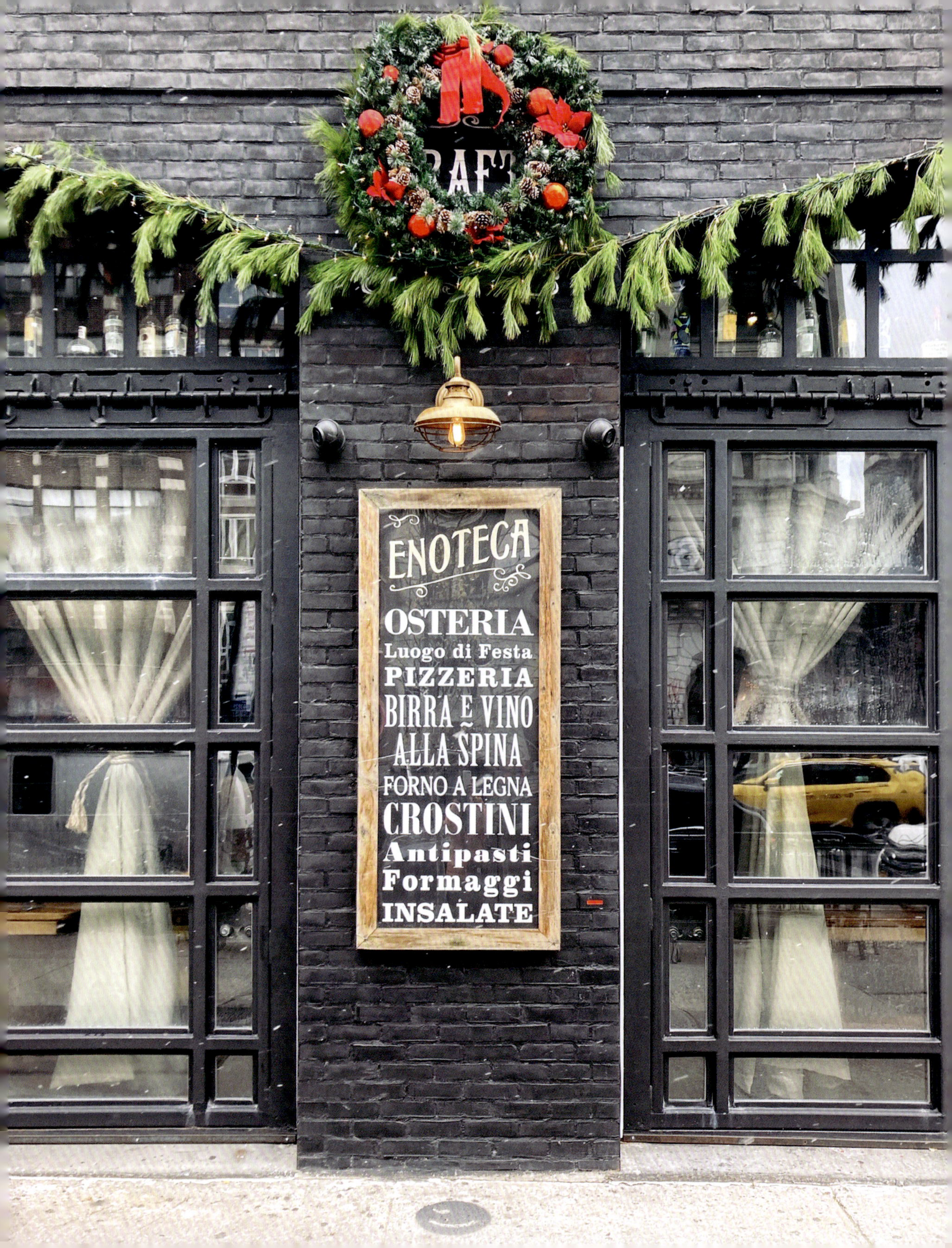
ENOTECA
OSTERIA
Luogo di Festa
PIZZERIA
BIRRA E VINO
ALLA SPINA
FORNO A LEGNA
CROSTINI
Antipasti
Formaggi
INSALATE

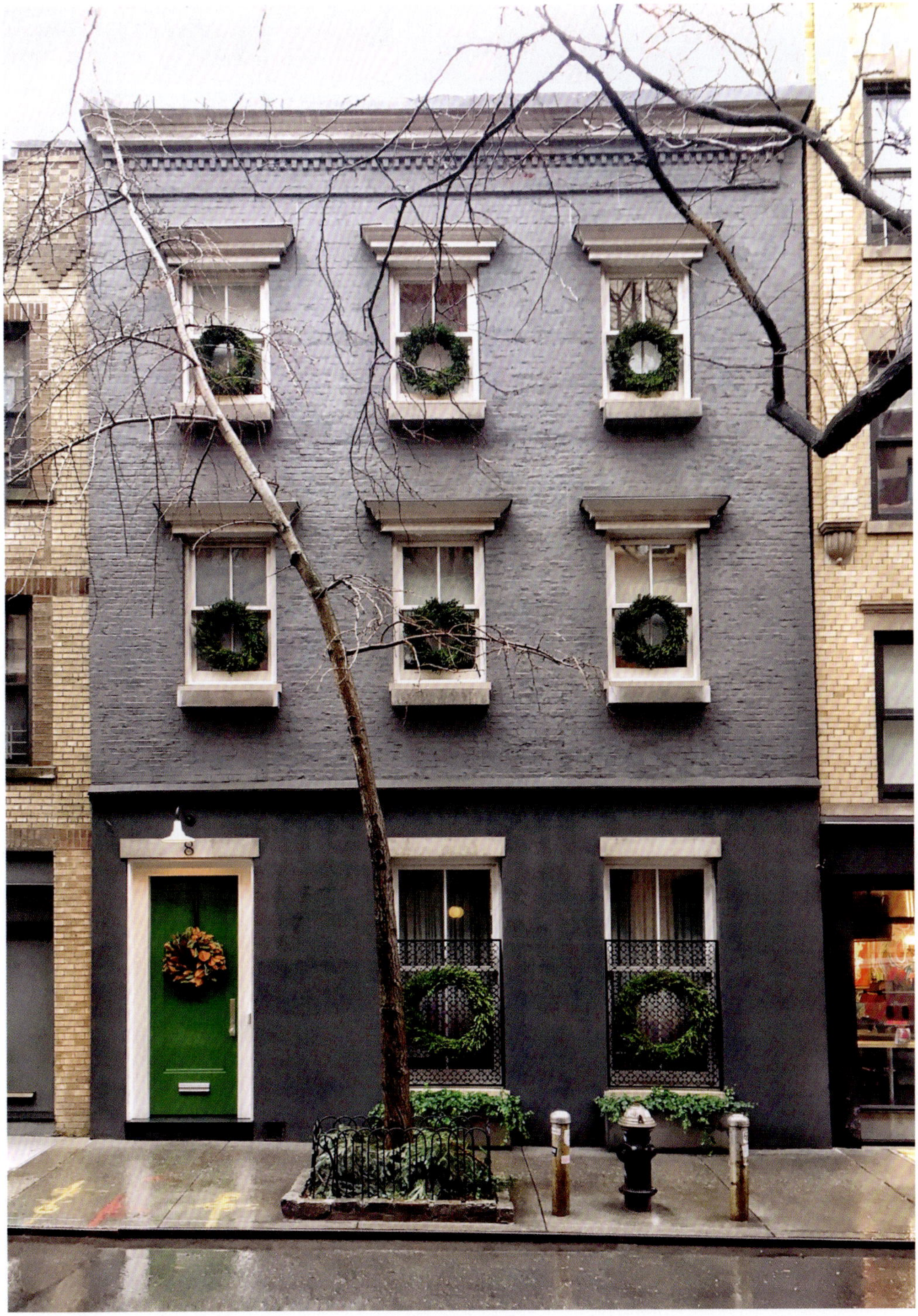

OPPOSITE: A simple garland and wreath complement Ainslie Bowery's rustic gray brick facade on Bowery on the Lower East Side. **ABOVE:** The unadorned green wreaths in every window are the perfect understated holiday accessories for this chic gray home on Morton Street in the West Village.

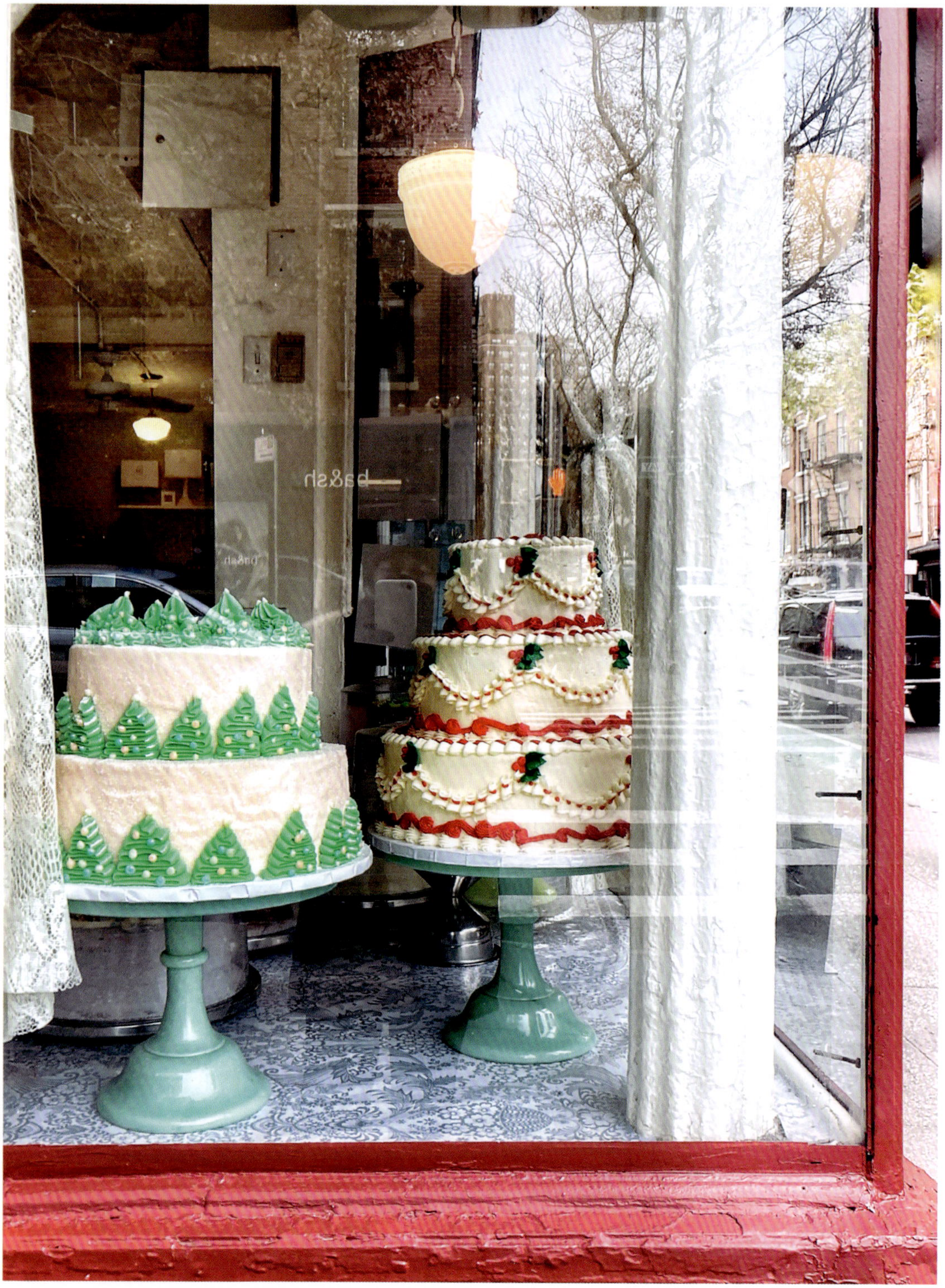

ABOVE: Festively decorated holiday cakes in the window of the original Magnolia Bakery, on the corner of West 11th and Bleecker Streets in the West Village

Downtown *Holiday* favorites

1. **John Derian, East 2nd Street between Bowery and Second Avenue:** A magical Christmas shop packed with more than thirty thousand ornaments.

2. **Washington Square Park Christmas tree, Fifth Avenue and Washington Square Park North:** The lighting of the Village's iconic tree takes place in mid-December.

3. **West 9th Street between Fifth and Sixth Avenues:** A whole block decked out with matching red bows, garlands, and wreaths.

4. **West 4th Street between West 12th and Charles Streets:** A townhouse with unique and creative displays, the Sant Ambroeus Christmas tree, and the Charles Street townhouse tree.

5. **Bleecker Street, between Bank and Grove Streets:** Many of the West Village's most charmingly decorated shops—perfect for window-shopping and actual shopping.

6. **Hudson Street between Bank and Grove Streets:** Lots of shops and restaurants, including Cursive Home for gifts and Dante West Village for drinking and dining.

7. **Union Square Holiday Market, Broadway between East 14th and East 17th Streets:** More than 175 vendors selling unique gifts and artisanal foods. Opens in mid-November.

8. **Lillie's Victorian Establishment, East 17th Street between Fifth Avenue and Broadway:** A restaurant and bar exploding with old-fashioned Christmas decorations.

9. **Balthazar, Spring Street between Crosby Street and Broadway:** A tastefully decorated cozy French bistro. Feels like you're celebrating the holidays in Paris.

10. **Feste and Champers, Crosby Street between Spring and Broome Streets:** A fabulous party and gift shop meets a Champagne bar and restaurant.

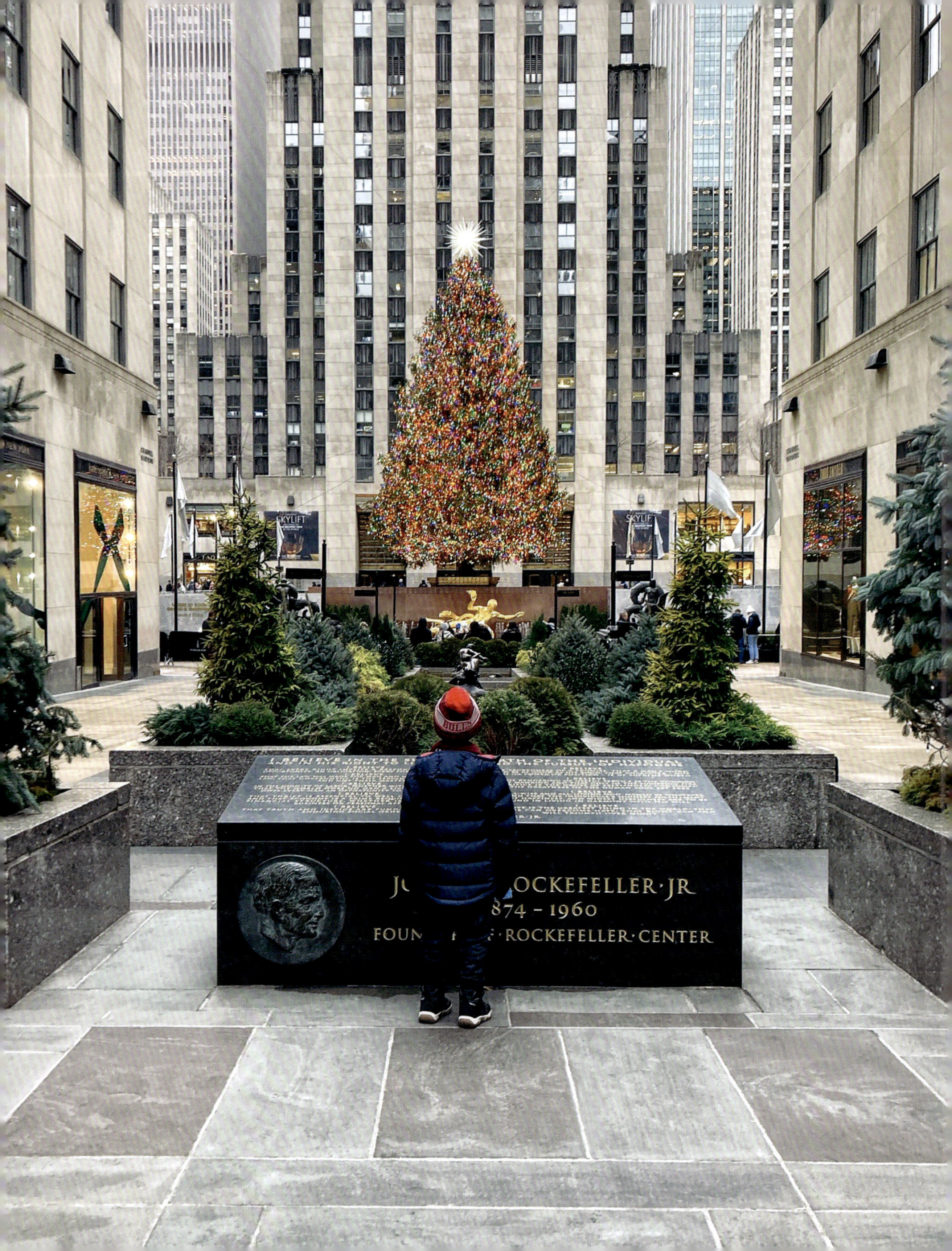
SKYLIFT
SKYLIFT
OCKEFELLER·JR
874 – 1960
ROCKEFELLER·CENTER

To my mother, who brought the Christmas cheer to our family for over six decades

Acknowledgments

My most heartfelt thanks go to all the New York City homeowners, businesses, florists, and designers whose fabulous decorations bring so much wonder and joy to our city every holiday season! Without your creativity and labors of love, there would be no *Walk With Me: New York, Holiday*.

A big thank-you to my Instagram friends and followers for enthusiastically pushing me to make this book. Your encouraging words were the gentle nudge I needed. I'm also indebted to the Instagram accounts whose posts led me to discover some of my favorite holiday spots.

It's hard to believe this is my third book with the fantastic team at Abrams. I couldn't ask for a more supportive editor than Rebecca Kaplan and a more talented (and patient), designer than Darilyn Carnes. You make it easy and fun—thank you!

A special thank-you to the brilliant Nim Ben-Reuven for the exceptionally beautiful calligraphy he created for the cover and inside pages.

To my wonderful agent, Kristin van Ogtrop, thank you for riding this exciting book wave with me.

Many thanks go to the dream team who've been generously contributing their expertise since my first book: Jenny Comita, a genius text whisperer, and Brian Luckey, a master photo fixer.

I'm so grateful to Vanessa Novak Spray, Noel Calingasan, Paula Flynn, Ellen Cohen, Rina Stone, Jennifer Alfano, Gary Goldsmith, Eve Karlin, Ruth Provenzano, Jacqueline Claire, Peter Som, and above all my family and friends for sharing their advice, location tips, and enthusiastic support.

Attempting to take photos with holiday crowds can be challenging and a lesson in patience, so I must give a big shout-out to all the people who graciously stepped out of the way when I asked them to move so I could get a clear shot. They always obliged with true holiday spirit and good cheer—and with offers to take my photo!

And finally, to my husband and partner-in-crime, Shawn Young, your unwavering support means everything to me. Thank you for being the best sounding board, a shoulder to lean on, and the one person whose opinion I value most. I've said it before and I'll say it again, I couldn't do it without you!

About the Author

SUSAN KAUFMAN (@skaufman4050) is a photographer, founding editor-in-chief of Time Inc.'s *People StyleWatch* magazine, and bestselling author of *Walk With Me: New York* and *Walk With Me: Hamptons*. Her photographs have appeared in numerous publications, including *Glamour, Hamptons, Country Living*, and *Australian Vogue*. A former fashion director at Condé Nast Publications, she splits her time between her Greenwich Village apartment and her home in Amagansett, New York, which she shares with her husband and their black Labrador, Sammy.